We dedicate this book to all of those individuals whose lives have been touched by gun violence and to those who have worked tirelessly towards creating solutions.

Contents

Figures   vii

Tables   ix

Foreword by   xi

Preface by Dr. Lisa A. Eargle and Dr. Ashraf Esmail   xiii

Acknowledgments   xv

Chapter One—Piercing the Silence: An Overview of Gun Violence—
Patterns, Profits, Protections and Policies   1
Lisa A. Eargle and Ashraf Esmail

Chapter Two—Shattered Self-Images: Narcissism, Egotistical Suicide
and School Shooters   19
Selina Doran and Mary Ann O'Grady

Chapter Three—From Egotistical and Anomic Suicide to Egotistical and
Anomic Homicide: Explaining The Aurora, Colorado Mass Shooting
Using Durkheim, Merton and Agnew   49
Dinur Blum and Christian G. Jaworski

Chapter Four—School Shooters: The Progression From Social Rejection
to Mass Murder   61
Martha Smithey

Chapter Five—Institutional Correlates of Intimate Partner Gun Homicides   82
Sheryl L. Van Horne

Chapter Six—(Il)legal Guns and Homicide: A Case Study of New Orleans   113
Jessica M. Doucet, Julia D'Antonio-Del Rio, and Chantel D. Chauvin

Chapter Seven—Do Firearms and Other Weapons Increase the Odds of
Injury During an Assault? An Offender-Based Analysis   134
Nicole M. Schmidt, Christopher A. Kierkus, and Alan J. Lizotte

Chapter Eight—No Help In Sight: The Impact of Trauma Center
Closures on Gun Violence Survival   154
Noam Ostrander and Anna Johnson

Chapter Nine—Gun Violence in the U.S.: A Muted Type of Terrorism   162
Reem A. Abu-Lughod

Chapter Ten—Applying A Disaster Process Framework to Studying Gun
Violence: The Gun-Assisted Violence as Disaster (GAVAD) Model   182
Lisa A. Eargle

Chapter Eleven—Framing Mass Gun Violence: A Content Analysis of
Print Media Coverage of the Virginia Tech and Sandy Hook
Elementary School Tragedies   214
James Hawdon, Laura Agnich, Robert Wood and John Ryan

Chapter Twelve—Satirizing Mass Murder: What Many Think,
Yet Few Will Say   233
Jaclyn Schildkraut, H. Jaymi Elsass, and Glenn W. Muschert

Chapter Thirteen—Voices From Gun Violence Prevention Interest
Groups: Prescriptive Solutions to Reducing the Problem   256
Selina Doran

Editors   287
Contributors   289

Figures

4.1   Social Rejection to School Mass Murder: Social Control, Social
      Learning, Moral Justification and Extremism   63
5.1   Gun Homicides by Victim-offender Relationship, 2000–2011   92
5.2   Offender's Age for All Gun-related Homicides, 2000–2011   94
5.3   Offender's Age for Intimate Partner Gun-related Homicides   95
5.4   Age of Victims of Gun Homicides, 2000–2011   97
5.5   Age of Victims of Intimate Partner Gun Homicides, 2000–2011   98
8.1   Chicago Homicide Numbers, 2003–2012   155
8.2   National Trauma Center Reimbursement Profile   157

Tables

1.1	Violent Crime Incidents and Victimization Involving Firearms	2
1.2	Firearm Usage in Violent Crimes, by Crime Type	3
1.3	Firearm Fatalities by Type	4
5.1	Independent Variables	87
5.2	Intimate Partner Gun Homicides, 2000–2011	93
5.3	A Comparison of Offender's Sex in All Gun-related Homicides Versus Intimate Partner Gun-related Homicides	93
5.4	A Comparison of the Race of the Offender in All Gun Homicides Compared to Intimate Partner Homicides, 2000–2011	96
5.5	A Comparison of the Sex of Victims in All Gun-involved Homicides Compared to Intimate Partner Gun Homicides	97
5.6	A Comparison of Victims by Race for All Gun-related Homicides Versus Intimate Partner Gun Homicides, 2000–2011	98
5.7	Independent Variable Descriptives	100
5.8	Bivariate Correlations	101
5.9	Principal Components Analysis for Urban Communities	103
5.10	Principal Components Analysis for Rural Communities	104
5.11	Negative Binomial Regression Analysis on Intimate Partner Counts of Homicides, 2000–2011	105
6.1	Descriptive Statistics	123
6.2	Correlation Matrix of Dependent, Explanatory, and Control Variables	124
6.3	Obliquely Rotated Principal Components Factor Pattern Matrices	125
6.4	Negative Binomial Regression Models Predicting Gun Homicide Counts in Orleans Parish Census Tracts	127
7.1	Variable Coding and Descriptive Statistics	140
7.2	Random-effects Logit Models	145
7.3	Fixed-effects Logit Models	147
8.1	Demographic Characteristics of Murder Victims and Perpetrators in Chicago, 2011	156

9.1   Murders in the U.S. 2010   167
10.1   Disaster Models and Their Stages   189
10.2   Disaster Phases, Component Stages and Definitions   190
10.3   Precursor Conditions and Their Examples, for Gun Violence   192
10.4   Warning Signs for Gun Violence   194
10.5   Catalysts for Gun Violence   195
10.6   Gun Violence Aspects   196
10.7   Gun Violence Impacts, Immediate and Long-term   197
10.8   Immediate Gun Violence Disaster Responses   198
10.9   Blame Assignment for Disaster Event, Directly and Indirectly   199
10.10   Recovery Efforts   200
10.11   Firearm Violence Prevention and Migration Efforts   201
11.1   Article Focus by Newspaper Location: Emergency Phase   223
11.2   Article Focus by Newspaper Location: Inhibition Phase   223
11.3   Article Focus by Newspaper Location: Adaptation Phase   224
11.4   Signs of Solidarity by Newspaper Location: Emergency Phase   225
11.5   Signs of Solidarity by Newspaper Location: Inhibition Phase   225
11.6   Signs of Solidarity by Newspaper Location: Adaptation Phase   225
11.7   Logistic Regression Predicting the Prevalence of Stories about
        Victims or Taking the Victim Frame   226
11.8   Logistic Regression Predicting the Prevalence of Stories
        Adopting the Solidarity Frame   226

Foreword

Across the United States, urban and rural areas are seeking a resolve to the culture of guns in America and its affect on the human capital. There is no panacea for addressing guns and the perpetual violence portrayed by individuals in possession of guns. However, *Gun Violence in American Society: Crime, Justice and Public Policy* have attempted to explore and scrutinize the complexity of gun violence in the American Society. The issues presented in this text were formulated by hypothesis and suggestive commentary. Presented are the causes and effects of 'violence ensued by individuals whom have chosen to resolve conflict with guns. Quantitative statistical analysis and qualitative methodological approaches helped yield answers to the researchers' theses and hypotheses.

In question, are short-term and long-term strains of gun violence and the burden it places on communities, schools public places medical practitioners, safety groups and such. Authors in this text attempt to share the disposition of national organizations such as the National Rifle Association (NRA). The intrinsic approach of the research conducted in this book provides a unique response to the subtle differences of why gun violence occurs. The extensive research performed presents a compelling proposition to regard for incidents such as the Sandy Hook massacre.

Federal, state, and local government agencies along with civilians are at odds with orchestrating a win/win solution to gun violence. Although statistics of gun violence fluctuates, between 1983 and 2012, occurrences of mass shootings revealed at least 78 incidents (Lemieux, 2014). Within the last five years, the culture of gun violence has accelerated (Lemieux, 2014). The authors in this text provide a vigorous and convincing argument to ensure that the culture of gun violence is not debunked with illogical fallacies. *Gun Violence in American Society: Crime, Justice and Public Policy* sets precedents of a more refined response to the culture of violence through a lens of social responsibility and the Second Amendment.

Gun Violence in American Society: Crime, Justice and Public Policy addresses the pathology and psychological persuasion of individuals that seek a resolute to ending social anomalies with violence. *Gun Violence in American Society: Crime,*

Justice and Public Policy answers to the causation of gun violence from a pragmatic scope. The context of this book implicates the cognitive dissonance of a mass shooter whom seeks to impose catastrophic damage for egotistical pleasures and fame. Lemieux (2014) propositioned that mass shooters tend to have isolated mental illnesses and are more likely under the auspices of psychiatric care. Further investigation of gun violence delves into a more micro response for understanding the signs and red flags that are easily missed. Authors in this text help readers to identify potential sociopaths in need of assistance who often go unattended or taken nonchalantly.

I highly recommend that *Gun Violence in American Society: Crime, Justice and Public Policy* reaches a conglomerate of people. Collegiate institutions, research organizations, associations, media outlets, and community organizers should review this book. *Gun Violence in American Society: Crime, Justice and Public Policy* in my humbled opinion is an easy read with justifiable data to support the authors' supposition of gun violence in the American Society.

Raymond M. Delaney Jr., Ph.D.
Associate Professor
University of Phoenix
College of Criminal Justice and Health Sciences

Preface

From the front pages of news websites, to opening stories of the local and national news programs, and in many entertainment venues, we are greeted daily with the images, sounds, and details of gun violence stories. Some recent examples of real life gun violence cases include the murders of three Muslim students in Chapel Hill, North Carolina (Campbell, 2015), the trial of the 'American Sniper' murderer (Stengle, 2015), shootings during a Mardi Gras parade in New Orleans (Plaisance and Burdeau, 2015), and a murder-suicide case involving a father and his daughter in New Mexico (Hoffer, 2015). Popular television series such as *CSI* and *Criminal Minds* (Parents Television Council, 2013) and movies such as *American Sniper* (Warner Brothers Pictures, 2014) and *Guardians of the Galaxy* (O' Hehir, 2014) involve gun violence. Many video games such as *Call of Duty* (Activision Publishing, 2014) and *Grand Auto Theft* (Rockstar Games, n.d.) also incorporate gun violence into their characters' actions. Gun violence is pervasive; it is everywhere. The effects of gun violence, its causes and solutions, however, continue to be sources of intense disagreement (Cook and Ledwig, 2010; Parsons and Johnson, 2014).

With the volume, *Gun Violence In American Society: Crime, Justice and Public Policy*, we seek to accomplish several objectives. First, we investigate how gun violence is created and perpetuated in society. Several chapters in this volume address these issues. Second, we demonstrate how a diversity of theoretical and methodological frameworks can be used to study gun violence. Theories used include Anomie, Social Strain, Social Control, Social Learning, and Social Disorganization theories. Terrorism and other disaster process frameworks are also used to elucidate the unfolding of gun violence events. Data collection methodologies include content analysis, secondary data analysis, interviews, and case studies. Data analysis techniques used include logistic and binomial regression, and GIS mapping.

Third, we examine the different situations in which gun violence can manifest itself. These range from school shootings, mass shootings, spree killings, domestic violence, violent crimes, to suicides, and accidents. Moreover, we explore the relationship between gun violence, different social groups, their communities, and social institutions. Finally, we hope to further the conversation on ways to prevent and mitigate gun violence and its impacts in the future. Some of the measures examined are gun control and gun rights legislation, elimination of the illegal weapons trade, holding weapons manufacturers accountable, improving mental health services, and improving gun safety training.

While this book does not examine every aspect of gun violence or by itself stop future incidents from occurring, we do believe it will facilitate more discussion of the issue. We also hope the book's publication will lead to additional insights, which can be applied in preventing and lessening the impact of future gun violence incidents.

Lisa A. Eargle, Ph.D. and Ashraf M. Esmail, Ph.D.

References

Activision Publishing. (2014). Call of Duty. Official website. http://www. callofduty. com/

Campbell, A. (2015). Craig Hicks was a threat with an `equal opportunity anger' neighbors say. Huffington Post, February 13. http://www.huffingtonpost. com/2015/02/13/craig-hicks-threatening-neighbors_n_6678098.html?utm_ hp_ref=mostpopular

Cook, P. J., and Ledwig, J. (2010). Five myths about gun control. Washington Post, June 13. http://www.washingtonpost.com/wp-dyn/content/article/2010/06/11/AR2010061103259.html

Hoffer, S. (2015). Police in New Mexico believe death of man, young daughter was murder-suicide. Huffington Post, February 13. http://www.huffingtonpost.com/ 2015/02/13/rio-rancho-suspicious-dea_n_6678352.html?utm_hp_ref=crime

O' Hehir, A. (2014). Guardians of the Galaxy: Marvel's goofy, exhausting and faintly fascist new franchise. Salon, July 30. http://www.salon.com/ 2014/07/30/guardians_of_the_galaxy_ marvels_goofy_exhausting_and_faintly _fascist_new_franchise/

Parents Television Council. (2013). An examination of violence, graphic violence and gun violence in the media, 2012–2013. http://w2.parentstv.org/main/Research/Studies/CableViolence/ vstudy_dec2013.pdf

Parsons, C. and Johnson, A. (2014). Young Guns: How Gun Violence is Devastating the Millennial Generation. Center for American Progress, February 21. https://www. americanprogress.org/issues/guns-crime/report/2014/ 02/21/84491/young-guns-how-gun-violence-is-devastating-the-millennial-generation/

Plaisance, S. and Burdeau, C. (2015). Shooting along Mardi Gras parade route in New Orleans kills 1, injures another. Huffington Post, February 13. http://www. huffingtonpost.com/2015/02/13/new-orleans-shooting_n_6675684.html?utm_hp_ref=crime

Rockstar Games. (n.d.) Grand Auto Theft website. www.rockstargames.com/ grandtheftauto/

Stengle, J. (2015). "American Sniper" said ex-marine was "straight-up nuts" Huffington post, February 11. http://www.huffingtonpost.com/ 2015/02/11/ american-sniper-trial_n_6665706.html?utm_hp_ref=crime

Warner Brothers Pictures. (2014). American Sniper: The official site. http://www. americansnipermovie.com/

Acknowledgments

The editors would like to thank all of the contributors to this volume, for their interest and hard work on addressing the issue of gun violence.

Chapter One

Piercing the Silence:
An Overview of Gun Violence—
Patterns, Profits, Protections, and Policies

Lisa A. Eargle and Ashraf Esmail

Introduction

In the following sections, numerous aspects of gun violence are examined. First, the extent of gun violence in the United States, how the United States compares to other nations, and the various types of firearm injuries and death are discussed. Second, the factors that are typically associated with gun violence are examined. Third, an overview of the types of firearm homicides that drive most of the discussion about gun violence is presented. Fourth, the consequences of gun violence for individuals and communities are presented. Fifth, a discussion of the extent of profits and employment in the gun industry is presented. Finally, the different perspectives and solutions proposed to address gun violence are investigated.

Extent of Gun Violence in the United States

Criminal Offenses

According to the National Crime Victimization Survey[1] (NCVS), in 2012 there were approximately 428,000 nonfatal firearm incidents in the United States, resulting in over 460,000 victimizations. The firearm violence rate for 2012 was approximately 1.8 incidents per 1,000 persons aged 12 years and older. These differ slightly from those for the year 2011, where there were approximately 415,000 firearm incidents, with over 468,000 victimizations. The firearm violence rate for 2011 was also approximately 1.8 incidents per 1,000 persons aged 12 years and older. In both years, violence incidents involving firearms comprised a relatively low percentage of all violent incidents—7.7 percent in 2011 and 6.6 percent in 2012 (Truman, Langton, and Planty, 2013).

As Table 1.1 shows, despite year-to-year fluctuations, the number and rate of violent incidents involving a firearm have slightly declined since 2005 (Truman and Rand, 2010). The percent of violent crimes involving firearms has slowly declined from 12 percent in 1993 to 8 percent in 2000 (Rennison and Rand, 2002), then fluctuated between 6 to 9 percent in subsequent years (Catalano, 2004, 2005, and 2006; Rand, 2008 and 2009; Rand and Catalano, 2007; Rennison, 1999, 2000 and 2002; Rennison and Rand, 2003; Truman, 2011; Truman, Langton, and Planty, 2013; Truman and Rand, 2010).

Table 1.1. Violent Crime Incidents and Victimization Involving Firearms[a]

Year	Incidents	Victims	% Violent Crimes	Victimization Rate[+]
2012	427,700	460,720	7.7	1.8
2011	415,160	467,930	6.6	1.8
2010	337,960	—	9.0	—
2009	326,810	352,810	8.0	1.4
2008	303,880	343,550	6.6	1.4
2007	348,910	394,580	7.1	1.6
2006	499,890	560,300	8.8	2.3
2005	419,640	477,040	8.9	2.0
2004	280,890	331,630	5.9	1.4
2003	385,040	467,350	5.6	2.0
2002	364,090	—	7.0	—
2001	524,030	—	9.0	—
2000	428,670	533,470	7.9	2.4
1999	457,150	562,870	6.8	2.5
1998	557,200	670,500	7.5	3.0

[a] does not include homicides; + per 1,000 population; —not reported by NCVS
References used: Catalano (2004, 2005, and 2006); Rand (2008 and 2009); Rand and Catalano (2007); Rennison (1999, 2000 and 2002); Rennison and Rand (2003); Truman (2011); Truman, Langton, and Planty (2013); Truman and Rand (2010).

In 2010, firearms were used in 29 percent of all robberies, 6 percent of all simple and aggravated assaults, and 7 percent of all sexual assaults and rapes[2] (Truman, 2011). As shown in Table 1.2, these percentages tend to fluctuate from year-to-year, ranging between 19 to 31 percent of all robberies, 5 to 7 percent of all assaults, and 1 to 7 percent of all rapes. The FBI's Uniform Crime Reports (UCR) show higher rates of firearm involvement in robberies and assaults (41.3 and 21.2 percent, respectively, in 2011) than the NCVS, but the UCR percentages are based upon crimes reported to the police, whereas the NCVS figures include both reported and unreported crimes.

According to the UCR, 67 to 69 percent of all homicides involve firearms (FBI, 2012). The number of firearm homicides, like other firearm violent crimes, has fluctuated from year-to-year; however, the number of firearm homicides has been generally declining over time, from over 18,000 cases in 1993 to approximately 11,000 cases in 2011. Homicides comprise a relatively small percentage of all firearm violence incidents, accounting for 3.2 percent or less of the cases (Planty and Truman, 2013).

Table 1.2. Firearm Usage in Violent Crimes, by Crime Type[a]

Year[b]	Assault N	Assault %	Robbery N	Robbery %	Rape N	Rape %
2010	184,700	6	140,640	29	12,630	7
2009	183,310	5	142,780	28	---	---
2008	184,240	5	119,640	24	---	---
2007	201,880	5	144,200	25	2,830	1
2006	---	—	—	—	—	—
2005	263,880	7	149,820	26	5,940	3
2004	196,030	5	84,860	19	—	—
2003	222,700	5	138,280	25	5,860	3
2002	235,280	5	117,480	25	11,330	4
2001	321,310	7	197,170	31	5,550	2
2000	339,870	6	187,060	26	6,550	3
1999	362,090	6	195,270	24	5,510	1
1998	475,400	7	182,200	21	12,800	4

[a] does not include homicides; [b] data not available for years 2011 and 2012; —not reported by NCVS

References used: Catalano (2004, 2005, and 2006); Rand (2008 and 2009); Rand and Catalano (2007); Rennison (1999, 2000 and 2002); Rennison and Rand (2003); Truman (2011); Truman and Rand (2010).

Noncriminal Offenses: Accidents and Suicides

Information on firearm accidents and suicides is not as readily available as the information for firearm usage in crimes. However, based on the reports that are available, there seems to be an increase in both types of incidents in recent years. Fatalities from firearm accidents increased from 606 cases in 2010 to 851 cases in 2011 (Hoyert and Xu, 2012). Prior to that, firearm accidents were responsible for 1543 deaths in 1993 and 875 deaths in 1998 (Gotsch, Annest, Mercy and Ryan, 2001).

Suicide deaths involving firearms has also changed over time. During the 1990s, the number of suicides by firearm decreased from approximately 19,200 in

1993 to approximately 17,000 in 1998 (Gotsch, Annest, Mercy, and Ryan, 2001). However, by 2010, the number of suicide by firearm cases had increased to 19,392 cases. In the following year (2011), the number of suicides involving firearms had increased by approximately 300 cases to 19,766 deaths (Hoyert and Xu, 2012).

Data on the percentage of firearm injuries and death by intent is also difficult to obtain. A study by Gotsch et. al (2001) suggests that the majority of firearm fatalities are intentionally self-inflicted (57.8 percent in 1998). The majority of nonfatal firearm injuries were the result of assault or legal intervention (71.9 percent in 1998). Table 1.3 displays the number and rate of firearm fatalities by type for multiple years. Higher numbers and rates are exhibited for suicides than for homicides or accidents, regardless of year. Over time, the rates for firearm fatalities declined until 2010. From 2010 to 2011, there was a slight increase in fatal firearm accidents; meanwhile suicide fatalities remained constant.

Table 1.3. Firearm Fatalities by Type

Cause		Year			
		1993	**1998**	**2010**	**2011**
Accident	N	1543	875	606	851
	Rate	0.6	0.3	0.2	0.3
Homicide	N	18,839	12,228	11,078	11,101
	Rate	7.3	4.5	3.8	3.6
Suicide	N	19,213	17,605	19,392	19,766
	Rate	7.4	6.5	6.3	6.3

N is the number of cases reported; Rate is the number of cases per 100,000 population
References used: Hoyert and Xu (2012) for the number of cases and rates for the years 2010 and 2011; Gotsch et. al (2001) for number of cases in the years 1993 and 1998. Rates for the years 1993 and 1998 were calculated using the number of cases from Gotsch et. al (2001) and historical population estimates from the U.S. Census Bureau (2000).

Extent of Gun Violence: the United States in a Global Context

Data for firearm deaths for different nations is even more difficult to obtain than data for the United States. One important source for data on homicides by firearms is the United Nations' Office on Drugs and Crime (UNODC) report. This source provides data for 112 nations[3] for various years in the 1995-2010 time period.[4] According to the UNODC, Honduras appears to have the highest firearm homicide victimization rates at 68.4 incidents per 100,000 population in the year 2010. The nation with the next highest rate is El Salvador, with 39.9 incidents in the year 2008. Nations with some of the lowest firearm homicide victimization rates are Japan (only 11 incidents and a rate of 0.0), Germany (rate of 0.2), India (rate of 0.3), and Canada (rate of 0.5).[5] Nations with firearm homicide victimization rates that are located in between these highest and lowest values are the Dominican Republic (16.3), South Africa (17.0), and Belize (21.8).[6] By comparison, the U.S. firearm homicide victimization rate is 3.2 incidents per 100,000 population in the year 2010, putting the U.S. in 14th place for the highest rate. As these figures indicate, there is wide variation in the firearm homicide victimization rates across nations (United Nations Office on Drugs and Crime, 2012).

Data for suicides by firearms is available from the World Health Organization (WHO) for 56 nations, for the late 1990s to early 2000s. The nation with the highest firearm suicide rate is Finland, with approximately 4335.2 cases per 100,000 population.[7] The nation with the second highest firearm suicide rate is Croatia, with approximately 4157.7 cases per 100,000 population. Nations with some of the lowest suicide by firearm rates are Kuwait (4.9), Peru (14.8), and South Africa (15.6). By contrast, the United States firearm suicide rate is 2415.1 cases per 100,000 population, with the 4th highest rate for reporting nations. Like firearm homicide rates, there is wide variation in firearm suicide rates across nations (Ajdacic-Gross, Weiss, Ring, Hepp, Bopp, Gutzwiller, and Rossler, 2008).

These results seem to suggest that firearms are more likely to be used in suicides than in homicides. Moreover, these results show that the United States does have relatively high rates of firearm homicides and suicides, in comparison to other nations. Data on firearm usage in crimes other than homicides is unfortunately not available internationally. Likewise, data on firearm accidents is also not available globally.

Correlates of Gun Violence

Gender

Males have higher firearm death and injury rates than females do. An analysis of state-level firearm death rates from the Kaiser Foundation (2013) shows that on average, the firearm death rate for males is approximately 6 times that for females. States have an average of 19.5 male and 3.3 female firearm deaths per 100,000 population.

This gap between male and female firearm death rates is maintained when examining firearm death by type. The male firearm death rate due to homicide is 6.2 cases per 100,000 population in 2011; the female firearm death rate due to homicide is 1.1 cases per 100,000 population (Planty and Truman, 2013). Of male suicides, 56 percent involved firearms; 30 percent of female suicides involved firearms (Centers for Disease Control, 2014).

In general, nonfatal firearm-related injury rates are much higher for males than for females (Gotsch et. al, 2001). For nonfatal firearm violence, the male rate is slightly higher than the female rate, at 1.9 cases per 1000 persons versus 1.6 cases per 1000 persons respectively (Planty and Truman, 2013).

Race and Ethnicity

In general, African Americans have higher firearm death rates than whites do. An analysis of state-level firearm death rates from the Kaiser Foundation (2013) for these two groups shows that on average, the firearm death rate for African Americans is almost 18 deaths per 100,000 population versus 10.3 deaths per 100,000 population for whites.

African Americans have a significantly higher and disproportionate rate of firearm homicide victimization than any other racial/ethnic group. In the year 2010, 54.8 percent of all gun homicide victims were African American, compared to 25 percent for non-Hispanic whites, 17.3 percent for Hispanics, 1.4 percent for Asians and 0.9 percent for American Indians. Yet, African Americans only comprise 12.8 percent of the U.S. population, while non-Hispanic whites comprise 64.8 percent of the population (Pew Research Center, 2013).

However, whites have significantly higher rates of suicide by firearms than African Americans do. Comparison of state-level gun suicide rates provided by the Washington Post in 2013 show that in every state, whites' gun suicide rates are 2 to 3 times that of African Americans (Chow, Keating and Stanton, 2013).

Age

According to the Bureau of Justice Statistics (2010), those aged 15 to 24 years are more likely to be victims of gun homicides than any other age group. The Pew Research Center found that 29.5 percent of gun homicide victims were between the ages 18 to 24 and that 39.9 percent were between the ages of 25 and 40 years (Pew Research Center, 2013). According to the Centers for Disease Control, firearm homicide is the second leading cause of injury death for those aged 15 to 24 and the third leading cause of injury death for those aged 25 to 34. Firearm suicide is the third leading cause of injury death for those aged 35 to 64 years and the fourth leading cause of injury death for those aged 64 and older, as well as those aged 15 to 24 years (Centers for Disease Control, 2010). Nonfatal firearm-related injury rates are also highest for those in their late teens and early 20s (Gotsch et. al. 2001).

Income

Those with lower incomes are more likely to be victims of firearm violence than those with higher incomes. Households with annual incomes below $7,500 have a firearm victimization rate of 8.4 per 1,000 population; households with annual incomes of $50,000 or more have a firearm victimization rate of 2.4 per 1,000 population (Perkins, 2003). An analysis of firearm deaths by type (homicide, suicide and accident) at the metropolitan-level finds a moderate, positive, and statistically significant relationship with percent impoverished population for all types of firearm death (Florida, 2012).

Region

The firearm death rate varies widely across states, from a high of 20.4 deaths per 100,000 population in Alaska, to a low of 3.2 deaths per 100,000 population in Hawaii (Kaiser Foundation, 2013). Analyses of the data show a pattern by region[8], where the average firearm death rate is significantly higher for the Southern and Western states than for the Midwestern and Northeastern states (13.3, 12.5, 9.5 and 6.8 respectively).

Firearm homicide rates are also higher in the South region than elsewhere. In 2010, the firearm homicide rate for the South was 4.4 cases per 100,000 population. By contrast, the rates for the Midwest, West, and Northeast were 3.4, 3.0, and 2.8 respectively (Planty and Truman, 2013). On the other hand, firearm suicide rates are higher in the West region than elsewhere. Analyses of white and black state-level firearm suicide rates from the Washington Post show that on average firearm suicide rates for the West are twice that of the Northeast region (109 versus 47 for whites, 38 versus 16 for blacks)[9]. The Midwest and South had average rates of 67 and 97 for whites and 29 and 33 for blacks, respectively (Chow et. al. 2013). Information on state or regional rates of accidental firearm deaths is unavailable.

For nonfatal firearm violence, there was no real appreciable difference between regions. The Midwest had the highest rate at 1.9 cases and the Northeast had the lowest rate at 0.9 cases per 1,000 population in 2010 (Planty and Truman, 2013). Information on state or regional rates of nonfatal firearm accidents is unavailable.

Urban Versus Rural

There seems to be no significant difference in overall firearm death rates between urban and rural areas. Firearm homicides are higher in urban areas than in rural areas, with the most urban areas experiencing 1.9 times the number of firearm homicides that the most rural areas experience. Firearm suicides are 1.54 times higher in the most rural areas than in the most urban areas (Branas et. al., 2004). Nonfatal firearm violence rates tend to be higher in urban areas (2.8 cases per 1000 population) than in suburban (1.2 cases) or rural areas (0.7 cases) (Planty and Truman, 2013). Information on nonfatal firearm accidents for urban and rural areas is unavailable.

Gun Ownership

An analysis performed on state-level data for the percentage of households with firearms and firearm deaths[10] shows a moderate, positive and statistically significant relationship between these two factors. However, this does not necessarily mean that firearm deaths occur in households with firearms. Many firearm victimizations occur outside of the victims' residence (Planty and Truman, 2013). It does not necessarily mean that owning a firearm will result in a firearm death either.

Gun Violence and Criminal Incidence Types

In this chapter so far, three types of gun violence have been discussed: firearm use in homicides, violent crimes like robbery, and suicide. There has also been some discussion of firearm accidents. In this section, the discussion focuses on different types of firearm homicide and assault incidents. These incidents are mass shootings, serial shootings, and acts of terrorism. These are the types of incidents that often get the most media attention and are most prominent in people's perceptions about gun violence (Pew Research Center, 2013).

Mass shootings are one incident events, where four or more victims are injured or killed by gun fire from an assailant (Bjelopera, Bagalman, Caldwell, Finklea, and McCallion, 2013). An example of this would be the Virginia Tech University shooting in April 2007. A troubled student at the University went on a premeditated rampage, killing 32 students and professors within a three-hour time period (Shapira, Jackman and Schneider, 2007). Serial shootings[11] occur when over a period of time, multiple victims are shot by a perpetrator (Bjelopera et. al, 2013). An example of this would be the DC Snipers of 2002 that shot 13 people, killing ten of them, during a 3 week period (White, 2012) or the recent 2014 Kansas City sniper, suspected of shooting at nine people, on different days as they entered or exited the freeway (Ellis, Cera, and Howell, 2014).

Acts of terrorism involving firearms are violent acts where people are injured and/or killed for political purposes, to undermine people's faith in their government or to get the government to capitulate to the terrorist organization's demands (FBI, n.d.). Several incidents involving members of the "Sovereign Citizens" movement have been involved in the murders of law enforcement officers in New Orleans, Louisiana, and Alamo, California, in 2012 and West Memphis, Arkansas in 2010. In 2013, a plot to kidnap and execute law enforcement officers by two avowed members of the movement was foiled in Las Vegas, Nevada (Southern Poverty Law Center, 2014). While other incidents may have been called terrorism in the media (such as the Fort Hood shootings, Sikh Temple shootings, or the Aurora Colorado theater shootings), since they do not clearly involve a political agenda, they are considered by some criminologists to be "mass shootings," stemming from mental illness, revenge, hate, or other motivations, and not acts of terrorism (Richinick, 2014).

In general, these types of incidents are still a relatively small portion of firearm incidents in the US (Wihbey, 2014). While mass shootings such as the Newtown, Connecticut, school shooting especially capture the public's attention (Pew Research Center, 2013), these types of events are not dramatically increasing over time (Fox and Delateur, 2013). Most criminal violence acts involving firearms are usually single-event, one or two victim(s) incidents, like criminal violence acts in general (Cooper and Smith, 2011). However, when these types of incidents occur often and repeatedly within a specific area, gun violence is often described in disease terms – as an epidemic that needs a cure. An example of this would be the over 400 gun homicides that occurred in Chicago during the year 2012 (Geier, 2012).

Consequences of Gun Violence

In addition to the homicides, assaults, suicides and accidents detailed earlier in this chapter, gun violence has other impacts on society as well. Some studies have connected exposure to gun violence to psychological issues, such as anger, anxiety, depression, and traumatic stress disorder. Because of victimization fears, people may obtain guns for self-defense purposes, increasing the likelihood of their use to settle disputes among family members and others in communities.

Those caught in the crosshairs of gun shots, in addition to psychological trauma, often experience debilitating physical injuries requiring extensive medical care, costing thousands of dollars, and reducing the employability of victims. To deal with the difficulties they face daily, many victims turn to alcohol and drugs to self-medicate, adding to the health problems experienced.

Communities frequented by gun violence experience population loss, directly from firearm deaths and indirectly from population flight and business closures. As more people and businesses leave an area, property values also begin to decline, making it harder for community leaders to recruit new desirable residents and enterprises. A stigma is placed on all those associated with a community deemed violent, regardless of their activities (Bieler, 2014).

Gun Profits

Despite the negative consequences produced by firearms use, firearm manufacturing and sales are financially lucrative industries. Approximately $6 billion in revenue is generated by the gun and ammunition industry annually in America. Approximately $5 billion in state and federal taxes were produced by firearms in 2012 (Sanburn, 2012). Remington Outdoor Company profits rose 52 percent over the year since the Sandy Hook school shooting, even though the company's Bushmaster rifle product was used by the shooter in the massacre. Sturm Ruger, the nation's top gun manufacturer, has also seen its profits dramatically rise (Huffington Post, 2013). Over 5 million new weapons were produced in the year 2011 alone. Additionally, three million plus firearms were imported into the U.S. in 2010.

Employment in firearms industries increased 30 percent between 2008 and 2011 (Sanburn, 2012). The state of South Carolina successfully recruited gun manufacturer Ithaca Gun Company to build a new facility in Horry County and create over 100 new jobs (South Carolina Radio Network, 2013). However, Ithaca Gun Company is not alone in its expansion; many other gun manufacturers are considering expansion and/or relocation to gun friendly states to take advantage of tax incentives and public support (Stone, 2013).

So who is buying all of these weapons, driving the increase in profits and employment? Most purchases are made by private American citizens, but government agencies such as law enforcement and the military comprise about 40 percent of all sales. Other nations, such as Canada and Australia, purchase these weapons as well (Plumer, 2012).

Perspectives on Addressing Gun Violence

When it comes to addressing gun violence, there are a variety of perspectives and solutions. Some have advocated increasing social control in society, by passing restrictive gun control laws, more enforcement efforts, and harsher punishments. Others have advocated understanding and changing people's worldviews about violence in general. Yet others have advocated education programs focused on responsible firearm use. Finally, many view gun violence as a public health issue and advocate greater accessibility to mental health care as a way to reduce the opportunities for violent behavior. In the following sections, the application of these perspectives in society in terms of legislation and programs is examined, beginning first with firearm legislation.

Major Firearm Legislation and Court Rulings

The first firearms related law came into being in December 1791, as the fourth article in the Bill of Rights (also known as the Second Amendment to the Constitution). It states "A well regulated Militia, being necessary to the security of a free State, the right of the people to keep and bear Arms, shall not be infringed" (National Archives, accessed 2014). In subsequent years, two different interpretations of what this Amendment states has emerged. One perspective, Individual Right theory, argues that governments cannot stop *individuals* from having firearms. Another perspective, Collective Rights theory, argues that Congress cannot prevent individual *states* from possessing firearms; there are no guarantees of individual rights to possess firearms and governing bodies can regulate firearms without infringing upon the Constitution (Cornell Law School, accessed 2014). It is the latter perspective that has generally guided firearm legislation until the first decade of the twenty-first century.

National Firearms Act (NFA) was originally enacted in 1934, but has been amended in subsequent years. It requires that certain firearms be taxed and registered. The Federal Firearms Act (FFA) was originally enacted in 1938, to require firearm manufacturers, sellers, and importers to obtain a federal license, maintain records on their customers, and refuse sales to certain categories of individuals. The Gun Control Act (GCA) of 1968 repealed the FFA and increased the restrictions of the NFA. The GCA set minimum age requirements for firearms purchasers, required all firearms to have a serial number assigned to them, and broadened of the category of persons prohibited from having firearms.

These restrictions were loosened with the Firearms Owners' Protection Act (FOPA) of 1986. Licensed dealers could now sell firearms at gun shows located within the dealers' state. Limits were set on the number of unannounced inspections of dealer sites that could be performed by the Bureau of Alcohol, Firearms, and Tobacco (ATF), the federal agency responsible for monitoring firearms in the US. Firearms dealers no longer had to maintain customer records of ammunition sales (except for armor piercing bullets) and could sell ammunition to out-of-state customers.

After the assassination attempt on President Reagan, his Press Secretary and other members of his cabinet, the Brady Handgun Violence Prevention Act (Brady Act) was enacted in 1993. It imposed a five-day waiting period before a handgun purchase was finalized and the weapon transferred to its owner. This allowed gun dealers to perform background checks on prospective handgun buyers, to make sure the buyers were not prohibited from having a gun. This background check system has become computerized since 1993, so the results of the check are almost immediate. In 1998, the check system was expanded to shotguns and rifle purchases as well. Individuals possessing a federal firearms license or a state-issued permit are exempt from the waiting period, allowing for fewer individuals to adhere to the Brady Act.

The Assault Weapons Ban of 1994 stopped the manufacture, sale and ownership of semi-automatic weapons and large capacity gun clips after September 1994 to the public. Semi-automatic firearms and large-capacity gun clips manufactured before September 1994 were excluded from these provisions. The law had a provision that required its reauthorization by Congress after 10 years of its enactment or it would expire. The law expired in 2004.

The Protection of Lawful Commerce in Arms and Child Safety Lock Acts were passed in 2005. This legislation allowed firearm manufacturers and sellers to be sued in civil court if a firearm or ammunition was used in criminal activity, if it could be established that the transferor was aware that the materials would be used for criminal purposes. Transferors could also be held liable if a defect in the product led to injury or death while being lawfully used. It also required that manufacturers, importers, and dealers of handguns to provide consumers with a secure gun storage or safety lock device free of charge or for a fee.

The National Instant Criminal Background Checks System Improvement Amendments Act (NICS Act) was passed in 2007. It provided monetary incentives to states that adopted the use of the NCIS database in performing background checks for firearm purchasers. The law also amended the rules regarding who would be deemed mentally ill and prohibited from purchasing a firearm. Grants were issued by the Attorney General's office to support state reporting of mental illness data on individuals to the NICS (Law Center To Prevent Gun Violence, 2012).

In the midst of these legislative changes, the Supreme Court in 2008 ruled in the *District of Columbia v. Heller* case that the Second Amendment does allow individuals to possess firearms, making the Washington DC ban on handguns illegal. However, the Court upheld rulings prohibiting the purchase of sawed-off shotguns by citizens and prohibiting criminals and mentally ill persons from acquiring firearms. Two years later, Chicago's ban on handgun possession was challenged before the Supreme Court in the *McDonald v. City of Chicago* case. The Court ruled that states have a right to possess arms, but not a majority decision about individuals' right to possess firearms for self-protection (Cornell Law School, accessed 2014).

In 2014, Georgia Governor Nathan Deal signed into law new rules that expanded the types of places where firearms could be carried, including government facilities, houses of worship, schools, and bars. Hunters could also install silencers on firearms they use. Those carrying these weapons must still undergo background checks before being allowed to purchase weapons. Many critics of this legislation argue that the relaxing of restrictions opens the door for further relaxing of restrictions and increases in shooting incidents (Bluestein, 2014).

Changing Views About Gun Violence

Politicians, psychologists, and others have long commented in blogs, on television interviews, and in newspaper articles about the pervasiveness of gun violence in movies, video games, and music lyrics, and the desensitizing effects it has on youths (Kain, 2013). The Motion Picture Association of America (MPPA) rating system developed the rating "PG-13" in 1984 to alert parents to content that was considered unsuitable for young children (Windolf, 2008). The placement of MPAA ratings on home video releases of films was added as well (Eugene Register-Guard, 1984). Tipper Gore, ex-wife of former Vice President Al Gore, successfully campaigned in 1988 to have parental advisory notices placed on music albums with offensive and violent lyrics (Siegel, 2005). Since the Aurora attacks and the Newtown shootings, these concerns about gun violence (and violence in general) in entertainment have been re-expressed (Horsey, 2013; Kain, 2013). Vice President Biden met with entertainment leaders at the White House to seek ways to reduce the amount of gun violence that appears in entertainment. President Obama called for more studies examining the relationship between violent entertainment and violent behavior in a national address devoted to gun violence in January 2013 (Stark, 2013). So far, studies on observing violence and violent behavior have produced inconsistent research results (Kain, 2013).

The Urban Institute joined with Virginia Commonwealth University to document the views of those who experienced gun violence first hand through photos and interviews. As a result, the document "Raising the Voices of Gun Violence" was produced. The idea is to humanize the statistics that are often reported, so that the researchers and the public can better understand the consequences of gun violence on individual lives and society (Bieler, 2014). Similarly, the conversation that author Frank Miniter had with a gang member is recounted in an interview about his latest book, *The Future of the Gun*, for the website The Blaze. The gang member supposedly stated to Miniter that there are two gun cultures in society: law abiding citizens whose weapon possession is restricted and criminals who illegally possess guns and seek to victimize the law abiding citizens. Many youth admire the illegal gun toting criminal because he is seen as having more power than the law abiding citizen (The Blaze, 2014). Those exposed to gun violence may turn to weapons as a way of feeling more secure in dangerous environments (Bieler, 2014).

Firearm Use Education Programs

The Committee to Reduce Firearm Violence in Massachusetts recommended in its report that standardized, accredited firearm safety courses which contain "live fire" training and other essential components become mandatory for receiving a gun license. At the time of the report, a variety of firearm educations programs existed in Massachusetts, of varying content and quality (Committee to Reduce Firearm Violence, 2014). The Prevention Institute takes this further by arguing gun owners should take gun safety refresher courses from time to time, not just once, to obtain a license (Prevention Institute, n.d.). While this would certainly reduce the number of accidental deaths from firearms, it is not clear how this would prevent firearm violence and suicides.

Firearm Violence As Health Issue

The Prevention Institute advocates restoring funding to the Centers for Disease Control to study health impacts of gun violence, creating a National Institute of Violence Prevention at the National Institutes of Health to track gun deaths like disease, and expanded coverage under the Affordable Care Act for those seeking mental health treatment (Prevention Institute, n.d.). The Urban Institute reports that exposure to gun violence, even if it does not result in violent acts, affects the mental health of children and their academic performance. Those injured by guns often have disabling injuries that impede their ability to work and pay their bills (Bieler, 2014). Still others advocate mental health screenings to restrict the mentally ill from acquiring firearms (Corcoran, n.d.). At this time, mental health screenings at gun purchases is almost nonexistent (Horowitz, 2012), although California and Colorado have passed legislation to strengthen the requirements (Corcoran, n.d.) after the Aurora movie theater attacks and the Southern California shooting spree. Those mental health screenings that do exist have eliminated 3,000 individuals with mental health issues from purchasing guns from licensed dealers; however, many others who should not have access still obtain firearms and create havoc, such as the Fed-Ex worker in suburban Atlanta who shot six people in 2014. In his suicide note, the shooter states "I am a socio-path. I want to hurt people" (Follman, 2014).

Conclusion

Every evening the local news, regardless of what city or town in America one is located, reports of another shooting event that has occurred. Sometimes it is the intended victims who are shot, sometimes innocent bystanders, or people just randomly selected. Sometimes it is a robbery that went horribly wrong, a domestic dispute that escalates into a shooting, or a deranged person on a rampage. Regardless of the details, gun violence is something that impacts many individuals, families and communities across America in many different ways. It also appears to be a phenomenon that will continue to affect us for some time to come, despite calls for ending gun violence and proposed solutions by many different constituencies. Moreover, it is an issue that wide disagreements about the causes and solutions continue to exist, making the situation even more intractable.

Notes

1. National Crime Victimization Survey (NCVS) is a questionnaire delivered in person or over the phone to residents aged 12 years and older, from a nationally representative sample of households, every 6 months for a 3-year period. The households included in the sample change at the end of those 3 years. In 2012, this produced a sample of approximately 92,000 households and 163,000 individuals. The crime data collected by the NCVS does not include homicide cases, as information collected is based upon interviews with living respondents (Truman, Langton, and Planty, 2013).
2. Numbers and percentages associated with sexual assaults and rape should be viewed with caution, as the number of sample cases that these estimates are based upon often fall below 10 (Truman, 2011).
3. There were 267 countries or world entities (Central Intelligence Agency, n.d.).
4. Not all nations have data reported for each year (United Nations Office on Drugs and Crime, 2012).
5. For the years of 2008, 2010, 2009, and 2009 respectively.
6. For the years of 2010, 2007, and 2010 respectively.
7. Death rates per 100,000 population are estimated using the suicide data from the World Health Organization (Ajdacic et. al. 2008) and year 2000 population numbers from the United Nations' Population Division (2000).
8. States were assigned to regions according to the U.S. Census Bureau's (n.d.) "Census Bureau regions and divisions with state FIPS codes."
9. Per 1 million people in racial category (Chow et. al. 2013)
10. Data on percentage of household with guns was obtained from the Washington Post (2013). Data on firearm death rates was obtained from the Kaiser Foundation for the year 2010. The chapter's author performed a correlation analysis to see if any statistical relationship existed between these factors, since stories of accidental child shooting occur from time to time in the media.
11. Some researchers make a distinction between serial and spree shooters. Serial shooters are considered to have a "cooling off period" between murders, where they return to normal life; spree shooters, on the other hand, are thought to remain in a killing mindset over time (Siegel, 2015). However, what exactly constitutes a "cooling off period" for

a killer cannot be easily and reliably determined (Bjelopera et. al., 2013). Hence, this distinction is not used in this chapter's discussion.

References

Ajdacic-Gross, V., Weiss, M. G., Ring, M., Hepp, U., Bopp, M., Gutzwiller, F., and Rossler, W. (2008). Methods of suicide: international suicide patterns derived from the WHO mortality database. Bulletin of the *World Health Organization, 86* (9): 726–732.

Bieler, S. (2014). Raising the Voices of Gun Violence. Urban Institute. http://www./ datatools.urban.org/Features/raising-the-voices-of-gun-violence/

Bjelopera, J.P., Bagalman, E., Caldwell, S. W., Finklea, K. M., and McCallion, G. (2013). Public mass shootings in the United States: Selected implications for federal public health and safety policy. *Congressional Research Service,* March 18. http://www.fas.org/sgp/crs/misc/R43004.pdf

The Blaze. (2014). The conversation with a former gang member that changed the worldview of this pro-gun author. *The Blaze,* August 14. http://www.theblaze. com/ blog/2014/08/14/the-conversation-with-a-former-gang-member-that-changed-the-worldview-of-this-pro-gun-author.

Branas, C.C., Nance, M.L., Elliott, M.R., Richmond, T. S., Schwab, C. W. (2004). Urban-rural shifts in intentional firearm death: different causes, same result. *American Journal of Public Health, 94* (10): 1750-1755.

Catalano, S. (2004). *Criminal Victimization, 2003.* Bureau of Justice Statistics.

———. (2005). *Criminal Victimization, 2004.* Bureau of Justice Statistics.

———. (2006). *Criminal Victimization, 2005.* Bureau of Justice Statistics.

Central Intelligence Agency. (n.d.) *CIA World Factbook.* http://www.cia.gov/ library/ publications/the-world-factbook.

Centers for Disease Control. (2010). 10 leading causes of injury deaths by age group highlighting violence-related injury deaths, United States–2010. http://www. cdc.gov/injury/wisqars/pdf/10lcid_violence_related_injury_deaths_2010-a.pdf.

———. (2014). Percentage of suicides among persons ages 10 years and older, by sex and mechanism, United States, 2005–2009. *National Suicide Statistics At A Glance.* http://www.cdc.gov/violenceprevention/suicide/statistics/ mechanism01.html

Chow, E., Keating, D., and Stanton, L. (2013). Gun suicide and homicide: statistics shaped by race. *The Washington Post,* March 22. http://www.washington post.com/wp-srv/special/national/gun-deaths

Committee to Reduce Firearm Violence. (2014). *Strategies for Reducing Gun Violence in the Commonwealth of Massachusetts: A Report to Speaker of the House of Representatives Robert DeLeo.* http://archives.lib.state.ma.us/ 2452/208093

Cooper, A. and Smith, E. L. (2011). Homicide Trends in the United States, 1980– 2008. *Bureau of Justice Statistics,* November.

Corcoran, M. (n.d.). Mental Health Checks When Purchasing a Gun. *The Work Threat Group, LLC.* http://workthreat.com/mental-health-checks-when-purchasing-a-gun/

Cornell Law School. (n.d.). "Second Amendment." *Wex Legal Dictionary.* Accessed 2014. http://www.law.cornell.edu/wex/second_Amendment

Ellis, R., Cera, D., and Howell, G. (2014). Ammo found beside road helped break Kansas City highway shooter case. *Cable News Network,* April 18 http://www.cnn.com/ 2014/04/18/kansas-city-highway-shootings/

Eugene Register-Guard. (1984). "Dealers will label ratings on cassettes." *Eugene Register-Guard*, August 11.

FBI. (n.d.). *Terrorism 2002–2005*. http://www.fbi.gov/stats-services/publications /terrorism-2002-2005/terror02_05.pdf

———. (2012). *Crime in the United States 2012: Expanded Homicide Data Table 8.*

Florida, R. (2012). The geography of U.S. gun violence. *The Atlantic Cities*, December 14. http://www.theatlanticcities.com/neighborhoods/2012/12/ geography-us-gun-violence/4171

Follman, M. (2014). Do Background Checks Work to Keep Disturbed People From Getting Guns? *Mother Jones*, May 22. http://www.motherjones.com/ mojo/2014/05/guns-mental-health-background-checks

Fox, J. A. and Delateur, M. (2013). Mass shootings in America. *Homicide Studies*, 20 (10): 1–21

Geier, K. (2012). 500 murders in Chicago in 2012; 435 caused by guns. *Washington Monthly*, December 30. http://www.washingtonmonthly.com/ political-animal-a/2012_12/500_murders_in_chicago_in_2012042087.php

Gotsch, K. E., Annest, J. L., Mercy, J. A., and Ryan, G. W. (2001). Surveillance for fatal and nonfatal firearm-related injuries–United States—1993–1998. *Morbidity and Mortality Weekly Report*, 50 (SS02): 1–32. Atlanta: Centers for Disease Control.

Horowitz, J. (2012). Aurora's Hard Truth: Mental Health Screening for Gun Buyers is Nearly Non-Existent. Huffington Post, August 1. http://www.huffington post. com/josh-horwitz/auroras-hard-truth-mental_b_1727695.html

Horsey, D. (2013). Rising movie gun violence gives rise to concerns over movie ratings. Los Angeles Times, November 13. http://articles.latimes.com/2013/ nov/13/entertainment /la-et-ct-horsey-on-hollywood-movie-violence-20131113.

Hoyert, D. L. and Xu, J. (2012). Deaths: preliminary data for 2011. *National Vital Statistics Reports*, 61 (6). Atlanta: Centers for Disease Control.

Huffington Post. (2013). Sandy Hook gun-maker profits up 52 percent in year since massacre. *Huffington Post*, December, 13. http://www.huffingtonpost.com/ 2013/12/13/ sandy-hook-gun-profits_n_444420134.html.

Kain, E. (2013). The Truth About Video Games and Gun Violence Do brutal games lead to mass shootings? What do three decades of research really tell us? *Mother Jones*, June 11. http://www.motherjones.com/politics/2013/06/ video-games-violence-guns-explainer

Kaiser Foundation. (2013). Number of deaths due to firearms per 100,000 population by race and ethnicity. http://kff.org/other/state-indicators/firearm-death-rate-by-race-and-ethnicity Law Center To Prevent Gun Violence. (2012). "Key federal acts regulating guns." May 21. http://smartgunlaws.org/key-federal-acts-regulating-guns/

National Archives. (n.d.). "The charters of freedom, a new world is at hand: Bill of Rights." Accessed July 14, 2014. http://www.archives.gov/exhibits/charters/bill_of_right_transcript.html

Perkins, Craig. (2003). Weapon use and violent crime. *Bureau of Justice Statistics.* Pew Research Center. (2013). Gun violence in America. *Pew Research Social And Demographic Trends.* http://www.pewsocialtrends.org/2013/05/07/gun-violence-inamerica/st_13-05-02_ss_guncrimes_o5_race/

Planty, M. and Truman, J. L. (2013). *Firearm Violence. 1993–2011.* Bureau of Justice Statistics.

Plumer, B. (2012). How the U.S. gun industry became so lucrative. *Washington Post*, December 19. http://www.washingtonpost.com/blogs/wonkblog/wp/ 2012/12/19/seven-facts-about-the-u-s-gun-industry/.

Prevention Institute. (n.d.) Gun Violence Must Stop. Here's What We Can Do to Prevent More Deaths. http://www.preventioninstitute.org/focus-areas/ preventing -violence-and-reducing-injury/preventing-violence-advocacy.html.

Rand, M. R. (2008). *Criminal Victimization, 2007*. Bureau of Justice Statistics.

———. (2009). *Criminal Victimization, 2008*. Bureau of Justice Statistics.

——— and Catalano, S. (2007). *Criminal Victimization, 2006*. Bureau of Justice Statistics.

Rennison, C. M. (1999). *Criminal Victimization, 1998: Changes 1997–98* with trends 1993–98. Bureau of Justice Statistics.

———. (2000). *Criminal Victimization, 1999: Changes 1998–99 with trends 1993–99*. Bureau of Justice Statistics.

———. (2002). *Criminal Victimization, 2001: Changes 2000-01 with trends 1993-2001*. Bureau of Justice Statistics.

——— and Rand, M. R. (2003). *Criminal Victimization, 2002*. Bureau of Justice Statistics.

Richinick, M. (2014). Why aren't mass shootings called terrorism? *Morning Joe*, MSNBC network, January 29. http://www.msnbc.com/morning-joe/why-arent-mass-shootings-called-terror

Sanburn, J. (2012). America's gun economy, by the numbers. *Time Business*, December 18. http://business.time.com/2012/12/18/americas-gun-economy-by-the-numers/print/

Shapira, I., Jackman, T. and Schneider, H. (2007). Gunman who killed 32 lived in a Va. Tech dormitory. *The Washington Post*, April 17. http://www. washingtonpost.com/wp-dyn/content/article/2007/04/17/AR200741700456 _pf.html

Siegel, L. J. (2015). *Criminology: The Core. 5th Edition*. Stamford: Cengage.

Siegel, R. (2005). Tipper Gore and family values. *National Public Radio*, January 11. http://www.npr.org/templates/story/story.php?storyId=4279560

South Carolina Radio Network. (2013). Ohio gun manufacturer to build new plant in Horry County. *South Carolina Radio Network*, October 17. http://www.southcarolina radionetwork.com/2013/10/17/ohio-gun-manufacturer-to-build-new-plant-in-horry-county/

Southern Poverty Law Center. (2014). *Terror From the Right: Plots, Conspiracies and Racist Rampages Since Oklahoma City*. http://www.splcenter.org/get-informed/ publications/terror-from-the-right

Stark, C. (2013). Obama calls out video games in gun violence address. *Mashable.com*, January 16. http://mashable.com/2013/01/16/obama-game-violence/

Stone, L. (2013). Gun manufacturers respond to tax incentives. Tax Foundation, August 13. http://taxfoundation.org/blog/gun-manufacturers-respond-tax-incentives.

Truman, J. L. (2011). *Criminal Victimization, 2010*. Bureau of Justice Statistics.

——— and Planty, M. (2013). *Criminal Victimization, 2012*. Bureau of Justice Statistics.

Truman, J. L. and Rand, M. R. (2010). *Criminal Victimization, 2009*. Bureau of Justice Statistics.

United Nations Office on Drugs and Crime. (2012) Homicide Statistics— *Homicides by Firearms*.

United Nations Population Division. (2000). Population in 1999 and 2000: all countries. *World Population Prospects: The 1998 Revision, Volume I: Comprehensive Tables*.

U.S. Census Bureau. (n.d.). Census Bureau regions and divisions with state FIPS codes. http://www.census.gov/maps-data/maps/pdfs/reference/us_regdiv.pdf

———. (2000). Historical population estimates: July 1, 1900 to July 1, 1999. http://www. census.gov/population/estimates/nation/popclockest.txt

White, J. (2012). Lee Boyd Malvo, 10 years after D.C. area sniper shootings:'I was a monster'. *The Washington Post*. September 29.

Wihbey, J. (2014). Mass murder. shooting sprees and rampage violence: Research roundup. *Journalist's Resource*, Harvard Kennedy School. http://journalistsresource. org/studies/government/criminal-justice/mass-murder-shooting-sprees-and-rampage-violence-research-roundup#sthash.pegGijls.dpuf

Windolf, J. (2008). Q & A: Steven Spielberg on Indiana Jones. *Vanity Fair*, January 2. http://www.vanityfair.com/culture/features/2008/02/spielberg-qanda200802/

Chapter Two

Shattered Self-Images: Narcissism, Egotistical Suicide and School Shooters

Selina Doran and Mary Ann O'Grady

Introduction

The authors of this chapter suggest that it has become necessary to examine environmental and socio-cultural factors in addition to the typical psychological assessments of individuals who [seemingly] engage in school shootings with or without a previous history of violent or aggressive behavior. Four school shooting case studies occurring in the U.S. within the ten-year period of 2003–2013 and meeting certain criteria (to be discussed in the methodology section) provide the material for analyses: Red Lake (2005), Amish schoolhouse (2006), Virginia Tech (2007), and Sandy Hook (2012). The chapter looks at the personalities and writings of school shooters in relation to suicide and narcissism.

To begin with, since most school shooters kill themselves following massacres, a useful starting point to assessing their behavioral conditions is to study suicide. Durkheim's (1987) *Suicide: A Study in Sociology* is renowned for interrogating conditions external to the individual and relating these to the conditions in which suicide occurs. Durkheim (1897/1952, 99) set out with the following mission: "without asking why [suicides] differ from one another we will first seek the social conditions responsible for them. . ." "Egotistical suicide" is a state of extreme individualism and worthless stemming from a lack of connection with society; this fits with the mindset of school shooters during their lives and as they plan their horrific attacks. This type of suicide has parallels with the personality condition "narcissism."

What this chapter intends to do is evince the narcissism of school shooters via examination of their personality traits and discourse analysis of their personal writings. Considering the narcissism literature, it certainly seems viable that the aggressive behavior of the perpetrators is related to threats of their unwarranted sense of superiority. Notably, it has been said that "a successful violent attack achieves a symbolic dominance over the other person, and so it affirms one's esteem to the extent of being superior over others" (Baumeister, et al., 1996, 11).

The layout of this chapter is as follows: Durkheim's theory of "egotistical suicide" is assessed and related to the literature on narcissism, providing theoretical foundations for the analyses; the methodological approaches of selecting case studies, discourse analysis of writings, and developing the model using a "grounded theory" approach are outlined in the next section; the profiles of the four school shooting case studies are thereafter discussed, relating writings to theories of narcissism and a Durkheimian understanding of suicide; lastly, the "deliverables" of a threat assessment model and suggestions for future research in this area are provided.

Theoretical Context

Suicide

Durkheim's (1987) *Suicide: A Study in Sociology* is renowned for interrogating conditions external to the individual and relating these to the conditions in which suicide occurs. A commentator on Durkheim's study noted that he treated suicide as both a social problem requiring a sociological solution and a moral one, which stems from the moralistic elements of society as an entity (Ramp, 2000, 88–89). Durkheim recognized that the true motives of suicide are somewhat a mystery, since only presumed reasons are recorded. Suicides in the study are, therefore, classified by causes rather than characteristics pertaining to the suicides themselves (Durkheim, 1897/2002, 99). In that sense, he is moving from micro-level analyses of individuals to the macro-level, structural conditions which influenced that individual to commit suicide:

> Disregarding the individual as such, his motives and his ideas, we shall seek directly the state of the various social environments (religious confessions, family, political society, occupational groups, etc.), in terms of which the variations of suicide occur (Durkheim, 1897/1952, 104).

In this chapter, the authors used Durkheim's framework as a lens for viewing the action of school shootings, but limitations of his text were scrutinized and challenged as appropriate.

Durkheim's (1897) theory of suicide was based on the four general typologies each with its specific motivating factors: egoistic, caused by social disconnect and isolation; anomic, caused by lack of purpose or societal role; fatalistic, caused by a desire to escape pain and oppression exerted by society or societal norms; and altruistic, caused by the perspective that the needs of the collective outweigh self-worth. The type pivotal to this chapter's discussion of narcissism is "egotistic suicide": the most prolific type of suicide characterized by a state of depression and apathy, where the individual lacks a desire to live. This state of "egoism" is said to occur when "the individual ego asserts itself to excess in the face of the social ego" (Durkheim, 1897/1952, 169); therefore, "we may call egoistic the special type of suicide springing from excessive individualism" (Durkheim, 1897/1952, 168). Social integration and collective sentiment are said to be the best mechanisms to restrain suicide, so when they weaken the individual is vulnerable to egoism (Durkheim, 1897/2002, 168). Religions and changing prejudices—the result of extensive education—lead to "excessive individualism," which breaks down society's ties to an individual; the more an individual interprets aspects of society, the more he will become alienated from it (Durkheim, 1897/1952, 209–210).

Lankford (2013) published a quantitative analysis comparing the characteristics and suicide tendencies of suicide terrorists—who tend to be driven by political ideologies—and those of rampage workplace, and school shooters between the years of 1990 and 2010. The attack characteristics served to explain the nature of the suicide attempt, where only 8 percent of the suicide terrorists' deaths were completely self-controlled and self-harming since the majority involved other individuals, such as suicide by airplane collision or suicide by cop. In sharp contrast, 89 percent of rampage shooters, 88 percent of school shooters, and 91 percent of workplace shooters had attempted to commit suicide by a self-controlled and self-harming method, which occurs with the arrival of law enforcement which forces the perpetrators to make the decision on how they want to die. In addition, Lankford (2013) discovered a significant difference in the attacks that included suicide notes or some type of written explanation where suicide terrorists, school shooters, and rampage shooters exhibited similar behaviors by writing notes or explanations in 50 percent to 67 percent of the cases, while only 11 percent of the workplace shooters provided a written note or explanation prior to their attacks. Workplace shooters were the most successful in suicide attempts at a rate of 91 percent. Ultimately, identifying the patterns shared by these four types of per-petrators may assist individuals who are charged with administering threat assessment, developing security initiatives, and conducting interventions or taking preventive measures in the lives of at-risk individuals.

Narcissism

A nexus exists between *egotistical suicide* and the condition "narcissism": a Freudian term based on the mythology of Narcissus, who was infatuated with his own image (Bushman and Baumeister, 1998, 220). The Narcissistic Personality Inventory (NPI) is a forced choice questionnaire consisting of forty items, based on the *American Psychiatric Association*'s DSM-III (1980) clinical evaluation and examines the following personality traits: sensation-seeking, a lack of empathy, creativity, (low) self-esteem, extraversion, psychoticism, dominance, and egocentricity. A seminal work by Kohut (1977) suggested that narcissism plays a role in both healthy and pathological conditions, but individuals who exhibit narcissistic disorders do not function as well during times of elevated stress or conflict due to insufficient coping mechanisms. These stressors may include a variety of environmental or situational factors, such as rejection in a personal or intimate relationship, or growing up in an internally dysfunction family which can result in feelings of rage, lack of empathy, and an inability to form peer relationships or friendships. The feelings commonly shared by this individuals include: feeling left out or feeling different from other family members or peers; or not being accepted for whom they are which sets up the dynamics for periods of intense self-doubt or anxiety that can be defended by narcissistic grandiosity punctuated by periods of boredom or emptiness and alienation. More notably, the criteria for the NPI are: a grandiose sense of self-importance or superiority; fantasies of success, power, beauty and so forth; exhibitionism, sensitivity to criticism; feeling indifferent towards others; exploiting interpersonal relationships and expecting favors without reciprocating; a lack of empathy; and alternating between over-idealizing and devaluating other people (Bradlee and Emmons, 1992, 823).

Several theorists (Baumeister, *et al.* 1996; Bushman and Baumeister, 1998; Feldmann, *et al.*, 1990; Kohut, 1977; Twenge and Campbell, 2003) have argued that narcissism is more likely to lead to aggression. Notably, Kohut (1977) theorized that individuals diagnosed as "severe borderline or narcissistic pathological" tend to fit that criteria of engaging in unprovoked violence directed toward unknown victims as a result of a cofactor or self-object which provides a framework or structure for the "damaged" self. Disappointments and other empathic failures may trigger bouts of narcissistic rage combined with fantasies of revenge and other violent crimes that may deteriorate into self-destructive acts, such as drug or alcohol abuse which in turn leads to a greater inability to inhibit risk-taking or violent and aggressive behaviors (Feldmann, et al., 1990). Baumeister, *et al.* (1996) refuted the axiom that violent attacks can be conflated with low self-esteem, hypothesizing instead that threatened egotism of unwarranted, highly favorable views of self (i.e. in narcissistic individuals) could result in violence and aggression. The element of having an ill-founded superior sense of worth is pertinent to this reaction, where "favourable views of self that are unwarranted, exaggerated, or ill-founded would be especially prone to disconfirmation by accurate feedback." As a result of this, "instances of minor, slight, or minimal feedback could elicit strong reactions from such insecure egotists, whereas secure egotists would dismiss such events as too trivial to be worth a response" (Baumeister, *et al.*, 1996, 9–10). Kohut (1977) purported that, in an attempt to mitigate his or her narcissistic vulnerability, the individual uses "self objects" to restore cohesion and reduce self fragmentation.

Interestingly, due to the depressive and apathetic state prior to an act of "egoistic suicide" and the passion involved in carrying out a violent act, Durkheim believes that this does not usually lead to homicide-suicide (Durkheim, 1897/2002, 322–323). On the contrary, it is maintained that the *anomic* type of suicide has the strongest link to homicide, due to its "state of exasperation and irritated weariness"

(Durkheim, 1897/2002, 324). In the case of the person who commits egoistic suicide, Durkheim (1897/2002, 322) alleged that "he cares little for human pain, [and so] he feels the weight of his personal sufferings less." Subsequent research conducted by Maris, *et al.* (2000), however, indicated that these four causes of suicide often interact, so that an individual may battle with multiple urges on the road to committing suicide. In addition, a list of specific risk indicators has been identified which include: social isolation, depression, humiliation or shame, a sense of hopelessness, rage, a stressful family life, the failure of a romantic relationship, failure at school or at work, and/or a precipitating crisis event. These parallel the school shooter characteristics identified by the *Federal Bureau of Investigation* (O'Toole, 2000) report.

Durkheim also makes some very interesting points on imitation and suicide that could be linked to the "copycat" nature of school shootings. Imitation is defined as "the immediate antecedent of an act is the representation of a like act, previously performed by someone else," which can occur between unconnected individuals (Durkheim, 1897/2002, 79). More importantly, "no imitation can exist without a model to imitate" (Durkheim, 1897/2002, 85) and that is where the "cultural script" of school shootings comes into play, prescribing a course of action (Newman, *et al.*, 2004, 230). The script infiltrated into society through the reporting and discussions of school shooting incidents becomes the "tool" as a coping strategy which school shooters use to try and solve their problems (Newman, *et al.*, 2004, 148). Paralleling this is Durkheim's (1897/2002, 85) acknowledgment that pertinent to the act of imitation is seeing the initial act; without this, the act of suicide will be non-existent. In the case of school shootings, these tend to be highly publicized and the ones that are particularly shocking (*Sandy Hook*, December 2012) or with the highest death count (*Virginia Tech*, April 2007) are notorious in nature. A further interesting point comes from Douglas (1967, 285) who argued that suicide is entrenched with meanings and so individuals' lives can be summed up through this action. For school shooters, the prospect of infamy through their act of homicide-suicide—more likely to come from particularly shocking and deadly attacks—is a driving force for them.

Fragile Male Identities

A commonality of school shooting incidents is that the perpetrators are male. Whitehead (2005) looked at masculinity as a risk factor in causing violent offending and purported that violence is indeed facilitated by the perpetrator equating it with manliness. Masculinity is a descriptive element of the cultural ideologies and observed behaviors of men. It has been pointed out that the term 'masculinity' in itself is problematic because, it is conceptually ill-defined, for masculinity is often conceived of differently, frequently within the same text (Collier, 1998, 16, 84). This gives some credibility to Treadwell and Garland's (2011, 3) assertions that "masculinity is multidimensional, varied and malleable" and there exists a "multiplicity of masculinities."

It has been acknowledged that there are various ways of "doing masculinity": crime is one of them (Messerschmidt, 1993, 81; Treadwell and Garland, 2011, 3). Most physical acts of violence are perpetrated by males (see Collier, 1998, 16, 84; Messerschmidt, 1993, 25–26, 80–81, 83; Treadwell and Garland, 2011, 3).The ideology of "hegemonic masculinity," which can be used to refer to particular characteristics, such as competitiveness, aggression, pride, 'machoness' and so forth, is also used as an explanation for the criminal behavior of males (Collier, 1998, 19). The absence of these characteristics suggests a lack of "masculinity" that translates into a "fragile male identity."

Since identity development is an ongoing social process (see Bauman, 2007; Erikson, 1968; Giddens, 1991; Jenkins, 2008; Mead, 1934) and "not even death freezes the picture: identity or reputation may be reassessed after death" (Jenkins, 2008, 17), school shooters seek to redefine their "fragile male identities" through their actions. Prior to that, perpetrators ensure their constructed "selves" are showcased by sending multi-media packages to news media outlets or uploading material to the internet: these have, therefore, been selected as units for analysis in this chapter. The "feedback" of others in the form of online reactions to school shooters fit with a social constructionist interpretation of identity construction: "It is not enough simply to assert an identity; that assertion must also be validated, or not, by those with whom we have dealings" (Jenkins, 2008, 42). Appropriately, it has been said that "the narcissist depends on others to validate his self-esteem" (Lasch, 1979, 10). School shooters, therefore, seek to reshape and showcase their newly constructed identities, albeit posthumously.

Qualitative Methodology/Grounded Theory

The data collection procedure for this research consisted of a qualitative document analysis (see Altheide, 1996) involving data collection from secondary sources, such as public and private documents: Internet posts and suicide notes respectively (Creswell, 2009). This section will go through each of the elements of selecting the case studies, conducting discourse analyses of writings, and developing a threat assessment model using a "grounded theory" approach.

Case Studies

The case study is said to be an "unappreciated and underutilised research tool" (Yin, 1992/2006, 83). For qualitative research into a specific type of incident like a school shooting, case studies are really the most viable approach. Newburn (2007, 911) said that the selection of case studies is: "not actually a methodological one, but a design one—something akin to sampling." Therefore, the steps involved in this process are: deciding upon the unit of analysis (i.e. the case); selecting single or multiple cases, specifying the criteria for this selection; and appropriating the most relevant data collection method (Yin, 1992/2006, 85–86). The selection of the four case studies included in this research were based upon the following criteria: date of shooting incident between the period of 2003 and 2013 so it was fairly recent cases; an attack which occurred at an educational institution of some kind; the killing of a minimum of four victims (as per the *FBI* definition of a mass shooting); and the access to documents and/or drawings constructed by the perpetrators, such as suicide notes, diaries, drawings, and so forth that would allow a detailed discourse analysis. In the beginning, this gave a population of ten potential case studies. After further investigation certain case studies were removed: instances where the perpetrator did not commit suicide (such as the Okios University shooting in Oakland), since this is a pertinent part of our hypothesis; incidents where no writings were left (such as the "Youth with a Mission" shooting in Colorado Springs); and gang-related shootings, rather than a specific attack against the institution. Consequently, four case studies were left that met the criteria: Sandy Hook Elementary School, Connecticut (2012); Virginia Tech University, Virginia (2007); Amish schoolhouse, Pennsylvania (2006); and Red Lake High School, Minnesota (2005). These were split between the two authors, with each being responsible for two specific case studies; although, to improve validity, the authors functioned as co-raters where the "profiles"—overview of incidents, key themes emerging, and discourse analyses of writings—developed by each author were checked by the other.

Constructing Profiles

For each of the case studies, the authors assessed print news media coverage to put together profile factsheets of perpetrators' lives before the incident and their behavior during the attack, including their deaths. Notable throughout this process was the disparity in the media coverage between the Virginia Tech and Sandy Hook incidents compared to the lesser-known ones of Red Lake and Amish schoolhouse: this suggests that the location and scope of the mass killings dictated the investment of time and interest put forth by the newspaper staff.

This was evident for both the less well-known cases of Red Lake and the Amish schoolhouse. In the case of the Red Lake incident, analyses were conducted using a series of *Minnesota Public Radio* in-depth feature articles and one-off articles from *FOX News, CNN, TIME* and the *New York Times*. What was illustrative in this case was the fact that there was not as much media attention given to this school shooting as previous cases and this was reflected in there being less coverage; also, there was little in the way of local news archives. The information that was collected on the Amish Shooting, conversely, tended to originate from local town newspapers, such as the *Bucks, County Courier Times, Delaware County Daily Times, The Mercury, The Times Herald*, and so forth.

For the highly publicized cases of Virginia Tech and Sandy Hook, there were a multitude of news coverage, so of key importance here was selecting which of those stories to analyze. In the end, the decision was made in the case of Virginia Tech to focus on the two local papers—which are most likely to interview local community members and have more saturated coverage than national sources —the *Roanoke Times* and *Richmond Times Dispatch*, alongside the newsweeklies *Newsweek* and *Time* which featured detailed and descriptive feature articles. As a supplement to this, the *Virginia Tech Review Panel* report, which gathered background information about the perpetrator's background and childhood using multiple sources, was consulted for additional information. The information that was collected on the Sandy Hook, Connecticut shooting originated from the *Associated Press State Wire*: Connecticut newspaper articles. The shocking nature of the event might that it had coverage in local and national press, but the local articles had the most information available given its geographical proximity to the incident and access to local community members as interview sources.

Discourse Analysis of Writings

School shooters have became increasingly proactive in the process of "managing" their identities after death, by preparing materials (suicide notes, manifestos explaining motives, blueprints of attack plan) knowing there will be media interest. These writings are especially relevant to the investigation since many of the incidents result in the death of the shooter due to suicide, suicide-by-cop, or other situational circumstances leaving no option for communication with the perpetrator post-event—these manifestos are rich territory for getting inside the heads of perpetrators and interrogating their motivations.

All four case studies left some form of legacy for analysis. The Red Lake (2005) shooter left an active online legacy to be analyzed: this revealed more about the identity he projected online and forum discussions provided an insight into the Neo-Nazi ideologies driving him. Part of Virginia Tech (2007) shooter's attack plan was to put together a multi-media package, consisting of twenty-seven video clips, an 800-word document and 43 captioned photos into the broadcast news station *National Broadcasting Company (NBC)*. It could be said that Cho's manifesto, showcased through saturated new media coverage and on video-sharing sites such as YouTube, created a "mega media spectacle" (Kellner, 2007), where consumers are seduced and fascinated by images within the media. The Amish school shooter (2006) wrote a suicide note to his wife and family, which is far less sophisticated than the more technologically savvy school shooters that followed after him leaving videos and Internet posts to document their legacies. At Robert Charles, IV's point in the timeline, it is not likely that he would have ever imagined that his handwritten note would have been scanned and uploaded to the Internet for a global audience. Since the Sandy Hook, Connecticut school shooting (2012), there has been a clamor for the release of additional information regarding the case and the authors here believed at the time of writing that these would be available for analysis. To retrieve these documents, one of the authors regularly liaised with the Connecticut State Attorney. The most recent telephone conference with State Attorney Sedensky in September 2013 revealed that the Sandy Hook school shooting incident is still classified as "under investigation," with the formal investigative report still to be written which suggests that it will be months—if ever—that these subpoenaed documents are released to the public. For that reason, the Sandy Hook writings were not able to be included in this chapter.

The technique chosen to analyze the writings of the Red Lake, Amish schoolhouse, and Virginia Tech perpetrators is "discourse analysis." The main purpose of this research method is to interrogate the textual descriptions within discourse by examining both semantics (dealing with denotations of words and sentences) on a micro-level to deal with small-scale meanings and macro-level to incorporate global ones and syntax (the arrangement and combination of words in sentences); and, secondly, pragmatically relating these findings to wider contextual dimensions, such as socio-cultural influences (van Dijk, 1988, 24-27). It has been stated that discourse is 'language in use' (Brown and Yule, 1983, 1). A Foucaultian perspective would argue that discourse is not just a piece of text—meaning assessing the units of language by themselves would be of little value—but a practice which *constructs* the meaning and affects ideas are translated into action. Consequently, this means that the context and functions of discourse must be addressed (Mayr and Machin, 2012, 7–8). A rather accurate summarizer of discourse then is Fairclough's (2012, 11) definition: "Discourses are semiotic ways of construing aspects of the world." What we are seeking to do here, therefore, is to evoke the key themes arising from the writings of school shooters and thereafter assess these through the analytical lens of narcissism and suicide theories. This is the most effective way of getting into school shooters' thoughts, allowing for the development of a threat assessment model (to be discussed in the "deliverables" section). The findings of the discourse analyses of writings will be outlined in the next section.

Grounded Theory Approach

Grounded theory provided the strategy of inquiry for these researchers to develop a general theory pertaining to the motives, methods, and behaviors of school shooters grounded in the views of the perpetrators. The "grounded theory" approach is one of developing theory through constant comparative analysis at all stages of the data collection and analysis process. It was conceptualized by Glaser and Strauss (1967) to diminish the "embarrassing gap" between theory and research. This process involved utilizing multiple stages of data collection, and the categorization, refinement, and identification of the inter-relationship among those categories of data (Charmaz, 2006; Strauss and Corbin, 1990, 1998) as cited in Creswell (2009). The two primary characteristics of grounded theory are a consistent comparison of data according with the emerging categories, and a theoretical sampling of the different groups in order to maximize the comparison and contrast of information. Through the development of theories, Bottom's (2000. 44) approach to "grounded theory" was taken into account:

1. Acknowledging that material will be entangled with some degree of theoretical context: narcissism literature and Durkheim's theory of suicide:
2. Engaging in the cultivation and testing of hypotheses throughout the research process, and being open to findings which may challenge pre-conceived expectations of results: in this case, counteractions to Durkheim's view that the "egotistic" type does not tend to lead to homicide-suicides;
3. Appreciating the point made by Glaser and Strauss that theory formulation is a 'process': this chapter had a two-fold method of assessing incidents and the perpetrators' lives and thereafter their writings;
4. Appreciating the relevance of concepts throughout all stages of the research: these authors acknowledge that there exist many findings outside the parameters set of narcissism and suicide theories: research here is only a snapshot into what is available.

Throughout the research carried out in this thesis, the continuing process of theory refinement, appreciating the importance-and limitations-of concepts, utilizing the appropriate type of sources and research methods, being open to new data which may surface, was adopted.

Profiling School Shooters and Incidents

Applying this to school shooters actually shows that the case studies demonstrate a lack of empathy for others and yet still feel they themselves are prosecuted by others matching the Narcissism Personality Inventory; therefore, narcissism is a driving force in allowing for this crossover from a state of depression and apathy —which school shooters are in—to a desire to kill others for a perceived injustice, namely "failing" to treat the perpetrators with the respect they believe they are owed. Moreover, it seems that school shooters seem to fall under the rubric of "overt narcissism," rather than its "covert" form, where sufferers lack energy and motivation of any kind (Twenge and Campbell, 2003, 262).Taking into considera-tion Durkheim's (1897/2002, 169) argument that for the individual in the state of egoism "life is intolerable unless some reason for existing is involved," it then becomes clear that for school shooters in that mind frame the plan of homicide-suicide—always planned well in advance—motivates them to continue living until they are ready to carry out their attack.

Red Lake

Overview of Incident

The Red Lake shooting was perpetrated at a school on Red Lake Indian Reservation, a poor and remote area of Minnesota, where four fifths of students at the school were poor enough to be entitled to free lunches. The perpetrator was a sixteen year old Native American. Jeffrey Weise, who lived with his grandfather, a tribal police officer, because his father committed suicide and his mother was in a nursing home. Weise supported a "National Socialist Government" and expressed admiration for Hitler and Nazism on Neo-Nazi websites and had swastikas on his notebooks. This is something he has in common with the Columbine perpetrators who would shout "Heil Hitler" in school. This is not uncommon, as these are all 'figures of power' that must have appealed to the shooters who felt inferior as men (Langman, 2009, 150).A threat at his school planned for Hitler's birthday was pinned on him because of his ideological beliefs,[1] although he was later cleared of this due to a lack of evidence.

At the time of the shooting, Weise was homeschooled for breaking the rules at school (unconfirmed what he did). There were rumors that his small group of friends was part of a "Darker" clique, which dressed in "Gothic black" clothes with spiked, dyed hair shaped to look like horns and piercings; plus, he wore a trench-coat to school reminiscent of gangsters who wore similar attire to conceal their weapons. The clique and clothing is reminiscent of the "Trench Coat Mafia" clique with regards to Columbine. It seems that focusing on a particular social group at school provides a "folk devil" (see Cohen 1972/2002) symbolizing the "threat" and resulting in stigmatizing of that group. At school, even though he was over six foot tall, he was still bullied a lot at school: some students describe him as quiet and non-threatening loner, even though he did have a small group of friends; one that he wounded called him a "cool guy," although admitted that Weise always talked about guns and killing; others were afraid of him and described him as "scary." It seems he was more of an extrovert online, with him experimenting with "online identities," some of them threatening and others were more submissive suggesting a desire to please his "audience" on particular sites.

Mirroring the Lanza case, Weise killed the relative with whom he lived (grandfather) prior to his school attack, plus the grandfather's companion. It seems that these were killings of convenience, however, so he could take his grandfather's bulletproof vest, gun belt and weapons. Weise fired two shotgun blasts in the air as a warning when he arrived at the school. The unarmed security guard confronted Weise and thereafter was shot in the chest and back. It seemed Weise killed the security guard because he was "in the way," although a fictional story he wrote had strange parallels: the main protagonist hated the security guard at his school for making him go through metal detectors and it ended up that the guard was the first to be killed by a zombie. Thereafter, Weise followed a 62-year old teacher to her classroom where he did the rest of his killing. In the classroom, Weise walked round the room in ninety seconds and shot students in the head at close-range as they hid under desks.

There is little doubt that Weise was inspired by the Columbine perpetrators. Not only did he share their Neo-Nazi beliefs and tendency towards racism, but he also replicated a number of aspects from their attack. Firstly, Weise wore similar attire of black hooded trench coat, military pants, bandana and military boots. During his shooting rampage, when a teacher said "God be with us," this provoked Weise to shoot her. He asked a male student whether he believed in God, the boy answered "No" and Weise turned and shot someone else instead.[2] Weise was also said to be grinning and waving as he fired at students, which paralleled the Columbine perpetrators laughing and taunting students (such as saying "Peekaboo!" to a girl hiding under a desk) before they shot them. This is a particularly disturbing aspect of the attack, for this suggests he derived enjoyment and pleasure in the acting of killing.

When tribal police officers entered the building, Weise was shot in the hip and leg. He yelled "I have hostages" to buy himself some time as law enforcement was closing in and shot himself in the same classroom where the majority of his victims lay. He shot himself under his chin, seemingly to ensure his suicidal attack would be successful. Again, this fits the pattern of school shooters killing themselves as law enforcement close in allowing them one final act of power: deciding when and how they die and removing any possibility of them being arrested (and thereafter being given the death penalty, although that would depend on the state). Overall, Weise killed two at home and seven at the school (five students, one security guard and a teacher), giving it one of the highest school shooting death tolls.

Online Writings

The archive of online material included profiles on sites, fictional stories he posted online, and discussions in forums. This allowed a deeper insight into his ideas, feelings and where he may have drew inspiration from. To begin with, the profiles he created were illustrative. On the site *New Grounds*, he listed two of his favorite films as the ones based on the Columbine shooting: *Elephant* and *Zero Day*. On *MSN* his profile lists his interests as revolving around killing and dying, plus his favorite things are school shootings and racial purity. His history is described as "accumulated rage" with brief glimpses of hope and it is stated that he cannot control his urges any longer, which is reflective of Freudian psychoanalytic theory. Accordingly, under the *Yahoo!* "occupation" heading, he lists "bein [sic] a problem." It is unclear to what he is referring to here: Being a burden to his grandfather? Causing trouble at school due to his beliefs? Exemplifying his feelings was a post on *LiveJournal* four months before the shooting about "things changing" and a "new me." This indicates that he was trying to make a fresh start. A month after that, however, he made a post that seemed to be rather self-deprecating and rage-induced in nature and suggested he was experiencing a wave of negative emotions. He criticized himself for being "naive" for expecting change and that a part of him has died and "he hates this shit"—it seems something disappointing must have happened to him around this time. There is also evidence of self-deprecation within the post with him stating "I really must be fucking worthless." This highlights a narcissistic identity as "the alternating feelings of grandiosity and worthlessness . . . are essentially responses to a fragile self-identity liable to be overwhelmed by shame" (Giddens, 1991, 178). He also references mothers who choose boyfriends over their children and others choosing alcohol over friendship. This is perhaps an oblique reference to how he feels about his parents: his father killed himself when Weise was eight and his mother was left brain-damaged after a car crash two years later. Kohut's research (1977) found that narcissistic behavior was intensified when there is an absence of a parent/caregiver. Weise's primary guardian became his grandfather and he was the first to be killed when Weise went on his shooting attack.

On the site *Above Top Secret*, Weise participated in a discussion with other users, posting that he was worried about the Native American omen about sighting a white owl, suggesting he was superstitious. One of the other users made a joke about "him killing himself" and Weise responded by revealing he had tried to commit suicide in the past; thereafter, other users provided supportive comments and advice. During his life, Weise used box cutters to slit his wrists and was on anti-depressants as a result of this, so this comment was truthful. The desire not to live fits the requirements for "egotistical suicide" (Durkheim, 1897). There were also references on *Yahoo!* to his depression and self-harm. He did not leave a suicide note, however, on the wrist-slitting occasion or prior to his shooting rampage—perhaps because he felt no one cared enough about him to want to read it.

By contrast, on the same site, he engaged in a dialogue about school shootings, explaining that he was the prime suspect of a threat made at his school. The school shooting threat on his school, where he almost gleefully stated that law enforcement were prepared for something to happen, suggested that he perhaps called in the threat to gauge their reaction to threats. Further, he stated that he fits the profile of a "school shooter" and lists all the reasons why: his military attire, shouting "Heil Hitler," having a clique similar to the "Trench Coat Mafia," not being popular, and partaking in Gothic subculture practices such as wearing black. This creates the question of whether he was trying to get caught by posting this. It certainly seems that was a way for Weise to "perform" a "school shooter identity" publicly, given he posted this on the internet.

Relating this to a Goffmanesque understanding of "performance" finds that "presenting self" to an audience as a means to gain acceptance from others: "when an individual plays a part he implicitly requests his observers to take seriously the impression that is fostered before them" (Goffman, 1959/1990, 28). To clarify, it is said that a person presents themselves to others in a certain way and if this presentation is *accepted* then elements of it become part of that person's identity. Depending on how important approval is to the presenter, therefore, the "audience" can either validate or refute someone's identity on the basis of their performance

(Jenkins, 2008, 71). This is similar to Mead's (1934, 178) argument that "the 'I' both calls out the 'me' and responds to it. Taken together they constitute personality." To clarify, the 'I' represents the "acting self" and the 'me' is the "the voice in part of others" (Mead, 1934, 177), therefore people's sense of self "arises through the taking of attitudes of others" (Mead, 1934, 174–175).This would be a way for Weise to gain attention and recognition, as it is said that the narcissist can only overcome his insecurity by "seeing his 'grandiose self' reflected in the attention of others . . . for the narcissist the world is a mirror" (Lasch, 1979, 10). The problem with this for narcissists is that "fictive mirrors offer grandiose highly unrealistic images in which the self can 'see' (and often mis-see) itself" (Martin, 1988, 140).

The clearest theme to emerge from his online postings was the extent of his Neo-Nazi ideologies. On *Yahoo*, his user name was in German and references "4/20," Hitler's birthday. His hobbies include "Being a Native American National Socialist" and his favorite quote is by Hitler and references "uninterrupted killing so the better may live,"—parallels with the "natural selection" beliefs of the Columbine perpetrator, Eric Harris—showing the Neo-Nazism has been incorporated into his identity. The Nationalist Forums (nazi.org) seem to be where Weise really expresses his feelings and thoughts, such as admiration for Hitler and his "courage" and "ideals." A collective identity is forged on there with other similar-minded people, with one user using terms like "combined minds" "nationalists" and "unite" to convey the sense of belonging and patriotism. This is an example of a "virtual community" that would have given Weise some sense of belonging. These communities are "interpersonal social networks" (Castells, 2000, 389) tied only to cyberspace. Bauman (2007, 111) describes these as "phantom-like cloakroom communities," as someone's mere presence makes them a member allowing them able to simply leave the community at any time.

Returning to Weise's profile now, he chose the user name "NativeNazi"— suggesting a merging of his beliefs into his identity—and engaged in a detailed dialogue on the site, no doubt motivated by the praise, encouraging comments, and questions he receives from other users who are surprised by the concept of a Native American National Socialist. Willingness was expressed by him to do more for the movement: he tried to recruit friends, but to no avail. Moreover, he is critical of the school for bestowing upon his peers "poisoned opinions" against Nazism and racial purity. Weise explained that after he read about the Third Reich he released that "they truly were doing it for the better." It seems he is particularly disgusted that his teachers and most students oppose his views—perhaps going some way to explain his inclination to carry out his attack at the school. The alienation he felt from the school and his peers do to his distinct prejudices shows a breakdown in social cohesion, creating the optimum conditions for a state of "egoism" to develop (Durkheim, 1897/2002, 168).

The dialogue on the site also persuaded him to think about the degradation of Native American culture. When speaking about the Red Lake reservation where he lives, Weise puts the word Indian in scare quotes to convey irony (see Fairclough,

1992, 123) and he also notes that there are few "pure blooded Natives" left. Of particular note is his disgust at the "Americanization" of Native American teenagers, arguing that they "walk, talk, act and dress like an African American." The school is once again a particular site of anger for him since the teachers at the school (bar one) are all White and they have called him racist—which he described as "silencing him"—for expressing his views that Native people should not be with White people to "keep their blood pure."[3] This could have been the development of his hatred for the school and provoked his idea of attacking the institution as a twisted form of "revenge."

Amish Schoolhouse

Overview of Incident

The problems of Charles Carl Roberts IV better known as the "Amish school shooter," were similar to Cho in that they also appeared to manifest at an early age. Roberts was devastated by the death of his newborn daughter, Elise in 1997 as she lived for only twenty minutes and he continued to carry anger and rage toward God and life in general. There were numerous references published by the media regarding his "torment" caused by memories of molesting two female relatives twenty years ago when he was aged twelve, and they were aged three and five, although his two female relatives deny any recollection of the incidents. This torment was believed to be ongoing as he struggled with impulses to do it again.

Roberts' penchant for revenge and contempt for female—particularly young girls to whom he seemed to feel irresistible urges—was illustrated during the school shooting incident where he specifically targeted female victims, while allowing the male students and the adults acting as teaching aides who had small children [reminiscent of his daughter, Elise] to exit the classroom unharmed. This is very similar to the Platte Canyon High hostage situation (Colorado, 2006), which involved an external attacker keeping female students hostage and letting male students and the teacher leave. Evidence found and confiscated from the crime scene had suggested that he, paralleling the sexual assaults of the Platte Canyon case, had been planning to sexually assault his female victims if allowed a sufficient amount of time—law enforcement arrived before he could go through with this—and blamed them for his conflicted sexual desire. Local police considered his comments credible enough to investigate him as a person of interest in an attempted, yet unsolved, local rape case in 2005: although, no evidence was found to prove he did this.

One striking facet of Roberts' school shooting incident is his sense of preparation and organization at least until the unanticipated quick response of the local police at the Amish school house where he had barricaded himself with his female victims. His high degree of organization is suggestive of an "instrumental homicide" as his primary motive, which typically entails detailed planning over time, and may also suggest a tendency toward "obsessive compulsive disorder" (OCD), where Roberts adhered to his daily routine prior to engaging in his mass killing spree. For example, he dropped his three children off that morning at their regular school bus stop and proceeded to call his wife to tell her that he would not be coming home, and that he loved her. He had prepared himself for a lengthy siege with multiple weapons, six hundred rounds of ammunition, tools such as ties to bind his victims, and a change of clothes. The media reported that Roberts had drafted a checklist of items to carry out his plans, which suggested that he had meticulously planned his attack for a week prior to the school shooting incident.

Interviews subsequently conducted with family and friends of the shooter revealed nothing in his behavior that would have raised an alarm to his ensuing actions since his wife described him as "a loving spouse and caring father, not a homicidal killer" which is a far cry from the executioner who fatally shot and killed ten young female victims. One media source described him as a milkman working for Northwest Food Products; while another described him as "the 32-year-old milk-truck driver who looked every bit the stereotypical mild-mannered, bespectacled, all-American dad."These descriptions hardly fit the profile of a school shooter, plus he was an external attacker: this continues to challenge researchers and forensic experts who are attempting to construct an assessment for individuals who are at higher risk for committing school shootings. In retrospect, the State Police Commissioner, Jeffrey Miller, commented that "he certainly was very troubled psychologically deep down and was dealing with things that nobody else knew he was dealing with." The description most fitting the "quiet loner" profile is that of his neighbor, Mary Miller, who called him "quiet–but pretty standoffish."

Suicide Notes

Roberts' contentious relationship with women was evidenced by the suicide note addressed to his wife, Marie, where he communicated his feelings of imperfection and unworthiness:

> I don't know how you put up with me all those years. I am not worthy of you, you are the perfect wife you deserve so much better. We had so many good memories together as well as the tragedy with Elise. It changed my life forever I haven't been the same since it affected me in a way I never felt possible. I am filled with so much hate, hate towards myself, hate towards God and unimaginable emptiness it seems like every time we do something fun I think about how Elise wasn't there to share it with us and I go right back to anger.

Further content analysis of Roberts' suicide note also suggests an overwhelming sense of guilt that his baby daughter had not survived to be able to share in all the good memories and fun activities that he and the rest of his family had experienced since her death. This analysis also suggests a sense of self-loathing, perfectionism, emptiness, and isolation which are all symptoms of "Narcissistic

Personality Disorder" that is characterized by an underlying fragile self-esteem, a sense of shame and/or humiliate, and an inability to tolerate criticism which often causes a narcissist to respond with anger, rage, contempt, and a desire to belittle others. All of these traits, alongside anger towards females, may be illustrated by an analysis of the crime scene involving ten females aged six to ten years who were bound, lined up in front of the classroom blackboard, and then shot execution style.

Virginia Tech

Overview of Incident

As a young child, Cho's problems centered on his unusually introverted nature and, after a medical procedure, his dislike of being touched.[4] Later on in his life, Cho was diagnosed with major depression and "selective mutism," choosing to remain silent in certain situations or in front of certain people. The first real "red flag" came in High School, when Cho wrote a paper for English class consisting of homicidal and suicidal thoughts and the need to "repeat Columbine."

A key theme from the analysis of Cho's life events was that he appeared to approach life with apathy. When he went to university, this pattern continued as he made little effort with his peers and professors. Cho's roommate, Joe Aust, described him as "extremely antisocial," as he ignored Joe whenever he tried to speak to him. His suitemates initially tried to make an effort to engage him, but Cho's strange behavior continued: at a party they took him to, Cho took out a knife at one point and started stabbing the carpet; he continuously referred to himself as "question mark" and had an imaginary girlfriend called Jelly; he burned papers in his dorm room and hid them under a sofa cushion; he phoned his suitemates pretending to be Cho's twin brother and asked to speak to himself.

In his classes, Cho's actions also raised some concerns: for a play-writing course, Cho wrote a play about a young man who hates the students at his school and wants to kill them, plus he writes a further three stories filled with gratuitous violence; his poetry class professor, Nikki Giovanni, felt he was trying to bully her with his disturbing behavior in class, such as sitting with a hat covering his head, always looking down, speaking in an inaudible tone, and refusing to make any changes to his work; when the poetry class professor told him to tone down the violent content in his poetry, Cho responded with "You can't make me."[5] Other students were afraid of him in the poetry class and so attendance fell. One of his peers from that module, Ann Brown, said "he was just off, in a very creepy way" and she used to joke that Seung Hui-Cho "was the kind of guy who might go on a rampage killing." Similarly, his suitemate, Andy Koch, made a similar remark: "We always said if someone were to shoot the school up, it would be Seung."

Further adding to his issues seemed to be Cho's lack of romantic success. In the poetry class, he took pictures of female students from his desk. Continuing this theme of sexual harassment, he stalked female students in person and online. A complaint was made after he turned up at a girl's dorm room and introduced himself as "Question Mark"—this complain about him undoubtedly would have fuelled his anger. Campus law enforcement got involved and Cho threatened to kill himself – his suitemates reported this immediately to them. The *New River Valley Community Services Board* evaluated Cho after his suicide threat and found him to be "an imminent danger to self or others"; he was thereafter temporarily detained at a psychiatric hospital.

Just over two months before the massacre in 2007, Cho made plans: he legally procured a .22 caliber Walther P22 handgun and a 9mm Glock 19 handgun, with state law meaning there was a waiting period between each purchase, many ammunition magazines, a hunting knife, and chains; he practiced shooting at an indoor range; he recorded his "manifesto" tapes at a local hotel. The night before the attack, there were reports of an Asian male loitering in Norris Hall and the doors were chained shut; there is the theory that it was Cho "practicing" before the main event the next day. On the day of the attack, Cho firstly shot student, Emily Hilscher, in her dorm room and thereafter killed the Resident Advisor, Christopher Clark, who was in the room next door and came to investigate the noise. There appears to be no link between Emily and Cho as they did not share any classes; however, she was an attractive girl and it is possible that she may have caught his attention when he was stalking female students. Following the first two murders, Cho went back to his room and prepared for the second and final part of his attack by changing clothes, applying his acne cream and brushing his teeth,[6] closing his email account and mailing his manifesto to *NBC*.

The most devastating part of Cho's attack was carried out in Norris Hall, where he chained the doors shut, put a note on them saying a bomb would go off if the chains were removed, and went on to murder thirty people. Chaining the doors shut[7] suggests that he was keen to exceed the death toll set by the previous "worst"[8] school shooting by delaying law enforcement intervention. The attack was methodological and brutal in nature, with multiple shots fired into each victim to ensure they were dead; this is similar to our other case study, the Amish school massacre. The medical examiner revealed that the thirty-two murdered by Cho had more than one hundred bullet wounds (each had been shot multiple times). Likewise, doctors treating survivors found their injuries to include at least three bullet wounds each. This corroborated what survivor, O'Dell, said: "There were [sic] way more gunshots than there were people in that room." When a magazine clip was empty, Cho reloaded his gun "in like two second" (quote from survivor, O'Dell) and resumed his attack. He tended to shoot the lecturers first (in a head shot, killing them instantly) and then executed the students row by row shooting multiple times. After he left room 207, he returned and repeated the same attack pattern. Survivors of the attack said Cho never spoke during the attack. One survivor, O'Dell, recalled: "I saw his eyes. There was nothing there, just emptiness almost." This suggests that Cho must have "depersonalized" his victims in order to be able to carry out his attack without any expression of emotion.

The end of the attack came when Cho heard the shotgun blast of law enforcement breaking through the doors he had chained shut, he killed himself with a shot to the face, denying them the chance to arrest him and/or shot him: this is a common pattern in school shootings. At 10:08am, Cho's body was discovered by police found amongst his victims in classroom 211 (which had the highest number of deceased victims) with two weapons near his body, no identification on him,[9] and what appeared to be a self-inflicted gunshot—from these circumstances, it seemed plausible to infer he was the shooter.

Manifesto

Cho's manifesto[10] suggests anger, feelings of "injustice" and persecution and the desire to "retaliate," the "front" he was projecting to everyone else clearly did not match how he was feeling inside. There is swearing throughout the manifesto, which is a simplistic form of intonation, used to convey the tone of anger. His manifesto is also filled with religious references about "sinners" and "spillers of blood"; suggesting a grandiose sense of self and omnipotence, he compares himself to Jesus and Moses, and claimed "By the power greater than God, we will hunt you down." A "grandiose sense of self-importance or superiority" and "fantasies of success and power" adhere to criteria of the "Narcissistic Personality Inventory" (Bradlee and Emmons, 1992, 823) Moreover, there is a reference to the Columbine (1999) perpetrators—a shooting that Cho was said to be fascinated with—as "martyrs" and makes a later point about starting a "revolution" for others who have been "wronged"—all these comments once again suggest narcissistic delusions of grandeur and omnipotence" (Lasch, 1979, 38). Further, in the manifesto and a letter he sent to the English department the previous day, he called himself by the pseudonym "Ax Ishmael," suggests that he wanted to replace his own identity with something else. There were even suggestions that he wanted to erase his identity altogether: at the university, he referred to himself as "question mark" numerous times; and, when Cho heard the police breaking down the door to arrest him, he shot himself in the face destroying what identified him as a person, physically wiping away his identity until the police could identify him. In this case, suicide was a "desperate act" (Durkheim, 1897/2002, xliii) as an attempt to reinstate Cho's sense of self-importance with the control over *how* and *when* his life ended. It could, therefore, be theorized that, as a final act of validation to their fragile male egos, school shooters want to make that decision to take their own lives rather than have that power taken away from them.

The opening line states "Oh the happiness I could have had mingling among you hedonists, being counted as one of you, only if [sic] you didn't fuck the living shit out of me." "You hedonists" likely refers to his peers and he accused them of destroying his happiness, showing a rudimentary dichotomy in Cho's mind of himself as the victim and people at the university as the ones who wronged him. Cho positions agency onto his victims for the attack he is about to commit:

> You had a hundred billion chances and ways to have avoided today, but you
> decided to spill my blood. You forced me into a corner and gave me only one
> option. The decision was yours. Now you have blood on your hands that will
> never wash off, you Apostles of Sin.

The quotes "you forced me into a corner" and "the decision was yours" exemplify
the fact that Cho holds his victims responsible for his actions. Further quotations
throughout his manifesto evince that he believed his victims to be the wrongdoers:

> "Only if [sic] you could have been the victim of your crimes."
> "To you sadistic snobs, I may be nothing but a piece of dog shit."
> "Your sin-ridden soul will slowly eat up your conscious for the heinous crimes
> you have committed."

The references to "crimes" and "sadistic snobs"—alongside later references to
"wanton hedonism," "menacing sadism," "fat surpluses, "and eating caviar and
drinking cognac—infers that Cho felt his peers were cruel, over-privileged, and
engaging in hedonistic practices. This was likely a way for him to "depersonalize"
his victims, for, as Clare (2000, 55) puts it: "violence is easier to enact when we
dehumanise the object of our anger." In reality, his peers made continuous efforts
to speak to him and invited him to social events; and his professors offered him
additional assistance, such as one-on-one sessions. The real mystery emerging is
why Cho, who clearly had trouble fitting in at university and seemed at best indifferent to being there, chose to stay on at Virginia Tech, rather than just dropping
out—this is something that will probably never be resolved; however, most likely,
it seems the first few years at university he was keen to be a writer, but, after poor
grades and constant complaints about his behavior, he then turned to the alternative
path of pursuing an attack against the institution itself. The apathy Cho projected
towards everything—his dorm room was sterile and bare of decorations; he ignored
his peers when they tried to speak to him; his lack of contribution to classes—fit the
state of egoism needed for "egotistical suicide," where the individual is in a state
of depression and lacks a desire to live (Durkheim, 1897/1952, 1897/2002). In the
case of Cho, it seems that he wanted to stay alive long enough to plan and thereafter
carry out his attack to appease his "overt narcissism" (see Twenge and Campbell
2003). When there are no other viable options, violence then acts as a mechanism
for overt narcissists to revalidate their sense of self-worth, gain respect—according
to their logic—and to release anger by retaliating against them whom they believed
to have disputed their sense of self-worth (Baumeister et al., 1996, 17; Twenge and
Campbell, 2003, 270). For school shooters, this is then transferred to a "cultural
script" which prescribes a course of action and influences an attack on the
institution of school itself (Harding et al., 2002; Larkin 2009; Newman et al.,
2004).

Accordingly, Cho became so driven by intense feelings of persecution and
paranoia that went on to inspire his revenge plan: "Are you happy now you have

destroyed my life" and finished his manifesto with the same rhetorical question: "Are you happy now?"At one point, he referred to horrible acts happening to "us": being raped and then being given stained toilet paper to clean it up, making the act even more deplorable because of the further humiliation—once again the reference to rape raised issues about whether anything like this ever happened to Cho at some point in his life. One particular line conveyed his future intentions to deal with this "persecution." "All the shit you've given me, right back at you with hollow points [photograph of hollow point bullets]." Later on, he expresses a desire to instill feelings in his victims: always living in fear, never knowing when he will strike and having physical reactions to this, such as a pounding heart; feeling constant guilt for committing "heinous crimes"; and the desire to kill themselves before "we hound you down and rip you, your friends and your family into small pieces." Having the power to evoke that kind of reaction will make Cho feel powerful; in his mind, he is reversing the wrongdoer-victim dichotomy he constructed earlier: "By destroying we create. We create the feelings in you [sic] of what it is like to be the victim." In his mind, his obsessive and extensively planned mission became about "diminishing one's opponent" (Govier, 2002, 20) in an attempt to vindicate himself. This mirrors Goffman's (1967) argument about "saving face" where "face" represents one's self image in a social order. By conflating masculinity with aggression and violence, Cho sought to validate his sense of grandiose self-worth (Bradlee and Emmons, 1992; Lasch, 1979) through his actions. The victims took on a symbolic role for Cho in that they were targeted for what they represented to him in his campaign of "revenge." The nature of 'revenge' is such that it is subjectively tied to individuals' conceptualizations of what is right and wrong (Govier, 2002, 13). The reality is that those brutally murdered and injured were innocent people who had done nothing wrong. The fact the perpetrator went into a number of different classrooms in Norris Hall (the site where the worst of the massacre occurred) showed he was not targeting any particular groups. Further, the particularly brutal nature of the attacks —a total of just over a hundred bullets were fired into the thirty-two killed and each of the survivors had been shot at least three times— suggests that the shooter intended to damage the university in general rather than having a vendetta against any specific persons.

Sandy Hook

Overview of Incident

The Sandy Hook shooting has parallels with a school shooting incident in Dunblane, Scotland. Similar ammunition was used, it involved an external attackers (adult male), and the victims were young children aged five and six and their female teacher. Lanza also shared several commonalities with Charles Carl Roberts, IV where he had no outstanding arrest warrants or criminal history, and he was an honors student at Newtown High School which he had previously attended. The shootings were also similar, as Lanza too carried an arsenal of carefully-chosen ammunition; it also shared a similarity where the victims were primarily female, some or all of them children, and shot multiple times at close range.] Both of these cases suggest that these killings are primarily "instrumental" in motive of wanting to accomplish a goal in contrast to "expressive" in motive, which typically suggests an emotional knee-jerk reaction. Typically, instrumental homicides involve a greater degree of planning in contrast to the reactive nature of expressive homicides.

His brother, Ryan Lanza described him as "My brother has always been a nerd . . . he wears a pocket protector;" while Lanza's friend, Joshua Milas said, "He was probably one of the smartest kids I know. He was probably a genius." These descriptions provided little insight into what triggered him into engaging in the second-deadliest (based on death toll) school shooting in U.S. history killing twenty-eight people, twenty of which were children, and including the gunman and his mother whom he murdered earlier that morning. However, additional comments provided by his mother, Nancy Lanza, to a divorce mediator in 2008 clearly stated that she realized that her son had "some disabilities"; and Richard Novia, the advisor of the high school technology club where Adam was a member, revealed that he was unable to feel pain or injury: "If that boy would've burned himself, he would not have known it or felt it physically." "It was my job to pay close attention to that." Lanza had been diagnosed with Asperger's Syndrome, which typically presents with social awkwardness, high intelligence, and a low threshold for frustration. Nancy Lanza was, therefore, reluctant to leave him alone, and was prepared to care for him as long as he needed it; she had even discussed moving out West to enroll him in a "special school or a center" during the past one and a half years, which may have caused her son additional stress since individuals diagnosed with autism are unable to tolerate changes in their routines or schedules.

Comments involving Lanza's behavior while in school show similarities with the Virginia Tech shooter: he was bright but awkward; he had no close friends; he wore the same clothes to school every day, a green shirt with khaki pants; Lanza rarely spoke in school, and gave a school presentation via computer without speaking a word; he hardly spoke to his classmates, and walked through school hallways awkwardly pressing himself against the wall. His silence continued after death since he did not leave a suicide note or manifesto detailing his motives for the mass killings; although, he did leave diaries and drawings that are currently sealed. Living at home mirrored his isolation at school since he spent most of his time in this mother's basement where he had a computer, flat-screen television, couches, and an elaborate video game setup. The media reported that Lanza showed an interest in a shooting video game called "Counter Strike," and played it with other students at school competing as either terrorists or counter-terrorists choosing an M4 military-style assault rifle and a Glock handgun similar to the weapons he used during the attack at the school.

Lanza's knowledge and familiarity with weapons did not end with video games, although he did enjoy working on computers, and playing violent video games that employed military-style assault rifles as weapons options. An in-depth review of online posts allegedly made by Lanza shows attentive edits that were made to Wikipedia pages for mass shootings; in addition, his posts on several general message boards for gun enthusiasts demonstrated the usual message board jargon and abbreviations for well-constructed sentences suggesting an intelligent and knowledgeable writing on the topic of guns at age seventeen. He dialogues about gun regulations and asks advice about how to obtain and modify models that were banned in Connecticut but still available for sale in other states.

Lanza foreshadowed his interest in mass killings by editing several pages addressing events which are similar to the Sandy Hood mass shooting (which particular ones have not been confirmed). Although Wikipedia did not confirm Lanza's identity, the *Hartford Courant* said that another user suggested Lanza spent time carefully editing mass shooting entries which often included a description of the shooters' precise weapons. He showed a particular interest in the 1988 mass shooting at *ESL, Inc.* which is a high tech software manufacturing company located in Sunnyvale, California where the shooter, Richard Farley killed seven people and wounded four other. *ESL, Inc.*'s mass shooting resembled the Sandy Hook incident since both shooters are suspected of shooting through glass doors to gain access to the building, despite the security measures in place. Both shooters carried thousands of rounds of ammunition in vests, and randomly shot individuals as they encountered them in the building. This creates the need for "target hardening" in schools, to try and block outsiders from entering the building.

Writings

Interest in the second-deadliest school shooting in U.S. history has spawned hundreds of newspaper articles and hours of media coverage which, subsequently, revealed the existence of several research warrants leading to the seizure of a collection of Lanza's journals and drawings. Since this case is still under investigation, and the Connecticut state attorney's final report has yet to be published, all these photos and documents that may provide significant insight into the psychology of school shooters remains sealed under the court's jurisdiction.

In March 2013, attorneys representing *The New York Times* as well as several additional media concerns have been requesting that the judge to allow documents relating to the investigation of the Sandy Hook school shooting to become public if State's Attorney Stephen Sedensky III files a request to extend the 90-day court order sealing the search warrant affidavits. Among the data likely revealed by these warrants would be inventories of items found when State Police investigators searched the Lanza's house and vehicles. Under Connecticut state law, search warrant affidavits usually become public record two weeks after they have been executed, but Sedensky cited the ongoing investigation as grounds to extend the 90-day extension which was due to expire March 27, 2013 (Pirro and Dixon, 2013). By the end of August 2013, State Attorney General George Jepsen has requested that a state judge compel Newtown officials to release Adam Lanza's school records to the state's Office of the Child Advocate. The motive underlying such a disclosure includes providing insight and preventing more horrors as a means of preventing future school shootings as well as providing the public with answers and protection in the hopes of identifying the signs/indicators of suicidal or homicidal children. Newtown has been particularly protective of the death certificates of the school shooting victims, and the investigators and prosecutors have yet to complete their criminal examination and release their report. In addition, the Connecticut state legislature conducted secret negotiations with criminal justice authorities as well as the victims' families to pass a law [June 2013] preventing public disclosure of photographs, crime scene video, and other information for at least one year which thereby serves to hinder any efforts to comprehend and potentially prevent future incidents of mass violence (*Courant* 2013).

Perhaps researchers should consider the following unanswered questions and how discovering the motivations might contribute to the information currently available on school shooters:

- Why did Lanza carry an arsenal of hundreds of rounds of ammunition in the form of multiple high-capacity clips that were sufficient to kill every student in the school if he was given enough time?
- Why did Lanza choose ammunition that was designed to inflict maximum damage to the victim by breaking up inside the victim's body tearing bone and tissue apart?
- Why did Lanza shoot his mother four times in the head with a 22-caliber rifle while she was still in her pyjamas in bed?
- Why did Lanza target all adult women and a majority of female child victims (eight boys and 12 girls)?
- Why were all the victims shot multiple times with a rifle, some at close range? Was this an instance of "overkill" where the shooter is emotionally driven to use greater force than what is necessary to kill?

Deliverables and Opportunities for Future Research

Since this is a unique research study that employs a novel approach for examining school shooters, the deliverables projected for this project include, but are not limited to, constructing an assessment that could possibly identify individuals who may exhibit a proclivity for becoming a school shooter. The authors also suggest that a complimentary assessment be constructed that will identify situations and/or environments that may exacerbate the tendency of individuals to become school shooters. It is also the opinion of the authors that theory should link to praxis, thereby suggesting the importance of disseminating the data/information generated through research to law enforcement, campus security, and policy makers that may contribute to constructing the strategies that will provide a greater measure of safety in academic environments for students, teachers, and faculty staff. This unique research study is additionally in the position to conceptualize a model that will systematically analyze online discourse for potentially threatening comments which could escalate into future school shootings.

Threat Assessment Model

The model developed wants to avoid profiling: generalizing the characteristics of a specific type of individual (Schneier, 2006, 134). Individuals are complicated beings and cannot just be compared against a checklist to decide on their intentions. Previous studies (O'Toole, 2000; Vossekuil *et al.*, 2002) have already demonstrated that there is no clear profile of a school shooter. Additionally, the danger in profiling is that "false negatives" slip under the radar because they do not meet certain characteristics, whilst "false positives" are wrongly accused for fitting the profile. This is reminiscent of type I and type II errors that can manifest in quantitative research methods where a type I error is defined as the incorrect rejection of a true null hypothesis while a type II error is defined as the failure to reject a false null hypothesis. The four case studies discussed and analyzed in this chapter are evident of the varying characteristics of school shooters. The Virginia Tech shooter was probably the most stereotypical interpretation of the "weird loner" who exhibited many strange behaviors, like violent writings, stabbing the carpet, referring to himself as "question mark," stalking females; more notably, the fact that other students were afraid of him definitely suggests that something was not right. The other three case studies appeared as a paradoxical combination of worrying behaviors and "appearing normal." Classmates described the Red Lake perpetrator as a "good listener" and a "cool guy," and purported that they did not believe he would go on a shooting spree, despite him being suspected of an earlier threat at the school. By contrast, teachers and classmates knew of his views on "racial purity" and the swastikas on his school notebooks; some even knew he identified as a Neo-Nazi and constantly spoke about guns and killing people. From this it may be inferred that *any* troubling behavior—whether this is accompanied by the student usually "appearing normal" or not—should be investigated, even just to offer a troubled student who may be depressed with no real thoughts of harming others some help. There tends to be a pattern throughout school shooting incidents that the pre-incident "warning signs" are either ignored or that those in the position to do something about the bizarre behavior seem to doubt their decisions about the actions they are witnessing.

Further, the four case studies analyzed in this chapter fit the state of "egoism," conceptualized by Durkheim, and the traits identified as pertaining to the personality condition "narcissism." From this, a more detailed and precise threat assessment model can be developed to be applied to everyday offline behaviors. The key themes emerging from the analyses conducted were: the perpetrators felt a sense of injustice at the world, and for the two internal perpetrators, this was directed at their school for challenging their views on racial purity (Red Lake) and university, most likely because the Virginia Tech perpetrator could not adjust to university life and seemingly blamed everyone else for this; the shooters felt persuaded either by specific persons, groups or just in general, with the feeling that they had suffered throughout their lives; blame is bestowed upon everyone else but the perpetrator for all their problems: this ties in with the sense of injustice and persecution they feel; a lack of romantic success in the case of the Virginia Tech shooter seemed to exacerbate matters, which led to stalking and harassment of female students; excessive individualism, where the perpetrators felt they were ostracized by others and hence there was a lack of connection to society; feeling some kind of shame (Amish schoolhouse shooter) and displays of self-hatred (Red Lake). Applying overt narcissism traits—covert narcissistic characteristics likely revolve around a general sense of hopelessness and despair, not any active plans to sustain a high sense of self-esteem and demonstrate superiority—to warning signs could be indicative of a potential case for threat assessment: over-reaction (commonly aggressive or passive-aggressive) to the slightest criticism, high self-esteem that needs constant validation, the desire to be infamous and extreme fantasies of success and power, delusions of grandeur, a feeling of superiority combined with a sense of worthlessness, and a sense of isolation from others in a particular environment and/or society in general. It has already been demonstrated in this chapter that four school shooters, of varying ages and with different motives, all adhered to the narcissism personality model to some extent and were all in a state of "egoism" at the time of the shooting, although the attack planning seemed to give them a goal to live for. Concurrently, all the perpetrators killed themselves before law enforcement could reach them: this shows the shooters want to enact power one last time by being the ones to end their own lives in a desperate act of suicide. It seems that perhaps the combination of homicide-suicide could encourage those with fragile, narcissistic identities in a state of excessive individualism to go through with the violent fantasies in their minds: they know that once they have gone through with the murders, the time will come where law enforcement either shoots them dead or arrests them; and, therefore, they go into the rampages with the clear intention of killing themselves at the end knowing that past school shooters have been seen as "martyrs" by admirers after their deaths.

Taking all this into consideration, it is advised that threat assessments take into account the factors the narcissism and egoism factors outlined above when investigating a potential threat. Clearly, what is important here is the *amount* of traits (individual, personality ones and environmental and life factors) present: aggregating these over a certain period of time should be indicative of someone's susceptibility to enacting a school shooting. If there was only evidence of one or two, for example, feeling isolated from school as a result of bullying and over-reacting to slight criticism, this could be attributable to other factors, such as the general insecurity of teenagers, hormones, and feeling pressure from schoolwork. It is when these are combined with more disconcerting aspects, like fantasizing about having power over others and then intensive shooting practice, that red flags should be raised. Online Intel can, thereafter, be utilized to make further assess-ments about whether any direct (specific and explicit details), indirect (more ambiguous but still a statement of intended action), veiled (disguised as something else such as 'I won't be around much longer) or conditional (something will happen if certain conditions are not met) threats have been made or the existence of other disturbing material.

Obviously if progress regarding the identification and neutralization of school shooters is going to continue and become effective, it has to be a collaborative effort among researchers, experts in the field, schools, policy makers/legislators, etc. This model is a starting point for seeking to explore features that may indicate a proclivity towards a school shooting; further development, organization and refinement will help to move this model and its practical application forward. Future research could also examine online commentary for each of the case studies covered here to find out more about the "admirers" of school shooters—this could also be developed into a threat assessment model to supplement the one developed within this chapter.

Notes

1.   It seems like this threat was him, perhaps to gauge the kind of response he would get to the threat and the security the school had in place. The fact that he was suspected of this attack meant that it is even stranger that people were incredulous when he shot up the school for real.
2.   Definite parallels to Columbine, where the first victim Rachel Scott was asked whether she believed in God, she replied "You know I do" and Eric Harris said "Go be with him then" and shot her in the head. In the library, the perpetrators also asked a couple of students the same question, with another one being killed and the other being injured when they both answered "yes." It seems in this case, Weise was willing to let ones go who refused to declare a belief in God.
3.   This conveys similar ideologies to Hitler's view of the "Ayran race" and the Norway (2011) mass shooter, Anders Breivik, with ideals of "racial purity" and being opposed to multiculturalism "diluting" this.
4.   This raises the question whether something sexual happened to him during the procedure. A lot of his later writings for his creative writing class revolved around sexual molestation of children by authority figures, with almost causal references to "ass raping" and the victim making plans to kill the abuser in retaliation.
5.   The intolerance of "old people" displayed in Cho's fictional play and the theme in his writings of teachers and stepfathers who are child molesters suggests a problem with authority figures. Although this is just surmising, maybe something sexual happened to him when he was a child, perhaps from someone in a position of authority.
6.   This seems a rather odd thing for someone who plans to die to do. The only real reason for this was to give the impression to his suitemates that he was going about his normal routine and nothing out of the ordinary was going on. There is also the possibility that Cho suffered from OCD, which would certainly fit in with the description of his dorm room was undecorated and "sterile."
7.   This appeared in the novel "We Need to Talk about Kevin," about a teenage boy who murders people at his school with a crossbow and blocks the exits with crowbars. It is not known whether Cho read this book, however, or whether this is a mere coincidence.

8.   This has been out in scare quotes because there is always an immediate link in news media content about the "worst" school shooting being the one with the highest death toll. In reality, as tragic as Virginia Tech was, probably Columbine or Sandy Hook is the "worst" in terms of the most heart-breaking and shocking because Columbine was the first of its kind to cause such devastation and Sandy Hook involved very young children.

9.   This, coupled with his self-inflicted gunshot wound to the face, seems he was trying to conceal his identity from law enforcement. He also scratched off the serial numbers on his weapons. All of this seems pointless, however, given he had recorded a confession video.

10.   This was also retrieved from the "School Shooters Info" website

References

Altheide, D. L. (1996) *Qualitative Media Analysis.* Thousand Oaks: Sage Publications.

Bauman, Z. (2007) *Consuming Life.* Cambridge: Polity Press.

Baumeister, R. F., L. Smart, and J. M. Boden. (1996) "Relation of Threatened Egoism to Violence and Aggression: The Dark Side of High Self-Esteem." *Psychological Review* 103 (1), 5–33.

Bottoms, A. E. (2000). *The relationship between theory and research in criminology* in R. King and E. Windcup (eds.). *Doing Research on Crime and Justice.* Oxford: Oxford University Press.

Bradlee, P. M. and R. A. Emmons. (1992) "Locating Narcissism within the Interpersonal Circumplex and the Five-Factor Model."*Personality and Individual Differences.* 13(7), 821–830.

Brown, G. and G. Yule. (1983). *Discourse Analysis.* Cambridge: Cambridge University Press.

Bushman, B. J. and R. F. Baumeister. (1998) "Threatened Egotism, Narcissism, Self-Esteem, and Direct and Displaced Aggression: Does Self-Love or Self-Hate Lead to Violence."*Journal of Personality and Social Psychology* Vol. 75 (1), 219–229.

Castells, M. (2000). *The rise of the network society.* (2nd ed.). Malden: Blackwell Publishers.

Clare, A. (2000) *On Men: Masculinity in Crisis.* London: Chatto and Windus.

Cohn, A. and A. Zeichner. (2006) "Effects of Masculine Identity and Gender Role Stress on Aggression in Men."*Psychology of Men and Masculinity* 7(4), 179–190.

Collier, R. (1998) *Masculinities, Crime and Criminology: Men, Heterosexuality and the Criminalised Order.* London: Sage Publications.

Courant. (2013) "Release Shooter Adam Lanza's File." Retrieved on September 2, 2013, from http://articles.courant.com/2013-08-25/news/hc-ed-adam-lanza-school-records-release-2013.

Creswell, J.W. (2009). *Research Design: Qualitative, Quantitative, and Mixed Methods Approaches.* (3rded.). Thousand Oaks, Ca: Sage Publications, Inc.

Douglas, J. D. (1967) *The Social Meanings of Suicide.* Princeton, NJ: Princeton University Press.

Durkheim, E. (1897/1952) *Suicide, A Study in Sociology.* Trans. J. A. Spaulding and G. Simpson; G. Simpson (ed). London: Routledge & Kegan Paul.

———. (1897/2002). *Suicide, A Study in Sociology. .* Trans. J. A. Spaulding and G. Simpson; G. Simpson (ed). London: Routledge & Kegan Paul.

Erikson, E. H. (1968) *Identity: Youth and Crisis.* London: Faber and Faber.

Fairclough, N. (2012). 'Critical Discourse Analysis.' In J. P. Gee and M. Handford (eds.).

The Routledge Handbook of Discourse Analysis. New York, London: Routledge, 9–20.

Feldmann, T.B., P.W. Johnson, and R.A. Bell. (1990). "Cofactors in the Commission of Violent Crimes: A Self-Psychology Examination."*American Journal of Psychotherapy*, 44(2), 172–179.

Giddens, A. (1991) *Modernity and Self-identity: self and society in the late modern age.* Cambridge, UK: Polity Press.

Glaser, B. and A. Strauss. (1967). *The Discovery of Grounded Theory: Strategies for Qualitative Research.* Hawthorne, NY: Aldine de Gruyter.

Goffman, E. (1967) *Interaction Ritual.* Chicago: Aldine Publishing Company.

Govier, T. (2002) *Forgiveness and Revenge.* New York, London: Routledge.

Harding, D. J., C. Fox, and J. D. Mehta. (2002) "Studying rare events through qualitative case studies: lessons from a study of rampage school shootings." *Sociological Methods Research* 31(174), 174–217.

Jenkins, R. (2008) *Social Identity* (3rd ed.) Oxon: Routledge.

Kellner, D. (2007) "Media Spectacle and the 'Massacre at Virginia Tech.'"*Fast Capitalism* 3.1 (1). *http://www.uta.edu/huma/agger/fastcapitalism/3_1/kellner. html*

Kohut, H. (1977) *The Restoration of the Self.* New York: International Universities Press.

Langman, P. (2009) *Why kids kill: inside the minds of school shooters.* New York: Palgrave MacMillan.

Lankford, A. (2013). "A comparative analysis of suicide terrorists and rampage, workplace, and school shooters in the United States from 1990 to 2010." *Homicide Studies: An Interdisciplinary & International Journal*, 17(3), 255–274.

Larkin, R. W. (2009) "The Columbine Legacy: Rampage Shootings as Political Acts." *American Behavioral Scientist*. 52: 1309–1326

Lasch, C. (1979) *The Culture of Narcissism: American life in an age of diminishing expectations.* London, New York: W. W. Norton and Company.

Maris, R.W., A.L. Berman, & M. M. Silverman. (2000). *Comprehensive textbook of suicidology.* New York, NY: Guilford.

Martin, J. (1988) *Who Am I This Time? Uncovering the Fictive Personality.* New York/London: W. W. Norton & Co.

Mead, G. H. (1934) *Mind, Self and Society: from the standpoint of a social behaviourist.* Chicago: University of Chicago Press.

Messerschmidt, J. W. (1993) *Masculinities and Crime: Critique and Reconceptualization of Theory.* Lanham, Maryland: Rowman and Littlefield Publishers Inc.

Newburn, T. (2007). *Criminology.* New York, NY; Oxfordshire, UK: Willan Publishing.

Newman, K. S., C. Fox, D. J. Harding, J. Mehta, and W. Roth. (2004) *Rampage: The social roots of school shootings.* Basic Books: New York.

O'Toole, M. (1999) "The School Shooter: A Threat Assessment Perspective." Washington, D.C: Federal Bureau of Investigation, Department of Justice.

Pirro, J., and K. Dixon. (2013). "Media, lawmakers seek Lanza documents." *News Times* Retrieved on September 2, 2013, from http://www.newstimes.com/ news/article/Media-lawmakers-seek-Lanza-documents-4370985.

Ramp, W. (2000) "The Moral Discourse of Durkheim's Suicide." In W. S. F. Pickering and Geoffrey Walford (ed.). *Durkheim's Suicide: A century of research and debate.* London, New York: Routledge, 81–96.

Schneier, Bruce. (2006) *Beyond Fear: Thinking Sensibly About Security in an Uncertain World.* Location: Springer.

Treadwell, J. and J. Garland. (2011) "Masculinity, Marginalisation and Violence: A Case Study of the English Defence League."British Journal of Criminology, 51 (4): 621–634

Twenge, J. M. and W. K Campbell. (2003) "'Isn't It Fun to Get the Respect That We're Going to Deserve?" Narcissism. Social Rejection and Aggression.'" *Personality and Social Psychology Bulletin,* 29, 261–272.

vanDijk, T.A. (1998). *Ideology: a multiple disciplinary approach.* London: Thousand Oaks, CA: Sage.

Vossekuil, B., R. A. Fein, M. Reddy, R. Borum and W. Modzeleski. (2002) "The Final Report and Findings of the Safe School Initiative: Implications for the Prevention of School Attacks in the United States." Washington, D.C: United States Secret Service and United States Department of Education.

Whitehead, (2005) "Man to Man Violence: How Masculinity May Work as a Dynamic Risk Factor." *The Howard Journal of Criminal Justice* 44 (4), 411–422.

Yin, R.K. (1992/2006). 'Case Study Design.' In D. De Vaus *Research Design. Volume IV.* London; Thousand Oaks, CA: Sage Benchmarks in Social Research Methods, 83–88.

Chapter Three

From Egoistical and Anomic Suicide to Egoistical and Anomic Homicide: Explaining the Aurora, Colorado Mass Shooting Using Durkheim, Merton and Agnew

Dinur Blum and Christian G. Jaworski

Introduction

After midnight on July 20, 2012, in a quiet suburb of Denver, a man dressed in body armor and a gas mask walked into a crowded movie theater and senselessly murdered twelve people, spraying gunfire inside. An additional 58 people were wounded. The crowd had gathered to watch the latest Batman film (*The Dark Knight Rises*). According to news reports following the shooting:

> Witnesses to the shooting said that a man appeared at the front of the theater about 20 minutes into the movie with a rifle, handgun and gas mask. He then threw a canister that released some kind of gas, after which a hissing sound ensued, and he then opened fire on the crowd packed into the early-morning screening of the film.

> We were maybe 20 or 30 minutes into the movie and all you hear, first you smell smoke, everybody thought it was fireworks or something like that, and then you just see people dropping and the gunshots are constant, witness Christ Jones told ABC's Denver affiliate KMGH. "I heard at least 20 to 30 rounds within that minute or two.

> A man who talked to a couple who was inside the theater told ABC News, they got up and they started to run through the emergency exit, and that when she turned around, she said all she saw was the guy slowly making his way up the stairs and

just firing at people, just picking random people. (Mosk, Ross, Esposito, and
Chumash, abcnews.com)

In less than thirty minutes, seventy people had been shot or wounded, making it one
of the worst mass shootings in American history.

Egoistical and Anomic Theories

The Federal Bureau of Investigation (FBI) defines mass murder as:

a number of murders (four or more, not including the shooter) occurring during
the same incident, with no distinctive time period between the murders. These
events typically involved a single location, where the killer murdered a number of
victims in an ongoing incident.

Thus, it is not only the number of casualties that defines the action, it is also the
time frame—it is a single act as opposed to having distinct time lags between
shootings.

Immediately after the Aurora attack, the focus of the media was on the man
who had done such a horrific act. The suspected perpetrator had surrendered
without a fight soon after the shooting and questions about his motives quickly
began to circulate among the police, the victims and our society. Initial reports said
that the suspect, James Holmes, had dyed his hair a bright orange and had described
himself as "the Joker," a reference to the homicidal psychopath of previous Batman
films (cnn.com, 7/20/12). Since then, much has been written about Holmes. What
were his motives? What were the circumstances that would lead such a man, who
was white, well educated, intelligent and from the upper middle class with a good
family, to senselessly gun down men, women and children? Was he mentally ill?
Or had there been recent circumstances that had led to such a despicable act?

Much attention has been given to the individual aspects and characteristics of
the shooter, but something remained unconsidered through the various news reports.
With all of the focus on the individual or psychological aspects of the suspect, no
broader social context was examined in an attempt to explain the shooting. We feel
this is an important piece if sociologists, criminologists, and police are ever to
understand the totality of these horrible crimes. By focusing exclusively on the
individual shooter's psychological factors, an important part -a broader societal
context or influence—is neglected.

With this in mind, we suggest that Emile Durkheim's theories of egoistic and
anomic suicide and Robert Merton's ideas on strain can be used as tools to help
understand mass shootings. Durkheim believed that when an individual has weak
ties to the community in which he or she lives or feels like an outsider , that
individual is at a higher risk of a certain type of suicide. He called this condition
egoism. A closely-related situation, termed anomie, was related to an individual
being under-regulated by society. For anomie to occur, a sudden major shift in a

person's life leads to a weakening of ties the person feels to the larger society, which exacerbates the stress the individual feels due to the changing circumstances. We believe the concepts of egoism and anomie can be applied to help explain Holmes' mass shooting in the Aurora theater. Robert Merton's idea of strain and responses to it is also applicable to this event. In addition to looking at individual psychological factors, an examination of social factors help explain why mass shootings happen, as well as offer insights in preventing them. While we may never be able to totally predict mass shootings, we hope incorporating broader social context will lend insight into social factors that go into these events. Given this awareness, interventions may be possible to reduce the likelihood of mass murders.

Background of James Holmes

Some background information about James Holmes is needed before we can apply Durkheim and Merton towards explaining this mass shooting. James Holmes is described as having a middle-class background, with both of his parents obtaining high educational levels. The *San Diego News-Tribune* wrote:

> Both his mother and father have excelled in the sciences. Arlene Rosemary Holmes is a registered nurse; Robert M. Holmes Sr. is a senior scientist in the San Diego office of FICO (Among other things, this multinational analytics firms provides credit scores). Robert had a glittering academic career—degrees from Stanford, UCLA and Berkeley—and his son showed signs of following in those over-achieving footsteps.

A lack of attachment to others is frequently a characteristic of homicide suspects. The British Broadcasting Corporation (BBC) reported that Holmes had no romantic attachments, but was involved in a video game group. However, outside of this group, there was no mention of Holmes having close friends. A former classmate, Breanna Hath, said, "There were no real girls he was involved with," she told the Washington Post. "It seemed he was really into a video game group that hung out together." (BBC). A former lab colleague, Billy Kromka, said Holmes had been one of the quieter people, and had spent much of his time immersed in his computer, often participating in role-playing online games." (BBC) It was also reported that Holmes received low scores on his comprehensive exams shortly before his suspected shootings and that after these exams he withdrew from school. This withdrawal would remove some of his social ties, as he no longer saw his coworkers or classmates. The *Union-Tribune* also reported that Holmes did not have an online presence besides his computer gaming group. By not being involved in Facebook or Twitter, he reduced his ability to connect with coworkers, classmates, or other people outside of a game setting.

Holmes and Holmes Typologies of Mass Murderers

Using Ronald and Stephen Holmes' typologies of mass murderers, it appeared that James Holmes could be considered either a psychotic mass killer or a disgruntled citizen mass killer (Holmes & Holmes, 2001).

We included the psychotic mass killer as a possibility, even if this type "appears to be very much in the minority of mass killers" (Holmes & Holmes, 2001, 106), given that in June 2013, James Holmes pled not guilty by reason of insanity to his charges (Dream, *LA Times*, 6/4/2013). For Holmes and Holmes, distinguishing characteristics of a psychotic mass killer was that said killer "is out of touch, at least at the time of the killing, with social reality. This killer may hear voices or see visions, but the source of the visions or voice rests within the impaired personality of the killer" (Holmes & Holmes, 2001, 107). Holmes and Holmes argued that "the psychotic mass killer hopes to gain a measure of psychological gain" (Holmes & Holmes, 2001,108), in that "the act does result in a form of psychological pleasure for the killer" (Holmes & Holmes, 2001, 108). For the psychotic mass killer, victims are "selected randomly; they happen to be in a space shared by the killer at the time of the murder" (Holmes & Holmes, 2001, 109), rather than being specifically sought by the killer. Given the random selection, the victims are unknown to the killer. Finally, Holmes and Holmes argue that this type of killer is geographically stable and does not travel far to seek victims. (Holmes & Holmes, 2001, 110)

As of the time of this writing, James Holmes' motives are not known to the authors, and will likely only be revealed during his trial. Thus, we cannot speak as to whether or not he heard voices or saw visions during his shooting in the theater. However, we do know that Holmes had no connection to his victims, nor did he travel far when he picked the cinema as his killing site. Once he entered the cinema, Holmes and his victims shared the same social and physical space.

Holmes and Holmes describe disgruntled citizen mass killers as "people who are so angry and upset with the way the world has treated them that they lash out with mass homicide" (Holmes & Holmes, 2001, 95). Similar to the psychotic mass killer, the disgruntled citizen mass killer "tends to be geographically stable" (Holmes & Holmes, 2001, 95). Additionally, the victims are randomly selected and are strangers to the killer (Holmes & Holmes, 2001, 98). The disgruntled citizen mass killer "perceives that society or a person has wronged him or her, and he or she must lash out with fatal violence at those people who are reminders of the society at large" (Holmes & Holmes, 2001, 97). While (again) we cannot speak as to James Holmes' mental state at the time of the killings, the idea that a person perceives that society has wronged them and lashes out using violence could be considered a form of responding to anomic circumstances. Holmes and Holmes argue that for this type of killer, "there is a personal gain here. The killer murders a group of persons who have no real role is not important to the killer. The gain is psychological to the point that the killer is demonstrating the wrongs of society.

People will now pay attention to his or her plight even though the killer may realize that because of his or her actions he or she will no longer be alive to bask in the 'reflected glory' over what he or she has done" (Holmes & Holmes, 2001, 97). Given this, we can understand James Holmes' shooting potentially exacting revenge on a world and society that he feels has wronged him. For example, if Holmes felt that his department wronged him by failing him on his comprehensive exams, he may have felt that people would pay attention to his situation if he responded with violence, even if he would not survive to see the aftermath of his actions.

For Holmes and Holmes, the types of mass killers are not mutually exclusive. Indeed, many of the typologies have overlapping characteristics. Thus, it is entirely possible that using their typologies, James Holmes falls into several categories. We had considered whether or not he also can be considered a disgruntled employee mass killer. However, that type of mass killer either "are often former co-workers of the killer" (Holmes & Holmes, 2001, 66) or happen to be at the former place of employment. Given that James Holmes did not commit his attack at his former university, nor did he target former co-workers, we felt that he could not be considered this type of mass killer, even if losing his employment as a graduate student served as an impetus for violence.

One thing in common with the typologies that Holmes and Holmes employ is an emphasis on the individual killer's mentality at the time the crime was committed. Possible larger, social factors are considered but not emphasized in their typologies. It is precisely these factors that we hope to expand on by using Durkheim and Merton's works.

Durkheim Theory on Suicide and Homicide

The parallels between suicide and homicide include an intense focus after the fact on the person committing the act, highlighting the fact that respect for life is considered normal, and both suicide and homicide violate this respect. Thus, both are considered deviant acts, and focus is turned to the actor, who is considered deviant. Because there is such heavy attention paid to the individual actor and their mindset, broader social forces at work often get ignored. While Durkheim never wrote about mass homicides, he did write about death, namely suicide, using a broader sociological context to explain an intensely private act. In his seminal work on the subject, Suicide, Durkheim identified that there would be a combination of social and individual traits that would lead an individual to kill themselves. Furthermore, there were detailed types of suicide. Of those, the two most important to understanding mass shootings would be egoism and anomie. We believe that by extrapolating Durkheim's work on suicide to mass murder we will find that the similar conditions that lead to suicide (and in particular egoistic and anomic suicide) are also related to mass shootings, such as the one that occurred in Aurora, Colorado.

In writing about suicide in general, Durkheim stated that suicides are more common in cities with an intense concentration of people. Furthermore, he argued that the causes given by the individual for the act are only superficial surface causes. Individual causes were merely manifestations of the general society. Durkheim further wrote that in "times of decadence" lacking in societal cohesion, suicides increase. Durkheim also wrote that most suicides occur in the upper classes. He argued that people of higher intelligence are more likely to commit suicide, and that low intelligence protects against suicide, leading to much lower rates for less intelligent people. Mental illness, for Durkheim, plays a very small part in explaining suicide. Durkheim said that suicides by mentally ill people are not all suicides. Rather, they are only one type of suicide. Finally, for Durkheim, men are far more likely than women to commit suicide.

Many of Durkheim's correlates of suicide can be applied to James Holmes. Holmes would have been considered to be of higher intelligence, as he was in a graduate program and had performed outstandingly as an undergraduate. Further, Holmes came from a large city and was from an upper middle class background. Additionally, Holmes faced distressing circumstances (not scoring well on his comprehensive exams and subsequently quitting graduate school), and may have not known how to cope with such a sudden change, leading to a loss of a support network and ultimately his shooting spree. Admittedly, our diagnosis is post-hoc —had the shooting spree not happened, we would not know if Holmes was a degenerate in Durkheim's (or anyone else's) sense of the word.

Durkheim described four types of suicide: Egoistic, Altruistic, Anomic, and Fatalistic. The types of suicide were related to social integration and social regulation of individuals in a given society. Egoistic suicide occurred when a person became socially isolated or felt he had no place in society, and this isolation was too much to bear, leading to suicide. Thus, it is a case of having too little integration. Altruistic suicide, on the other hand, can be viewed as being the opposite of egoistic suicide. Rather than having too little integration into a society, altruistic suicide can be understood as an individual being too integrated into a given society, with the group identity becoming the individual's identity. For example, suicide bombers kill themselves in order to promote a group goal and identity. Anomic suicide was related to sudden, unexpected changes to which the individual did not know how to react. These changes would be related to under regulation in society. An example of this would be suicide following a sudden, unexpected job loss. Finally, fatalistic suicide was related to overregulation in society. This would include someone feeling like they are constantly being monitored and the stress from this constant monitoring is too much to bear, and death is viewed as an escape from this constant regulation.

The ideas of egoistic and anomic suicide fit the description of James Holmes' shooting spree very well. Durkheim argued that intellectual growth may increase egoistic suicide rates because intellectual growth is coupled with weakening traditions and moral individualism. Thus, as a person learns more and sees the world in a new light, the traditions and worldview they had are replaced, which can lead to social isolation from those who are operating under more traditional world views and who are more collectively oriented. Durkheim contends that once traditions are gone, they cannot be artificially reconstituted. Durkheim also focused on the role of religion in promoting or preventing suicides. He argued that strong religious traditions prevent egoistic suicide. However, he did not believe this was due to any divine prohibitions. Rather, it was the decline of the community acting as a mechanism of social cohesion and social control. He wrote that communities composed of obligatory beliefs and strong connections protect members from self-murder. Given that the only community mentioned with respect to James Holmes was an online gaming group – and one that did not meet in person – there was no sense of social control or of obligation to a bigger group that Holmes belonged to. Based on news reports, Holmes had few, if any, friends, and a former classmate of his said Holmes "was obsessed with computer games and was always playing role playing games. 'He did not have much of a life apart from that and doing his work. James seemed like he wanted to be in the game and be one of the characters." (Gye, Keneally, and Bates; dailymail.co.uk) For Durkheim, religious communities were his focus, and with the decline of traditional religions, intellectualism is all that remains. He argued that intellectualism was related to social isolation because the established traditions (e.g., religious traditions) were being replaced, and one sacrifice with this trade-off was having a support network of people one interacted with in religious settings (such as friends one would see at services). Durkheim argued that community is the main preventer of egoistic suicide. Communities that place a higher value in the individual and less emphasis on community or the group will have much higher suicide rates, regardless of population size. When society no longer has a "moral compass," or a general sense of strong collective beliefs, the uncertainty produced inspires indulgence in immoral acts, including committing suicide. Related to this indulgence, when the social environment changes suddenly, suicide rates abruptly rise. These changes can be related to both egoistic and anomic suicides. Durkheim also contends that while suicide rates may vary across locations, the social conditions that affects egoistic suicide rates are consistent and to some extent general. When a society has lost its "moral compass" and uncertainty drives immoral acts, imitation spreads drive for egoistical suicide. The example set becomes dangerous because societal indifference lessens the revulsion these horrific acts should inspire. Durkheim argues that the imitative power of egoistic suicide is not the imitation itself, but rather is in the problems nested in the "soul" of the society. If the society were not already ailing, imitation of egoistic suicides would not take place.

Durkheim emphasized social solidarity in his writings, and argued that solidarity makes a big difference in whether or not individuals commit suicide (or, in this case, homicide). Durkheim believed that during "times of decadence," suicides would increase. While this term goes undefined, Durkheim makes it very clear that societal cohesion of the society as a whole is extremely important.. "Suicide," or in our understanding, homicide, "varies inversely with the degree of integration of the social groups of which the individual forms a part." When society begins to unravel, and close bonds between people begin to fray, suicides will increase drastically. When society as a whole becomes more individualistic, there comes the rise of suicides stemming from "excessive individualism." This rise in individualism could be the "times of decadence" that Durkheim predicted would lead to higher suicide rates. This worldview is the opposite of a tightly knit community. "There is, in short, in a cohesive and animated society a constant interchange of ideas and feelings from all to each and each to all, something like a mutual moral support, which instead of throwing the individual on his own resources, leads him to share in the collective energy and supports his own when exhausted." When this strong sense of community and attachment declines, unconnected individuals will begin to strike out violently at an increasing rate because they have no support network to keep them grounded and supported.

For Durkheim, there are some factors that lower the chances of egoistic suicide occurring. He argues that minorities will commit considerably less egoistic suicides. Typically, intolerance for minority groups raises communal protections among the persecuted. Essentially, one of the products of persecution or intolerance towards minority groups leads to increased cohesion within minority groups. He also asserted that there are far more unmarried people committing egoistic suicide than married people. All things being equal, unmarried people will kill themselves about twice as much as married people. This can be understood as the marital relationship providing strong social ties for people, with single people not having these ties. Robert Agnew summarizes Durkheim thusly:

> Durkheim's theory clearly focuses on the absence of society. Deviance ultimately is caused by the failure of society (or its organs) to regulate individual goals adequately. The absence of such regulation is what Durkheim means by anomie. . . . The absence of society does not free individuals to satisfy their universal desires in the most expedient manner. Rather, the absence of society leads individuals to develop unlimited or unattainable goals, and the failure to achieve these goals leads to 'anger and all the emotions customarily associated with disappointment' (Durkheim 1951: p. 284). It is these emotions that drive individuals to suicide and violence." (Agnew 1997, 31)

We can see that the Aurora theater shooting fits the pattern established by Durkheim. An intelligent, well-educated but lonely, isolated young man decided to commit mass slaughter instead of suicide. The suspect's race, social class, educational level, and marital status were all predicted by Durkheim. While it may be hard to define societal breakdown and moral compass, especially as they relate to the twenty-first century United States, there is no doubt that James Holmes felt loneliness, isolation and a lack of community felt by so many who commit suicide or mass murder. Presumably, once James Holmes withdrew from graduate school, it signaled a failure to achieve his goal, and this shortcoming fueled anger within him, and he acted on this anger by shooting inside the theater.

Merton's Explanation of Anomie

Building on Durkheim's notion of anomie, Robert Merton (1964) explained deviance as a reaction to strain a person feels based on their acceptance or rejection of societal goals and the means needed to achieve them. Merton described five adaptations to strain. People who accepted both societal goals and the means to achieve them were termed conformists, and were not considered deviant. An example of conformity would be accepting attaining wealth as a goal, with working a legal job as the means to attain the goal. Another adaptation would be accepting societal goals but rejecting the means to achieve them. Merton termed these people innovators. An example would be selling drugs to make money quickly—the goal of attaining wealth remains, but the means to achieve it is rejected. The third adaptation would be rejecting the goals of society but accepting the means. These people were defined as ritualists. This can be understood as someone who continues to go to work at a low-paying job, with no hopes of achieving wealth through the job. The fourth group, and the one that we feel is best related to the phenomenon of mass shootings, is retreatist. Retreatists are people who reject both societal goals and means. One can think of this either as a person joining a monastery, or more cynically as the Unabomber, who went into reclusion and lived alone in a cabin in Montana. The last group Merton described was rebels; those who, like retreatists, reject both the goals and means of a society, but go further and substitute new goals and means.

Agnew argues that there is one distinct difference between Durkheim's and Merton's theories:

> In Durkheim, we find that anomie at the societal level (i.e., the failure to regulate individual goals) leads to strain at the individual level. This strain, involving he pursuit of unlimited or unattainable goals, leads to anger/ frustration and may drive the individual to suicide and violence. In Merton, strain at the individual level, involving the failure to achieve monetary success, is perhaps the major cause of anomie at the societal level (i.e., the low emphasis on legitimate norms by the cultural system). Individual-level strain in Merton is a function of the larger cultural and social environment; specifically the strong emphasis on monetary success by the cultural system, the systematic denial of opportunities for such success by the stratification system, and the pressure by the social and cultural system to adopt comparative reference groups from higher strata. (Agnew 1997, 45)

Thus, we are left to reconcile whether individual-level strain is a catalyst for strain at the societal level or whether general societal strain leads to individual-level strain. Ultimately, this distinction may not be especially useful/ Rather, it is the presence of strain that an individual internalizes—this strain can be either from the societal level, from the individual level, or have both levels felt in tandem – and that fuels negative emotions and the desire to act on them with violence, either against oneself (i.e. suicide) or by inflicting pain and harm onto others.

Many of the characteristics of James Holmes and his mass shooting fit with the theories of Merton and Durkheim. Holmes was unmarried and reportedly had broken up with his girlfriend days before the shooting spree Aurora, Colorado. (Gye, Keneally, and Bates; dailymail.co.uk) Given his professional situation—that he had just failed his comprehensive exams and withdrew from graduate school, he was facing a sudden, unexpected change which he may not have known how to deal with, not the least of which was the loss of a support network at work, compounded with losing a support network in the form of a significant other in his personal life. From what has been written, Holmes had few communal ties outside of his gaming group, was intelligent, and came from a well-off family. While one can argue that Holmes' engagement in graduate school was an acceptance of higher education as either a societal goal, mean to achieve a goal (such as launching a career after obtaining a Ph.D), or both, his withdrawal from graduate school suggests a rejection of education as a goal and/or a means to attain a goal. To the best of our knowledge, Holmes, as a young Caucasian male, was not a minority and outside of his gaming group, had few social ties. Given these few ties, combined with the stress of not doing well on his comprehensive exams and withdrawing from school, Holmes may have felt isolated and lost, and felt that shooting was a response to these stresses. One aspect to point out is that Merton's theory of strain centers on economic strain, and possibly status attainment (i.e. achieving a respected status takes time and can be achieved in certain ways, but you may have people either circumventing these ways or replacing a conventional status with one of their own) and as such, is somewhat limited. In order to account for broader areas of social strain, we also examine Robert Agnew's (2006) strain.

Agnew's General Strain Theory

In his General Strain Theory, Agnew defined strain as "events or conditions that are disliked by individuals" (Agnew, 2006, 4). He identified three sources of strain: when individuals lose something they value; when individuals are treated badly by others; and when individuals are unable to achieve their goals (2006, 4). Thus, the scope of strains expands upon Merton's idea of strain. Merton's conception of strain is Agnew's third type of strain. In addition to adding two new dimensions of strain, Agnew contends that there are objective strains, which are "disliked by most people or most people in a given group" (2006, 10) and subjective strains, which is an "event or condition that is disliked by the particular person or persons being examined" (2006, 10). One can identify James Holmes failing his comprehensive exam as a subjective strain, in that he was unable to finish his goal of completing graduate school. Leaving graduate school may have both been a response to this strain as well as a strain in that he lost something valuable to him—his years of studying and work went unrewarded with the goal of a doctorate. Agnew argues that crime is one way individuals cope with strain. One such coping mechanism is that, in the interim, "crime allows individuals to obtain revenge against those who have wronged them, or, if this is not possible, against more vulnerable targets" (2006, 14). Further, "strains lead to negative emotional states (including anger), which are conducive to crime" (2006, 31). One can view Holmes' shooting spree as a way of him coping with his negative emotions related to his problems in graduate school, and turning his anger on a group of vulnerable people (targets), rather than on the people he may have felt accountable for his problems. Two main sources of strain for adults that Agnew identifies are unemployment and marital problems. Given that graduate school was Holmes' source of income and work, and that he had reportedly broken up with his girlfriend shortly before his shooting spree, one can view these two events occurring close to one another as creating a high amount of strain, with violent crime being Holmes' outlet and way of coping.

Conclusion

In this chapter, we have attempted to highlight is that there are social causes to mass shootings. This piece is not written in an attempt to diminish psychological findings or diagnoses. Indeed, feelings of isolation likely have both social and psychological roots. The purpose of this chapter is to explain social causes of mass shootings, not justify them. We write this in an attempt to focus on factors that are typically under-reported or outright ignored in analyses and media portrayals of mass shootings. One can look at some of the factors discussed in this paper and apply them to at least one other mass shooting in the same state—the Columbine High School shooting in Littleton, Colorado. In that specific shooting, there were two per-petrators, both of them adolescent Caucasian males who felt isolated from most of high school society despite being part of a small clique. They claimed this feeling of isolation as a source of rage and as the impetus for shooting their classmates. It is important to note that there have been multiple mass shootings in the United States since James Holmes' shooting, including the murder of 26 children at an elementary school in Connecticut, six deaths in a shooting inside a college in Santa Monica, California, and four deaths, including the gunman, in a shooting in a business in St. Louis, Missouri.

Given this spate of violence, one possible intervention to consider is the implementation of support networks in schools and jobs. While co-workers can be a support network in and of themselves, having both formal and informal mechanisms may provide some much-needed social support, and a way to alleviate feelings of social isolation. Ideas for formal mechanisms include workplaces hiring counselors for people to vent to during their employment as well as after – i.e. having someone in place who can advise workers with respect to stresses of the workplace, as well as during transitional periods when workers are either leaving their workplace for a new one or when they are preparing to retire. Informal mechanisms could include people working as teams and meeting regularly for both work-related goals but also to see how everyone is doing – a mechanism of informal social control. The main idea behind these mechanisms is to reduce feelings of isolation and increase feelings of belonging and of community. Such interventions might not prevent all future mass shootings, but may reduce the likelihood of these horrific acts happening and save lives in the future.

References

Agnew, Robert. 2006. *Pressured Into Crime: An Overview of General Strain Theory*. Los Angeles: Roxbury Publishing

British Broadcasting Corporation. 2012. "Profile: Aurora shooting suspect James Holmes." July 30, 2012.

Deam. Jenny. 2013. "Judge Accepts James Holmes' Insanity Plea in Colorado Shooting." *Los Angeles Times*. June 4, 2013.

Durkheim. Emile. 1997 (orig. 1897; 1951). *Suicide : A Study in Sociology*. Translated by John A. Spaulding and George Simpson. New York: Free Press

Gye, Hugo. Meghan Keneally. and Daniel Bates. 2012. "Dark Knight Gunman

Faced Eviction and 'Broke Up With Girlfriend' Just Before Killing Spree." Dailymail.co.uk. July 24, 2012.

Holmes, Ronald M. and Stephen T. Holmes. 2001. *Mass Murder in the United States*. New Jersey: Prentice Hall.

Lilly, J. Robert. Francis T. Cullen and Richard A. Ball. 2002. Criminological Theory: Context and Consequences, Third Ed. Thousand Oaks: Sage.

Merton, Robert K. 1964. "Anomie, anomia, and social interaction: Contexts of deviant behavior. "In M.B. Clinard (Ed.). Anomie and deviant behavior (pp.213–242). New York: Free Press

Mosk, Matthew, Brian Ross. Pierre Thomas. et al.2012. "Aurora Suspect James Holmes' Mother: 'You Have the Right Person.' Abcnews.com. July 20, 2012.

Passas, Nikos and Robert Agnew, eds. 1997. The Future of Anomie Theory. Boston: Northeastern University.

Pearson. Michael. 2012. "Gunman Turns 'Batman' Screening Into Real-Life 'Horror Film." Cnn.com. July 20, 2012.

Rowe. Peter and John Wilkens. 2012. "Quiet, unassuming San Diegan accused of mass murder." *San Diego Union-Tribune*. July 20, 2012.

Chapter Four
School Shooters: The Progression from Social Rejection to Mass Murder

Martha Smithey

Introduction

School shooters appear to be evil, fanatical, frightening, and sociopathic. And the outcomes of their actions make this appearance seem very correct. In recent years, the number of school shootings in the United States has declined since the early 1990s but the number of victims per school shooting has increased (Fox, Levin, & Quinet, 2012) indicating a transformation of school shootings from single-victim murders to mass murders. The transition to multiple victims explains why the horror and fear of school shootings is much greater than it was a few decades ago. Kaiser (2005) concluded that since 1996 the U. S. has witnessed the onset of a "very disturbing form of adolescent violence, the mass random shooting of students in public schools" (p.102). Mass shooting on a school campus refers to several injuries many of which are life-threatening or lethal.

Mass murder is the killing of three of more victims as part of a single ongoing event. According to Duwe (2004), who studied mass murder during the twentieth century, it is generally agreed among researchers that the definition of mass murder depends on the total amount of time over which the murders take place and the number of persons killed. School shooting are defined as murder occurring on a school campus with one or more victims. This definition is inclusive of single- and double-victim homicides but the trends of offending and victimization rates of school shootings described at the beginning of this chapter suggest that school shooters are increasingly committing mass murder to redress their grievances. This trend lead McGee and DeBernardo (1999) proposed a profile of a "class room avenger" who, among other characteristics, has a history of attachment difficulties.

Characteristics of mass murderers include slaughtering their victims in one event, targeting people they know or with whom they are familiar, motivated by revenge, and using efficient weapons of mass destruction such as automatic, high-powered firearms (Fox & Levin, 2011).

The horror caused and the fear induced by school shooting is well-founded by the increasing numbers of injury and death from school shootings in the past few years. Yet understanding school shooters is our best option for effective prevention. Such an attempt is made in this chapter which by focusing on the progression of social rejection to mass murder in the school environment.

Increasingly school shooters share characteristics with extremists who commit mass murder including social marginalization, a lifestyle of discontent shared with peer groups with similar discontent, the development of dogmatism, intolerance for dissimilar others, and experiencing rejection, failure, and loss (Gruenewald, 2011; Wilcox, 2007). School shooters tend to have been bullied and rejected youth and often form groups among themselves that foment hate and prejudice toward their antagonists (Meloy et. al., 2004; O'Toole, 2000). Those who do not form groups with other rejected youth remain socially isolated and are typically described as a "loner" in the psychological research on school shooters (Kaiser, 2005; McGee & DeBernardo, 1999). However, while "loners" may refer to a single shooter, they are not necessarily alone. They interact with others through selected means of mass media to create a social environment that is similar to the environment of hate groups and may even interact with hate groups online. In the end, both types develop and foment hate that leads to the extreme behavior of school mass murders.

Additionally, it is important to look at the similarities across different types of homicides and homicide offenders to better isolate trends and develop a more in-depth understanding of how individual social factors can produce a multitude of negative outcomes. According to Gruenewald (2011) "General crime pattern studies have focused less on explaining the most common forms of homicide but instead have analyzed the similarities and differences across complex homicide subtypes. This method of research has facilitated a more in-depth understanding of particular forms of homicides" (p. 181). Given the current trends and change in method from single- or double-homicide school shooting to mass shootings, such a level of understanding is needed to address this social problem.

Using existing literature, I focus on the similarities between bullying, hate crimes, extremism, and mass murder. I theoretically model the progression from being a victim of bullying to committing mass murder at school. The similarities of these types of criminals make it worthwhile to study them as a single phenomenon along a progression from rejection to hate. By doing so, I address the problem of the origin and process of the creation and continuation of hate within the school environment that culminate in a school mass murder. I explain the progression with an integration of social control theory (Hirschi, 1969), social learning theory (Burgess & Akers, 1966; Sutherland, 1947; Sykes & Matza, 1957), and moral justification theory (Katz, 1988) (see Figure 4.1). Finally, I offer suggestions for preventing violence in schools.

Figure 4.1. Social Rejection to School Mass Murder: Social Control, Social Learning, Moral Justification, and Extremism

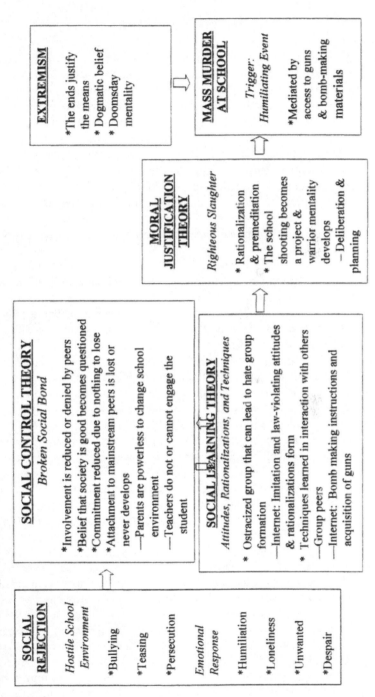

Social Rejection

Smith and Thompson (1991) define bullying as a set of behaviors that is intentional and causes physical and psychological harm to the recipient. Olweus (1993), a prominent researcher on bullying, defines a victim of bullying as "a student [who] is being . . . exposed repeatedly and over time, to negative actions no the part of one or more other students . . . and the bully [is] more powerful than the victim" (p. 9). He defines "negative actions" as acts that intentionally inflict or attempt to inflict injury or discomfort upon another. They include verbal abuse, such as name calling, taunting, and teasing, or physical abuse, such as kicking, pinching, hitting, restraining, or pushing. Leary, Kowalski, and Phillips (2003) characterize "bullying and malicious teasing [as actions] aimed rather indiscriminately [at] . . . students who are powerless and unpopular". Theses definitions can be generalized into bullying behaviors are intentional repeated harm committed by persons with the social ability to do so.

Bullying is prevalent in our schools. Whitney and Smith (1993) found that 27 percent of junior high/middle school children reported being bullied occasionally and 10 percent reported victimization on a weekly basis. Other studies show a range between 7 and 27 percent of students being bullied on a frequent basis (Butsche & Knoff, 1994; Hoover, Oliver, & Hazler, 1992; National Institute on Child Health and Development, 2009; Nansel et. al., 2001; O'Moore & Hillery, 1989; Vieira da Fonseca, Garcia, & Perez, 1989). These numbers are disturbingly high and suggest that anywhere from one out of four to one out of fourteen children are victims of chronic abuse and humiliation. Given typical sizes of middle/junior high and high school classes, these numbers suggest that at least two to seven per class are experiencing some degree of emotional abuse at school.

The likelihood of being a frequent, chronic victim appears to increase as victims who are repeatedly targeted advance in grades. Borg's (1999) research on the extent and nature of bullying among primary and secondary school children found that the "hard core of regular bullies remains large as the students progress in grade-levels but the victim pool shrinks to such an extent that the same victims become the targets of several bullies acting singularly or in groups (p. 144). Thus a student who is bullied throughout middle/junior high school and then continues being bullied in high school becomes increasingly targeted. This is due to the number of "regular" offenders growing with each grade advance while the victim pool shrinks. Consequently, the amount and degree of victimization intensifies and becomes more ubiquitous and relentless for that victim. Additionally, Davidson and Demaray (2007) found a trend of reporting less bullying as grade level increases. For those whose victimization becomes chronic, the likelihood of seeking help diminishes. This is due to the belief that school officials can intervene lessens.

There are clear trends in the types and location of bullying behaviors. The abuse is not just teasing and name-calling. Borg (1999) studied victimized students and found that physical abuse was the most common type of bullying with 61 percent reporting, followed by isolation with 36.3 percent of victims reporting. Several researchers have found that the majority of bullying occurs on the school's playground and in the classroom (Borg, 1999; Siann et. al., 1994; Whitney & Smith, 1993). That the classroom is a prime spot for experiencing humiliation is particularly devastating for the victim since he or she is required to spend the majority of their time in that location. This underscores the victim's perception that school officials can or will not effectively intervene. That the playground is a prime spot is particularly painful for the victim since isolating oneself to avoid the potential for interaction to become humiliated only contributes to the chronic despair of the victim. The increasing despair and decreasing attempts to seek help create social alienation and disconnection with the school environment.

Social Control Theory

According to Hirschi (1969), individuals obey society's rules and laws because they are bonded to society by four elements. One element is their attachment to others, which is achieved typically through the giving and receiving of love from important and significant others such as family, friends, and teachers. Such attachment results in feelings of being accepted and wanted. Another element is involvement in the everyday activities of their social world. For an adolescent, school is a major part of their social world and participating in school events and organizations structures the hours of their day with socially rewarded and supported activity. Another element is commitment. People invest time toward fulfilling the goals their society has taught them are important for being a "good person". The invested time toward achieving the cultural goals becomes cached as part of the trajectory toward achieving the status of a "good person". This cache is part of the reward structure of society since it can be used as leverage by society to reward acceptable social behavior or punish unacceptable social behavior. The loss of status or "stake in conformity" (Toby, 1957) is often used as punishment and results in the loss of the effort, resources, and time invested in achieving the socio-cultural goals. The last element of the social bond is belief that society's ways of doing things, rules, and laws are good and morally correct. Having this belief is essential to the motivation to follow the rules and obey the law; else the person would be motivated toward law-violation.

In totality, the presence of these four elements in a person's life forms a strong bond with society. The weakening of one or more elements weakens the entire bond. When a person's bond is weakened or broken, they are more likely to commit crime including acts of violence.

Broken Social Bond

Bullying breaks the social bond of the victim or impedes the development of one in the first place. The rejection experienced in a hostile school environment breaks or weakens the victim's social bond. The removal of an individual from conventional activity marginalizes him which makes it difficult to attach to others, commit to goal fulfilling behavioral trajectories, to be involved in school activities, and to believe that society is fair and morally just. Bullying and teasing leading to marginalization has been identified as a frequent motive in school shootings (Fox & Burnstein, 2010; O'Toole, 2000; Newman et. al., 2004). The consequences of bullying include marginalization resulting in humiliation and lack of respect which create motive, a need for revenge. or the restoring one's self to a place of non-marginalization. The typical school structure tacitly allows bullying and emotional abuse among students by having many places where students are unsupervised and little or no support from school personnel regarding interpersonal relations with other students. Aronson (2004) delineated the stratification of students and power in school settings and concluded there is a

> . . . poisonous social atmosphere prevalent at most high schools in this country—an atmosphere characterized by exclusion, rejection, taunting, and humiliation . . . an iron-clad hierarchy of cliques—with athletes, class officers, cheerleaders, and preppies at the top. At the bottom are students who do not fit in. The teenagers near the top of the hierarchy are constantly rejecting, taunting, and ridiculing those near the bottom. Those in the middle often join in as a way of differentiating themselves from those at the bottom (p. 355).

The emotions experienced by the bullied victims include loneliness due to isolation, feeling singled out for persecution, and chronic fear of public humiliation. Hoover, Olive, and Hazler (1992) found that approximately 14 percent of boys and girls suffer severe trauma from bullying abuse. Studying the emotional responses of victims to bullying, Borg (1998) found that about one-third reported feelings of vengefulness. anger, and self-pity. About one-fourth reported feeling helpless. The effect of these emotions is exponential and pervades every aspect of the youth's life and activities.

Consequently, belief in society being good and moral becomes questioned by the bullying victim because unfair and discriminatory environments undermine the credibility of the social control agents and mechanisms that are attempting to form the social bond. Credibility is important in gaining Durkheim's (1897 [1951]) social sentiment needed for social cohesion and belonging. Belonging to primary groups such as family and peers is needed for the victim to care about their society. If they do not care about their society. then they are not compelled to follow its rules. Also, sympathy and empathy are lost which leads to reduced commitment. When the victim has nothing to lose (Toby, 1957), they are no longer subject to wanting the "rewards" of society. There is a big sense of loss with no expectation that they will ever get the reward. The rewards and quality of life compels persons to commit toward socially approved paths of goal fulfillment. Commitment also compels persons to care about others in their community become diminished greatly due to the social rejection. For bullying victims. attachment to peers or their culture (i.e.

school) is lost or never developed. This results in reduced involvement since potential friends or peers are either afraid to appear as the victim's friend and therefore risk being bullied also or they want to befriend the bully who may be a popular student.

Although parents may be a positive source of attachment, they are powerless to change the school environment and cannot substitute for peer activity and acceptance. Once the bulled victim has been "ostracized," he is now poised to become a hater. The student is no longer connected to the school environment (which for an adolescent is society) and will actively "remove" himself from this environment by becoming a loner or seeking others who have also been rejected.

The chronic experience of rejection leads to isolation: Borg (1999) studied victims of bullying and concluded "there are many pupils out there who are silently suffering great physical and psychological pain, humiliation, and stress" (p. 152). Reduced involvement is the result of potential friends or peers either being afraid to appear as the victim's friend and risk being bullied also or the potential peers want to befriend the bully who is often a popular student.

Popular students are more effective bullies due to their ability to command a large audience. The lack of sanctions or deterrent methods applied to bullying by popular students results in the larger school system seeming unjust and uncaring. For adolescents, the school system represents society-at-large. Consequently, belief in society is questioned because unfair and discriminatory environments undermine the credibility of the social control agents and mechanisms that are attempting to form a bond. Durkheim (1897 [1951]) argues that social sentiment needed for social cohesion and commitment to the goals and culture of society.

Acceptance and belonging is necessary for the victim to care about their society, especially during adolescence. This makes middle and junior high school students especially vulnerable to the negative and traumatic emotions of bullying. This is an age period where youth experience increasing pressure from peers and society while maturing physically and psychologically, and beginning to experience separation from parents. Collectively, these changes result in increased stress for most adolescents (Feldman, 2006). Meloy et. al. (2004) found that this age period correlates with adolescent mass murderers who tended to around 17 years of age, "a time of late adolescence when separation from the nuclear family, the establishment of an occupational or career path, and the search for an intimate partner pose both opportunities and potential crises" (p. 301).

Chronic, humiliating social rejection from the environment that represents society to the individual will result in rejecting the society at a minimum and the need to harm society at a maximum. If individuals reject their society, then they are not compelled to follow its rules.

Commitment to conventional activities is reduced because in a hostile environment, sympathy and empathy are not taught or fostered. This leads to reduced commitment. When the victim has nothing to lose (Toby, 1957), they are no longer subject to wanting the "rewards" of society. A big sense of loss can lead to no expectation reward. Fox and Levin (2011) found loss to be a major contributor to the likelihood committing mass murder. Ad adolescent whose bond is broken is one where he once experienced reward and worked toward meeting societal expectations. The loss of a broken bond can be acute or chronic. Acute loss is more salient. The rewards and quality of life which compels many to care about their community are damaged or absent due to the social rejection. Attachment to peers or their culture (i.e. school) is lost or never developed. As previously mentioned, the emotions experienced by the bullied victim include isolation, persecution, and chronic public humiliation which constitute the sense of "loss."

Social Learning Theory

Attitudes, Rationalizations, and Techniques

The ostracized persons now have the potential to become haters or a hate group. According to social learning theory, group members share attitudes and beliefs that lead to hatred of others (Burgess & Akers, 1966). Research on hate murderers shows that the hate and techniques used to commit mass murder are developed and socialized through interaction with like-minded persons (Gruenewald, 2011). Researching school shootings, Vossekuil et. al. (2000) found that in one-half of the cases the attackers were influenced or encouraged by others. For the bullied victim, hate is the motivation for revenge and the bully's willingness and the need to restore honor or stop potential to harm others is the rationalization. The techniques of how to kill, assault, and bomb targets are actively taught through interaction with each other or through internet usage. The internet assists in the fomentation of hate by providing models of persons seeking revenge which can be imitated by the bullied victim. Language, text, games, and videos are sources of content for law-violating attitudes and rationalizations that become violent behavior.

There are numerous hate groups that provide rationalizations, techniques, and hateful attitude development. Law enforcement estimates place the number of active hate groups in the U. S. as high as 900 or more. Organized hate groups form for the purpose of recruitment and collaborations people who share a variety of biased attitudes and activities (Grimes, 2011). The vast majority, if not all, hate groups have websites to disseminate their rationalizations and justifications for hate against another group. The website actively encourages hate behavior and crimes and recruit persons to enroll in their group through establishing like-mindedness of emotion and belief regarding the immorality and evil behavior of others. The characteristics of the websites are much like those of extremists and include detailed instructions on hate activity such as bomb-making instructions or how to access and modify guns. There are other websites that provide the same information that are not directly tied to any one or more hate groups. Potential school shooters can access those sites in addition or in place of hate group sites.

The course of learning to hate through interactions with others can include neutralizing the any degree of the existence of a bond by implementing techniques of neutralization (Sykes & Matza, 1957). Neutralization theory assumes society is a collective conscience and that people are compelled to follow society's rules but, when faced with a compelling force to commit crime, they must "neutralize" their internalized understanding of the conventional expectations held by society including not harming others. Sykes and Matza describe techniques or mental exercises that dissuade any feelings of remorse or guilt from choosing to act counter to those expectations, including the planning and commission of mass murder.

One technique is condemning the condemners where offenders rationalize their offending with the belief that everyone does bad behavior so they are no worse than anyone else. Often those condemned by the offenders have not acted in a manner that can be deemed deviant, harmful, or criminal. However, for bullying victims the application is more complex. An added dimension of this technique addresses the use of lethal violence to redress the emotional abuse experienced by the victim. Bullying is the condemnation of persons who are perceived as weak, unattractive, and socially awkward. The social rejection and unwantedness that bullying victims experience lead to the condemned (*i.e.* the bullying victim) in turn condemning the condemners (*i.e.* the bullies). This allows the would-be school shooters to justify their intention to act on their hate because not only are they the condemned after the act of revenge, the bullies are the condemned due to the creation and sustaining of the hostile environment.

School shooters also deny the victim. With this technique, the offender rationalizes that the recipient of the harmful, deviant, or criminal behavior deserves what will happen or has happened because they are not victims of a crime but rather viewed as offenders who need to be punished. Once the hate is internalized and permeates much of the thought and behavior of the bullied victim, the bullies are viewed as deserving the violence being planned against them; therefore the bullies as targets for revenge are not viewed as "victims" but rather as offenders.

For some school shooters, there may be an appeal to higher loyalties—another technique of neutralization. Here the shooter believes that they are stopping the bully from harming others, either presently or in the future. In this sense, the shooter's higher loyal consists of other who are vulnerable to the victimization of bullies.

The techniques of neutralization, rationalizations and justifications are amplified through group interaction or internet interaction. In this way, the justification of mass murder and other techniques of hate and revenge are learned in interaction with others.

Adult mass murderers typically act alone after the accumulation of long-term failure. The triggering event is some type of loss, usually a job or intimate partnership (Fox & Levin, 2011). The likelihood of group formation is very low in these cases because the disgruntled person is removed from access to others like him or with similar experiences. In the cases of intimate partner loss, a restraining order may be issued. In the case of the school shooter, the law and parents force the youth to remain in the social environment that has produced his rejection and despair. This increases the likelihood that the bullying victim's hate will increase and that he will identify and connect with others who have similar experiences with the school environment. Even if there are such persons in the work place, the dismissed employee will not have the same level of contact as a student would have with other victims on a daily basis. Consequently, group formation of potential school shooters is greater due to the forced interaction with the school environment.

Meloy et. al. (2004) found that approximately 25 percent of school shootings are done inh a group with two or more offenders. The group appears to deliberate and commit the mass murder as a unified entity. It is unclear to what degree all the offenders agree with or intend to carry out the shooting. Work by Wintrobe (2006) on the political economy of extreme rationalism found that:

> solidarity denotes unity or oneness of purpose. Sometimes solidarity is motivated by empathy or identification, as when we feel for others who have experienced a misfortune that could have happened to us. The desire for group identification seems to be fundamental characteristic of human beings (p. 9).

In other words, the nature of the group with which one identifies often has a common focus based on experience or cause. In the case of school shooters, the nature of solidarity is revenge or "reforming" the school environment to stop the harm. The group members may have varying degrees of revenge and desire for harming the bullies. Yet those who participate in the school shooting appear as a unified front. The conformity to the group's horrific behavior is similar to the conformity often observed within extremist groups which is usually greater than within the wider society. This solidarity creates an unquestioned conformity so the group of school shooters not only has a strong like-mindedness but appear to outsiders to be acting as one.

Moral Justification Theory: The Mass Murder Trigger

According to Katz (1988), understanding crime is:

> understanding how individuals strive to make a meaningful world when confronted with strong feelings of fear, anxiety, and alienation. Criminals make their world meaningful in ways that provide the moral and sensational motivations leading to crime. A criminal act is a "project" through which the criminal is trying to transcend a moral challenge and achieve a moral dominance that he faces in the immediate situation. This achievement is morally meaningful to the criminal and involves that person's perceptions of right and wrong or justice and injustice" (p. 9).

The moral challenge faced by a chronically, systematically bullied student is to escape or end a situation that is otherwise inexorably humiliating. With chronic despair comes a "martyrdom aspect" of not caring about the costs because the reward of being a "moral" person is worth the cost. Katz (1988, p. 9) uses the phrase "righteous slaughter" to describe the rationalizations and murders of killers who have some degree of intimacy with their victims. These murderers believe their lethal actions are correct because they are upholding the moral good and that the killer interprets the lethal event as one in which the victim was doing something the killer cannot ignore. The event often is a humiliating experience for the killer who believes their behavior was the "good" behavior and the victim's behavior was the "bad" behavior.

In fact, Meloy et. al. (2004) found that the "clinical and situational aspects of mass murderers as they moved toward the commission of a mass murder included the development of a 'warrior mentality'" (p. 292).

The school shooter develops the warrior mentality and the mass shooting becomes deliberated as a project or mission with detailed planning and discussion of the technique of the event. Mediating effects in the ability to effectively plan and enact the mass murder include the availability of guns, bomb making instructions, and bomb-making materials. The internet provides successful venues for overcoming these obstacles. Loners and hate group members use it for bomb making instructions and information on the acquisition of guns. Also, guns are available due to family and acquaintances having guns easily available.

Extremism

Extremism is taking a belief to its limit or way beyond reasonable behavior (Wilcox, 2007). The social interaction of the rejected youth and the subsequent formation and fomenting of hate can lead to extreme hate behavior. The bullying-victim-turned-hater now exhibits characteristics of extremism (Wilcox 2007). One such characteristic is that the school shooter believes that the ends justify the means whether this is revenge, restoring honor, or stopping further harm to him and others by killing the bully. In the case of revenge as motive, the shooter is acting from the emotional pain of the chronic humiliation. The violence can be a combination of expressive release and attempt at restoration of honor. In the case of eliminating harmful persons as motive, the shooter sees his mission as removing harmful elements of society, much like a mission serial killer (Fox & Levin, 2011). Regardless of motive, an expedient way of achieving the extremist goals is a mass murder and the targets are located in the school setting.

The shooter becomes dogmatic in his belief by having rigid, unyielding beliefs that are narrow in scope. Gruenewald (2011), studying extremist murderers, found that they were primarily motivated by ideology and belief. This applies to school shooters as well. The development of the dogmatic belief is that other options for redressing his pain and grievances/victimization have not worked and are less efficient with little or no potential for gaining the desired outcome which is revenge or restructuring the hostile environment. At some point there may have been consideration of alternative options including varying tactics in social interaction with potential peers or the bully, seeking help from teachers and other school personnel, or seeking comfort and assistance from home, but past experience with the school officials may have lead the bullying victim to believe these options are no longer viable.

Once in this dogmatic state, the shooter then is unwilling to listen to others who have beliefs outside their dogmatic, narrow scope. Suggestions, conversations, or digital communications with others about their hatred of certain persons or the school may be met with attempts of minimizing the seriousness of the situation or refusal to believe the situation can be resolved through other means.

A doomsday mentality develops. Having experienced the limited, mandatory social environment of hostility at school with little intervention from teachers and parents, society now seems fatalistic. The ability to project onto the future a positive view of life and social environments outside or after high school is a mental exercise for which the bullied victim has few resources to imagine left and, due to age, the victim has had limit opportunity to find. The doomsday mentality is exacerbated by groupthink emergent from interaction with the other haters, who have little skill or ability also to envision a non-hostile social environment or an alternative course of action.

School shooters, like extremists, may also have belief in conspiracy theory that others are plotting against them. Gruenewald (2011) found in a study of far-right extremist homicides that the perpetrators were suspicious of central federal authority. As bullying victims transform into haters, their suspicion of the authority of teachers and school administrators grows and can become a dogmatic belief that the whole school is against them.

Another characteristic of extremists that holds for school shooters is that they have come to live a lifestyle of discontent. Wintrobe (2006), who studied the rationality of extremism, refers to "the calculus of discontent" (p. 75) which casts the actor as rational. He concluded that extremists have big goals and that the effective attainment of the goals requires elaborate planning. Those with extreme beliefs also use extreme methods. As a rational actor, they have "calculated their method in the best possible course available to them" (p.76), regardless of how irrational others view their actions. The school shooter's discontent is with the current structure of the school environment that allows emotional and physical abuse between students. To restructure a school environment is an extreme undertaking, especially when the hierarchy-power structure of the school allows bullying to go largely unchecked. When the school authority is unable or unwilling to reorder the school structure to hold abusers accountable, the task appears impossible to the victim who has now developed extremist characteristics. The reordering of the school becomes viewed as increasingly necessary to eliminate the abuse. Whether a lone shooter or group, the discontent is exacerbated by hating and agitating against others who they perceive as needing to be stopped emerges. The victims start viewing the bullies as using extreme, harmful behavior and become the target of the extremist goals and behavior of the bullying victims and view other students and school personnel as complicit in the emotional abuse and humiliation. The combination of dogmatic belief, conspiracy, and discontent become the motivating emotions behind the planning of the school mass murder. The extensiveness of these emotions may be the force that has led them to multiple victims instead of targeting just those who repeatedly bullied them.

Finally, extremists view collateral damage as a necessary "evil." School shooters are aware that students who are not viewed as complicit may be hurt or killed and, in some cases, have selectively told potential victimization to stay out of the away. In a few cases they have told them in advance of the school shooting to not come to school on the day of the planned mass murder.

Mass Murder at School

Once the social bond is broken and the lone hater or hate group has rationalized and justified their actions to the point of extremism, the bullying victim is now poised for a transformation to a mass murderer, the motive is revenge and restoration of honor. The outcome is terrorism of the rejecting environment. Research on rampage mass murder and school shootings provide evidence of this transformation

Aronson's (2004) research revealed that rejection and the accompanying humiliation was the dominant issue underlying every one of the rampage killing in the U. S. that he studied. In fact, a football player who was injured during the Columbine school shooting admitted to having teased and rejected the Columbine shooters. School mass murders are an attempt to overcome the humiliation and repair the damaged reputation. Mullen (2004) analogizes motives for school shootings with "running Amok" as a means to restore honor or lost status:

> Amok within the Mayan culture was said to be a mechanism used by young men following some form of public humiliation to regain face and social prestige with the manner of their death being a vindication of their courage and potency (p.321).

In this analogy, the killer proclaims their power by going for "high public infamy". This is a form of revenge for the rejection and humiliation and is a way of re-establishing validity for their inclusion in the social environment. Kaiser's (2005) work on school shooters corroborates this with his finding that humiliated youth who commit school mass murder often do so from the need to restore their honor and reputation.

Weeber's (2011) research on extremism and terrorism suggests another motive that is plausible for a school shooter. He writes that "extremists seek a radical restructuring of the society in which they live" (p.225) and that "terrorism is closely associated with extremism" (p.229). Much like an extremist, the school shooter may seek a radical reordering of the school environment or believe he is working toward that goal. In this sense, the school shooter may view himself as a reformist but he has chosen a terrorizing, extreme method and is motivated to fulfill his goal at any cost including his own death.

The ability to commit mass murder is mediated by gun availability, internet access to bomb-making instructions, and the likelihood that the injuries sustained by the victims are lethal. This likelihood increases as the power of the weapon increases (DeVoe e.t al., 2002; Stolzenberg & D'Alessio, 2000). Indeed, the trend in mass murders indicates a higher level of revenge and rage with an increase in high body-count killings since 1980 (Duwe, 2004). With this extreme emotional state and "warrior mentality" (Meloy et. al., 2004, p. 292), only one humiliating event is needed to trigger the mass murder.

Once a school shooting has occurred, the media provides the audience that the school shooter imagined. Driven by journalistic values, the images and message intended by the school shooter are not defined by him but rather by the media. This is due to what the media determine and shape as a "newsworthy story". According to Farnen and Payerhin (1990), the media and the portrayal of violence is based on "predominant journalistic values require news to be about unexpected, sensational, and conflictive events. Violent groups are more are more than willing to supply an ample measure of each ingredient required for a newsworthy story" (p. 103). They contend that the media provide discrete knowledge of an issue or event rather than in-depth knowledge about the controversy or public policy. This results in a recreation, replacement, or displacement of the accuracy of details and context of the mass murder. Sanders (1990) refers to this as a creating a "meta-reality" for which the media selectively combine sights, sounds, images, and symbols (p.98). Moreover, the media often contribute to the goals of the shooter. A sensational, news story produces a much larger audience for the shooter's intended message and greater and more immediate identity establishment or re-establishment occurs. Essentially, the school shooter has been in an honor contest with the bully (Luckenbill, 1977). The size of the audience is the determining factor in who "wins" the contest, (although often both competitors end up injured or dead), one wittingly and one unwittingly. The desired end for the bullying victim is a "status-conferral" (Lazarsfeld & Merton 1971, p. 104) which the media provide for the school shooter by singling out this form of terrorism for the mass audience. The media attention defines the behaviors and opinions as significant enough to deserve public notice.

School shooters are similar to terrorists competing against a society or government for the dissemination of messages and control in that they invoke widespread fear. But they are dissimilar to these other types of terrorism because school shootings are on the interpersonal level and include persons known by the shooter.

The Solution: Change the School Environment

Not all bullying victims seek revenge or to restore honor. Borg (1998) studied the response of victims to bullying and found that about one-third did nothing, one-third did not seek parental help, about one-fifth sought teacher help, and only one in six sought help from the principal. These numbers show that while one in three feel anger and the need for revenge, fewer than one in five attempt the legitimate avenue of seeking help from school authorities. This speaks loudly about the level of comfort and anticipation of support these students have for the school power-holders. Borg attributed this to school officials not taking bullying seriously enough and suggested that

> The reason why so many victims feel helpless . . . may well be the result of the often widespread skepticism on the part of teachers and school administrators in regard to the seriousness of bullying (p.440).

There is a wider skepticism at the societal level regarding school or legal intervention in bullying. Many people believe that bullying is "normal" and that it teaches students to defend themselves. They argue that immediate confrontation with the bully by the victim would curtail their victimization, prevent chronic bullying and the subsequent emotions accompanying it, and stem bullying of others. This belief that youth should be allowed to manage their own bullying experiences assumes that children are capable agents of informal social control and leaves this increasingly dangerous social problem unattended by adults. This is not a solution and it relieves the school (and society) from any responsibility for changing the school environment to provide intervention that assures the safety of our children (see also Fox & Levin, 2011). Moreover, the belief that bullying teaches toughness implies that bullying victims deserve their abuse because they are too weak to defend themselves. This belief contributes to the lack of seriousness on the part of the school regarding the consequences of bullying and leaves some children with no place to turn except depression, suicide, or homicide.

On some level, school shooters are acting radically to restructure their social environment. The need to eliminate what they perceive as a painful, humiliating environment is believed by them to be eliminating an emotionally abusive environment in which they and other non-targeted person are compelled to participate by society's laws and parental demands. Methods to restructure the environment in a less radical way are either believed to be non-existent or have been met with failure. Perceptions that there are no socially acceptable ways to restructure the environment are founded in interactional patterns with persons of authority who minimize or are dismissive of the student needs. This is due to current school conditions that are far from ideal and do not have the economic resources nor social structure for sufficient focus on the well-being of students.

The ideal school setting produces a constant, healthy focus on *all* students. Advancing knowledge, creativity, and critical thought requires a degree of knowledge about each student. While this is idealistic, the goal should be a social setting that facilitates the accomplishment of this ideal to the highest degree possible. Not only would the amount of bullying be reduced, but higher quality education and reduced criminal behavior (such as drug use, theft, etc.) would be achieved.

The schools have opportunity to act toward this end. There is a time lag between victimization and externalizing stress as a school shooter during which the school authorities can intervene in both the aggressive, emotional abuse perpetrated by bullies and the rejection and hate felt by bullying victims. During this lag time the bullying victim's sense of powerlessness becomes more profound and despairing which can eventually lead to the need to regain power, even if at all costs. Wintrobe's (2006) calculus of discontent where extremists rationally plan to carry out complex tasks helps us understand the lag of time from the onset of victimization to the onset of planning mass murder. As bullying victims experience growing isolation and discontent, the likelihood of a mental transition from premeditation of mass murder to deliberation increases.

Conclusions drawn by several researchers imply a lag effect and focus on a time interval during which "buffering" can occur. There is a time interval from which the victim's state of mind transitions from internalized to externalized distress. If the internalized stress is dissipated, then externalized stress does not occur. Internalized distress is buffered by support from teachers, classmate, and others in the school setting with adult support being a more consistent and effective mediator than peer support (Davidson & Demaray, 2007; Demaray & Malechi, 2003; Kochenderfer-Lass and Skinner, 2002). Emotional, instrumental, informational, and appraisal support were all found to be important for dissipating internalized stress and for validating the bullying victim as a worthy, credible person. Davidson and Kilpatrick concluded that:

> stable social support networks may provide ongoing feelings of security.... If one believes that support resources will be available in times of crisis, this belief improves that persons' coping ability to handle such a crisis. [This either] works as a coping mechanism or as a primary and/or secondary appraisal (2007, p. 385).

The research found also that school counselors are an important part of a positive, proactive environment that addresses bullying and bullying victimization. To be proactive, the dichotomy of victim or bully needs to be eliminated because it does not serve to address the problems of emotional abuse and interpersonal conflict. Espelage, Bosworth, and Simon (2000) examined the social context of bullying behaviors in early adolescence and suggest that counselors conceptualize bullying as a continuum of behaviors rather than focusing on identification of "the bully" (p. 332) to more effectively address and reduce a hostile school environment. This applies to victimization as well. Rather than discrete categories of victims and offenders, deconstructing the events into continuums with degrees of bullying and victimization would allow more customized intervention.

In addition to responding to bullying with a formal means of reporting bullying and a predetermined school response, the research points to the need to restructure the school environment so that support mechanisms that do not formally label a student as a victim or bully can displace the development of hate by chronic victims and to dissipate the need to be abusive by bullies. Supportive, positive interaction with adults and classmates would create an accepting group with which the victim could develop a positive social bond. If the control over the interaction is such that victim feels supported and accepted and becomes involved in conventional activities that bolster the bond, the negative feeling and distress from the victimization can be channeled into social skills and support for others. In this way, hate formation is circumvented or dissipated. Left to their own devices, students lack the skills and motivation to transform this anger into a more effective resolution to their distress than mass murder or suicide (Klomek et. al., 2009; National Institute on Child Health and Development, 2009; Young & Leventhal, 2008).

The needed changes in the school environment described so far are *interactional* changes, where attitudes and interactions among school personnel and students would become be proactive in regard to bullying. But there are needed changes in the organizational structure as well. Smaller school size and additional personnel would strengthen the interactional, monitoring, and social attitude changes that are needed to reduce the hostility and conflict in the school environment.

Smaller schools with smaller classes would increase learning and create a better supervised setting. Cotton (1993) reviewed 103 studies that investigated associations between high school size and factors such as academic performance, social behavior, dropout rates, and parental involvement and concluded that smaller schools (400-600 students) are beneficial to students in all domains of function. This change would also reduce the alarming rate at which teachers are leaving the profession.

Fox and Levin (2011) advocate smaller schools along with a zero tolerance of bullying and labeling anywhere on the campus or at school-related activities. Smaller schools would lower the teacher-to-student ratio and allow a greater degree of teachers knowing the students on an individual level, increase student-teacher and student-to-student interaction and supervision. Kaiser (2005) found that smaller groups are more apt and able to police themselves thus increasing the informal social control that is assumed by the belief that victims are capable of stopping bullying with immediate confrontation.

Another way to increase adult attention to and supervision of students is adding another layer of personnel who supervise hallways, buses, campus grounds, lunchroom, and other places where students congregate. Some schools attempt to achieve this with community volunteers and often utilize retired persons to assist in supervising and teaching. While the volunteer program is beneficial to the students and retired persons, it is insufficient for ensuring a supportive, supervised, non-hostile school environment where children can thrive. A formal layer of personnel whose function is to assist teachers and to supervise non-classroom areas and activities is needed. This layer could consist of lay persons who have some degree of experience or who would receive training on working with and supervising youth. This change not only creates a safer environment for the children, it allows teachers to focus their attention and energy on education instead of supervising hallways, cafeterias, or campus areas.

Finally, as pointed out by Fox and Levin (2011), blaming parents of the school shooters is not a solution. Such blame assumes that bad kids are products of bad homes. This is more often *not* the case than is the case. Parental responsibility laws have increased stress and pressure on parents which has largely resulted in an increase of violence and hostility toward the children in the home. Peer and media influence overpower positive parenting and, in the cases of school shooters, bullied and rejected students tend to hang out with other bullied and rejected students. This breeds a collective hate toward the bullies and rejecters.

Conclusion

School shootings have transformed from single- or double-victim homicides to mass murders during the past few decades. The primary causative factor is chronic school bullying during which victims experience humiliation, isolation, and social rejection. These feelings transform into hate and break the bullying victim's bond with school and the larger society. Either as a loner who interacts with internet sources that foster hate or as a member socially marginalized group whose members foster hate, the social learning of attitudes and techniques of hate and violence lead to defining their situation as one that requires revenge, restoration of honor, or elimination of the hostile school environment. Moral justification of the mass murder as a "righteous slaughter" results in the adoption of extremism tendencies and poises the school shooter for a triggering, humiliating event. The bullying victim's internalized stress then becomes externalized as a mass murder.

Understanding the school shooter's motives and rationales are important for many reasons including the safety of children, creating a healthier and more effective learning environment, attendance and retention of students, and better establishment of authority and responsibility of school personnel for the well-being of children. A hostile school environment increases the likelihood of a school mass murder as it creates socially rejected youth who are motivated and feel morally justified in gaining revenge for the emotional abuse and loss of social status. School environments need to change to eliminate bullying with smaller schools and class sizes, a zero-tolerance of bullying, support mechanisms for bullied youth, and additional school personnel to increase supervision of youth during class and non-class activities.

References

Aronson, E. (2004). How the Columbine High School tragedy could have been prevented. *Journal of Individual Psychology, 60*, 34–47.

Batsche, G., & Knoff, H. (1994). Bully and victims: Understanding a pervasive problem in the schools. *School Psychology Review, 3*, 165–174.

Borg, M. G. (1998). The emotional reaction of school bullies and their victims. *Educational Psychology, 18*, 433–444.

Borg, M. G. (1999). The extent and nature of bullying among primary and secondary school children. *Educational Research, 41,* 137–153.

Burgess, R. L. and Akers, R. L. (1966). A differential association-reinforcement theory of criminal behavior. *Social Problems, 14,* 128–147.

Cotton, K. (1996). *Affective and social benefits of small-scale schooling.* Charleston, WV: Clearinghouse on Rural Education and Small Schools.

Davidson, L. M. and Demaray, M. K. (2007). Social support as a moderator between victimization and internalizing-externalizing distress from bullying. *Social Psychology Review, 36,* 383–405.

Demaray, M. K. and Malecki, C. K. (2003). Perceptions of the frequency and importance of social support by students classified as victims, bullies, and bully/victims in a urban middle school. *School Psychology Review, 32,* 471–489.

DeVoe, J. F., Ruddy, S. A., Miller, A. K., Planty, M., Peter K., Kaufman, P., Snyder, T. D. Snyder, Duhart, D. T. and Rand, M. R. (2002). *Indicators of school crime and safety.* U. S. Department of Education, National Center for Education Statistics, and U. S. Department of Justice, Bureau of Justice Statistics.

Durkheim, E. (1897 [1951]) *Suicide.* Trans. John A. Spaulding and George Simpson. New York: The Free Press.

Duwe, G. (2004). The patterns and prevalence of mass murder in twentieth-century America. *Justice Quarterly, 21,* 729–761.

Espelage, D. L., Bosworth, K., and Simon, T. R. (2000). Examining the social context of bullying behaviors in early adolescence. *Journal of Counseling and Development, 78,* 326–333.

Farnen, R. F., and Payerhin, M. (1990). Decoding the mass media and terrorism connection: Militant extremism as systemic and symbiotic processes. In Sanders, C. R. (Ed.) *Marginal conventions: Popular culture, mass media and social deviance,* pp. 98–116. Bowling Green, OH: Bowling Green State University Press.

Feldman, R. S. (2006). *Development across the life span.* Upper Saddle River, NJ: Prentice Hall.

Fox, J. A. and Burstein, J. (2010). *Violence and security on campus: From preschool through college.* Santa Barbara, CA: Praeger.

Fox, J. A. and Levin, J. (2011). *Extreme killing: Understanding serial and mass murder.* Thousand Oaks, CA: Sage Publications.

Fox, J. A., Levin, J., and Quinet, K. (2012). *The will to kill: Making sense of senseless murders. 4th edition.* Upper Saddle River, NJ: Prentice-Hall.

Grimes, Jennifer (2011). Hate crimes. In Chambliss, W. J. (Ed.) *Crime and criminal behavior,* pp. 127–138. Washington, DC: Sage.

Gruenewald, J. (2011). A comparative examination of homicides perpetrated byfar-right extremists. *Homicide Studies, 15,* 177–203.

Hirschi, T. (1969). *Causes and prevention of juvenile delinquency.* New York: Wiley.

Hoover, J. H., Oliver, R., and Hazler R. J. (1992). Bullying: Perceptions of adolescent victims in the Midwestern USA. *School Psychology International, 13,* 5–16.

Kaiser, D. A. (2005). School shootings, high school size, and neurobiological considerations. *Journal of Neuropathy, 9,* 101–115.

Katz, J. (1988). *Seductions of crime: Moral and sensual attractions in doing evil.* New York: Basic.

Klomek, A. B., Sourander, A., Niemela, S., Kumpulainen, K., Piha, J., Tamminen, T., Almqvist, F., and Gould, M. S. (2009). Childhood bullying behaviors as a risk for suicide attempts and completed suicides: A population-based birth cohort study. *Journal of the American Academy of Child & Adolescent Psychiatry, 48,* 254–261.

Kochenderfer-Ladd, B., and Skinner, K. (2002). Children's coping strategies: Moderators of the effects of peer victimization? *Developmental Psychology, 38,* 267–278.

Lazarsfeld, P. and Merton, R. K. (1948). Mass communication, popular taste and organized social action. In Schramm, W., and Roberts, D. F. (Eds.) *The process and effects of mass communications.* Pp. 554–578. Urbana, IL: University of Illinois Press.

Leary, M. R., Kowalski, L. S., and Phillips, S. (2003). Teasing, rejection, and violence: Case studies of the school shootings. *Aggressive Behavior, 29,* 202–214.

Luckenbill, D. F. (1977). Criminal homicide as a situated transaction. *Social Problems, 25,* 176–186.

McGee, J. and DeBernardo, C. (1999). The classroom avenger. *Forensic Examiner, 8,* 16–18.

Meloy, J. R., Hempel, A. G., Gray, B. T., Mohandie, A. S., Shiva, A., and Richards, T. C. (2004). A comparative analysis of North American adolescent and adult mass murderers. *Behavioral Sciences and the Law, 22,* 291–309.

Mullen, P. E. (2004). The autogenic (self-generated) massacre. *Behavioral Sciences and the Law, 22,* 311–323.

Nansel, T. R., Overpeck, M., Pilla, R. S., Ruan, W. J., Simons-Morton, B. and Scheidt, P. (2001). Bullying behaviors among US youth: Prevalence and association with psychosocial adjustment. *Journal of the American Medical Association, 285,* 2094–2100.

National Institute on Child Health Developmetn (2009). *Child Development and Behavior Branch Report.* U. S. Department of Health and Human Services, National Institutes of Health. Retrieved from http://www.nichd.nih.gov/publications/pubs/Documents/cdbb_council_2009.pdf

Newman, A. F., Fox, C., Harding, D.J., Mehta, J., and Roth, W. (2004). *Rampage: The social roots of school shootings.* New York: Basic Books.

Olweus, D. (1993). Bully/victim problems among schoolchildren: Basic facts and effects of a school-based intervention program. In S. Hodgins (Ed.), *Mental disorder and crime* (pp. 317–349). Thousand Oaks: Sage.

O'Moore, A. M. and Hillery, B. (1989) Bullying in Dublin Schools. *Irish Journal of Psychology, 10,* 426–441.

O'Toole, M. E. (2000). The school shooter: A threat assessment perspective.*Critical incidence response group report.* Washington, DC: Government Printing Office.

Sanders, C. R. (1990). A lot of people like it: The relationship between deviance and popular culture. In Sanders, C. R. (Ed.) *Marginal conventions: Popular culture, mass media and social deviance.* pp.3–13. Bowling Green, OH: Bowling Green State University Press.

Siann, G., Callaghan, M., Glissov, P., Lockhart, R. and Rawson, L. (1994). Who gets bullied? The effect of school, gender, and ethnic group. *Educational Research 36,* 123–134.

Smith, P. K. and Thompson, D. (1991) *Practical approaches to bullying.* London: Fulton.

Stolzenberg, L. and D'Alessio, S. J. (2000). Gun availability and violent crime: New evidence from the national incident-based reporting system. *Social Forces, 78,* 1461–1482.

Sutherland, E. H. (1947). *Principles of criminology.* Philadelphia: Lippincott.

Sykes, G. M. and Matza, D. (1957). Techniques of neutralization: A theory of delinquency. *American Sociological Review, 22,* 664–670.

Toby, Jackson (1957). Social disorganization and stake in conformity: Complementary factors in the predatory behavior of hoodlums. *Journal of Criminal Law, Criminology, and Police Science, 48,* 12–17.

Vieira da Foseca, M. M., Garcia, I. F. and Perez, G. Q. (1989). Violence, bullying and counseling in the Iberian Peninsula. In Roland, E. and Munthie, E. (Eds.) *Bullying: An international perspective,* pp. 22–34. London: Fulton.

Vossekuil, B., Reddy, M., Fein, R., Borum R.,and Modzeleski, M. (2000). *USSS safe school initiative: An interim report on the prevention of targeted violence in schools.* Washington, DC: US Secret Service, National Threat Assessment Center.

Watson, S. W. (2007). Boys, masculinity, and school violence: Reaping what we sow. *Gender and Education, 19,* 729–737.

Weeber, S.C. (2011). Terrorism and extremism. In Chambliss, W. J. (Ed.) *Crime and criminal behavior,* pp. 225–238. Washington, DC: Sage.

Whitney, I. and Smith, P. K. (1993). A survey of the nature and extent of bullying junior/middle and secondary schools. *Educational Research, 35,* 3–25.

Wilcox, Laird (2007). What is extremism? Style and tactics matter more than goals. In George, J. and Wilcox, L. *American extremists: Militias, supremacists, klansmen, communist, & others,* pp. 54–62. New York: Prometheus Books.

Wintrobe, R. (2006). *Rational extremism: The political economy of radicalism.* Cambridge University Press: New York.

Young, S.K. and Leventhal, B. (2008). Bullying and suicide: A review. *International Journal of Adolescent Medicine and Health, 20,* 133–154.

Chapter Five

Institutional Correlates of
Intimate Partner Gun Homicides

Sheryl L. Van Horne

Introduction

Little research has focused on intimate partner homicides outside cities. This study examines the impact of structural factors on intimate partner homicides in rural counties, comparing them to urban areas across the United States. Expanding on the paucity of research on rural crime, this research applies the systemic reformulation of social disorganization theory, which highlights the importance of institutions, and this study adds civic engagement and religious participation as additional institutions that play a key role in regulating community interactions and reflecting communal values.

Despite decreases in homicides across the country since 1992, intimate partner homicide has remained relatively stable over time. According to Supplementary Homicide Report Data, between 2000 and 2011 there were 113,650 homicides using guns across the United States out of 169,723 total homicides. Gun deaths overall were 49 percent lower in 2010 compared with 1993 (Cohn et al., 2013). Although the rate of gun violence has declined since 1993, trajectories differ in certain types of homicide and in different types of locations. According to survey research over 23 percent of women and 11 percent of men report some type of physical intimate partner violence in their lifetime (Centers for Disease Control and Prevention, 2008). Research indicates that gun presence and use impacts the outcome of the domestic dispute. For example, one study indicated a fivefold increase in homicide risk for women when her partner possesses a gun (Cambell et al, 2003). Furthermore, when a gun is used in a domestic dispute the abuse is twelve times more likely to end in death (Salzman, Mercy, O'Carroll, Rosenberg &

Rhodes, 1992). Research on intimate partner homicides, therefore, should examine the type of instrument used.

As homicides differ according to type they should be disaggregated by victim-offender relationship and by type of place. A significant body of research indicates that intimate homicides differ significantly from stranger and acquaintance homicides with respect to the significance and magnitude of the effects of structural variables (Parker & Smith, 1979; Parker, 1989; Williams & Flewelling, 1988; Kovandzic, Vieraitis & Yeisley, 1998). When all homicides are combined together important differences based on victim-offender relationship information, or type of homicide, are masked and findings might appear inconsistent (see Land et al., 1990). In addition to a need for homicides to be disaggregated by victim-offender relationship, they also need to be disaggregated by type of place. Most of the research has focused on homicides in cities, nearly neglecting homicides in rural communities. Yet, nearly one in ten homicides occurs in communities identified as rural and some of the counties with the highest rates of homicides are classified as rural counties (Kposowa & Breault, 1993). Previous research has indicated that the last two decades of the twentieth century had the highest homicide rates (Zahn & McCall, 1999) and that trends in rural counties do not always mimic those in urban areas (see Weisheit & Donnermeyer 2000). To be more specific, from 1966 to 1997 violent crime in urban areas increased until about 1991 then declined, whereas in rural areas there was a constant increase throughout that period (Weisheit & Donnermeyer 2000). Hence, the type of place matters and further comparisons between rural and urban places are needed.

Theoretical Framework

Social disorganization theory provides a macro-level framework suitable to examining intimate partner homicides to further examine structural forces beyond the individual him or herself. Social disorganization arose out of the classical Chicago school studies by Wirth (1938) and Shaw and McKay (1942). Shaw and McKay (1942) examined crime rates in Chicago neighborhoods from 1900 to 1930 noting that they remained relatively unchanged, despite changes in the population. They found that structural processes (poverty, racial/ethnic heterogeneity, and residential mobility) explained delinquency, expanding beyond Park and Burgess (1925) who indicated that cities expand and "grow radially in a series of concentric zones or rings" (Palen, 1981, 107). According to Park and Burgess, the transition zones were of the utmost concern, since it led to residents being displaced due to the outward push of the business district. Shaw and McKay tested Burgess' model by examining juvenile court records and found that juvenile delinquency was related characteristics of the neighborhoods and not the nature of the individuals within those neighborhoods. Originally, the theory focused on three primary variables: poverty, ethnic heterogeneity and population mobility.

Social disorganization theory combines demographic variables (ethnic/racial heterogeneity, poverty) and demographic processes (for example, population mobility) with the structural components of a community that impact the community's ability to informally control itself (Shaw & McKay, 1942), making it a valuable theoretical foundation for the study of homicides. Decades after its initial inception, a new understanding of how social disorganization affected communities arose where the impact of institutions within the communities became the focus of criminological studies. Research by Kornhauser (1978) and Bursik (1988) indicated that disorganization affects the way communities regulate themselves and share the value of living free of predatory crime. Kasarda and Janowitz (1974) underscore the importance of institutions in the socialization process. This theoretical shift with respect to the systemic reformulation of social disorganization theory sparked a renewed interest in a theoretical perspective that had sat relatively dormant for decades. Additional research expanded the understanding of social disorganization and led to a new reformulation of social disorganization theory that incorporates the importance of institutions to the understanding of structural causes of crime, often referred to as the systemic reformulation of social disorganization theory. Kasarda and Janowitz (1974) understood the local community to be a "complex system of friendship and kinship networks and formal and informal associational ties rooted in family life and ongoing socialization processes . . . fashioned by the large scale institution of mass society" (329). Through this conceptualization of the social disorganization model, one of the most important variables is length of residency in that the longer one resides in an area the more likely they will be assimilated to the culture (Kasarda & Janowitz,1974). Poverty can influence mobility and racial heterogeneity (Bursik & Grasmick, 1993).

Relatively few studies examine the impact of a range of social disorganization variables on homicide rates in rural or non-metropolitan areas on a broad scale, though there are some notable exceptions. Weisheit and Wells (2005) compared metropolitan and nonmetropolitan counties using data from 1994–1998. While they did examine the victim-offender relationship as one of their variables, it was not discussed in any detail within the article, leaving the gap not completely bridged. Osgood and Chambers (2000) argue for an expanded analysis, since they examined data from only four states. Crime rates in rural areas do not necessarily mirror crime rates in urban areas, and have even increased in some areas (Cameron, 2001; Lee & Hayes, 2005). The rate of intimate partner homicides has been significantly higher than suburban or urban areas across the country with large cities having the lowest rates and seeing the largest decline in the past thirty years (Fox & Zawitz, 2007). A number of researchers have argued that it is important to disaggregate homicides (see for example: Williams and Flewelling, 1988; Maxfield, 1989; Flewelling & Williams. 1999; Kubrin, 2003). This research seeks to add to the macro level understanding of intimate partner homicides in both rural and urban areas, expanding on the role and impact of institutions by incorporating an examination of voter participation and religious participation. By incorporating institutions into the analysis, this study examines the "relatively stable configuration of statuses, roles, values, and norms that emerge from the basic functional requirements of a society" (Messner and Rosenfeld, 1999, 28). Through the inclusion of religious and political institutions, this analysis adds to the understanding of the impact of institutional factors on intimate partner gun homicides.

Understanding Rurality

Before examining the structural correlates of intimate partner gun homicides in rural communities, it is important to understand what rural means and how it is similar to and different from urban places. There are a number of different ways of conceptualizing rurality, and its definition has changed significantly over time. In order to understand what rurality means there are four different possible conceptions: a demographic or ecological understanding that focuses on population density, a social structural conception that focuses on close kinship ties and informal social control, an economic understanding that focuses on the occupations of residents, cultural in that rural residents share common values. Generally the first two conceptions of rurality go hand-in-hand. Dewey (1960) found a significant relationship between population size and differences in anonymity, the division of labor, heterogeneity, formal interactions, and status symbols. While these differences may be predominantly related to population size, it is important to note that even within the category of rural there are still differences within rural communities that may not be related to population size at all. In fact, another conceptualization of rurality focuses on geographic isolation. Places that are more geographically isolated are likely to have fewer outside influences.

What little recent research exists suggests that such notions of associating rurality with an idyllic place far removed from big city influences and crime is inaccurate. While rural communities have typically been thought of as "small, unconcentrated and relatively isolated from the influence of large metropolitan centers" (Miller & Luloff, 1981, 610), rural communities are becoming more urbanized. Social cohesion, wholeness and reciprocity, while often associated with rural communities (Hogg & Carrington, 1998), are not necessarily going to be found in smaller places. The majority of the literature about rural areas describes rural culture as conservative, traditional, slow to change, and a bit fatalistic (Bealer et al., 1965; Loomis, 1950; Miller & Crader, 1979; Sorokin & Zimmerman, 1929). Consistent with the current literature examining structural factors, for the purpose of this analysis rural counties are defined by population size, wherein there is no city with population greater than twenty-five hundred and counties have fewer than fifty thousand inhabitants.

Furthermore, there are some key differences in the institutional makeup of rural communities that may play a more significant role, regardless of the conceptualization of rurality. The central Appalachian region has experienced strong levels of out-migration (Duncan, 2001), underemployment, a decline of two-parent families (Friedman & Lichter, 1998), and economic underdevelopment (White, 1987). Across the country there are rural areas with high violence and homicide rates (Montell, 1986). This could be a result of changes in the rural population, deteriorating rural economies, and family disruption. In fact, Sampson (1986) found differences in victimization data for rural areas, noting that different structural factors may play a role. Thus, there are some significant differences in rural communities that may impact intimate partner homicides. There has been, and continues to be, an association between urban areas and crime, but "by neglecting rural settings, researchers have ignored important data that may yield new insight into the factors that explain crime rate variations across diverse geographic communities" (Lee & Ousey, 2001, 582). Rural communities need further investigation and this research seeks to fill some of the current gaps in knowledge.

Methods

Utilizing recent Uniform Crime Report Supplementary Homicide Report data (2000–2011), U.S. Census data (2000), a study of County Characteristics (2000–2007), and the Association of Religion Data Archives (ARDA) Religious Congregations and Membership Study of 2000, this study investigated how the systemic reformulation of social disorganization theory explains intimate partner homicides involving guns in metropolitan areas, as well as in rural counties. Supplementary Homicide Reports are considered to be one of the sources of data with the most in-depth information about homicides (Pampel & Williams, 2000). The unit of analysis is the county. With the exception of the ARDA data, datasets were downloaded from the Inter-university Consortium for Political and Social Research (IPCSR) and merged together using SPSS 19. Negative binomial regressions were run using Stata SE10. For the independent variables, a number of sources provided the pertinent data (see Table 5.1), including U.S. Census Bureau data from Gallup-Black's study *Rural and Urban Trends in Family and Intimate Partner Violence in the United States* (ICPSR #4115) which provided the following data: population size and population density, Gini household index of inequality, poverty rates, county type, percentages of female headed households with children under 18, percent nonwhite, divorce rates, population mobility, high school dropout rates, and the percent of the population born in state. Additionally, some independent variables were derived from ICPSR #20660, including, *County Characteristics, 2000–2007* including the dissimilarity index, unemployment, votes in the presidential election, and the residential population over 18 (to determine percent voting). Intimate partner homicides include homicides committed by current or former spouses, common law spouses, current boyfriends and girlfriends, and homosexual partners. Only homicides involving a gun of some sort are examined here, and all gun types were combined.

Table 5.1. Independent Variables

Variables	Measure	Data Source
Dependent		
Intimate Partner Gun Homicides	Pooled county-level counts of intimate partner gun homicides, 2000–2011	Supplementary Homicide Reports
Independent		
Poverty	Percent of the population below the poverty line	Rural and UrbanTrends
Gini household inequality index	Gini household index	Rural and UrbanTrends
Female headed household with a child under 18	Percent of female headed households with children under 18	Rural and UrbanTrends
Percent non-white	Percent of the population that is not white	Rural and UrbanTrends
Dissimilarity Index	The ratio of white to black residents	County Characteristics 2000–2007
Unemployment	Percent of the population over 16 who are not employed	County Characteristics 2000–2007
Divorced	Percent of the population that is divorced	Rural and UrbanTrends
Population density	Population per square mile	Rural and UrbanTrends
Population size	The county population size	Rural and UrbanTrends
Population mobility	Percent of the population who have moved within the past 5 years	Rural and UrbanTrends
Born in state	Percent of the population that was born in the state they resided in in 2000	Rural and UrbanTrends
High School Dropouts	Average percent of individuals over 25 who did not completed high school (1995–1999)	Rural and UrbanTrends
Voter Participation	Percent of county residents over 18 who voted in the 2000 Presidential election	County Characteristics 2000–2007
Religious Participation	Percent of county residents over 18 registered with a religious organization in 2000	ARDA's Religious Congregations and Membership Study of 2000

Concentrated Disadvantage

Disadvantage and inequality lead to a weakening of the legitimacy of social norms, making it difficult for communities to maintain social control (Logan & Messner, 1987). Homicide data in the United States indicate that homicide offenders are more likely to be economically disadvantaged (Harries, 1990; Martinez & Lee, 1999;

Short, 1997; Wolfgang, 1958, Peterson & Krivo, 1999). An increasing number of scholars (Bursik, 1988; Wilson, 1987) have argued for a new construct to measure concentrated disadvantage because of studies examining the structural correlates of crime indicating that there are certain areas that are highly impoverished, with many female-headed single parent households with children under 18, a high percentage of the population living in poverty, and a higher Gini household inequality index value. All these indicators tend to be highly correlated with one another.

Concentrated disadvantage can impact community attachment and reflect a greater level of disorganization within a community. As Sampson and Groves (1989) indicate socioeconomic deprivation leads to a reduction in community attachment and weakened social ties. Parker, Stults and Rice (2005) found that concentrated disadvantage was significant, but that it also varied somewhat by race in the cities over 100,000 that they analyzed. The spatial overlap of populations with concentrated disadvantages isolates that population, leading to a greater potential for crime. Recent research found significant support for a correlation between concentrated disadvantage and crime (Lee, 2000; Krivo & Peterson, 1996). Research applying a social disorganization framework has found that concentrated disadvantage is consistently one of the most, if not the most, important factor contributing to crime. Studies of homicide offenders indicate that they are more likely to be poor and economically disadvantaged as well (see Wolfgang, 1958; Harries 1997; Martinez & Lee, 1999). Poverty and other forms of disadvantage impact crime.

In addition to poverty, studies incorporate other aspects of concentrated disadvantage including aspects of family structure. A number of studies have found that family structure correlates such as female headed households with young children are correlated with higher crime rates (see for example Sampson, 1986; Osgood & Chambers, 2000; Wilson, 1987, 1996; Albrecht, Albrecht & Albrecht, 2000; Snyder & McLaughlin, 2004). For example, Albrecht and Albrecht (2007) found that counties with a greater proportion of female headed households had greater economic inequality. Prior research reveals significant correlations between high poverty rates, low income levels, and female-headed, single-parent families (Eggebeen & Lichter, 1991; Lichter & Eggebeen, 1993; Rountree and Warner 1999; Lichter & Jensen, 2001).

Additionally, the racial difference of household composition in a community could be an indicator of differences in norms and values that might lead to more crime. A few studies (Osgood & Chambers, 2000; Sampson & Groves, 1989; Warner & Pierce, 1993) examine dissimilarity in their examinations of social disorganization theory. This indicator ranges from 0 (no dissimilarity) to .5 (the most dissimilarity). A score of zero would indicate more ethnic homogeneity, while a .5 would indicate the most ethnic heterogeneity. This score is calculated by the following formula: $1-\sum(p_{i2})$ where p_i is the proportion of households that are white or nonwhite (Blau, 1977; Osgood & Chambers, 2000). The dissimilarity index is highly correlated with the racial makeup in the county, but offers insight into the structural demographics of the counties.

Population Structure Component

Additional indicators that may be significant are the combination of population density and population size to form a population structure component. In areas of higher population density and areas with more people overall, informal controls may be significantly weakened; neighbors will be less likely to know one another, and, therefore, be less able to know when something is amiss in their community, for example. In areas of higher population density, there may also be a greater degree of anonymity and a lesser degree of shared norms or collective efficacy. In sum, densely populated areas along with residential mobility can increase the opportunities for crime (Shaw & McKay, 1942; Stark, 1987). Land et al. (1990) created a population structure component through a principal component analysis of the natural log of the unit population size and the natural log of population density which was found to be statistically significant, and empirically relevant. Areas where there are more people per square mile and more people overall may also have higher counts of intimate partner gun homicides.

Residential Stability/Instability Component

One of the key variables historically in the application and understanding of social disorganization theory is residential stability. The more transitory people in a community, the less cohesiveness in that community, the less unified the community, and the greater likelihood of competing norms and lack of assimilation to community norms. The more stable the community, the better able it is to maintain community attachment. Sampson and Groves (1989, 787) found that residential stability was more important than urbanization with respect to its impact on friendship networks. Kassarda and Janowitz (1974) viewed population stability as more important than the size of the community. Sampson (1995) reviewed numerous studies that analyzed the impact of poverty on crime rates, finding that when poverty was combined with residential mobility, it is associated with an increase in violent crime. Stability is operationalized as the percent of residents who did not move within the past five years [in 2000] and the percent of the population born in the state in which they currently reside. The expectation is that greater residential instability is positively correlated with intimate partner gun homicides in rural areas as well as urban ones.

Unemployment

Arthur (1991) found that unemployment, poverty, public aid, and race were related to both property and violent crime rates in 13 rural Georgia counties. Unemployment here is operationalized as the percent of people over 16 who did not work. Historically, few studies found a significant relationship (or looked for one) between unemployment and crime when examining social disorganization theory.

Matthews, Maume and Miller (2001) found a relationship between unemployment and homicides. The greater the percentage of the population in the work force, the greater the similarity of values and the greater likelihood of pro-social and shared values.

Education

The systemic reformulation of social disorganization theory examines the institutional factors that could impact disorganization in an area. Individuals are socialized by the educational system to conform to societal expectations. The fact that someone completed high school indicates that they are more committed to community institutions like the labor market and the schools themselves. Additionally, students learn compliance in the schools as well as better problem-solving techniques so that they want to avoid violence and can utilize non-violent mechanisms for dispute resolution. In one study, high school dropouts in rural areas shared the same regression space with other variables related to concentrated disadvantage, including poverty, female headed households, unemployment and percent black (Lee, 2008). According to the literature, accounting for concentrated disadvantage is crucial to understanding homicides.

Divorce

Family structure correlates with higher crime rates (see for example Sampson, 1986). Family stability can be defined as the extent to which family units in a particular area conform to the traditional nuclear family. Schwartz (2006) found that family structure was even more important for male homicides, compared to homicides committed by females, though it was significant for both. According to Schwartz, family structure was the most significant variable on homicide rates in counties with more than 20.000 people.

Voter Participation

Voting can also be an indicator of participatory norms and involvement in community life. This is a variable that is not often utilized, although there are a couple of studies in which it has been related to crime rates (Coleman, 2002). Voting is generally considered a civic duty in support of democracy (Almond & Verba, 1965), although the proportion of the population who view voting as a moral obligation is not evenly distributed; regular voters, women, older people, and religious people were found more likely to hold that belief (Blais, 2000). Voter participation in an election, especially a national one, can be thought of as a measure of conformity in that it can be a good picture of conformity at one particular point in time, demonstrating how a particular community can hold its members to a widely accepted goal (Coleman, 1990; Elster 1989). As Coleman

(2002: 257) notes it is possible to use voter turnout "as a standard measure of the degree of conformity across units of analysis." Other studies have found links between voting and other positive social behaviors like responding to the census (Knack & Kropf, 1998) and donating to charities (Knack 1992). Sampson and Raudenbush (1999) and Sampson et al. (1997) emphasize the importance of social cohesion, finding that violent crime is lower in areas where residents are willing to intervene and where social cohesion is high. This demonstrates the importance of informal social control. In areas of higher voter participation it can be presumed that those communities are more cohesive, in that there is a larger component of the community with the similar understanding of the importance of voting. Coleman (2002) found that voter conformity, or participation, impacts various crimes at the state and county levels. Lee (2008) found voter turnout to be significant in predicting violent crime, including murder, when included in a factor containing civic associations per 1000 and civically engaged religions. Voter participation in this study is operationalized as the combined factor of the percent of residents over 18 who voted in the national 2000 presidential elections. It is a direct measure of institutional involvement and an indirect measure of agreement on other social issues.

Religious Participation

This study expands the examination of institutions by incorporating religious participation by using the percent adjusted adherents in ARDAs 2000 study. County-wide data on religious participation are examined here as well. Very few studies have examined the connection between religion and crime; however, it is yet another socializing institution that can reduce crime rates. Religious participation in this study is operationalized as being registered with a religious institution. While registration itself does not mean that a person entirely proscribes to the religion or attends ceremonies regularly, it may mean that areas with higher participation rates are more likely to have similar values and to be socialized more similarly. So. crime should be lower in those areas. since informal social control networks and institutional controls should be stronger in those areas. In fact, using 1990 data, Tolbert, Lyson, and Irwin (1998) found that the percentage of the population attending churches that were civically engaged was significantly correlated to lower levels of inequality, poverty, and unemployment. Irwin, Tolbert, and Lyson (1997, 1999) found that church membership was negatively associated with out-migration. Furthermore, research indicates that the presence of civic institutions have a greater impact on rural areas (Beggs. Haines & Hurlbert, 1996). Lee and Bartkowski (2004) found that churches per capita impacted violent crime rates in rural areas.

As with non-gun homicides. homicides involving guns are not evenly distributed across the country. Some communities are more criminolgenic than others. It is expected that areas where there is greater disadvantage, more people and higher population density, greater population instability, a higher proportion of divorces, more unemployment, a greater proportion of high school dropouts, less voter participation and a smaller percentage of the population registered as members of a religious organization, the greater the intimate partner gun homicide counts in both urban and rural counties across the country.

Data and Results

Figure 5.1 provides an overview of gun homicides throughout the country by victim-offender relationship from 2000 until 2011. Of the 113, 650 gun homicides, 8670 (7.6 percent) were between intimate partners, 4367 (3.8 percent) involved other family members (excluding spouses and former spouses), 26,235 (23 percent) were between acquaintances, 19, 766 (17.4 percent) were between strangers, and 54,612 (48 percent) involved relationships that were undetermined. This research examines intimate partner gun homicides described at the top of the bars.

Figure 5.1. Gun Homicides by Victim-Offender Relationship, 2000–2011

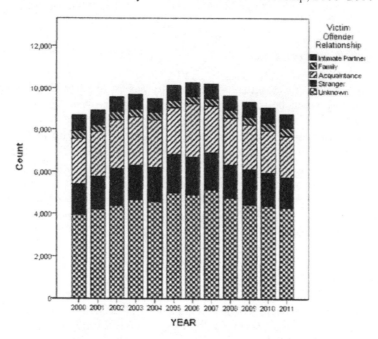

Table 5.2 provides a breakdown of the victim offender relationship in intimate partner homicides from 2000 through 2011 by frequency and percent. Wife and girlfriend account for nearly three quarters of the intimate partner gun homicide victims.

Table 5.2 Intimate Partner Gun Homicides, 2000–2011

	Frequency	Percent
Boyfriend	636	7.3
Common-law husband	73	.8
Common-law wife	290	3.3
Girlfriend	2681	30.9
Homosexual relationship	87	1.0
Husband	818	9.4
Wife	3670	42.3
Ex-husband	78	.9
Ex-wife	337	3.9
Total	8670	100.0

The charts below provide information about all instances of intimate partner gun homicides compared with all gun homicides from 2000 to 2011. The first set of charts focus on offender characteristics while the second focus on victim characteristics. Characteristics of intimate partner gun homicides stand out as considerably different from overall gun homicides in important demographic respects, including sex (especially of the victim), race and age.

Offender Characteristics

Table 5.3. A Comparison of Offender's Sex in All Gun-related Homicides versus Intimate Partner Gun-related Homicides

Sex of Offenders in Gun Involved Homicides—2000–2011		
Female	Male	Unknown
3.38%	61.52%	35.10%
Sex of Offenders in Intimate Partner Homicides Involving Guns—2000–2011		
18.46%	81.54%	—

The offender's sex in homicides in general is overwhelmingly male. Males are more likely to be involved in violence in general, and deadly violence more specifically. While homicides have among the highest clearance rates by police, there are still a great deal of homicides (35 percent) where the police do not know who the offender is. Once a suspect is known, the relationship can be classified and the second chart depicts the sex of the offender in known intimate partner homicides. Intimate partner homicides tend to be the most accurate of homicide data, since standard police procedure when someone is killed is to look to the closest family members, especially the significant other or former significant other. Over eighty percent of all intimate partner homicides known to police are committed by males.

As depicted in Figure 5.2, most offenders in gun homicides are younger individuals, in their teens and twenties. The older the offender, the fewer gun homicides they are involved in. Individuals in their twenties account for the highest proportion of gun-related homicides. In terms of trends over time, younger individuals have a less steady pattern, with a spike in gun homicides in 2006 that was most pronounced for teens and individuals in their twenties. Despite that brief increase in gun homicides they have been declining since then within those age groups, although gun homicides for individuals in their thirties have been increasing since 2008. The number of gun homicides for offenders in their thirties, forties, fifties and sixties tended to be relatively stable over the twelve years examined. Offenders under thirty, however, peaked in 2006 and have since declined.

Figure 5.2 Offender's Age for all Gun-related Homicides, 2000–2011

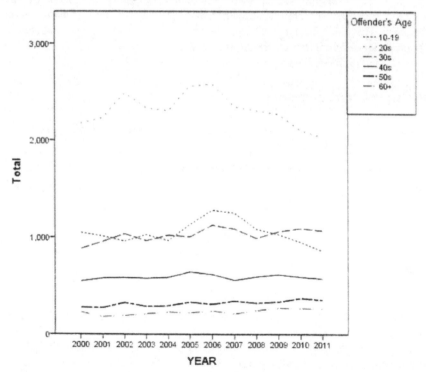

Figure 5.2 indicates the ages of all known offenders involved in gun homicides. Over half of the ages of known offenders of gun homicides in general are under 30 years old, whereas nearly 75 percent of perpetrators of intimate partner homicides

are committed by individuals between twenty and fifty. Thus, perpetrators of intimate partner homicides tend to be older. The most frequent age group of known intimate partner offenders involved in gun-related homicides tend to be the thirties and forties, followed by twenties and then fifties. In examining trends over time, intimate partner gun homicides committed by those in their twenties and thirties has followed a downward trend. Numbers of intimate partner homicides involving guns where the offender was in his/her forties have been more erratic.

Figure 5.3 Offender's Age for Intimate Partner Gun-related Homicides, 2000–2011

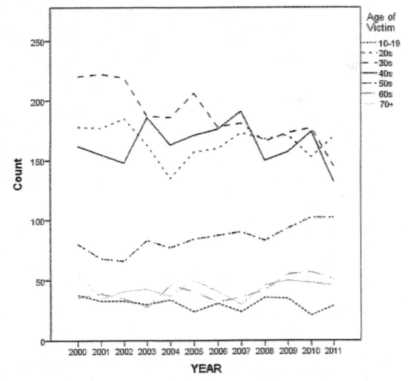

While the race is unknown in over a third of all gun homicides, one can clearly see the disproportionate and higher percentage of blacks involved in gun homicides overall. Intimate partner homicides are most often committed by whites. The figure on the right reveals over two thirds of intimate partner homicides committed with guns were committed by whites. It is important to note that there may be more intimate partner homicides within the unknown category, but as police are most focused on those closest to the victim, intimate partner data categories are likely to be the most accurate.

Table 5.4. Comparison of the Race of the Offender in all Gun Homicides compared to Intimate Partner Homicides, 2000–2011

Race of Offenders in Gun Involved Homicides—2000–2011	
Asian/Pacific Islander	0.86%
Black	34.55%
American Indian or Alaskan Native	0.31%
Unknown	36.13%
White	28.14%
Race of Offenders in Intimate Partner Homicides Involving Guns—2000–2011	
Asian/Pacific Islander	1.81%
Black	29.84%
American Indian or Alaskan Native	0.50%
Unknown	1.05%
White	67.00%

Victim Characteristics

This section examines the sex, age and race of the victims of intimate partner homicides committed with guns, compared to all gun homicides, revealing significant differences in all demographic categories examined.

While most victims of fatal gun violence are male, victims of intimate partner gun violence are overwhelmingly female. Figure 5.6 displays a comparison between victims of gun related homicides and intimate partner gun-related homicides. Over eighty percent of victims of gun homicides are male, while over eighty percent of victims of intimate partner gun homicides are female.

The majority of gun violence homicide victims are mostly in their 20s over the dozen years, with nearly twice as many victims in their twenties compared to those in their thirties, the second most common age category of victims. The overwhelming majority tend to be under 40. Gun homicides for those under 30 tend to have the most variability over time, with those over 50 remaining relatively steady over the twelve years. Teens as victims of gun violence peaked in 2006, while those in their twenties declined in 2004 and rose again, declining after 2007.

Table 5.5 A Comparison of the Sex of Victims in all Gun-Involved Homicides Compared to Intimate Partner Gun Homicides, 2000–2011

Sex of Offenders in Gun related Intimate Partner Homicides, 2000–2011	
Male	Female
81.54%	18.46%
Sex of Victims of Intimate Partner Gun-related Homicides, 2000–2011	
19.21%	80.79%

Figure 5.4 Age of Victims of Gun Homicides, 2000–2011

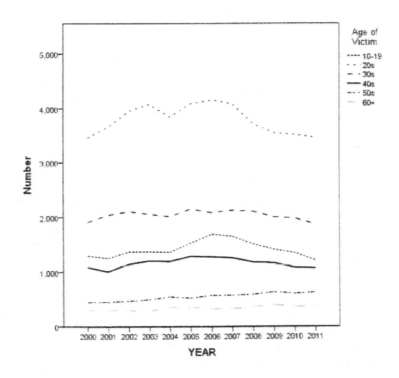

Figure 5.5 Age of Victims of Intimate Partner Gun Homicides, 2000–2011

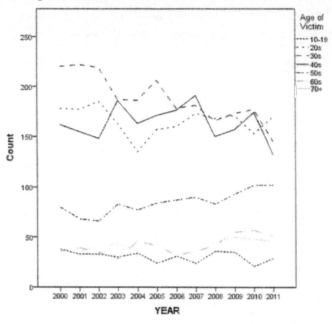

Table 5.6 A Comparison of Victims by Race for all Gun-related Homicides versus Intimate Partner Gun Homicides, 2000-2011

Race of Victims in Gun Involved Homicides. 2000–2011	
Asian/Pacific Islander	1.60%
Black	54.94%
American Indian or Alaskan Native	0.50%
Unknown	1.00%
White	41.95%
Race of Victims in Intimate Partner Homicides Involving Guns. 2000–2011	
Asian/Pacific Islander	2.05%
Black	27.50%
American Indian or Alaskan Native	0.61%
Unknown	0.87%
White	68.97%

Individuals in their thirties and forties tend to account for the highest percentage of victims of intimate partner gun homicides. Homicides involving intimate partners in their fifties increased over the dozen years examined, while intimate partner gun homicides involving victims in other age categories either increased or remained about the same. There is more fluctuation over time in the proportion of intimate partner gun homicide victims.

One can clearly see the differences in racial patterns of victims depending on whether one is examining all gun-involved homicides across the country or just those between intimate partners. Black victims account for over half of victims in gun homicides, while white victims account for just over forty percent of all victims of gun homicides. Intimate partner gun-related homicide victims are more proportionate with the race of the general population, with nearly seventy percent of victims falling into the white racial category.

Table 5.7 provides a brief overview of the basic descriptive information of the variables utilized in the study. In this particular research two sets of data analyses are conducted: one examining urban counties and the other examining only rural counties. Therefore, the first two sub-columns provide information about the minimum and maximum for the variables in all counties and the second column includes the means and standard deviations for urban counties, while the third column describes the means and standard deviations for the rural counties.

Bivariate Correlations

According to the bivariate correlations, there is considerable overlap between some of the key variables. The GINI household index and poverty are highly correlated with one another (.795, p<.01). Percent nonwhite and the Dissimilarity Index are even more highly correlated with one another (.939, p<.01). As one would expect, the natural log of population size and the natural log of population density are highly correlated with one another (-.665). Because of these high correlations, a principal component analysis is needed as such multicollinearity violates the assumptions of regression analysis. Although this does not allow variables to be examined individually, it allows them to be a part of the analysis. (See Table on pages 102–103)

Principal Component Analysis

Since there are many variables to consider, many of which are correlated with one another, and since it is important to maintain statistical power, a principal component analysis is run to reduce the factors. This is also consistent with a large number of studies previously discussed which examine the impact of such concepts as concentrated disadvantage, the population structure component, residential instability, and civic engagement (see Land et al., 1990; Lee, 2008). In order to examine specific institutional correlates separately, divorce, high school dropouts, voter participation, and religious affiliation variables are excluded from the variables input into a varimax rotated principal components analysis.

Table 5.7. Independent Variable Descriptives

	All Counties		Metropolitan		Rural	
	Min	Max	Mean	SD	Mean	SD
Percent living below the poverty line	2.12%	50.89%	11.23%	4.95	15.84%	6.42
Gini household index	.36	.58	.46	.02	.46	.03
Female headed household with a child under 18	0%	26.90%	9.77%	3.15	7.53%	3.64
Dissimilarity index	.01	.5	.24	.14	.15	.16
Percent non-white	0.16%	86.70%	17.35%	14.26	13.20%	19.43
Unemployment	1%	29.80%	4.06%	2.27	5.83%	3.34
High school dropouts	3.65%	66.16%	20.76%	7.00	28.34%	9.05
Population size	790	9519338	450112	860515	11199	5467
Population density	.39	66951	747.23	2930.19	24.39	19.53
Born in state	15.81%	96.51%	64.31%	14.70	69.89%	14.54
Moved in the last 5 years	9.52%	72.01%	45.47%	7.217	37.42%	6.75
Percent divorced	0%	16.95%	9.86%	1.58	9.41%	2.00
Voter participation	4.84%	89%	51.55%	8.45	55.90%	9.35
Religious Participation	5.97%	100%	48.81%	12.91	47.65%	19.92

Table 5.8. Bivarite Correlations

	1	2	3	4	5	6	7	8	9
1. IP homicides									
2. % poverty	.186**								
3. GINI hh Index	.229**	.795**							
4. Fem hh w/child	.278**	.675**	.625**						
5. Dissimilarity	.369**	.504**	.443**	.679					
6. % nonwhite	.360**	.529**	.449**	.748**	.939**				
7. unemployment	.086*	.547**	.405**	.248**	.207**	.233**			
8. HS dropouts	.042	.640**	.444**	.270**	.257**	.283**	.283**		
9. Ln Pop size	.574**	.075*	.192**	.286**	.384**	.342**	.342**	.469**	
10. Ln Pop density	.350**	.009	.135**	.396**	.389**	.402**	-.110**	.055	-.252**
11. Born in state	-.187**	.061	.146**	-.012	-.243**	-.186	.065**	-.223**	-.665**
12. % moved in last 5 yrs	.191**	.057	-.033	.180**	.311**	.229**	-.180**	.221**	-.263**
13. % divorced	.130**	.227**	.237**	.370**	.107**	.082	.067	.116**	.069*
14. % voted	-.206**	-.584**	-.391**	-.394**	-.483**	-.465**	-.342**	-.585**	.097**
15. % religious	.014	.042	.081	.009	-.050	-.063	.005	.054	.044

Bivarite Correlations (continued)

	10	11	12	13	14
1. IP homicides					
2. % poverty					
3. GINI hh Index					
4. Fem hh w/child					
5. Dissimilarity					
6. % nonwhite					
7. unemployment					
8. HS dropouts					
9. Ln Pop size					
10. Ln Pop density					
11. Born in state	-.225**				
12. % moved in last 5 yrs	.146**	-.580**			
13. % divorced	-.031	-.139*	.214**		
14. % voted	-.078	.170**	-.269**	-.178**	
15. % religious	.155**	.255**	-.281**	-.201**	.147**

Table 5.9 identifies three components where the data are statistically overlapping. The first component is consistent with prior research identifying concentrated disadvantage. The second component is consistent with Land et al. (1990) research combining the natural log of population size and the natural log of population density, creating a population structure component. The third factor represents residential instability incorporating the percent of the population not born in state and those who moved within the last five years.

Table 5.9. Principal Components Analysis for Urban Communities

	Component 1	Component 2	Component 3
Poverty	.899		
Gini household Index	.832		
Female headed households	.848		
Dissimilarity Index	.747		
Percent non-white	.779		
Population size		.847	
Population density		.912	
Percent born in state			−.859
Moved within last 5 years			−.870
Eigenvalue	3.987	1.974	1.148
Variance explained	44.300	21.934	12.760

Similarly, with the data from the rural counties, Table 5.10 depicts the three components that are derived from the data: concentrated disadvantage, a population structure component, and a component representing residential stability (as opposed to the urban data in which the signs are reversed). In both factor analyses the concentrated disadvantage component explains the most variance, though it explains a greater percentage of variance within urban counties.

Table 5.10. Principal Components Analysis for Rural Counties

	Component 1	Component 2	Component 3
Poverty	.775		
Gini household Index	.615		
Female headed households	.893		
Dissimilarity Index	.865		
Percent non-white	.925		
Population size		.948	
Population density		.954	
Percent born in state			−.848
Moved within last 5 years			−.881
Eigenvalue	3.511	1.831	1.576
Variance explained	39.030	20.348	17.511

Analysis

While many researchers in the past have analyzed homicide data by employing ordinary least squares (OLS) linear regression, homicides are such a rare occurrence that any findings that they might have concluded may be due to statistical error even if those studies attempted to normalize the distribution through the calculation of the natural log of homicides. Since the dependent variable is intimate partner gun homicide counts, and since count data are utilized. Poisson regression is more appropriate (Cameron & Trivedi. 1998). Poisson regression is used with count variables and is discrete, not continuous, like the curve assumed with ordinary least squares regression, making it a better statistical fit for this analysis. Negative binomial regression is a form of Poisson regression, but may be more appropriate since Poisson regression assumes equal means and variance. Negative binomial regression allows researchers to examine homicide count data without the assumption that the data are not overly-dispersed in part because it provides a residual variance term that helps control for the over-dispersion in the data (Gardner, Mulvey & Shaw. 1995; Osgood, 2000 and Paternoster & Brame, 1997). When analyzing rare crime counts with "small populations and low-base rates" (Osgood, 2000: 21) negative binomial regression may be the best alternative. Negative binomial regression has been successfully employed in analyses of homicide count data at the macro level (Paternoster & Brame. 1997; Paternoster.

Brame, Bachman and Sherman, 1997; Sampson & Laub, 1997; Braga, 2003; Parker, 2004; Van Horne, 2009; Van Horne, 2010). When using data where there many of the units of analysis have zeros, small values, and discrete dependent variables, negative binomial regression is a better statistical tool.

Table 5.11 presents the results of two negative binomial regression equations predicting intimate partner gun homicide count totals for the years 2000 through 2011. To assess the overall model fit, one can use a likelihood ratio test, which is computed as twice the difference between the log-likelihoods of the models being compared. This value is then compared with the χ^2 distribution, with degrees of freedom equal to the difference in the number of parameters between the two models being compared (Osgood & Chambers, 2000). In this case the first model is being compared with a model with only a dispersion parameter and an intercept. The χ^2 value−2126.47 which is highly significant (p <.001), suggesting that the model fits the data very well. While the rural model was statistically significant, the χ^2 value= 49.36 (p< .05) and not all of the variables were statistically significant.

Table 5.11. Negative Binomial Regression Analysis on Intimate Partner Counts of Homicides, 2000–2011

	Urban Model N=741	Rural Model N=485
Concentrated Disadvantage	.286***	−.017
	(.041)	(.083)
Population Structure Component	.884***	.385***
	(.035)	(.098)
Population Instability/Stability Component	.341***	−.084
	(.039)	(.099)
Unemployment	.046**	.011
	(.016)	(.024)
High School Dropouts	.020**	.033**
	(.008)	(.013)
Percent divorced	.133***	.011
	(.020)	(.040)
Voter Participation	−1.38**	2.02
	(.564)	(1.085)
Religious Participation	−.006*	−.010*
	(.002)	(.004)
Likelihood ratio chi-square	−1940.24	−460.196
Likelihood ratio χ^2	2126.47***	49.36*
Pseudo R^2	.173	.051

In terms of the individual predictors of intimate partner gun homicide counts, everything that was expected to be correlated with intimate partner gun homicide counts was statistically significant in the urban analysis. Concentrated disadvantage, the population structure component, population stability, percent divorced, voter participation, unemployment, and religious participation were all statistically significant as applied to counties that experienced intimate partner gun homicides and significant in the direction one would expect. In a negative binomial regression model the beta coefficient refers to the proportion change in the dependent variable when the independent variable changes by one unit (Cameron & Trivedi, 1998). For example, a one unit change in concentrated disadvantage the difference in logs of expected counts would be expected to increase by 0.286 units, while holding all other variables in the model constant. Concentrated disadvantage positively correlates with intimate partner gun homicide counts in urban areas and, in fact, was one of the strongest predictors although the population structure component and residential instability were even stronger predictors. The change expected in log count for a one-unit increase in the population structure component was .884, holding all other variables constant.

In the rural model, the population structure component, high school dropouts and religious participation were statistically significant. The population structure component was the most significant factor in the rural model. For a one unit change in population structure the difference in logs of expected counts would be expected to increase by 0.385 units, while holding all other variables in the model constant. Furthermore, voter participation was the only variable where the direction of the relationship was the opposite of what was expected, though it was not significant.

Discussion

As predicted, the systemic reformulation of social disorganization theory applies well to intimate partner gun homicides in urban areas. While the model was statistically significant for rural counties, many of the key variables significant for urban areas were not for the rural communities. These findings have important policy implications and theoretical implications. With more recently emerging literature on the importance of civic engagement, this research highlights the importance of further investigation of voter participatory norms, especially in urban areas. Additionally, religious participation must be investigated further. While the percent of the population who are registered with a religious institution is not the best measure of the potential impact of religion as an institution, even this operationalization of religion is significant and serves as a buffer against intimate partner gun homicides in both types of geographic areas- rural and urban. In rural communities, education was also a significant factor.

Most importantly, however, this research highlights the importance of disaggregating by community type and the need for additional research on homicides in rural areas, though further research is clearly warranted. Policies cannot be one size fits all and must consider the type of location. What works in urban communities to reduce intimate partner gun homicides may not work in rural communities. Even amongst rural counties, the population structure matters. Hence, policy or program change should also take size and population density into account.

Despite the decline in homicides over the past twenty years, homicide is still a serious problem in many locations. With the availability of guns comes an increased likelihood of their use, potentially resulting in homicide. There are indications that research should be disaggregated by gun type, which this study does not do. However, trends in gun homicides differ by type of gun. For example, homicides involving handguns increased considerably in the late 80s and then declined in 2008, while homicides involving other types of guns were low in 1999 and have increased slightly since then (Cooper and Smith, 2011). Further research is warranted in this area and the statistics about do not disaggregate by victim-offender relationship.

Additional research is needed to examine rural areas in greater depth and new theoretical models may be needed to understand crime in those communities. This research highlights key differences between homicides depending on the type of communities in which they occur. Research should also expand beyond rural and urban and include an examination of suburban communities as well. Different typologies of communities may be worth researching as well. Agrarian rural communities may differ significantly from mining communities in terms of the interrelation of institutions. This research demonstrates the importance of the population structure component in rural areas, so a focused analysis of those communities is warranted as well.

References

Albrecht, D. E., C. M. Albrecht, & S. L. Albrecht. (2000). Poverty in non-metropolitan America: Impacts of industrial, employment, and family structure variables. *Rural Sociology*, 65(1): 87–103.

Albrecht, D. E. & Albrecht, C.M. (2007). Income inequality: The implications of economic structure and social conditions. *Sociological Spectrum*, 27(2): 165–181.

Almond, G.A. & S. Verba. (1965). *The civic culture, political attitudes and democracy in five nations, an analytic study*. Boston, MA: Little Brown.

Arthur, J. A. (1991). Socioeconomic predictors of crime in rural Georgia. *Criminal Justice Review*, 16: 29–41.

Bealer, R. C., F. K. Willits & W. P. Kuvlesky. (1965). The meaning of 'rurality' in American society: Some implications of alternative definitions. *Rural Sociology*, 30(3): 255–266.

Beggs, J. J., V.A. Haines & J. S. Hurlbert (1996). Revisiting the rural-urban contrast: Personal networks in nonmetropolitan and metropolitan settings. *Rural Sociology*, 61 (2): 306–325.

Blais, A. (2000). *To vote or not to vote- The merits and limits of rational choice theory*. Pittsburgh, PA: University of Pittsburgh Press.

Blau, P. M. (1977). *Inequality and heterogeneity: A primitive theory of social structure*. New York: Free Press.

Braga. A. (2003). Serious youth gun offenders and the epidemic of youth violence in Boston. *Journal of Quantitative Criminology*. 19(1): 33–54.

Bursik. R. J. Jr. (1988). Social disorganization and theories of crime and delinquency: Problems and prospects. *Criminology*, 26(4): 519–551.

Bursik R. J. Jr. & H. G. Grasmick. (1993). Neighborhoods and crime: The dimensions of effective community control. New York: Lexington Books.

Cameron, A. C. & P. K. Trevedi (1998). *Regression Analysis of Count Data*. New York: Cambridge University Press.

Cameron. J. G. (2001). *A spatial analysis of crime in Appalachia. final report.* (NCJ 189559). Washington. DC: United States Department of Justice. National Institute of Justice.

Campbell. J.C.. D. Webster. J. Koziol-McLain. C. Block. D. Campbell. M. A. Curry, F. Gary, N. Glass. J. McFarlane. C. Sachs. P. Sharps. Y. Ulrich. S. A. Wilt, J. Manganello, X. Xu. J. Schollenberger. V. Frye. and K. Laughon. (2003) Risk factors for femicide in abusive relationships: Results from a multisite case study. American Journal of Public Health 93:1089–97.

Centers for Disease Control and Prevention. (2008) Adverse health conditions and health risk behaviors associated with intimate partner violence- United States. 2005. *Morbidity and Mortality Weekly Report*, 57(5): 113–117.

Cohn. D.. P. Taylor, M.H. Lopez. C.A. Gallagher, K. Parker and K.T. Maass. (2013) *Gun homicide rate down 49% since 1993: Public unaware: Pace of decline slows in past decade.* Washington. D. C.: Pew Research Center.

Coleman. J. (1990). *Foundations of social theory*. Cambridge. MA: Harvard University Press.

Coleman, S. (2002). A test for the effect of conformity on crime rates using voter turnout. *Sociological Quarterly*, 43(2): 257–276.

Cooper, A. and E. Smith (2011). *Homicide trends in the United States, 1980–2008.* (NCJ 236018). Washington D. C.: USDOJ. Bureau of Justice Statistics.

Dewey, R. (1960). The rural-urban continuum: Real but relatively unimportant. *American Journal of Sociology*, 66: 60–66.

Eggebeen, D.J. & D.T. Lichter. (1991). Race, family structure, and changing poverty among American children. *American Sociological Review*, 56: 801–817.

Elster, J. (1989). *The cement of society: A study of social order.* New York, NY: Cambridge University Press.

Flewelling. R. L.. & K. R. Williams (1999). Categorizing homicides: The use of Disaggregated data in homicide research. In M.D. Smith, and M. A. Zahn (eds). *Homicide: A sourcebook of social research.* (pp. 96–106). Thousand Oaks, CA: Sage Publications.

Fox, J. A. & M. Z. Zawitz (2007). Homicide Trends in the United States. Washington D.C.: USDOJ. Bureau of Justice Statistics.

Friedman, S. & Lichter, D. T. (1998). Spatial inequality and poverty among American children. *Population Research and Policy Review*, 17: 91–109.

Gallup-Black, Adria. Rural and Urban Trends in Family and Intimate Partner Violence in the United States. 1980–1999. ICPSR04115-v1. New York City, NY: New York University [producer]. 2004. Ann Arbor, MI: Inter-university Consortium for Political and Social Research [distributor]. 2005–04–07. doi:10.3886/ICPSR04115.v1

Gardner, W.. E. P. Mulvey, & E. C. Shaw (1995). Regression analyses of counts and rates: Poisson, overdispersed poisson. and negative binomial regression. *Psychological Bulletin*, 118: 392–404.

Harries, K.D. (1990). *Serious violence*. Springfield, IL: Charles C. Thomas.
———. (1997). *Serious violence: Patterns of homicide and assault in America. 2nd Edition.* Springfield, IL: Charles C. Thomas.
Inter-university Consortium for Political and Social Research. County Characteristics, 2000–2007 [United States]. ICPSR20660-v2. Ann Arbor, MI: Inter-university Consortium for Political and Social Research [distributor]. 2008-01-24. doi:10.3886/ICPSR20660.v2
Irwin, M.D., C.M. Tolbert, & T.A. Lyson. (1997). How to build strong home towns. *American Demographics*, 19: 42–47.
———. (1999). There's no place like home: Nonmigration and civic engagement. *Environment and Planning A* 31: 2223–38.
Kasarda, J. D., & M. Janowitz. (1974). Community attachment in mass society. *American Sociological Review*, 39 (June): 328–339.
Knack, S. (1992). Civic norms, social sanctions, and voter turnout. *Rationality and Society*, 4: 133–56.
——— & M. E. Kropf. (1998) For shame! The effect of community cooperative context on the probability of voting. *Political Psychology*, 19(3): 585–599.
Kornhauser. R. R. (1978) *Social sources of delinquency*. Chicago: University of Chicago Press.
Kovandzic, T.V., L.M. Vieraitis, & M.R. Yeisley. (1998). The structural covariates of urban homicide: Reassessing the impact of income inequality and poverty in the post-Reagan era. *Criminology*, 36(3): 569–599.
Kposowa, A.J. & K. D. Breault. (1993). Reassessing the structural covariates of U.S. homicide rates: A county level study. *Sociological Focus*, 26(1): 27–46.
Krivo, L.J. & R.D. Peterson. (1996). Extremely disadvantaged neighborhoods and urban crime. *Social Forces*, 75:619–649.
Kubrin, C.E. (2003). Structural covariates of homicide rates: Does type of homicide matter? *Journal of Research in Crime and Delinquency*, 40(2): 139–170.
Land, K. C., P. L. McCall, & L. E. Cohen. (1990). Structural covariates of homicide rates: Are there any invariances across time and social space. *American Journal of Sociology*, 95(4): 922–963.
Lee, M.R. (2008). Civic community in the hinterland: Toward a theory of rural social structure and violence. *Criminology*, 46(2): 447–477.
———. (2000). Concentrated poverty, race, and homicide. *Sociological Quarterly* 41: 189–206.
Lee, M.R., & J.P. Bartkowski. (2004). Love thy neighbor? Moral communities, civic engagement, and juvenile homicide in rural areas. *Social Forces*, 82(3): 1001–1035.
Lee, M. R. & T. C. Hayes. (2005). Decline in homicide victimization and the changing share of homicide victimization in rural areas during the 1990s: A research note. *Criminal Justice Studies*, 18(4): 393–401.
Lee, M. R., & G.C. Ousey (2001). Size matters: Examining the link between small manufacturing, socioeconomic deprivation, and crime rates in non-metropolitan communities. *Sociological Quarterly*, 42(4): 581–602.
Lichter, D.T. D.J. Eggebeen. (1993). Rich kids, poor kids: Changing income inequality among American children. *Social Forces*, 71(3):761–780.
Lichter, D.T. L. Jensen. (2001). Rural poverty and welfare before and after PRWORA. *RuralAmerica*, 16(3):28–35.
Lilly, J. R., F. T. Cullen & R. A. Ball. (1989). *Criminological theory: Context and consequences*. Newbury Park, CA: Sage Publications.

Logan, J.R. & S.F. Messner (1987). Racial residential segregation and suburban violent crime. *Social Science Quarterly*. 68: 510–525.

Loomis, C. P. (1950). The nature of rural social systems: A typological analysis. *Rural Sociology*, 15(June): 56–174.

Martinez, R. Jr., & M.T. Lee (1999). Extending ethnicity in homicide research: The case of latinos. In M.D. Smith and M. A. Zahn (eds.) *Studying and preventing homicide: Issues and challenges*. Thousand Oakes. CA: Sage Publications.

Matthews, R. A., M. O. Maume, & W. J. Miller. (2001). Deindustrialization, economic distress, and homicide rates in midsized rustbelt cities. *Homicide Studies*, 5(2): 83–113.

Maxfield, M.G. (1989). Circumstances in Supplementary Homicide Reports: Variety and validity. *Criminology*, 27: 671–695.

Messner, S.F. & R. Rosenfeld (1999). Social structure and homicide. In M.D. Smith and M.A. Zahn (eds.) *Homicide: A Sourcebook of Social Research*. Thousand Oaks. CA: Sage Publications.

Miller, M. K. & K. W. Crader (1979). Rural urban differences in two dimensions of community satisfaction. *Rural Sociology*, 44(Fall): 489–504.

Miller, M. K. & A. E. Luloff. (1981). Who is rural? A typological approach to the examination of rurality. *Rural Sociology*, 46(4): 608–625.

Montell, W. L. (1986). *Killings: Folk justice in the upper South*. Lexington: University of Kentucky Press.

Osgood, D. W. (2000). Poisson-based regression analysis of aggregated crime rates. *Journal of Quantitative Criminology*, 16: 21–44.

Osgood, D. W. & J. M. Chambers. (2000). Social disorganization outside the metropolis: An analysis of rural youth violence. *Criminology*, 38(1): 81–116.

Palen, J. J. (1981). *The urban world* (3rd ed.). New York: McGraw-Hill.

Pampel, F. C. & K. R. Williams (2000). Intimacy and homicide: Compensating for missing data in the SHR. *Criminology* 38: 661–680.

Park, R. and E. Burgess (1925[1967]). *The City*. Chicago: University of Chicago Press.

Parker, K. F. (2004) Industrial shift, polarized labor markets and urban violence: Modeling the dynamics between the economic transformation and disaggregated homicide. *Criminology*, 42(3): 619–646.

Parker, K. F., B. J. Stults, & S. K. Rice. (2005). Racial threat, concentrated disadvantage and social control: Considering the macro-level sources of variation in arrests. *Criminology*. 43(4): 1111–1134.

Parker, R.N. (1989). Poverty, subculture of violence, and type of homicide. *Social Forces*. 67(4): 983–1007.

——— & M.D. Smith. (1979). Deterrence, poverty and type of homicide. *American Journal of Sociology*. 85: 614–624.

Paternoster, R., & R. Brame (1997). Multiple routes to delinquency? A test of developmental and general theories of crime. *Criminology*. 35: 45–84.

Paternoster, R., R. Brame, R. Bachman, & L. Sherman (1997). Do fair procedures matter? The effect of procedural justice on spouse assault. *Law and Society Review*, 31: 163–204.

Peterson, R.D., & L.J. Krivo (1999). Racial segregation, the concentration of disadvantage, and black and white homicide victimization. *Sociological Forum*. 14(3): 465–493.

Rountree, P. M. & B. D.Warner (1999). Social ties and crime: Is the relationship gendered? *Criminology*. 37(4): 789–814.

Salzman, L. E., A. Mercy, P. W. O'Carroll, M. L. Rosenberg, and P. H. Rhodes. (1992) Weapon involvement and injury outcomes in family and intimate assaults. *Journal of the American Medical Association*. 267: 3043–3047.

Sampson, R. J. (1987). Urban Black Violence: The effect of male Black joblessness and family disruption. *American Journal of Sociology*. 93(2): 348–382.

——. (1995). The Community. In J. Wilson and J. Petersilia (eds.), *Crime*. San Francisco, CA: ICS Press.

Sampson, R. J., & B. W. Groves. (1989). Community structure and crime: Testing social disorganization theory. *American Journal of Sociology*. 94:774–802.

Sampson, R.J., & J. H. Laub (1997). Socioeconomic achievement in the life course of disadvantaged men: Military service as a turning point, circa 1940–1965. *American Sociological Review*. 61(3): 347–367.

Sampson, R.J. & S.W. Raudenbush (1999). Systemic social observations of public spaces: A new look at disorder in urban neighborhoods. *American Journal of Sociology*. 105(3): 603–651.

Sampson, R.J., S.W. Raudenbush, & F. Earls (1997). Neighborhoods and violent crime: A multilevel study of collective efficacy. *Science* 277: 918–924.

Schwartz, J. (2006). Family structure as a source of female and male homicide in the United States. *Homicide Studies*, 10(4): 253–278.

Shaw, C. R. & H. D. McKay (1942). *Juvenile delinquency in urban areas*. Chicago: University of Chicago Press.

Short, J.F. Jr. (1997). Poverty, ethnicity, and violent crime. Boulder, CO: Westview.

Snyder, A. R. & D. K. McLaughlin. (2004). Female-headed families and poverty in rural America. *Rural Sociology*, 69 (1): 127–149.

Sorokin, P., & Carl C. Zimmerman. (1929). *Principles of Rural-urban Sociology*. New York: Henry Holt and Co.

Stark, R. (1987). Deviant places: A theory of the ecology of crime. *Criminology*, 25(4): 893–909.

Tolbert, C.M., T.A. Lyson, & M.D. Irwin (1998). Local capitalism, civic engagement, and socioeconomic well-being. *Social Forces*. 77(2). 401–428.

United States Department of Justice. Federal Bureau of Investigation. Uniform Crime Reporting Program Data: Supplementary Homicide Reports, 2000 [Data file]. ICPSR03448-v1. Ann Arbor, MI: Inter-university Consortium for Political and Social Research [distributor]. 2002. doi:10.3886/ICPSR03448 2001 [Data file]. ICPSR03722-v1. Ann Arbor, MI: Inter-university Consortium for Political and Social Research [distributor]. 2003. doi:10.3886/ICPSR03722 2002 [Data file]. ICPSR03999-v1. Ann Arbor, MI: Inter-university Consortium for Political and Social Research [distributor], 2004. doi:10.3886/ICPSR03999 2003 [Data file]. ICPSR04125-v1. Ann Arbor, MI: Inter-university Consortium for Political and Social Research [distributor], 2005–07–06. doi:10.3886/ICPSR04125 2004 [Data file]. ICPSR04465-v1. Ann Arbor, MI: Inter-university Consortium for Political and Social Research [distributor], 2006–08–18. doi:10.3886/ICPSR04465 2005 [Data file]. ICPSR04723-v1. Ann Arbor, MI: Inter-university Consortium for Political and Social Research [distributor], 2007–06–11. doi:10.3886/ICPSR04723 2006 [Data file]. ICPSR22401-v1. Ann Arbor, MI: Inter-university Consortium for Political and Social Research [distributor], 2008–07–08. doi:10.3886/ICPSR22401.v1 2007 [Data file]. ICPSR25103-v1. Ann Arbor, MI: Inter-university Consortium for Political and Social Research [distributor], 2009–06–10. doi:10.3886/ICPSR25103.v1 2008 [Data file]. ICPSR27650-v2. Ann Arbor, MI: Inter-university Consortium for Political and Social Research [distributor],

2010–05–10. doi:10.3886/ICPSR27650.v2 2009 [Data file]. ICPSR30767-v1. Ann Arbor. MI: Inter-university Consortium for Political and Social Research [distributor], 2011–08–04. doi:10.3886/ICPSR30767.v1 2010 [Data file]. ICPSR33527-v1. Ann Arbor. MI: Inter-university Consortium for Political and Social Research [distributor]. 2012–06–19. doi:10.3886/ICPSR33527.v1 2011 [Data file]. ICPSR34588-v1. Ann Arbor, MI: Inter-university Consortium for Political and Social Research [distributor]. 2013–04–26. doi:10.3886/ICPSR34588.v1

Van Horne. S. L. (2009) Spousal homicide across the United States: Community correlates, the importance of place, and implications for comparative studies" *The International Journal of Interdisciplinary Social Sciences* 4(7): 75- 96.

———. (2010). *The importance of place: A national examination of the structural correlates of intimate partner homicides* (Doctoral dissertation. Rutgers University-Graduate School-Newark). Ann Arbor. MI.

Warner. B. D. & Pierce. G. L. (1993). Reexamining social disorganization theory using calls to police as a measure of crime. *Criminology*. 31: 493–517.

Weisheit. R. A.. & J. F. Donnermeyer (2000). Change and continuity in crime in rural America. (pp. 309–358) In G. LaFree (ed.) *The nature of crime: continuity and change*. Washington. D.C.: U.S. Department of Justice.

Weisheit. R. A. & Wells. L. E. (2005). Deadly violence in the heartland: Comparing homicide patterns in nonmetropolitan and metropolitan counties. *Homicide Studies*. 9(1): 55–80.

White. D. (1987). A social epidemiological model of central Appalachia. *Arete*. 12, 47–66.

Williams. K. R.. & R. L. Flewelling. (1988). The social production of criminal homicide: A comparative study of disaggregated rates in American cities. *American Sociological Review*, 53(3): 421–431.

Wilson. W. J. (1987). *The truly disadvantaged*. Chicago: The University of Chicago Press.

Wirth. L. (1938). Urbanism as a way of Life. *American Journal of Sociology*, 44(1):1–24.

Wolfgang. M. E. (1958). *Patterns of criminal behavior*. Philadelphia, PA: University of Pennsylvania Press.

Wolfgang. M. E.. and F. Ferracuti (1967). *The subculture of violence*. London. England: Tavistock Publication Limited.

Zahn. M.A. and P.L McCall (1999). Homicide in the 20th Century United States: Trends and Patterns. In M.D. Smith and M.A. Zahn (eds.) *Studying and preventing homicide: Issues and challenges*. Thousand (10–30) Oaks. CA: Sage Publications.

Chapter Six

(Il)legal Guns and Homicide:
A Case Study of New Orleans

Jessica M. Doucet, Julia M. D'Antonio-Del Rio and Chantel D. Chauvin

Introduction

With several recent mass murders involving offenders with easy access to multiple, high-powered firearms, activists are calling for changes to gun legislation in the U.S. The shooting at Sandy Hook Elementary School in Newtown, CT, left 26 dead at the hands of Adam Lanza in 2012 (*The New York Times*, 2012). Lanza carried with him multiple firearms, including a semiautomatic rifle (Barron, 2012). This was the second deadliest school shooting in American history, following the attacks on Virginia Tech in 2007 (*The New York Times*, 2012). In addition to school shootings, the mass murder at an Aurora, CO, movie theater by James Holmes left 12 dead and 58 wounded, and caused a frenzy of media attention and attempts at legal reformation. Holmes also carried several weapons, including an AR-15 assault rifle, a Remington 12-gauge shotgun, and a .40 caliber Glock handgun, as well as more than 6,000 rounds of ammunition (Frosch & Johnson, 2012). These examples of gunmen with relatively easy access to firearms and ammunition have reignited debates regarding gun legislation in the U.S. by both the public and government officials.

Though these events have brought the issue to the forefront, the debate over gun control legislation has been heated for several decades. Researchers examining the gun-crime relationship have come to different conclusions regarding how gun availability influences crime rates, with some predicting guns increase crime, while others predict guns decrease crime (Agnew & Brezina, 2012). While each analysis adds additional information to the literature, no firm conclusions have been drawn.

These inconsistent findings could be due to the varied measures of gun availability utilized. In prior research gun permits, gun magazine subscriptions, and gun crimes (to name a few) have been used in an effort to enumerate gun availability. Some of these proxies are the best available measures in many cases, though they may not accurately reflect gun accessibility (Kleck, 2004). Furthermore, most of the prior research fails to distinguish between legal and illegal firearm availability, even though the type of access may dictate its explication of the gun-crime link (Stolzenberg & D'Alessio, 2000).

The current manuscript aims to advance the literature by separately examining the influence of legal and illegal firearm access on gun homicides in New Orleans, LA. The city provides a unique case study because it has a long history plagued by crime and violence and has been touted as one of the most dangerous cities in the country. Furthermore, the city is located in a state with some of the most lenient firearm laws. In an effort to protect the rights of gun owners, Louisiana has held on to its lax regulations even in the midst of a national firearm debate. Using concealed carry permits and gun violations to measure legal and illegal gun availability, respectively, this study seeks to determine which type of access can predict gun homicides in Orleans Parish census tracts.

Literature Review

Gun Availability and Crime

There has been a plethora of research conducted to determine the impact gun availability has on crime rates, particularly violent crime rates (see among others, Bronars & Lott, 1998; Duggan, 2001; Kleck & Kovandzic, 2001; Kovandzic & Marvell, 2003; Lott & Mustard, 1997; Miller, Hemenway, & Azrael, 2006). These studies have provided mixed results, with some indicating that increased gun availability increases crime (Blumstein, 1995; Cook, Molliconi, & Cole, 1995; McDowall, 1991; Sloan et al., 1990), while others report a reduction in crime rates (Lott, 1998; Lott & Mustard, 1997) or no net effect (Kleck, 1997; Kleck & Kovandzic, 2001).

These studies provide a number of hypotheses to explain why gun availability may influence levels of crime. One explanation predicting a positive association between availability and rates of violent crime, particularly homicide, is the Zimring-Cook hypothesis. It states that more interpersonal conflicts will result in fatalities or severe injuries if individuals carry guns, due to the more serious damage inflicted by guns than other weapons (Cook, 1983; Kleck & McElrath, 1991; Newton & Zimring, 1969;). Others hypothesize that having armed citizens may further encourage the use of guns by criminals who are now at an increased risk of facing an armed victim. Additionally, if criminals believe a potential target is armed, they may be quick to react to any threat with lethal violence (Ayres & Donohue, 2003). Furthermore, having a gun may lead a criminal to target a victim previously thought to be too tough to challenge by using the gun to coerce a victim into compliance (Luckenbill, 1982).

Support for these hypotheses has been found in numerous studies concluding that gun availability increases homicide rates. Using gun production as a proxy for gun availability, Kleck (1979) found that homicide rates in the United States increased as gun availability increased. Similarly, in several studies conducted in Detroit, gun availability, operationalized in three different ways, was found to increase homicides (Fisher, 1976; McDowall, 1991; Newton & Zimring, 1969). Newton and Zimring (1969) and Fisher (1976) measured gun availability through handgun permits and licenses respectively, while McDowall (1991) used robberies and suicides committed with a gun as a proxy. Furthermore, gun ownership is linked to increased homicide rates by Duggan (2001). In his study, gun ownership is determined based on state-level sales data from gun magazines. The studies discussed above are only a sample of the research that has found gun availability increases homicide rates. Additionally, these conclusions are drawn in studies conducted at various levels of analysis utilizing an array of gun availability measures.

As with any highly debatable issue, however, there are also arguments supporting gun availability. Proponents have provided explanations for how increased gun availability may reduce crime rates. One theory is that gun-wielding victims can deter criminals. Based on the rational choice perspective put forth by Cornish and Clarke (1986), offenders are rational beings who conduct a cost-benefit analysis when deciding whether or not to commit crime. Supporters of the theory argue that knowing there is an increased potential of encountering an armed victim, criminals may choose to not commit crime as the risks would outweigh the benefits of doing so (Lott, 1998; Lott & Mustard, 1997). Support for this argument can be found in a survey of incarcerated felons conducted by Wright and Rossi (1986). Belief that a potential victim may be armed deterred 40 percent of the felons interviewed from committing a crime. A majority of those same individuals reported being more fearful of an armed victim than a law enforcement officer (Wright & Rossi, 1986). Additionally, research has found that potential victims are more likely to avoid injury if they have a gun present when defending themselves (Kleck & DeLone, 1993).

These hypotheses are supported by a number of studies, including those conducted by Lott (1998) and colleagues (Bronars & Lott, 1998; Lott & Mustard, 1997), which have found a negative association between gun availability and crime rates. Based on exit poll surveys, Lott (1998) concluded that increased gun ownership resulted in reduced state homicide rates. Lott and Mustard (1997) find further support in their examination of concealed carry permits in U.S. counties from 1977 to 1992. Additionally, in a study of violent crime in Illinois, Bordua (1986) found in a county-level analysis that gun ownership was negatively associated with violence, particularly homicide. Gun ownership was measured as the average annual number of firearm owner identification cards issued by the state over an eight-year period. As with the studies that found a positive relationship, these analyses have been conducted using various units of analysis and measures of gun availability; however, they find support for a negative relationship between gun availability and violent crime.

Though the gun debate has been a topic of interest with each side garnering support, research on gun availability and crime became increasingly important as states started to pass right-to-carry laws. These laws grant concealed carry permits to any individual who meets certain criteria as laid out by the law. Those individuals do not have to provide a reason for carrying a concealed weapon, nor can they be turned down if they meet the basic requirements. These laws as a result have made carrying a concealed handgun in public much easier. They have gained popularity in the past several decades, as states make an effort to thwart criminal activity (Cramer & Kopel, 1995; Lott, 1998; Lott & Mustard, 1997).[1] Consequently, researchers began to assess their impact on crime rates as these laws became more common across the country. In fact, much of the research referenced above was not only conducted to determine how gun availability influences crime rates in general, but, more specifically, to determine the immediate and long-term effects of right-to-carry laws on crime rates. As with general tests of gun availability, some studies concluded that enacting these laws increases crime (Ayres & Donohue, 1999; Donohue, 2003; Kleck & Kovandzic, 2001), while others concluded that they reduce violence (Bronars & Lott, 1998; Lott, 1998; Lott & Mustard, 1997; Plassmann & Whitley, 2003).

The above research illuminates the complex relationship between guns and crime. In reviewing the literature as a whole, however, an important aspect to the gun-crime relationship appears to be lacking—a differentiation between legal and illegal gun access. In assessing the influence of gun availability on rates of violence, the conclusions drawn are based on varying measures of legal or illegal gun access. Researchers have failed to acknowledge that "both legal and illegal gun availability may be important in predicting violence rates, but in different ways" (Stolzenberg & D'Alessio, 2000, p. 1465). Additionally, by focusing on the effects of right-to-carry laws in recent decades, research on the impacts of illegally carried weapons was pushed aside. Stolzenberg and D'Alessio (2000) recognized this deficit and attempted to address it in their research by parsing out legal and illegal gun availability. Measuring legal guns through concealed carry permits, the authors found that these guns have little to no impact on various measures of violence, specifically violent crime and gun crime, including gun crimes committed by juveniles. More importantly, they find that illegal gun availability, measured as the rate of stolen guns, is positively related to violent crime and measures of gun violence (Stolzenberg & D'Alessio, 2000). This study reinforces the importance of examining the effects of illegal versus legal guns on violent crime separately.

Additionally, the inconsistent findings of prior research could be explained by the diverse measures of firearm availability and varying levels of analysis. Gun availability is measured through a number of proxies including registration or license rates (Bordua, 1986), gun production (Kleck, 1979), gun magazine subscriptions (Duggan, 2001), or crimes and suicides committed with a gun

(McDowall, 1986, 1991). Prior studies also utilized various levels of analysis, from city-specific to nationwide. While researchers are aiming to find an answer that fits all, it is possible that the intricacies of the gun-crime relationship vary based on place. If this is the case, there cannot be a one-size fits all answer for the gun-crime problem.

In an effort to contribute to the gun-crime literature, the current study seeks to determine the separate impacts of legal and illegal gun availability on gun homicide rates. To do so, gun homicides committed in Orleans Parish, Louisiana, are analyzed at the census-tract level. What follows below is a brief history of New Orleans and an explanation as to why the city provides an interesting case study that may further illuminate the relationship between guns and violence.

New Orleans as a Case Study

A Brief History of Crime in New Orleans

Orleans Parish, Louisiana, presents a unique opportunity to study the issue of violent crime, particularly homicide. *Nouvelle-Orléans*, named in honor of the Duke of Orléans, was settled by the French in 1718. Since its founding on a swampy crescent of the Mississippi River, New Orleans has experienced a distinctive history of trials and tribulations. Early settlers of the city were confronted with disease, an often intolerable environment, and an influx of criminals from the jails of Paris. The levels of violence experienced by the first New Orleanians, arguably, set the standard for crime to continue throughout the city's history. Lax views on alcohol and gambling, as well as rampant corruption within the government, led to increasingly high levels of theft, assault, and homicide. By the time the Spanish took control of the city in the 1760's, the government of New Orleans had garnered a reputation for its poor quality and inefficiency, which continued to be prevalent in the consequent takeover by France in 1800. Finally, in 1803, France sold Louisiana (including New Orleans) to the United States; however, there was little change to the corruption and criminal activity by citizens and government officials alike (Asbury, 2008; Taylor, 2010).

New Orleans continued to carry a reputation as being one of the nation's most perilous places, "for crime, bloodshed and murder were considered commonplace" (Taylor, 2010, p. 22). Around the start of the Civil War, reporters detailed crime in the Crescent City: "newspapers were almost constantly filled with reports of murders, robberies, and assaults, and of the activities of gangs of incendiaries, who frequently fired sections of the city and plundered under cover of conflagrations" (Asbury, 2008, p. 315). At the time, there were no permits required for the possession of firearms, and men customarily carried them. Furthermore, the majority of homicides were committed in the swamp, the outskirts of the city, and were never reported to the police (Asbury, 2008).

At the start of the twentieth century, New Orleans citizens saw continually high rates of violent crime, corruption, and vice. By the 1950's, most city cleanups were superficial and did little to support vast changes in the system (Ellis, 2010). Still, New Orleanians' relaxed attitudes toward vice did not help to generate change in the political and legal atmosphere. "The visible, blatant excesses of Vieux Carré vice [. . .] were the tip of a much larger Louisiana iceberg. Behind the B-girls, hookers, gaming, and dope lay a much larger criminal octopus" (Ellis, 2010, p. 63). Big businesses and organizations were reluctant to bring their facilities to New Orleans, because of the rampant government corruption. Also, the city's experience with racketeering and crime by known members of the city's Italian crime families was notorious (Ellis, 2010; U.S. Department of Justice, n.d.). In the late 1970's and early 1980's, a series of high-profile murders of tourists in the French Quarter were brought to the attention of the country (Ellis, 2010). However, although crime was increasing, public trust of the New Orleans Police Department (NOPD) was extremely low. Many believed that the city's police were "more concerned with the profits of corruption and internal politics than preventing crime or apprehending criminals" (Ellis, 2010, p. 159). By the 1990's, an investigation of the NOPD by the federal government shed light on the excessive levels of brutality and corruption that plagued New Orleans (Ellis, 2010). It appeared that criminals ran the streets of New Orleans, and there was nothing that could be done to quell the loss of life and property.

Around the beginning of the new millennium, government and police corruption were at an all-time high. Most citizens' primary complaint about the area was the police. Many people criticized the use of extreme brutality and "indifference to open black gang warfare, whose whizzing bullets were cutting down young innocents and 'gangstas' alike" (Ellis, 2010, p. 203). New Orleans' black-on-black murder rate began to rise dramatically in certain parts of the city, where poverty, deprivation, discrimination, and drug use were most detrimental (Ellis, 2010). However, the most profound event of the early 21st century in New Orleans was the disastrous impact of Hurricane Katrina, which affected every aspect of life in the city, including violence and crime. Looting of businesses and homes created an atmosphere of trepidation to returning residents (Frailing & Harper, 2010). Those who remained throughout the storm or returned shortly after were met with horrendous living conditions, including the threat of violent crime.

In the years following the storm, New Orleans has consistently been pronounced one of the most dangerous cities in America, with a violent crime rate reaching 1,019.40 per 100,000 in 2008. Furthermore, the homicide rate has fluctuated between 49.11 per 100,000 (in 2010) and 63.60 per 100,000 (in 2008) in the years following Hurricane Katrina, for which reliable population counts are available. When compared to the 2008 national homicide rate (5.40 per 100,000) and Louisiana homicide rate (11.90 per 100,000), the extreme level of violence displayed in New Orleans is apparent (U.S. Federal Bureau of Investigation, 2009a, 2009b). A history replete with violence and vice, issues with corruption within the local government and law enforcement, and extremely high violent crime and homicide rates make New Orleans a unique case for the study of legal and illegal guns.

Gun Legislation in New Orleans

In addition to its criminal past, New Orleans has also shared the relatively lax laws in Louisiana concerning the possession of firearms. In a recent publication titled *Gun Laws Matter 2012: Understanding the Link Between Weak Laws and Gun Violence*, the Law Center to Prevent Gun Violence ranked Louisiana 45 out of 50 with some of the weakest gun statutes in the U.S. They analyzed 29 firearm policy areas and found that Louisiana does not prohibit the possession of assault weapons, .50 caliber rifles, or large capacity ammunition magazines; does not require gun dealers to apply for a state license; does not require gun owners to register their weapons or obtain a license; and does not impose a waiting period on the purchases of firearms, among other lenient regulations (Law Center to Prevent Gun Violence, 2012). The Law Center also cited the fact that "in 2009, Louisiana had the second highest number of gun deaths per capita among the states" and "plays a significant role in gun trafficking" (Law Center to Prevent Gun Violence, 2012).

In addition to the lax gun regulations, Louisiana citizens are given the right to protect oneself and one's property with deadly force. Stand Your Ground laws, as they are called, "enable an individual to use deadly force even in situations in which lesser force would suffice or in which the individual could safely retreat to avoid further danger" (Gerney & Parsons, 2013). The existence of these laws has been brought to the forefront of the gun violence debate as a result of George Zimmerman's murder trial and subsequent acquittal for the death of Trayvon Martin. However, even before enacting similar Stand Your Ground laws in 2006, Louisiana had long protected the rights of citizens with "castle laws," allowing any Louisianian the right to use, even deadly, force to protect oneself on one's own property (McGaughy, 2013). Today, RS 14:19 of the Louisiana State Legal Code provides that "a person who is not engaged in unlawful activity and who is in a place where he or she has a right to be shall have no duty to retreat before using force or violence [. . .] and may stand his or her ground and meet force with force" (Louisiana State Legislature, 2012a).

Although Louisiana does not require a permit, license, or the registration of firearms, the Louisiana State Police do mandate the possession of permits for concealed handguns. In particular:

> Act 4 of the First Extraordinary Session of the 1996 Legislature amended and re-enacted R.S. 40: 1379.3 providing for the issuance of statewide concealed handgun permits by the Deputy Secretary of the Department of Public Safety & Corrections (DPS). The permit grants statewide authority to a citizen to carry a concealed handgun on his person. A handgun is defined as "a type of firearm commonly referred to as a pistol or revolver originally designed to be fired by the use of a single hand and which is designed to fire or is capable of firing fixed

cartridge ammunition." It does not include "shotguns or rifles that have been altered by having their stocks or barrels cut or shortened" (Department of Public Safety & Corrections, 2010).

This legislation does not allow for the carrying of a concealed weapon in certain locations, for example law enforcement offices, prisons, or jails; the state capitol building; churches, synagogues, or mosques; or schools designated as "firearm free zones." The permittee must produce the weapon when requested to do so by a law enforcement official, and cannot carry and conceal the handgun while under the influence of alcohol or drugs. Finally, if the permit-holder is arrested for a misdemeanor or felony, he or she must notify the deputy secretary of public safety within 15 days (Department of Public Safety & Corrections, 2010). While there are certain restrictions regarding who can carry a firearm and under what circumstances, the relatively lenient Louisiana laws portray the extent of the protections afforded to gun owners. Because New Orleans is such an integral piece of the Louisiana landscape, these laws and legal provisions greatly affect the culture of violence that is prevalent in the city.

Summary and Expectations

Previous research on gun availability and violent crime provides inconsistent findings with some concluding more guns increase crime, while others conclude guns decrease crime. These discrepancies leave policy makers and citizens alike unsure of the true nature of the relationship. With the exception of Stolzenberg and D'Alessio (2000), most researchers have focused on either legal or illegal guns. These researchers have failed to acknowledge that legal access and illegal access may both be important in predicting the relationship, but in different ways. Additionally, most of this research has utilized a wide array of gun availability measures and varying units of analysis. It is possible that the gun-crime relationship depends on place, making a one-size-fits-all model unrealistic. In an attempt to improve on the available research, the current study analyzes the impact of legal and illegal gun access on gun homicide rates in Orleans Parish, Louisiana. New Orleans was chosen as the study area given its violent history as well as its location in a state with some of the most lenient gun laws nationwide. It is expected that legal and illegal guns will predict gun homicide, but in different directions. Specifically, legal gun access, measured through concealed carry permits, will work to reduce gun homicides, while illegal gun access, measured through weapons violations, will increase gun homicide rates.

Data and Measures

Data for this study were gathered from various sources, including the American Community Survey, the Zip Code Business Patterns, the Louisiana Department of

Safety, and the New Orleans Police Department. The American Community Survey's (ACS) 2009 release of their five-year estimates, collected from 2005 to 2009, are utilized to obtain information on demographic variables needed for the analysis. The 2008 Zip Code Business Patterns contain information on all known establishments with paid employees based on the Employer Identification Number given to companies by the Internal Revenue Service (U.S. Census Bureau 2012). The Louisiana Department of Safety produces an annual report on concealed carry permits issued, revoked, suspended, or denied each year. Finally, the New Orleans Police Department provided all of the crime data utilized in this study. The variables obtained from these data were measured at the census-tract level. Upon combining the information, comprehensive data were available for 177 of the 181 census tracts within Orleans Parish, Louisiana.[2]

Dependent Variable

The dependent variable for this study is the number of gun homicides within each census tract in Orleans Parish from 2007 to 2010. While there are issues with reporting crime in the United States, homicide tends to be a reliable indicator of the level of serious crime because they are more likely to come to the attention of the police. Additionally, determining if a homicide occurred is not subject to police discretion like other violent crimes (Gove, Hughes, & Geerken, 1985). Data on gun homicides were obtained through a public records request filed with the New Orleans Police Department. The homicides reported are those that were brought to the attention of the police through calls for service, which give a more accurate measure of the occurrence of crime than arrest data.

Explanatory Variables

The explanatory variables of interest are measures to capture illegal guns and legal guns. Legal guns are captured by measuring the number of concealed carry permits issued within each census tract per every 1,000 people over the age of 21. The number of concealed carry permits was obtained from the Louisiana Department of Safety's Annual Legislative Reports from 2007 to 2009 compiled by the Concealed Handgun Permit Unit. The permit information is based on the number of permits that were issued by the department over the three-year period.[3] This report provided counts within zip codes that were then apportioned to census tracts based on the population within the tract.

Illegal guns are measured as the number of gun violations per 1,000 people within the census tract. These data were obtained from the New Orleans Police Department through a public records request. Gun violations are coded as such whenever a person is caught illegally carrying a gun, including, but not limited to, a felon or juvenile possessing a firearm, possession of a firearm on school property or in firearm-free zones, or possessing or dealing a firearm without a serial number

(Louisiana State Legislature, 2012b). As with the gun homicide data, these reports are based on calls for service, which provide a more accurate depiction of crime than arrest reports.

Control Variables

In studying gun homicide, there are several potentially confounding variables that must be controlled due to their known association with violent crime rates (among others, see Land, McCall, & Cohen, 1990: Laub & Sampson, 2003; McCall, Land, & Parker, 2010). To account for their influence, the following variables were drawn from the 2009 ACS five-year estimates and measured within census tracts: proportion of persons who are black (black), proportion of households that are female-headed (female-headed households), proportion of persons living below the poverty line (poverty), proportion of persons unemployed (unemployment), proportion of persons 25 and older who are high school dropouts (high school dropouts), proportion of households that are renter occupied (renters), proportion of persons who did not live in the same house as the prior year (turnover), and proportion of persons between the ages of 15 and 24 (age structure). Additionally the natural log of the population (lnpop) is included to reduce problems with the skewed distribution of the population across census tracts.

The final control variable is the number of religious organizations per 1,000 people. This variable was drawn from the 2008 Zip Code Business Patterns. Included within this measure are organizations that promote religious activities, as well as churches, monasteries, religious temples, synagogues, and mosques (U.S. Census Bureau, 2011). Because Orleans Parish is located in the South, it is important to control for the influence of religion on violence. The literature regarding religion and violence, as well as the southern subculture of violence, notes that certain religious denominations are associated with increased homicide rates (Beyerlein & Hipp, 2005; D'Antonio-Del Rio, Doucet, & Chauvin, 2010; Ellison, Burr, & McCall, 2003; Lee & Bartkowski, 2004;). Additionally, those religious denominations that support corporal and capital punishment, believe in a wrathful God, and have "an eye for an eye" mentality tend to be more prevalent in southern states (Ellison & Musick, 1993; Ellison & Sherkat, 1993). To ensure this potential effect is captured, the religious organizations variable was included in the analyses. Because the data are only available at the zip code level, they were apportioned to census tracts based on the population.

Descriptive Statistics and Data Reduction

Table 6.1 presents the descriptive statistics for the dependent, explanatory, and control variables. Both the average gun homicides and the average gun homicide rate for the years 2007 to 2010 are included. These statistics reveal that on average there were approximately 3.3 homicides within a census tract over the four-year period. Additionally, the average yearly gun homicide rate was approximately 61 per 100,000 people. This rate nearly 12 times higher than the national average homicide rate of approximately 5.2 per 100,000 people from 2007 to 2010 (U.S. Federal Bureau of Investigation, 2011).

The measure of gun violations reveals that there were more than twice as many gun violations during the four-year period as there were gun homicides. Additionally, on average slightly more than four concealed carry permits were issued per 1,000 individuals 21 and over during the four-year period.

The descriptive statistics of the control variables reveal that on average, 62 percent of census tract populations are black, 22 percent of households are headed by females, 25 percent of households live below the poverty line, 14 percent are unemployed, 21 percent are high school dropouts, 37 percent are renters, 24 percent were not living in the same house one year prior, and 14 percent are between 15 and 24 years old. Additionally, on average there is less than one religious organization per 1,000 people.

Table 6.1. Descriptive Statistics

	Mean	Standard Deviation
Dependent Variables		
Gun Homicide Count	3.33	3.80
Gun Homicide Rate*	60.78	85.15
Explanatory Variables		
Gun Violations	7.27	14.73
Concealed carry permits per 1,000 people 21+	4.34	4.54
Control Variables		
Black	.62	.35
Female headed households	.22	.20
Poverty	.25	.17
Unemployment	.14	.11
High school dropout	.21	.15
Turnover	.24	.12
Renters	.37	.15
Religious organizations per 1,000 people	.74	.69
Ages 15 to 24	.14	.10
Ln Population	7.30	.70

*Rates for total population per 100,000 people per year

Table 6.2. Correlation Matrix of Dependent, Explanatory, and Control Variables

	1	2	3	4	5	6	7	8	9	10	11	12
1 Gun homicide count (2007-2010)	1	—	—	—	—	—	—	—	—	—	—	—
2 Concealed carry permit per 1,000 people 21+	-.044	1	—	—	—	—	—	—	—	—	—	—
3 Gun violations per 1,000 people	.214	.247	1	—	—	—	—	—	—	—	—	—
4 Black	.547	-.026	.161	1	—	—	—	—	—	—	—	—
5 Female headed households	.350	.301	.159	.481	1	—	—	—	—	—	—	—
6 Poverty	.413	.141	.120	.510	.631	1	—	—	—	—	—	—
7 Unemployment	.270	-.051	-.020	.549	.343	.521	1	—	—	—	—	—
8 High school dropout	.422	.027	.469	.583	.405	.464	.412	1	—	—	—	—
9 Turnover	.061	.033	.107	-.064	.056	.111	-.033	-.080	1	—	—	—
10 Renters	.302	.009	.170	.298	.551	.620	.316	.400	.232	1	—	—
11 Age structure (15 to 24)	.141	-.056	-.095	.214	.010	.192	.266	.002	.175	.111	1	—
12 Religious orgs per 1,000 people	.052	.732	.466	.009	.440	.291	.000	.204	.050	.255	-.195	1

A bivariate correlation matrix was created and examined because of the known association between several of the control variables included in the present study. As shown in Table 6.2, multiple variables are highly correlated with one another.

The correlated variables are conceptually distinct; however, statistically they may be capturing some of the same variance. By indexing these variables, we are able to more succinctly analyze the core concepts while reducing issues of multi-collinearity. An obliquely rotated principal components factor analysis was therefore conducted for the correlated control variables, as displayed in Table 6.3.

Based on conventional standards, factors that produced an eigenvalue greater than one and variable factor loading scores greater than .5 were kept for inclusion in the regression analyses (Land et al., 1990; McCall et al., 2010). The first factor that was created measures resource disadvantage. The variables included are black, poverty, female-headed households, unemployed, and high school dropouts. This index was expected as the variables included within it have been shown in prior criminological research to be interrelated (Bursik & Grasmick, 1993; Land et al., 1990; McCall et al., 2010; Morenoff, Sampson, & Raudenbush, 2001; Sampson, Raudenbush, & Earls, 1997; Wilson, 1987, among others). A second index measuring residential instability was also created and includes the variables turnover, renters, and age 15 to 24.

Table 6.3. Obliquely Rotated Principal Components Factor Pattern Matrices

	Factor Loading Scores	
Resource Disadvantage		
Poverty	.818	
Black	.817	
Female headed households	.742	
High school dropouts	.741	
Unemployment	.729	
Instability		
Turnover		.746
Renters		.685
Age structure		.577
Eigen Value	2.967	1.359

Analytical Methods

Spatial regression techniques have become increasingly common in statistical analyses to take into account the fact that observations across space are not independent from one another (Anselin, 1988; Baller, Anselin, Messner, Deane, & Hawkins, 20001; Sampson, Morenoff, & Earls, 1999). Homicides experienced in one tract may not be independent of homicides that occur elsewhere, because census tract boundaries are not concrete delineations of space. To determine if significant spatial dependence exists, a Moran's I statistic is generated. This statistic indicates significant autocorrelation if it is higher than .20 (Anselin, 1988). To obtain a Moran's I statistic, a first order rook contiguity weight matrix was generated as it is required to estimate the statistic. The Moran's I value for the four-year gun homicide rate was .2035, justifying the use of a spatial variable to account for autocorrelation. A spatial lag variable was created and examined to determine if it significantly reduced the Moran's I value. Analysis of this variable revealed a statistic of .0369, indicating that the inclusion of a spatial lag variable adequately addresses the issue of spatial autocorrelation. The lag variable was therefore carried over into the regression analyses to capture the spatial dependence that exists between Orleans Parish census tracts.

To analyze the impact of legal and illegal guns on gun homicides in Orleans Parish census tracts, negative binomial regression techniques were utilized. Many scholars have recognized the need to use different statistical methods when predicting statistically rare events, due to the potential for non-linear relationships (see Long & Freese, 2006; Osgood, 2000; Osgood & Chamber, 2000). Within the current dataset, approximately 27 percent of census tracts experienced zero gun homicides and approximately 21 percent experienced only one over the four-year period. Additionally, because homicide rates are dependent on population size, which varies across census tracts, homogeneity of error variance cannot be assumed. Because of the skewed distribution of the dependent variable and heteroskedasticity of error variance, the assumptions of standard regression analyses are violated. To correct these issues, negative binomial regression is utilized because it does not rely on the assumption of linearity.[4] In addition, the model was also offset by the natural log of the population. By offsetting the model by the natural log of the population, the coefficients within the analysis can be interpreted as rates rather than counts. Furthermore, robust estimation was used to provide robust standard errors to adjust for heterogeneity within the model (Long & Freese, 2006).

Results

Table 6.4 reports the results for the models predicting counts of gun homicides in Orleans Parish census tracts. The first model includes only the control variables as well as the spatial lag variable. Including the spatial lag in each model makes the model results more conservative as it becomes more difficult to attain statistical significance when spatial dependence is controlled. In this model, resource dis-advantage is positive and significantly related to gun homicides. This finding is expected and is consistent with prior criminological literature (see Land, et al., 1990, among others).

Table 6.4. Negative Binomial Regression Models Predicting Gun Homicide Counts in Orleans Parish Census Tracts

	Model 1		Model 2		Model 3	
Gun Violations			0.033*	(0.015)		
Concealed Carry Permits					-0.065**	(0.022)
Resource Disadvantage Index	0.832***	(0.099)	0.792***	(0.084)	0.823***	(0.095)
Instability	-0.013	(0.107)	-0.041	(0.090)	-0.039	(0.106)
Religious Organizations	0.323	(0.259)	0.081	(0.219)	0.691**	(0.227)
Population Size (ln)	-0.322*	(0.162)	-0.132	(0.134)	-0.192	(0.151)
Spatial Lag	-0.285	(0.278)	-0.294	(0.227)	-0.353	(0.254)
Maximum Likelihood R²	0.472		0.534		0.491	

Unstandardized coefficients reported with robust standard error in parentheses

† p ≤ .10; *p ≤ .05; **p ≤ .01; ***p ≤ .001

Model 2 includes the first independent variable—gun violations. The gun violations measure is positively and significantly related to gun homicides at the .05 level. For a more detailed interpretation of the coefficients, the standardized percent change is calculated to determine the strength of the variable in predicting gun homicides. To determine the percent change, the unstandardized coefficient is multiplied by its standard deviation and the exponential is taken. The resulting value is then subtracted from one and multiplied by 100.[5] Analysis of the percent change reveals that for each additional gun violation per 1,000 people, the gun homicide rate increases 62.6 percent.

Model 3 includes the second key independent variable measuring concealed carry permits. This variable is negative and significantly related to gun homicides at the .01 level. The standardized percent change indicates that for each additional concealed carry permit per 1,000 people 21 and over, the homicide rate within a census tract decreases by 25.6 percent. Additionally, both resource disadvantage and religious organizations are positive and significantly related to gun homicides within Orleans Parish census tracts. While used as a control variable, the positive, significant value of religious organizations is noteworthy. The percent change reveals that for each additional religious organization per 1,000 people, homicide increases more than 61 percent. This finding may be surprising, though it is not completely unexpected given the culture of honor that tends to dominate the south.

While both of the independent variables are significantly related to gun homicides in the predicted directions, they are not equally effective in predicting the homicide rate. The illegal possession of firearms appears to have a stronger effect on gun homicides as the percent change is 37 percent higher than that of legal guns. Additionally, the maximum likelihood R^2 value is greater for the second model ($R^2 = .534$) than the third model ($R^2 = .491$), indicating a better fitting model when illegal guns are included in the analysis. These R^2 values provide support for the conclusion that illegal guns are a better predictor of gun homicides than legally carried firearms.[6]

Discussion and Conclusion

Gun violence has been extensively studied in recent decades, with renewed interest over the last several years following a string of mass murders in the United States. Each new study attempted to further explicate the relationship between gun availability and crime by utilizing various measures or levels of analysis. Additionally, these studies examined either legal or illegal gun access, failing to recognize the predictability of both. The conclusions drawn from these studies are as varied as their methods and techniques. Some research finds that increased gun availability increases crime rates, while others find it decreases crime or has no net effect (Blumstein, 1995; Cook, Molliconi, & Cole, 1995; Kleck, 1997; Kleck & Kovandzic, 2001; Lott, 1998; Lott & Mustard, 1997; McDowall, 1991; Sloan et al., 1990). The current manuscript aimed to expand this literature by examining the influence of both legal and illegal gun access on gun homicide rates in Orleans Parish census tracts.

The influence of gun availability on gun homicides varies based on the type of access analyzed. Guns that are legally on the street, represented by the rate of concealed carry permits, reduce gun homicide. This finding supports the theories that gun-wielding victims have the ability to deter criminal activity. However, when guns are illegally held, measured through the rate of gun violations, gun homicides increase dramatically; supporting the idea that more guns means more crime. These findings tend to support both sides of the gun debate. However, an important distinction must be made. While both legal and illegal gun access are able to predict gun homicides, the predictive power is not the same. Illegal guns are better at predicting gun homicide rates than legal guns as evidenced in the percent change values (a 63 percent increase versus a 26 percent decrease respectively) and the pseudo-R^2 values, which indicates the illegal gun measure is a better predictor of gun homicides.

Additionally, the results also show that religious organizations serve to increase gun homicides. While this variable is used as a control and may seem counterintuitive, it is important to note that the effect may be explained by the subculture of violence evident in the South. Based on prior research, certain religious affiliations, particularly evangelical Protestantism, are associated with increased crime rates (see Beyerlein & Hipp, 2005; D'Antonio-Del Rio et al., 2010; D'Antonio-Del Rio & Lee, 2009, among others). The South tends to be dominated by the Protestant beliefs of a wrathful and vengeful God, which supports capital and corporal punishment, as well as defending oneself and property against threats. It is possible that this positive, significant relationship is being driven by the strongly held religious beliefs regarding a person's right to defend their life and property.

The current study is not without its limitations, though these shortcomings may serve to guide future research on gun violence. One potential limitation is the measurement of legal and illegal gun access. This shortcoming is not new to the debate regarding the gun-crime relationship. The measure for legal access, concealed carry permits, is unfortunately not an exact count of permits in a census tract, but rather an appropriation made based on the number of permits issued in each zip code. This proxy measure was used because it was the best available measure of legal guns in the city. Louisiana, as discussed earlier, does not require gun owners to register their firearms and any information collected by the state is not publicly available. Some researchers have utilized a similar measure, but there could arguably be a more accurate count of firearm ownership made available in the future.

An additional limitation is that this is a case study using cross-sectional data. As a result, these findings are not necessarily generalizable to the population as a whole nor do they show long-term trends of the effects of guns on violent crime. While this may be seen as a limitation, as discussed above, it is also possible that the inconsistent findings in prior research are due to the gun-crime relationship being place-specific. With regard to the use of cross-sectional data, the literature would benefit from an analysis of the long-term influence of legal and illegal gun access in New Orleans.

While the gun debate is far from over, each additional study into the relationship between guns and violence is vital. However, it would be beneficial to come to a consensus on the most accurate measures of legal and illegal gun access in an effort to determine the true nature of the relationship. The present research is a step in this direction. Also as demonstrated by the current study, recognizing the separate, but equally important, influence of legal and illegal guns is another piece of the complicated gun-crime puzzle.

Notes

The authors would like to acknowledge partial funding for this research by the Francis Marion University Professional Development Committee.
1.   Even though the implementation of right-to-carry laws has sparked much debate and has been widely studied, not all states have these laws in place nor are they the only laws that allow citizens across the United States to carry concealed weapons. In fact, as of July 2013, all 50 states allow concealed weapons to be carried in public though 13 states do not have right-to-carry laws (Long, Garcia, & Pearson, 2013). These states

either have unrestricted laws (allowing citizens to carry guns in public without a permit) or "may-carry" laws (allowing local jurisdictions to dictate who may and may not carry a concealed weapon) (Ayres and Donohue 1999). However, because right-to-carry laws have been enacted in a majority of states, prior research has focused on these laws specifically.

2.   Orleans Parish, Louisiana, is a county-equivalent. The parish consists of the city of New Orleans and the city of Algiers.

3.   This number does not take into account whether or not permits were later revoked or had not been renewed.

4.   A likelihood-ratio test used to detect overdispersion produced a significance level less than .001, indicating that negative binomial regression techniques are appropriate. This model corrects for overdispersion by adding a parameter to reflect the "unobserved heterogeneity among observations" (Long and Freese 2006: 372).

5.   These standardized percent changes can be interpreted as rates instead of counts because the regression analyses were offset by the natural log of the census tract population.

6.   The R^2 values provided with negative binomial regression are not equivalent to a traditional R^2 value. These values cannot, therefore, be interpreted in the same way. However, these values can be compared across models to determine the goodness of fit of the model.

References

Agnew, R., & Brezina, T. (2012). *Juvenile delinquency: Causes and control* (4th ed.). New York, NY: Oxford University Press.

Anselin, L. (1988). *Spatial econometrics: Methods and models.* Norwell, MA: Kluwer Academic Publishers.

Asbury, H. (2008). *The French Quarter: An informal history of the New Orleans underworld.* New York, NY: Basic Books.

Ayres, I., & Donohue, J. J. (1999). Nondiscretionary concealed weapons laws: A case study of statistics, standards of proof, and public policy. *American Law and Economics Review.* 6, 436–470.

Ayres, I., & Donohue, J. J. (2003). Shooting down the more guns, less crime hypothesis. *Stanford Law Review,* 55, 1193–1314.

Baller, R. D., Anselin, L., Messner, S. F., Deane, G., & Hawkins, D. F. (2001). Structural covariates of U.S. county homicide rates: Incorporating spatial effects. *Criminology,* 39, 561–590.

Barron, J. (2012, December 14). Nation reels after gunman massacres 20 children at school in Connecticut. *The New York Times.* Retrieved from http://www.nytimes.com/2012/12/15nyregion/shooting-reported-at-connecticut-elementary-school. html?pagewanted=all

Blumstein, A. (1995). Youth violence, guns, and the illicit-drug industry. *Criminal Law and Criminology.* 86, 37–58.

Bordua, D. J. (1986). Firearms ownership and violent crime: A comparison of Illinois counties. In J. M. Byrne & R. J. Sampson (Eds.), *The social ecology of crime* (pp. 156–188). New York, NY: Springer Verlag.

Bronars, S. G., & Lott, J. R. (1998). Criminal deterrence, geographic spillovers, and the right to carry concealed handguns. *American Economic Review,* 88, 475–479.

Bursik, R. J., & Grasmick, H. G. (1993). *Neighborhoods and crime: The dimensions of effective community control.* Lanham, MD: Lexington Books.

Cook, P. J. (1983). The influence of gun availability on violent crime patterns. In M. Tonry & N. Morris (Eds.), *Crime and justice: An annual review of research* (pp. 49–89). Chicago, IL: University of Chicago Press.

Cook, P. J., Molliconi, S., & Cole, T. B. (1995). Regulating gun markets. *Journal of Criminal Law and Criminology,* 86: 59–92.

Cornish, D. B., & Clarke, R. V. (1986). *The reasoning criminal.* New York, NY: Springer Verlag.

Cramer, C. E., & Kopel, D. B. (1995). Shall-issue: The new wave of concealed handgun permit laws. *Tennessee Law Review,* 62, 679–757.

D'Antonio-Del Rio, J. M., Doucet, J. M., & Chauvin, C. D. (2010). Violent vindictive women: A re-analysis of the southern subculture of violence. *Sociological Spectrum,* 30, 484–503.

D'Antonio-Del Rio, J. M., & Lee, M. R. (2009). Violent women? Southern culture and gendered patterns of lethal violence. *International Journal of Sociological Research,* 2, 63–81.

Department of Public Safety & Corrections. (2010). *Concealed Handgun Permit Unit.* Retrieved from http://www.lsp.org/handguns.html

Donohue, J. (2003). The impact of concealed carry laws. In J. Ludwig & P. Cook (Eds.), *Evaluating gun policy: Effects on crime and violence.* Washington, DC: Brookings Institution.

Duggan, M. (2001). More guns, more crime. *Journal of Political Economy,* 109, 1086–1114.

Ellis, S. S. (2010). *Madame Vieux Carré: The French Quarter in the twentieth century.* Jackson, MS: University Press of Mississippi.

Fisher, J. C. (1976). Homicide in Detroit. *Criminology,* 14, 387–400.

Frailing, K., & Harper, D. W. (2010). Crime and hurricanes in New Orleans. In D. L. Brunsma, D. Overfelt, & J. S. Picou (Eds.), *The sociology of Katrina: Perspectives on a modern catastrophe* (pp. 55–74). Lanham, MD: Rowman & Littlefied Publishers, Inc.

Frosch, D., & Johnson, K. (2012, July 20). Gunman kills 12 in Colorado, reviving gun debate. *The New York Times.* Retrieved from http://www.nytimes.com/2012/07/21/us/shooting-at-colorado-theater-showing-batman-movie.html?pagewanted=all

Gove, W. R., Hughes, M., & Geerken, M. (1985). Are uniform crime reports a valid indicator of the index crimes? An affirmative answer with minor qualifications. *Criminology,* 23, 451–501.

Gerney, A., & Parsons, C. (2013). License to kill: How lax concealed carry laws can combine with stand your ground laws to produce deadly results. *Center for American Progress.* Retrieved from http://www.americanprogress.org/issues/guns-crime/report/2013/09/17/74132/license-to-kill/

Kleck, G. (1979). Capital punishment, gun ownership, and homicide. *American Journal of Sociology,* 84, 882–910.

———. (1997). *Targeting guns: Firearms and their control.* New York, NY: Aldine de Gruyter.

———. (2004). Measures of gun ownership levels for macro-level crime and violence research. *Journal of Research in Crime and Delinquency,* 41, 3–36.

Kleck, G., & DeLone, M. (1993). Victim resistance and offender weapon effects in robbery. *Journal of Quantitative Criminology,* 9, 55–82.

Kleck, G., & Kovandzic, T. (2001). The impact of gun laws and gun levels on crime rates. Paper presentation at the Annual Meeting of the American Society of Criminology. Atlanta, GA.

Kleck, G., & McElrath, K. (1991). The effects of weaponry on human violence. *Social Forces, 69,* 669–692.

Kovandzic, T. V., & Marvell, T. B. (2003). Right-to-carry concealed handguns and violent crime: Crime control through gun decontrol? *Criminology, 2,* 363–396.

Land, K. C., McCall, P. L., & Cohen, L. E. (1990). Structural covariates of homicide rates: Are there any invariances across time and social space? *American Journal of Sociology, 95,* 922–963.

Laub, J. H., & Sampson, R. J. (2003). *Shared beginnings, divergent lives: Delinquent boys to age 70.* Cambridge, MA: Harvard University Press.

Law Center to Prevent Gun Violence. (2012). *Louisiana state law summary.* Retrieved from http://smartgunlaws.org/louisiana-state-law-summary

Long, J. S., & Freese, J. (2006). *Regression models for categorical dependent variables using Stata.* College Station, TX: Stata Press.

Long, R., Garcia, M., & Pearson, R. (2013, July 9). General assembly overrides governor's veto of concealed carry bill. *Chicago Tribune.* Retrieved from http://articles.chicagotribune.com/2013-07-09/news/chi-illinois-concealed-carry_1_harrisburg-democrat-gun-bill-quinn

Lott, J. R. (1998). *More guns, less crime: Understanding crime and gun control laws.* Chicago, IL: University of Chicago Press.

Lott, J. R., & Mustard, D. B. (1997). Crime, deterrence, and right-to-carry concealed handguns. *The Journal of Legal Studies, 26,* 1–68.

Louisiana Department of Public Safety and Corrections. (2008). *Concealed handgun permit unit: Annual legislative report, 2007–2008.* Retrieved from http://www.lsp.org/pdf/chAnnualReport07–08.pdf

Louisiana Department of Public Safety and Corrections. (2009). *Concealed hand gun permit unit: Annual legislative report, 2009.* Retrieved from http://www.lsp.org/pdf/chAnnualReport09.pdf

Louisiana State Legislature. (2012a). *RS 14:19.* Retrieved from http://www.legis.la.gov/legis/law.aspx?d=78336

———. (2012b). *RS 14:95.1.* Retrieved from http://www.legis.la.gov/legis/Law.aspx?p=y&d=78740

Luckenbill, D. F. (1982). Compliance under the threat of severe punishment. *Social Forces, 60,* 811–825.

McCall, P. L., Land, K. C., & Parker, K. F. (2010). An empirical assessment of what we know about structural covariates of homicide rates: A return to a classic 20 years later. *Homicide Studies, 14,* 219–243.

McDowall, D. (1986). Gun availability and robbery rates: A panel study of large U.S. cities, 1974–1978. *Law and Policy, 8,* 135–148.

———. (1991). Firearm availability and homicide rates in Detroit, 1951–1986. *Social Forces, 69,* 1085–1101.

McGaughy, L. (2013, July 19). Understanding Louisiana's stand-your-ground and castle laws. *The Times-Picayune.* Retrieved from http://www.nola.com/politics/index.ssf/2013/07/louisiana_stand_your_ground_zi.html

Miller, M., Hemenway, D., & Azrael, D. (2006). State-level homicide victimization rates in the US in relation to survey measures of household firearm ownership, 2001–2003. *Social Science and Medicine, 64,* 656–664.

Morenoff, J. D., Sampson, R. J., & Raudenbush, S. W. (2001). Neighborhood urban inequality, collective efficacy, and the spatial dynamics of urban violence. *Criminology*, 39, 517–559.

Newton, G. D., & Zimring, F. E. (1969). Firearms and violence in American life. *A staff report to the national commission on the causes and prevention of violence*. Washington, DC: U.S. Government Printing Office.

The New York Times. (2012, December 14). The shootings at Sandy Hook Elementary School. *The New York Times*. Retrieved from http://www.nytimes.com/interactive/2012/12/14/nyregion/The-shooting-at-the-Sandy-Hook-Elementary.html

Osgood, D. W. (2000). Poisson-based regression analysis of aggregate crime rates. *Journal of Quantitative Criminology*, 16, 21–44.

Osgood, D. W., & Chambers, J. M. (2000). Social disorganization outside the metropolis: An analysis of rural youth violence. *Criminology*, 38, 81–115.

Plassmann, F., & Whitley, J. (2003). Confirming more guns, less crime. *Stanford Law Review*, 55, 1315–1370.

Sampson, R. J, Morenoff, J. D., & Earls, F. (1999). Beyond social capital: Spatial dynamics of collective efficacy for children. *American Sociological Review*, 64, 633–660.

Sampson, R. J., Raudenbush, S. W., & Earls, F. (1997). Neighborhoods and violent crime: A multilevel study of collective efficacy. *Science*, 277, 918–924.

Sloan, J. H., Kellermann, A. L., Reay, D. T., Ferris, J. A., Koepsell, T., Rivara, F. P., Rice, C., Gray, L., & LoGerfo, J. (1990). Handgun regulations, crime, assaults, and homicide. *New England Journal of Medicine*, 319, 1256–1262.

Stolzenberg, L., & D'Alessio, S. J. (2000). Gun availability and violent crime: New evidence from the national incident-based reporting system. *Social Forces*, 78, 1461–1482.

Taylor, T. (2010). *Wicked New Orleans: The dark side of the big easy*. Charleston, SC: The History Press.

United States Census Bureau. County Business Patterns. (2012). *How the data are collected (coverage and methodology)*. Retrieved from http://www.census.gov/econ/cbp/methodology.htm

———. North American Industry Classification System. (2011). *2007 NAICS definition. 813110 religious organizations*. Retrieved from http://www.census.gov/cgi-bin/sssd/naics/naicsrch?code=813110&search=2007% 20NAICS%20Search

United States Department of Justice. (n.d). *FBI New Orleans division: A brief history*. Retrieved from http://www.fbi.gov/neworleans/about-us/history-1/history

United States Federal Bureau of Investigation. Crime in the United States. (2009b). *Table 5: Crime in the United States, by state, 2008*. Retrieved from http://www2.fbi.gov/ucr/cius2008/data/table_05.html

United States Federal Bureau of Investigation. Crime in the United States. (2009a). *Table 6: Crime in the United States, by metropolitan statistical area, 2008*. Retrieved from http://www2.fbi.gov/ucr/cius2008/data/table_06.html

United States Federal Bureau of Investigation. Crime in the United States. (2011). *Table 1: Crime in the United States by volume and rate per 100,000 inhabitants, 1992–2011*. Retrieved from http://www.fbi.gov/about-us/cjis/ucr/crime-in-the-u.s/2011/crime-in-the-u.s.-2011/tables/table-1

Wilson, W. J. (1987). *The truly disadvantaged: The inner city, the underclass, and public policy*. Chicago, IL: University of Chicago Press.

Wright, J. D., & Rossi, P. H. (1986). *Armed and considered dangerous: A survey of felons and their weapons*. New York, NY: Aldine de Gruyter.

Chapter Seven

Do Firearms and Other Weapons Increase the Odds of Injury During an Assault? An Offender-Based Analysis

Nicole M. Schmidt, Christopher A. Kierkus and Alan J. Lizotte

Introduction

It is commonly believed that armed offenders are more dangerous than unarmed offenders and that assaults involving weapons usually lead to serious consequences for crime victims (Newton & Zimring, 1969). This belief is based on the assumption that weapons make it possible for offenders to inflict more damage on their victims. The public believes that the presence of lethal weapons increases the extent of danger to which crime victims are exposed. For instance, typically it is assumed that an assault involving a gun is more dangerous than one involving a knife. This is referred to as the "objective dangerousness doctrine" (Zimring, 1972) or the "weapon instrumentality effect" (Cook, 1991; Kleck, 1997). Empirical research suggests that the relationship between the type of weapon used in an assault and the seriousness of the incident is complex. In fact, the presence of certain weapons may decrease the probability that victims will be attacked and hurt, although it may increase the chances that any injuries inflicted will be serious or fatal (Cook, 1980, 1987; Kleck & McElrath, 1991; Zimring, 1968, 1972).

Most of what is known about the relationship between weapon selection and injury is based on victimization data (see for example Melde & Rennison, 2008). To date, only one major study (Wells & Horney, 2002) has examined this issue from the offender's standpoint. The difference between the victim's and the offender's perspective is potentially important for several reasons. Victimization studies are likely to under report weapon effects in some situations while over reporting them in others. For example. victims who are assaulted by armed offenders who do not actually use the weapon may report that they have suffered unarmed assaults. Conversely, some unarmed offenders, no doubt, claim that that they are carrying weapons when in fact they are not. Victims who believe these claims may report that they have suffered armed assaults even though technically they did not. Unfortunately, we do not know the proportion of armed and unarmed assaults reported in victimization surveys representing "false positives" and "false negatives." Hence, it is important to replicate research using victimization data with offender data. More importantly, the measurement issue discussed above raises a theoretical concern: victimization studies have a difficult time separating weapon instrumentality effects (Cook, 1991; Kleck, 1997) from offender effects (Wells & Horney, 2002) If a victimization study shows that people attacked with a certain type of weapon are particularly likely to be injured there are at least three possible reasons why this might occur.

One reason may be that "bigger weapons put bigger holes in people." Offenders armed with large caliber firearms may kill and severely injure more individuals than offenders armed with other kinds of weapons (e.g., knives). A second reason may be that offenders armed with certain weapons may be qualitatively different from other kinds of offenders. For example, serious offenders who are intent on causing harm may arm themselves with the most deadly weapons. With victimization data, only the most basic offender characteristics (e.g., sex, race) are reported, so these studies cannot examine adequately the effect of offender-related variables. Finally, offenders armed with deadly weapons may be emboldened to carry out more serious attacks even if the weapons are never used. For example. offenders who carry guns may be more willing to become involved in physical altercations than unarmed offenders because they feel that they are carrying a "trump card" should the fight turn against them. In a victimization study, if a victim is unaware that an offender is armed, the attack will be viewed as an unarmed assault.

If either the second or the third scenario is accurate, it may not be the inherent destructive potential of the weapon that exerts a causal influence on injury. Rather. weapon instrumentality effects may be spurious to offender variables. Disentangling and correctly specifying these causal relationships has important policy implications (Wells & Horney, 2002). If the causal chain is based truly on weapon instrumentality, then policies that restrict certain weapons are likely to reduce injuries resulting from crime. However, if offender variables drive the causal sequence then policies that focus on weapons will be ineffective. Worse, if it is empirically true that the presence of deadly weapons decreases the probability of injury (Cook. 1980, 1987; Kleck & McElrath, 1991; Meithe & Sousa, 2010; Zimring, 1968, 1972), policies designed to restrict such weapons may have the perverse effect of increasing the total amount of injury.

Mindful of these concerns. the present study investigates the relationship between offender characteristics, the type of weapon used during an assault incident, and the injury outcome for the victim from the perspective of the offender.

By incorporating offender characteristics along with weapon type, we aim to isolate the effects of certain kinds of weapons on victim injury and develop plausible explanations for why these relationships exist.

Prior Research

The available literature suggests that the relationship between weapon selection and victim injury is complex. In some instances, the presence of a firearm may protect victims from the risk of injury. Luckenbill (1982) has argued that robbers armed with guns are better able to ensure compliance with their demands than unarmed robbers or perpetrators armed only with personal weapons. Cook (1982) calls this phenomenon "the instrumental violence pattern" (p. 249), arguing that victims are less likely to resist offenders who carry firearms. Results from a study by Skogan (1978) provide the empirical basis for his argument. In a national survey of robbery victims, Skogan found that only 8 percent of the subjects resisted perpetrators armed with guns while 15 percent resisted those armed with other weapons.

Heavily armed perpetrators may not actually have to attack or injure victims to achieve their objectives. They can exercise power by threatening the use of force as opposed to actually using it (Cook, 1982; Kleck & McElRath, 1991). This argument is supported by empirical research (Block, 1977; Cook, 1982; Cook & Nagin, 1979; Hindelang, 1976; King, 1987; Meithe & Sousa, 2010; Tark & Kleck, 2004; U.S. Bureau of Justice Statistics, 1986). For instance, Cook (1982) demonstrated that 73.5 percent of victims were hurt when attacked during unarmed, noncommercial robberies, but only 22.1 percent suffered the same fate during robberies where the perpetrator was armed with a gun. More recently, Tark and Kleck (2004) reported that 33.3 percent of victims were hurt when attacked with a gun, 40.6 percent were injured when attacked with a non-gun weapon, and the greatest proportion (47.6 percent) were hurt when assaulted by an unarmed offender. Similarly, Meithe and Sousa (2010) found that offenders armed with guns were considerably less likely to injure carjacking victims than offenders who did not use (or at least claim not to have used) a firearm. Moreover, victims may be protected from injury by the fact that an offender is more likely to miss a victim when firing a gun than when attacking with some other type of weapon or no weapon (Kleck & McElrath, 1991). Empirically, Wells and Horney (2002) found that offenders who attacked victims with guns had 58 percent lower odds of inflicting injury relative to unarmed offenders. However, offenders armed with other kinds of weapons had 78 percent higher odds of hurting their victims.

Once the decision to use force is made, however, the presence of a weapon, particularly a firearm, appears to increase the probability that a victim will suffer serious injury or death. An early study by Wilson and Sherman (1961) showed that guns were approximately three times as lethal as knives when used in criminal attacks. This finding was replicated by Block (1977) who reported a similar ratio. Zimring (1968) showed that the death rate from criminal attacks involving firearms was five times greater than attacks perpetrated with knives. This ratio was affirmed by Cook (1982), who reported that the rate of fatalities in robberies involving guns was 9.0 per 1,000, which is approximately five times higher than the 1.7 per 1,000 that occur during armed robberies involving other types of weapons. Kierkus (2002) found that robbers armed with firearms are more likely to kill multiple victims when compared to both unarmed robbers and those armed with personal weapons, such as clubs and knives; the odds of a multiple homicide taking place during a robbery involving a long gun are 1.991 to 1 relative to a robbery that does not involve a weapon. With respect to serious injury, Wells and Horney (2002) reported that offenders who use guns increase the odds that the victim will be badly hurt by a factor of more than 60 relative to unarmed attackers. The odds ratio relative to offenders armed with other weapons also is substantial (about 14 times greater).

As noted earlier, there are several possible theoretical explanations for these findings. The most intuitive is that differences in the inherent destructive potentials of the weapons lead to differences in lethality. It also is possible that serious offenders who have a higher inherent probability of injuring victims are more likely to carry firearms than to go unarmed or carry other weapons. Kleck (1986) provided empirical support for this by finding that felons incarcerated for gun-related offenses had longer and more serious violent criminal records than those incarcerated on non-gun related charges. Similarly, Cook (1982) argues that professional offenders, those who set clear goals for committing a crime, are the ones most likely to carry lethal weapons compared to other armed robbers. Finally, it is possible that some offenders who carry lethal weapons are more likely to engage in serious violent behavior for non-instrumental reasons. Called the "excess violence pattern," the belief is that robbers armed with guns sometimes injure or kill victims simply for fun (Cook, 1982, p. 262). Conversely, unarmed robbers and those armed with personal weapons are unlikely to engage in this type of behavior because they find direct physical assaults, such as beating or stabbing the victim physically distasteful. Kleck (1997) agrees, stating, "guns provide a more . . . antiseptic way of attacking others, and could allow some attackers to bypass their inhibitions against close contact with their victims" (p. 221).

In summation, the relationship between weapon selection and the risk of injury is complex. It seems that the presence of a weapon, particularly a firearm, reduces the probability of victims being injured during an assault but increases the probability that any injuries sustained will be serious or fatal (Cook, 1982; Kleck & McElrath, 1991; Wells & Horney, 2002) and that multiple victims will be killed (Kierkus, 2002), but methodological considerations prevent these conclusions from being viewed as definitive. The Wells and Horney (2002) study represents the most systematic and methodologically advanced examination of these issues. The injury and serious injury odds ratios reported by these authors are compelling because they control for offender intent and they compare different incidents involving the same offenders. These results suggest that weapon instrumentality effects are strong. Wells and Horney's (2002) study is an important contribution to the literature on weapon instrumentality effects but their sample consists exclusively of incarcerated males; hence, it is not known if their findings can be generalized to a broader population of offenders. It is possible that incarcerated men are qualitatively different from other offenders in terms of both weapons selection tendencies and patterns of weapons use.

The present study attempts to disentangle further weapon instrumentality effects from offender effects in a community sample of high-risk adolescents. We build on previous research in several ways. First, we estimate both random-effects and fixed-effects models. This allows us not only to compare the injury outcome of an assault when the same offender uses a different type of weapon during a different assault incident (fixed-effects model) but also to include time-stable offender characteristics as predictors (random-effects models) to examine more extensively offender versus weapon effects. Second, we include several time-varying offender characteristics in our models to control for potentially important offender characteristics that have not been investigated in previous research. In particular, we focus on gang membership because prior research has demonstrated a very strong link between gang membership, gun carrying, and crime (Bjerregaard & Lizotte, 1995; Lizotte, Krohn, Howell, Tobin, & Howard, 2000; Lizotte & Sheppard, 2001; Thornberry, Krohn, Lizotte, Smith, & Tobin, 2003). Finally, rather than classifying weapon types as no weapon, gun, and other weapon, we use a broader classification of weapon types to investigate whether specific kinds of non-gun weapons have different effects on injury.

Methods

Sample and Data

This study used data from the Rochester Youth Development Study (RYDS), a longitudinal study of antisocial behavior (Thornberry et al., 2003). The study follows a panel of youth from their early teenage years (mean age 14 at Wave 1) through adulthood (mean age 31 at Wave 14). The present study will analyze data from Waves 4 through 9 where subjects are, on average, aged 15.5 to 18. Subjects and their primary caregiver were interviewed in person biannually from 1988 through 1992. These waves were selected because they span the adolescent years, a period known for high levels of criminal behavior, and contain key variables needed for the analysis.

The initial sample consisted of 1,000 seventh and eighth grade students attending Rochester public schools in 1988. The retention rate for the time frame considered exceeds 85 percent and subject loss is not differential (Thornberry et al., 2003). In order to maximize the amount of variation on key measures of anti-social behavior, the RYDS oversampled youth who were at high risk of offending. This was accomplished in two ways. Males were oversampled by a ratio of 75 percent to 25 percent, because they are more likely than females to be serious and chronic offenders, and youth living in census tracts with high area arrest rates were assigned a higher probability of selection than those in tracts with lower area arrest rates.

The unit of analysis for the present study is assault incident. Each case represents an offender self-reported armed or unarmed assault that occurred between Wave 4 and Wave 9 of the study, so it is possible that the same subject appears multiple times in the data set. For instance, a subject that reported an unarmed assault in Wave 5, an armed assault in Wave 7, and both an unarmed and an armed assault in Wave 8 would contribute four cases to the total sample. This procedure yields 1,034 assault incidents for analysis.[1] Note that while the random-effects models will use all 1,034 cases, the fixed-effects models will use only cases where an offender has committed more than one assault and where the injury outcome varies across assaults.

Measures

We investigated two categories of independent variables, assault incident type and offender characteristics, to predict our offender-reported outcome measures, injury and hospitalization. There were limitations with using offender-reports to measure injury outcomes, but offender data provides a breadth of information that is unavailable in victimization data. Studying weapon effects using multiple data sources and multiple methods is important and informative (Wells & Horney, 2002); this study presents another perspective in examining this issue. The coding and descriptive statistics for each measure are displayed in Table 7.1.

Assault incident type. The primary independent variable is the type of assault incident. The offender is asked to report information on the most serious armed and unarmed assault (separately) that occurred during the interview time frame, so these are not representative of all assaults committed by this sample during the study period. Assault incidents are classified into one of five categories: unarmed, gun, knife, club, or street weapon. Unarmed assaults comprise the majority, with 84.8 percent of the sample reported as such. Assaults involving a gun (handgun, shotgun, or long gun) comprised 3.1 percent of the sample of incidents, while 3.7 percent of assaults involved a knife or other cutting/stabbing instrument.[2] Finally, 7.1 percent of assaults involved a club or instrument designed to inflict blunt force trauma, while about 1 percent involved a street weapon, such as a rock, brick, or broken bottle.[3] Incidents that could not be classified into any of these categories were excluded.[4] The number of such incidents was trivial (1.1 percent).

Time-stable offender characteristics. Time-stable offender characteristics include sex, race, and low self-control. Sex is included because previous research has shown that most gun carrying adolescents, particularly those who own and/or carry a gun for protection, are male and the majority of firearms offenses are committed by males (Bankston & Thompson, 1989; Cao, Cullen, & Link, 1997; Kulig, Valentine, Griffith, & Ruthazer, 1998). The offender in each incident was classified as either male (81.0 percent) or female (19.0 percent). Frequently it is

Table 7.1. Variable Coding and Descriptive Statistics

Variable	Coding	Mean	SD	N
No Weapon	Assault with no weapon, 0=No, 1=Yes	.85	.36	1034
Gun	Assault with a gun, 0=No, 1=Yes	.03	.17	1034
Knife	Assault with a knife, 0=No, 1=Yes	.04	.19	1034
Club	Assault with a club, 0=No, 1=Yes	.07	.26	1034
Street Weapon	Assault with a street weapon, 0=No, 1=Yes	.01	.12	1034
Male	Male gender, 0=No, 1=Yes	.81	.39	1034
Female	Female gender, 0=No, 1=Yes	.19	.39	1034
White	White race, 0=No, 1=Yes	.15	.36	1034
African-American	African-American race, 0=No, 1=Yes	.69	.46	1034
Hispanic	Hispanic ethnicity, 0=No, 1=Yes	.16	.36	1034
Low Self-Control	Twelve-item scale, higher scores indicate lower self-control; α=.85	2.38	.44	972
Age	Age at assault wave	16.7	1.17	1034
Live with Both Parents	Live with both parents at assault wave	.24	.43	1033
Drug Use	Drug use at assault wave, 0=No, 1=Yes	.34	.47	1034
Gang Membership	Gang member at assault wave, 0=No, 1=Yes	.22	.41	1032
Peer Gun Ownership	Peers owned guns for protection at assault wave, 0=No, 1=Yes	.63	.48	981
Injury	Assault caused injury, 0=No, 1=Yes	.72	.45	1016
Hospitalization	Assault caused hospitalization, 0=No, 1=Yes	.19	.39	987

assumed that African-Americans and Hispanics are more likely to carry firearms and other weapons than whites, and some studies support this contention (e.g., Kingery, Biafora, & Zimmerman, 1996), but other researchers dispute this (e.g., Kulig et al., 1998). It also is not apparent that increased carrying by certain racial groups is associated with increased levels of violence (Kingery et al., 1996). Since the relationships between race, weapon use, and violent behavior are far less consistent than those involving sex, we include this as another offender characteristic. We measure race using three dichotomous outcomes. Offenders were classified as White (15.2 percent), African-American (69.2 percent), or Hispanic (15.6 percent).

We included low self-control as it is conceivable that individuals with lower self-control may be more likely to use a weapon and/or may be more likely to inflict injury than individuals with higher self-control. We measure self-control at Wave 10 using a twelve-item scale where higher scores indicate lower self-control. Although this measure is taken after the assault incidents included in the study, Gottfredson and Hirschi (1990) contend that self-control is stable over the life course; therefore it should not matter when this variable is measured. The average level of low self-control is 2.38 on a four-point scale.

Time-variant Offender Characteristics

Time-variant offender characteristics include age, living with both parents, drug use, gang membership, and peer gun ownership. Offender age at the time of the incident is measured in years (mean = 16.7, SD = 1.17). Living with both parents is a dichotomous measure of family structure that distinguishes offenders who live with both of their biological parents at the time of the incident (24.4 percent) from subjects who do not (75.6 percent). It is well known that children who do not reside in traditional two parent families have an elevated risk of involvement in delinquency (see Free, 1991; Kierkus & Baer, 2002). Drug use is a dichotomous measure of whether the offender used drugs during the wave in which the assault occurred. Thirty-four percent of this sample reported drug use during the assault wave. We include this variable because research has shown that subjects who are involved with drugs are more likely to be violent than individuals who are not (Lizotte et al., 2000).

Gang membership is a dichotomous measure distinguishing respondents who classify him or herself as a gang member during the assault wave (15.6 percent) from subjects who are not currently gang members (84.4 percent). Gang membership is included as a measure of offender seriousness. Subjects who identify themselves as gang members have a high probability of being serious, chronic offenders who are well acquainted with using violence for instrumental purposes (Thornberry et al., 2003). It is expected that if offender characteristics play a role in injury outcome, offender gang membership will be a significant predictor of victim injury and hospitalization. Finally, peer gun ownership is a dichotomous variable assessing whether the offender's peers report owning a gun for protection during the wave in which the assault incident occurred. Approximately 63 percent of the sample reported having peers who own guns for protection. This measure helps describe the offenders in the study. It is plausible that offenders who associate with peers who own guns for protection are part of a culture that regularly experiences gun violence. They may be more likely to use guns in assault situations, which in turn may influence the probability of victim injury (Lizotte, Howard, Krohn, & Thornberry, 1997; Lizotte et al., 2000).

Injury Outcome

This dichotomous variable assesses whether the offender self-reported that the assault incident resulted in an injury. The offender was asked simply whether the person was hurt during the assault.[5] If the response was yes the incident was assigned a value of 1, otherwise it was assigned a value of 0. Seventy-two percent of assaults resulted in injury to the victim.

Hospitalization Outcome

The second outcome in this analysis assessed whether someone was taken to the hospital from the assault. This variable is designed to differentiate simple injuries from serious injuries. An incident was assigned a value of 1 on hospitalization according to one of two criteria: 1) the offender specifically indicated that someone was taken to the hospital, needed medical attention, or needed to see a doctor as a result of the assault or 2) the description of the incident indicated that the injury inflicted would prompt a reasonable person to seek medical attention.[6] If a determination of the seriousness of injury could not be made based on the description given, the case was coded as missing.[7] It may seem tautological to classify a gun assault that ended in the victim being shot as a hospitalization (because then a gun assault would be, by definition, a hospitalization), but this is not true for two reasons. First, not all gun assaults ended in a victim being injured (e.g., if the gun was not fired or the offender shot and missed the victim). Second, out of the 187 assault incidences resulting in a hospitalization, 19 involved guns and only four of those were classified as such because the offender specifically stated that they shot their victim. Most were classified as a hospitalization because they stated that the victim required medical attention. Although not as sophisticated an injury measure as that proposed by some recent investigators (e.g., Safarik & Jarvis, 2005), this operationalization of serious injury was designed to be comparable to Wells and Horney (2002, p. 279), and is consistent with the approach taken by other recent studies of injury (e.g. Tark & Kleck, 2004).

Hypotheses and Analytic Strategy

The primary goal of this study was to examine the extent to which offender characteristics versus weapon instrumentality influence the injury outcome during an assault in an offender-based, community sample of high-risk adolescents. If weapon instrumentality (Cook, 1991; Kleck, 1997; Zimring, 1972) is the primary mechanism responsible for the relationship between the type of weapon used during an assault and the resulting injury, then weapon type will have a strong and significant relationship to injury when controlling for offender characteristics. On the other hand, if offender characteristics drive the causal relationship as some have suggested (see Cook, 1982; Kleck, 1986, 1997), then certain offender-related variables will predict injury while weapon type will not. A clarification of the effects of these two variables will imply a rethinking of previous conclusions drawn exclusively on the basis of victimization studies.

A secondary goal of this study was to examine the extent to which different weapon types make injury and hospitalization more or less likely. We anticipate that offenders who are heavily armed will be less likely to injure their victims than those who are less heavily armed. We base our hypothesis on two theoretical grounds. First, heavily armed offenders may be able to obtain what they want simply by threatening the use of force (Cook, 1982; Kleck & McElRath, 1991; Meithe & Sousa, 2010). Second, offenders armed with firearms may be less likely to hit their victims when attempting an attack (Kleck & McElRath, 1991; Wells & Horney, 2002). We also anticipate that offenders who are heavily armed will be more likely to inflict a serious injury (defined as hospitalization) on their victims than offenders who are less heavily armed. This hypothesis is based primarily on the findings reported by Wells and Horney (2002), as well as on victimization data analyzed by Wilson and Sherman (1961), Zimring (1968), and Cook (1982).

Given that both of the dependent variables in the analysis are dichotomies, we will estimate two logit models for each outcome variable. The first model predicts the outcomes using a random-effects logit, while the second predicts the outcomes using a fixed-effects logit. Random- and fixed-effects models are two methods of analyzing panel data that effectively control for unobserved explanatory variables in samples with repeated observations of sample members (Petersen, 2004). Although similar in this respect, random- and fixed-effects models make different assumptions about unobserved variables, and correspondingly have different advantages and disadvantages. The random-effects model assumes that the unobserved variables, or error terms, are uncorrelated with the observed explanatory variables (Petersen, 2004; Wooldridge, 2002). This is a strong assumption, one that is not always appropriate, making this a primary disadvantage of the random-effects approach (Petersen, 1993, 2004). The fixed-effects model, on the other hand, makes no assumptions about the correlation between the unobserved and observed variables, but simply allows there to be a correlation and controls for all unmeasured variables in the model (Petersen, 2004; Wooldridge, 2002), which is a significant advantage (Petersen, 1993, 2004). The fixed-effects model can control for unmeasured effects, but also has limitations. This model can only estimate the effects of variables that change over time and it uses the data inefficiently because individuals who do not vary over time on the observed variables are excluded from the model (Petersen, 1993, 2004).[8] The random-effects model does not control for unmeasured effects, so it has the advantages of being able to estimate the effects of both time-variant and time-constant variables and use data from all individuals, even those who do not vary on the outcome over time, making it more efficient (Petersen 1993, 2004).

The previous discussion is not meant to suggest that one method is superior to the other. In fact, as Petersen (2004) notes, these two models are merely "different ways of describing the data, each yielding relevant insight in its own right" (p. 334). Both methods have their advantages and uniquely contribute to examining the above hypotheses. The random-effects analysis uses the data more efficiently and allows us to assess the impact of time-constant offender characteristics on our outcomes. The fixed-effect analysis controls for all unmeasured variables and, rather than focusing on between-person effects like the random-effects model, allows us to examine how within-person change over time affects our outcomes (Petersen, 2004). Put more simply, the fixed-effects analysis compares offenders to themselves and will tell us how the outcome of an assault changes when the type of weapon used by an individual changes across assaults.

Results

Table 7.2 presents the equations for the random-effects logit models predicting injury and hospitalization during an assault.[9] As noted earlier, in addition to being more efficient, the random-effects model also allows one to examine whether unchanging (i.e., time-stable) personality characteristics affect the outcome because it focuses on between-person effects, rather than within-person effects. This was useful for our purposes because we are attempting to separate out weapon-effects from person-effects. Specifically, we wanted to determine whether offender characteristics predict injury during an assault (i.e., a type of person effect), and whether weapon use predicts injury during an assault (i.e., a weapon instrumentality effect), or both.

Column 2 in Table 7.2 displays the equation predicting whether or not an injury occurred during an assault. The time-stable predictors, sex, race, and low self-control, do not significantly predict injury. One time-variant offender characteristic, gang membership, significantly predicts injury. The odds of an assault resulting in injury are over two times higher for gang-affiliated offenders than non-gang members. This relationship is expected given the evidence that gang members commit more crime while belonging to a gang and are more likely to carry weapons (Thornberry et al., 2003).

There also is an effect of weapon-type on injury. Offenders who use a club have an odds of inflicting injury that is nearly four and a half times higher than offenders who use no weapon. This effect is stronger than that of gang membership. In contrast, the other, more serious, weapon types (i.e., gun, knife) do not significantly predict injury. Importantly, this effect remains significant when comparing the coefficient for offenders who use clubs to the coefficients for offenders who use guns ($p=.04$) and who use knives ($p=.009$). Even compared to more serious weapons, clubs induce more injury.[10]

Table 7.2. Random-effects Logit Models

	Injury			Hospitalization		
	b	SE	Odds	b	SE	Odds
Male	.34	.24	1.40	.44	.34	1.55
African-American	−.25	.28	.78	−.61	.34	.54
Hispanic	−.32	.35	.73	−.59	.44	.55
Low Self-Control	.22	.22	1.25	−.28	.28	.76
Age	−.12	.08	.89	.09	.10	1.09
Live with Both Parents	−.00	.21	1.00	−.77	.31	.46*
Drug Use	.30	.21	1.35	.31	.24	1.36
Gang Membership	.81	.25	2.25***	1.00	.25	2.72***
Peer Gun Ownership	.33	.18	1.39	.65	.25	1.92**
Gun	−.04	.54	.96	2.10	.55	8.17***
Knife	−.26	.45	.77	−.36	.58	.70
Club	1.46	.50	4.31**	.28	.37	1.32
Street Weapon	.24	.88	1.27	.86	.77	2.36
Overall χ^2		36.84***			60.91***	
N		904			878	

* p<.05 **p<.01 ***p<.001

Similar to the injury model, time-stable offender characteristics do not predict hospitalization, but gang membership does. Gang members have nearly three times higher odds of inducing a hospitalization compared to non-gang members. Apparently, gang members are serious about their assaults. Unlike the injury model, however, two additional time-variant offender variables significantly predicted hospitalization: living with both biological parents and having peers who own guns. The odds of inflicting a serious injury resulting in hospitalization were cut in half for offenders living with both biological parents at the time of the assault. It seems that an intact family can buffer the seriousness of an assault, which is good news for those living in intact families. Conversely, outside the home, associating with peers who own guns also results in odds of hospitalization from an assault that are two times higher than associating with peers who are not gun owners. Perhaps peer gun ownership provides a signal to offenders that the use of excessive violence during an assault is acceptable. In essence, travelling in a dangerous world requires aggressive physical responses.

Although more of the offender characteristics predict hospitalization than injury, the largest effect on the odds of hospitalization comes from the type of weapon used during the assault. Using a club predicts injury, but it does not predict hospitalization. The only weapon type that has a significant impact on hospitalization is a gun. The odds of inflicting a serious injury resulting in hospitalization is over eight times higher for offenders who use a gun than those who use no weapon during an assault. Moreover, this effect continues to be significant when comparing the coefficient for gun to knife ($p=.001$) and gun to club ($p=.005$).[11]

To summarize the results thus far, it appears that fixed individual characteristics such as gender, race/ethnicity, self-control, and age have little impact on injury and hospitalization. Offender characteristics that are variable over time such as living with both parents, gang membership, and peer gun ownership, along with weapon instrumentality effects, do influence injury and hospitalization. In addition, the results support our assertion that the extent of injury will vary depending on the type of weapon used during the assault. Specifically, we hypothesized that offenders who are less heavily armed during an assault, such as those using a club, would be more likely to inflict injury, but that offenders who are more heavily armed, such as those using a gun, would be more likely to inflict serious injury resulting in hospitalization. The results support this contention. The results do not support our contention that the use of a gun during an assault will reduce the likelihood of injury or that the use of a lesser weapon would decrease the odds of hospitalization. We find no significant effect of using a gun on injury, which is in contrast with previous research that relied on an offender based sample (i.e., Wells & Horney, 2002).

Although we controlled for several offender characteristics in the random-effects model it is conceivable that offender characteristics are still operating to predict injury and we simply did not capture this in the included measures. In other words, it is possible that some unmeasured offender characteristic predicts the type of weapon used by the offender, and what appears to be a direct effect of weapon type on injury and hospitalization is actually an indirect effect of this unmeasured variable. To investigate this issue further, we estimated fixed-effects logit models, which control for any unmeasured personal characteristics that could be influencing our outcomes. Essentially, this method allows us to compare the outcome of an assault within individuals. For example, we can determine the outcome of assaults for offenders when they use a knife, compared to the outcome for those same offenders when they use a gun, compared to the outcome for those same offenders when they use no weapon. This removes all person-effects from the model because we are comparing injury outcome within-individuals, but across weapon types. The equations predicting injury and hospitalization are presented in Table 7.3.

Controlling for all unmeasured person-effects, both gang membership and using a club during an assault continue to predict injury. As Table 7.3 demonstrates (column 2), both effect sizes are comparable to those in the random-effects model but the interpretation is slightly different. The odds of an offender injuring their victim while they are a gang member is over two times higher than the odds of injury being inflicted by that same person while he/she is not a current gang member. The gang provides a context where injuring a victim is more likely, regardless of the type of person or the type of weapon used during an assault. Despite controlling for all unmeasured offender characteristics, a strong weapon instrumentality effect remains. When offenders use clubs during assaults they have nearly four times the odds of injuring their victims compared to assaults where those same offenders use no weapons. In this analysis. the coefficient for club did not significantly differ from the coefficients for gun or knife, but this could be a function of the smaller sample size: both tests were significant at the .10 level.

Table 7.3. Fixed-effects Logit Models

	Injury			Hospitalization		
	b	SE	Odds	b	SE	Odds
Age	−.06	.13	.94	.18	.17	1.20
Live with Both Parents	−.42	.57	.66	−.90	.72	.41
Drug Use	−.12	.33	.89	−.02	.35	.98
Gang Membership	.76	.38	2.14*	.49	.38	1.63
Peer Gun Ownership	−.21	.28	.81	.09	.33	1.09
Gun	−.20	.73	.82	2.27	.86	9.68**
Knife	−.22	.58	.80	.10	.70	1.11
Club	1.36	.58	3.90*	−.21	.40	.81
Street Weapon	−.54	1.08	.58	1.36	1.28	3.90
Overall χ²		13.83			17.26*	
N		380			301	

* p<.05 **p<.01 ***p<.001

The same variables predict injury in the random- and fixed-effects models, but not for hospitalization. Controlling for unmeasured person-effects, only weapon type continues to predict whether an assault resulted in hospitalization. The odds of hospitalization is nearly ten times higher for offenders when they use a gun compared to those same offenders assaulting someone without using a weapon. This odds ratio is even higher than in the random-effects model, and equates to an almost 900 percent increase in the odds of hospitalization. Moreover, this effect is still significant when comparing the gun coefficient to knife (p=.039) and club (p=.009). Guns cause more hospitalizations than no weapon. using a knife. or using a club. It is interesting that the effects of living with both parents, gang membership. and peer gun ownership disappear when one holds constant offender factors. When one examines the between person-effects. these variables appear to have an effect on the odds of hospitalization. but when one compares offenders to themselves. changes in their family structure, gang member status, and associations with gun-owning peers do not affect the odds of seriously injuring their victims.

Specifically, when comparing individuals to themselves in the fixed-effects models we only find one non-weapon effect—being in a gang increases injury in assaults compared to when the same subjects are not in gangs—while there are weapon instrumentality effects for both injury and hospitalization.[12] By comparison, the random-effects models that compare subjects to each other show several non-weapon effects of peer gun ownership, gang membership, and family structure on hospitalization. We take this to mean that subjects who possess these attributes do so in a more stable way that impacts their seriously injuring others. It also is worth noting that prior research has shown that knives produce more injury than guns. We find that knives and guns produce no more injury than no weapon at all. Rather, clubs are more likely to produce injury compared to assaults involving no weapon. Perhaps these findings speak to the intent of these adolescents. Young offenders who carry knives may not be motivated to use them. Gun carriers may also lack the motivation and intent to use the gun during an assault, except when they do use them the result is disastrous.

Discussion

This study investigated how the type of weapon used during an assault affects the injury outcome for the victim. We built on the work of Wells and Horney (2002) by examining whether a weapon instrumentality effect exists in a community-based sample of high-risk adolescents (as opposed to a sample of convicted offenders), and by classifying weapons into more specific categories than "no weapon," "gun," or "other weapon." In addition to investigating whether weapon instrumentality effects, offender characteristics, or both, predict the injury outcome of an assault, we tested the hypothesis that heavily armed offenders are less likely to inflict injury, but more likely to inflict serious injury, while less heavily armed offenders are more likely to inflict injury, but less likely to inflict serious injury.

The findings of this study suggest that both offender characteristics and weapon instrumentality effects influence whether an assault results in an injury or hospitalization. Across offenders in our sample, being a gang member increases the odds that a victim will be injured or hospitalized, while associating with gun-owning peers increases the odds that a victim will be hospitalized. Within offenders, the odds of injuring a victim continue to be significantly higher during periods of active gang membership compared to periods of non-gang activity.

A few of our offender-related variables predict injury and hospitalization, but the type of weapon used during assaults has a stronger effect than any offender characteristic. Current gang members have two to three times higher odds of injuring or hospitalizing their victims than non-gang members. The odds of offenders injuring their victims when using a clubs or blunt instruments is nearly four and a half times the odds of offenders who use no weapon, and is about four times the odds relative to instances where they themselves use no weapon. The results for hospitalization are even more obvious. The odds of gun-wielding offenders hospitalizing their victims are over eight times greater than the odds of offenders who use no weapon. When offenders use guns, the odds of hospitalizing the victims are almost ten times greater relative to that same offenders carrying out the attacks with no weapon.

A second focus of this study was to determine whether different weapons have different effects on injury and hospitalization. We anticipated that offenders armed with guns would be less likely to injure, but more likely to hospitalize (i.e., seriously injure) their victims, while less heavily armed offenders would be more likely to injure but less likely to seriously injure their victims. We found partial support for these hypotheses. First, less heavily armed offenders, specifically those using clubs or blunt objects, were significantly more likely to injure their victims than unarmed offenders, and in the random-effects model, significantly more likely to injure their victims than offenders armed with guns or knives. It is possible (although we have no method of confirming this) that the victim played a role in this effect. For example, the victim may see a club or blunt object as a non-deadly weapon and consequently be more likely to escalate the situation, and in turn increase their risk of injury. Second, heavily armed offenders, namely those carrying guns, were significantly more likely to hospitalize their victims than unarmed offenders or offenders using knives or clubs.

These results are consistent with the findings of Wells and Horney (2002) (also see Cook, 1982; Kleck, 1997; Wilson & Sherman, 1961; Zimring, 1968), although the magnitude of our effects differs in some respects. First, we find a stronger effect for the increased victim injury for offenders using clubs than they did for offenders using weapons other than a gun. This could be because we separate out the other weapons, so the null effects of knife or street weapon use being combined with clubs/blunt objects could be reducing the overall magnitude of their other weapon effect. In addition, Wells and Horney's (2002) odds ratio for the effect of gun use on hospitalization was over 60: substantially higher than our finding of nearly ten. This could be due in part to the difference in our samples. They used a sample of incarcerated male offenders, while we used a community sample of adolescents. It is plausible that their sample contained more seasoned offenders, who were more likely to actually hit their victims when firing a gun, thus leading to substantially higher odds of hospitalization.

Our study, however, does not find support for the hypothesis that using a gun during an assault reduces the likelihood of an injury, or that using a lesser weapon reduces the likelihood of hospitalization. This is in contrast to previous research showing that the presence of a gun can actually reduce injury (Cook, 1982; Kleck & McElRath, 1991; Meithe & Sousa, 2010; Tark & Kleck, 2004; Wells & Horney, 2002). The significance of this finding is unclear, but the discrepancy again may be due to our sample. Perhaps these youthful, inexperienced offenders do not fully realize the power that wielding a gun can have in terms of ensuring victim compliance. Somewhat related, it is possible that many of these assaults were unplanned; thus, the offender did not bring the weapon into the assault with the intention of robbing the victim, meaning there was no intent to control the victim with a weapon.[13]

One thing is clear from our findings: decreasing the availability of firearms to adolescents has the potential to have a substantial impact on reducing the amount of serious injury inflicted during assaults. The effect size of gun presence on hospitalization is substantial, and is far stronger than any effects of offender-related characteristics. Moreover, the notion that the presence of a gun may reduce the likelihood of injury during an assault does not hold for our sample. Therefore, not only does the presence of a gun not prove beneficial in terms of limiting injury, but it is also extremely detrimental in terms of the seriousness of any injury that does occur.

This study makes a few important contributions to the literature. First, we confirm that there is a strong weapon instrumentality effect at work in this community sample of high-risk adolescents. Comparing across offenders, and comparing offenders to themselves, we find that weapon use during an assault had stronger effects on injury and hospitalization than any offender variable. Moreover, the weapon effect varied depending on the type of weapon. Specifically, youth who use clubs/blunt objects are significantly more likely to injure their victims, while adolescents who use guns are significantly more likely to hospitalize their victims. This is consistent with other research; but, in contrast to previous research we do not find that using a gun reduces the likelihood of injury in our sample. The weapon effects are stronger than offender characteristics, but one offender-related variable stands out as important in influencing injury. Gang members are more likely to injure their victims during an assault than non-gang members, and this finding holds true even when we compare offenders during periods of gang activity to themselves during periods of non-gang activity. Interestingly, when comparing offenders to themselves, the odds that a victim will be hospitalized is no different for current gang members than the odds for non-gang members. Clearly, the gang fosters the use of violence in an assault, but it does not necessarily affect the seriousness of injury that results.

We controlled for several offender characteristics in this analysis, but unfortunately were unable to account for offender intentions or for differing stages of the assault. This is a limitation as other research has demonstrated that offender intent significantly predicts injury outcome, and that examining the process of the assault incident matters (Tark & Kleck, 2004; Wells & Horney, 2002). It would be very informative if future research could incorporate these two factors into an investigation of weapon instrumentality in a community context. In addition, extending the time frame to include both adolescents and adults would be ideal.

Acknowledgments

Support for the Rochester Youth Development Study has been provided by the Office of Juvenile Justice and Delinquency Prevention (86-JN-CX-0007), the National Institute on Drug Abuse (DA005512), and the National Science Foundation (SBR-9123299, SES-9123299). Work on this project was also aided by grants to the Center for Social and Demographic Analysis at the University at Albany from NICHD (P30-HD32041) and NSF (SBR-9512290). We thank Robert Apel for helpful comments on an earlier draft of this paper and Elle Teshima for clerical assistance with the final draft.

Correspondence concerning this article should be addressed to Christopher A. Kierkus, School of Criminal Justice, Grand Valley State University, Grand Rapids, MI 49504. Email: kierkusc@gvsu.edu

Notes

1. These incidents are contributed by a total of 439 unique offenders. The highest number of incidents contributed by any one offender is ten, the mean is 2.2, and the standard deviation is 1.4.
2. This includes the following specified other weapons: pen.
3. This includes the following specified other weapons: synthesizer, chair, brass knuckles, household items, skateboard, padlock, and hammer.
4. Specified other weapons coded as missing include ring, dog, car, and mace.
5. The question is worded such that it asks about injury to the assault victim, as opposed to a bystander or person otherwise not involved in the incident
6. This includes situations such as the following: broken bones, broken nose, stitches, knocked teeth out, concussion, internal bleeding, being shot, being killed, and being paralyzed.
7. The following specified situations were coded as missing: shot them (because it was classified a non-weapon assault), mace, hit with object, threw bottle, just threatened (because it was classified a weapon assault), bit them, showed weapon to scare (because it was classified a weapon assault), and kicked were coded as missing.
8. This is because the equation for the model includes a dummy variable for each individual, thus controlling for all time-invariant characteristics of that individual (see Petersen, 2004 for a more detailed discussion).
9. Note that in the hospitalization analysis, we present results including assaults that do not result in injury. In supplemental analyses, we restricted the analysis to cases that resulted in injury and the results are substantively similar but with larger odds ratios.
10. The test between the club and street weapon coefficient was not significant, but this is likely because such a small portion of the sample reported using a street weapon (<2 percent).
11. Again, the coefficient did not significantly differ from that of street weapon users.
12. Note that in the hospitalization models, the comparison group included both no injury and less serious injury assaults. To see if the weapon instrumentality effect of guns held, we estimated two additional models: one comparing hospitalizations only to less serious injuries and one comparing hospitalization only to no injuries. Guns continued to produce significantly more hospitalization when compared only to subjects who have

been injured in both the random- and fixed-effects models. There was no significant effect for gun assaults when the comparison group was no injury, suggesting that gun assaults are no more or less likely to result in serious injury than no injury compared to no weapon assaults.

13. We attempted to explore this further by examining the effect of weapon use on injury outcome in the context of a robbery. Unfortunately there were too few reported robberies in our sample across Waves 4 to 9 (n=22).

References

Bankston, W. B., & Thompson. C. Y. (1989). Carrying firearms for protection: A causal model. *Sociological Inquiry.* 59(1). 75–87.

Bjerregaard. B., & Lizotte. A. J. (1995). Gun ownership and gang membership. *Journal of Criminal Law and Criminology.* 86, 37–58.

Block. R. (1977). *Violent crime.* Lexington. MA: Lexington Books.

Cao. L., Cullen. F. T., & Link. B. G. (1997). The social determinants of gun ownership: Self-protection in an urban environment. *Criminology.* 35(4), 629–657.

Cook, P. J. (1980). Reducing injury and death rates in robbery. *Policy Analysis. (winter).* 21–45.

Cook. P. J. (1982). The role of firearms in violent crime. In M.E. Wolfgang, & N. A. Weiner (eds.), *Criminal violence* (pp. 236–289). Newbury Park. CA: Sage.

Cook. P. J. (1987). Robbery Violence. *The Journal of Criminal Law and Criminology.* 78(2). 357–376.

Cook. P. J. (1991). The technology of personal violence. In M. Tonry (ed.), *Crime and Justice: A Review of Research* (pp. 1–72). Chicago. IL: University of Chicago Press.

Cook. P. J., & Nagin. D. (1979). *Does the weapon matter?* Washington. DC: Institute for Law and Social Research.

Free. M. D., Jr.   (1991). Clarifying the relationship between the broken home and juvenile delinquency: A critique of the current literature. *Deviant Behavior. 12*(2). 109–167.

Gottfredson. M. R., & Hirschi. T. (1990). *A general theory of crime.* Palo Alto. CA: Stanford University Press.

Hindelang. M. J. (1976). *Criminal victimization in eight American cities.* Cambridge. MA: Ballinger.

Kierkus, C. A. (2002). Do guns make robberies more deadly? An analysis of the impact of weapons on the lethality of weapons related homicide. Presidential paper from the *American Society of Criminology Annual Meeting.* 2002.

Kierkus, C. A., & Baer. D. (2002). A social control explanation of the relationship between family structure and delinquent behaviour. *Canadian Journal of Criminology.* 44(4). 425–458.

King, J. W. (1987). Situational factors and the escalation of criminal violence. Paper presented at the *Annual Meeting of the ASC.* Montreal. Canada.

Kingery, P. M., Biafora. F. A., & Zimmerman. R. S. (1996). Risk factors for violent behaviors among ethnically diverse adolescents: Beyond race/ethnicity. *School Psychology International. 17*(2). 171–186.

Kleck. G. (1986). Evidence that Saturday night specials not very important for crime. *Sociology and Social Research. 70.* 303–307.

Kleck, G. (1997). *Targeting guns: Firearms and their control.* New York. NY: Aldine de Gruyter.

Kleck, G., & McElRath, K. (1991). The effects of weaponry on human violence. *Social Forces, 69*, 669–692.

Kulig, J., Valentine, J., Griffith, J., & Ruthhazer, R. (1998). Predictive model of weapon carrying among urban high school students: Results and validation. *Journal of Adolescent Health, 22*(4), 312–319.

Lizotte, A. J., Howard, G. J., Krohn, M. D., & Thornberry, T. P. (1997). Patterns of illegal gun carrying among young urban males. *Valparaiso University Law Review, 31*(2), 375–393.

Lizotte, A. J., Krohn, M. D., Howell, J. C., Tobin, K., & Howard, G. J. (2000). Factors influencing gun carrying among young urban males over the adolescent-young adult life course. *Criminology, 38*(3), 811–834.

Lizotte, A. J., & Sheppard, D. (2001). *Gun use by male juveniles: Research and prevention.* U.S. Department of Justice, Office of Justice Programs, Office of Juvenile Justice and Delinquency Prevention.

Luckenbill, D. F. (1982). Compliance under threat of severe punishment. *Social Forces, 60*, 811–825.

Miethe, T. D., & Sousa, W. H. (2010). Carjacking and its consequences: A situational analysis of risk factors for differential outcomes. *Security Journal, 23*(4), 241–258.

Melde, C., & Rennison, C. M. (2008). The effect of gang perpetrated crime on the likelihood of non-lethal victim injury. *American Journal of Criminal Justice, 33*(2), 234–251.

Newton, G. D., & Zimring, F. E. (1969). *Firearms and violence in American life. A staff report to the National Commission on the Causes and Prevention of Violence.* Washington, DC. Government Printing Office.

Petersen, T. (1993). Recent advances in Longitudinal Methodology. *Annual Review of Sociology, 19*, 425–454.

Petersen, T. (2004). Analyzing panel data: Fixed- and random-effects models. In M. Hardy & A. Bryman (eds.), *Handbook of Data Analysis* (pp. 331–345). London: SAGE Publications.

Safarik, M. E., & Jarvis, J. P. (2005). Examining attributes of homicides: Toward quantifying qualitative values of injury severity. *Homicide Studies, 9*, 183–203.

Skogan, W. (1978). *Weaponry use in robbery: Patterns and policy implications.* Evanston, IL: Northwestern University, Center for Urban Affairs.

Tark, J., & Kleck, G. (2004). Resisting crime: The effects of victim action on the outcomes of crimes. *Criminology, 42*(4), 861–909.

Thornberry, T. P., Krohn, M. D., Lizotte, A. J., Smith, C. A., & Tobin, K. (2003). *Gangs and delinquency in developmental perspective.* New York, NY: Cambridge University Press.

U.S. Bureau of Justice Statistics. (1986). *The Use of Weapons in Committing Crimes.* Washington, DC: Special Report. U.S. Government Printing Office.

Wells, W., & Horney, J. (2002). Weapons effects and individual intent to do harm: Influences on the escalation of violence. *Criminology, 40*(2), 265–296.

Wilson, H., & Sherman, R. (1961). Civilian penetrating wounds of the abdomen. *Annals of Surgery, 153*, 639–649.

Wooldridge, J. M. (2002). *Econometric Analysis of Cross Section and Panel Data.* Cambridge, MA: The MIT Press.

Zimring, F. E. (1968). Is gun control likely to reduce violent killings? *University of Chicago Law Review, 35*, 721–737.

Zimring, F. E. (1972). The medium is the message: Firearm caliber as a determinant of death from assault. *Journal of Legal Studies, 1*(1), 97–124.

Chapter Eight

No Help in Sight: The Impact of Trauma Center Closures on Gun Violence Survival

Noam Ostrander and Anna Johnson

Introduction

The prevalence of firearms among the US civilian population is notoriously high. There are almost as many guns (294 million) (United States Department of Justice Bureau of Alcohol, Tobacco, Firearms, and Explosives, 2011) as people (308 million) (US Census Bureau, 2012), though the proportion of households with guns appears to be dropping and ownership varies by region and with urban-rural demographics (Brennan, 2012).

Firearms are the most common weapon used in violent crimes. Firearms are especially dominant in homicide statistics. In 1993, the rate of firearm-related homicide murders was 6.6/100,000. This rate dwindled to 3.3/100,000 in 2009. However, firearms account for an increasing percentage of homicides—69.6 percent in 1993 versus 73.7 percent in 2009. Additionally, based on the National Vital Statistics Report data on deaths in United States during 2009, nearly 20,000 people use firearms every year to commit suicide. When those individuals are included in the numbers, more than 60,000 US citizens were killed or injured due to firearms in 2009. These numbers have increased in the past few years. In 2013, the Centers for Disease Control and Prevention estimated that more than 100,000 Americans suffer gunshot wounds each year: over 31,000 die and over 73,000 are treated in hospital for non-fatal firearm injuries (CDC, 2013). The majority of homicides (68 percent) are still committed with guns, and most of these victims are male (85 percent in gun homicides and 90 percent in gun assaults). Victimization rates are considerably elevated for minority groups such as African-Americans and Hispanics.

While high profile, mass shootings like the ones at Sandy Hook Elementary and the Aurora, Colorado movie theater draw considerable public attention, shootings in impoverished urban areas remain a significant location for gun violence in the United States. This chapter will not focus on the reasons for that difference. Rather, the attention in this chapter will look at the inner city shootings and the closures of trauma centers that would have treated the victims of these shootings. To situate this chapter, Chicago's gun violence from 2012 will be utilized for a case study. Following that case study, national trends in trauma center closures will be detailed. Finally, this chapter will consider the consequences of these closures.

Chicago: 2012 Murder Capital of the US

Over the past few years, Chicago has been in the spotlight for a re-framing of gun violence as a public health hazard in the United States. In 2012, Chicago led the nation with 506, which was a 16 percent increase from the previous year (New York Times, 2013; Chicago Police Department, 2012). This increase might represent a particular spike for 2012, in a trend that has been lower than the early 2000s.

Figure 8.1. Chicago Homicide Numbers 2003–2012

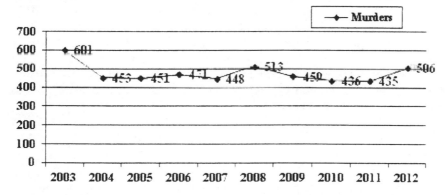

Of those 506 murders, approximately, 87 percent were due to firearms (Washington Monthly, 2012). In total, more than 2,000 people were shot in Chicago during 2012 (Bloomberg, 2013). These staggering numbers led the media to label Chicago as murder capital of the United States in 2012, with many media outlets noting the greater number of shooting deaths in Chicago than the US military deaths in Afghanistan, which was an active war zone in 2012. In examining the demographic profile of individuals who are victims and perpetrators of gun violence in Chicago, a similarity emerges.

Table 8.1. Demographic Characteristics of Murder Victims and Perpetrators in
Chicago, 2011 (Chicago Police Department, 2012)

	Victims	Perpetrators
Gender	Male: 90.1%	Male: 88.4%
Age	Mode: 20-23	Mode: 17-18
Race	African American: 75.3	African American: 70.5%
Ethnicity	Hispanic/Latino: 18.9%	Hispanic/Latino: 24.3%
Prior Arrest Record	76.9%	87.3%

In a side by side comparison, the demographic profiles of victims and perpetrators are nearly identical. This comparison is important as it highlights the reality that often the victims have been perpetrators of violent crimes, and perhaps even homicides. In many instances, shootings in Chicago are often followed by retaliatory shootings across gang lines. In these cases, a perpetrator of a shooting may quickly become the victim of a shooting.

While the cost in terms of lives lost, personal and community trauma is difficult to fathom, researchers at the University of Chicago have tried to calculate the total cost of these shootings. The estimated cost per year for gun violence in Chicago averages approximately $2.5 billion per year, or $2,500 per household in Chicago (Adler et al., 2009). Nationally, the average cost of gun violence is $100 billion, which equals roughly the salary for 2 million police officers (Bloomberg, 2013). While these figures take into account the public cost for police officer salaries, acute emergency care, and rehabilitation for people with gunshot wounds, it does not account for the money lost through business closures or lost potential revenue for victims and survivors. Additionally, it does not account for the terror among residents who live in high crime neighborhoods, nor does it account for the children kept in doors to protect them from violence.

Trauma Centers

Hospitals in the United States often have trauma centers that are ranked for one through five depending on their capacity to offer intensive care for acute injuries. Level 1 trauma centers maintain the highest level of surgical care at any time of the day, while Level 5 trauma centers usually stabilize, evaluate, and transfer trauma victims to a higher level trauma center. Gunshot injuries and other serious traumatic injuries in the United States are typically taken to Level 1 trauma centres (Cook, Lawrence, Ludwig, and Miller, 1999). These are hospitals that are equipped to provide the highest level of emergency care to individuals with traumatic injuries like gunshots. Provided they have available capacity, these hospitals must treat any individual who comes in with traumatic injuries. Because many of these patients are indigent and lack financial means to pay for their care, trauma centres often lose money treating patients with traumatic injuries. Many patients injured by gun violence are uninsured, indigent, and cannot pay for their care, so taxpayers ultimately cover much of the cost of their hospital treatment.

Figure 8.2. National Trauma Center Reimbursement Profile (Trauma Center Association of America, 2013)

National Trauma Center Reimbursement Profile

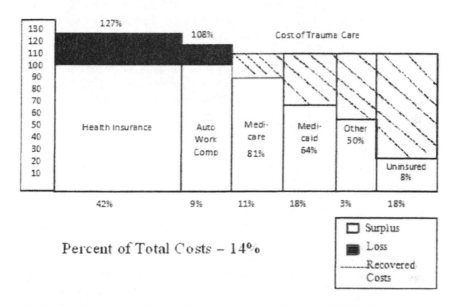

Percent of Total Costs – 14%

As Figure 8.2 illustrates, trauma centers that provide care to a high mix of patients who are uninsured or have Medicaid or Medicare coverage, often lose money providing these services. These patients create a heavy financial burden on trauma centers and municipalities (Cook, Lawrence, Ludwig, and Miller, 1999). Furthermore, even when patients are covered under Medicaid, there is often a significant delay between the time of care and the payment for services from the state. As an extreme example, Maine hospitals currently have up to a three year wait to receive reimbursements for treating Medicaid patients (Levitz and Radnofsky, 2013). This long delay in payment may compromise the financial health of the hospital providing care to survivors of gun violence and other traumatic injuries. In Chicago in 2011, 670 patients were treated for gun injuries in Cook County hospitals at an average cost of $52,000 per patient. This translates into approximately $34 million per year at the taxpayers' expense for acute care. In addition to the acute care, survivors of gun violence may need significant rehabilitation. The average health costs in the first year of a traumatic spinal cord injury range from $311,000 to $953,000 (DeVivo, Chen, Mennemeyer, and Deutsch, 2011). Again, this cost is often at the public expense.

Hospitals across the country have responded to the unreimbursed cost of treating such injuries by closing their trauma units. For example, the University of Chicago Medical Center closed its trauma center in 1988, which left many residents on the south side of Chicago, where many shootings occur, approximately 5 miles away from the nearest trauma center. This response is not uncommon among urban trauma centers that serve blighted areas. Between 2001 and 2007, more than 69 million citizens lost geographical access to a trauma center. Sixteen million needed to travel more than 30 minutes to find a trauma hospital, which is particularly serious when timely treatment can make a significant difference between level of impairment, life, and death (Yuen-Jan Hsia and Shen, 2011). These closures have created what Crandall and her colleagues (2013) call "trauma deserts."

Most often, these closures directly affected residents of impoverished urban communities, where violence is more common than other area. Additionally, with fewer trauma centers in a region, the remaining trauma centers may become overwhelmed with individuals needing urgent care for life-threatening injuries. These closures have mainly affected residents of impoverished urban communities, where much gun violence occurs. In those facilities that have remained open, patients are staying fewer days due to cost-cutting measures (Kroll, 2008).

While trauma centers are closing in urban areas, the US is experiencing a boom in trauma centers opening overall. The vast majority of these new trauma centers are operating in suburban communities. In these communities, traumatic injuries are more likely the result of automobile accidents, and individuals who are admitted often have health and car insurance to cover the high costs of care (Kaiser, 2012). In these situations, the traditional notion of trauma centers operating at a financial loss is turned into a profit generating unit for hospitals. This disparity between the profit-generating trauma centers in the suburbs and a profit-losing trauma centers in urban areas is likely to be exacerbated in the next 5-10 years as Medicare and Medicaid programs are cut by $556 billion and $12 billion, respectively (Budget OoMa, 2008; Rudowitz, 2008).

Returning to Chicago

Chicago again provides an example of the effect of Level 1 trauma center closures. For many years, the vast majority of shootings in the city were concentrated in the west and south sides of the city. In the south side of Cook County, there has not been a Level 1 trauma center since 1988 when the University of Chicago Medical Center (UCMC) closed its Level 1 trauma center. The UCMC closure resulted in a trauma desert on the south side of the city. As an aside, UCMC maintains a pediatric Level 1 trauma center, but has restricted its services to youth who are 15 years old and younger. For the purposes of gun violence in Chicago, many of the victims, while still younger than 18 years old, are still too old to be cared for at that trauma center. The only other Level 1 trauma center near the south side of Chicago is Advocate Crist Medical Center, which is located outside of Cook County, but still in a nearby suburb. This medical center has seen a spike in trauma patients going from 380 in 2007 to 1002 in 2012. While this increase cannot be linked directly to the closure of the University of Chicago Medical Center's trauma center, it might represent the stress that falls on other Level I trauma centers in the area to treat seriously wounded individuals. Compared to the south side, the west side of Chicago, has three Level I trauma centers with John H. Stroger, JR Hospital of Cook County, Mount Sinai, and Loyola University Medical Center, which is just outside the Cook County limits.

Aside from the need for other Level I trauma centers to serve more patients when a hospital decides to close their trauma unit, transportation times from the scene of a shooting to the trauma center may also be affected. The Illinois Department of Public Health tracks average travel times by zip code throughout the state. Within Chicago, the areas most affected by gun violence also have longer travel times from the scene of the shooting to a Level I trauma center. The longest average run time is in the far south at 24 minutes, while the shortest run time is in the east, more affluent area, at seven minutes. For context, the professional standard for ambulance run times in Chicago is 20 minutes. It should be noted that these times track ambulance times once they have picked up the wounded individual until they arrive at the hospital. For scenes where a shooting has occurred, these times may be further delayed if there is still a danger of additional shootings present on the scene. Unfortunately, data does not exist to demonstrate how the travel times have changed since the closure of the University of Chicago Medical Center's trauma center.

Crandall and her colleagues (2013) drove home the significance of travel time in their analysis of the Illinois State Trauma Registry data from 1999–2009. Based on that analysis, gunshot victims who were shot within five miles of a Level I trauma center had a crude mortality rate of 6.42. For individuals who were shot more than five miles from a Level I trauma center, their crude mortality rate was 8.73. This translates into approximately 6.3 additional deaths a year, just based on expanded travel times. The example that Chicago provides is utilized in order to underscore the points that closures of Level I trauma centers increases the amount of time people with serious injuries must wait before they receive medical care, and creates greater stress on the trauma network within a geographic area.

A Way Forward

In the financial context of inner-city hospitals losing money through level one trauma centers, the question emerges of how to address the problem. At the current time, it is unclear how the Affordable Care Act (ACA) implementation might have an impact. However, it seems unlikely that the ACA will reach members of the population discussed in this chapter. Indeed, many of the victims of gun violence might qualify already for Medicaid, but have yet to sign up for the program. For those who make too much money to qualify for Medicaid or its expansion, it also seems unlikely that they would buy health insurance despite the penalty that is attached to not having insurance. If this is true, then a large portion of trauma care provided to inner city victims of gun violence would still come at the public expense and be a financial loss for the treating hospital.

Avenues to support hospitals providing trauma care have three main courses. First, at the state level, Medicaid reimbursement times must be reduced. As noted above, many states wait many months before the services they provide to patients covered under Medicaid. This long delay in payments causes hospitals with a high Medicaid patient mix additional financial stress. Second, Medicaid reimbursement amounts must be increased. This avenue comes with many challenges. As states have been hit hard with the recent financial downturns, many do not have the means to increase funding to Medicaid. As an example of that, some states have opted out of the ACA Medicaid expansion because they lack the needed funds to cover more of their citizen. This opt out is particularly striking because the federal government would provide 90 percent of the addition funds needed. Thus, the states that have opted out of the expansion are not even able to cover 10 percent of the cost of that expansion. Because of this reality, the ACA, which was meant to provide health insurance coverage to nearly every US citizen, may still leave millions of people without coverage. Finally, level one trauma centers should receive additional stipends for providing needed care to inner city neighborhoods to offset the losses they incur, which threatens their ability to remain operational.

References

Adler, R., Cook, P., Ludwig, J., and Pollack, H. (2009). Gun violence among school-age youth in Chicago. The University of Chicago Crime Lab.

Brennan, A. (August 1, 2012) "Analysis: Fewer gun owners own more guns." CNN. Retrieved from: http://edition.cnn.com/2012/07/31/politics/gun-ownership-declining/index.html.

Budget Office of Management. (2008). Fiscal Year 2009 Budget. Washington D.DC.: US Government Printing Office.

Chicago Police Department. (2012). 2011 Chicago Murder Analysis report. https://portal.chicagopolice.org/portal/page/portal/ClearPath/News/Statistical%20Reports/Murder%20Reports/MA11.pdf

Cook, P., Lawrence, B., Ludwig, J., and Miller, T. (1999). "The medical costs of gunshot injuries in the United States." Journal of American Medical Association 282, pp. 447-454.

Crandall, M., Sharp, D., Unger, E., Straus, D., Brasel, K., Hsai, R., and Esposito, T. (2013). "Trauma deserts: Distance from a trauma center, transport times, and mortality from gunshot wounds in Chicago." American Journal of Public Health 103 (6), pp. 1103-1109.

Davey, M. (January 2, 2013). "In a soaring homicide rate, a divide in Chicago." New York Times. Retrieved from: http://www.nytimes.com/2013/01/03/us/a-soaring-homicide-rate-a-divide-in-chicago.html?pagewanted=all&_r=0

DeVivo. M.J.. Chen. Y.. Mennemeyer, S.T.. and Deutsch. A. (2011). "Costs of Care Following Spinal Cord Injury." *Topics in Spinal Cord Injury Rehabilitation* 16/4, pp. 1–9.

Geier, K. (December 30. 2012). "500 murders in Chicago in 2012: 435 caused by guns." *Washington Monthly*. Retrieved from: http://www.washingtonmonthly.com/political-animal-a/2012_12/500_murders_in_chicago_in_2012042087.php.

Jones, T. and McCormick. J. (May 22. 2013). "Chicago killings cost $2.5 billion as murders top N.Y.'s." *Bloomberg*. Retrieved from: http://www.bloomberg.com/news/2013-05-23/first-lady-s-chicago-shows-gun-toll-for-city-that-bleeds.html

Kaiser Family Foundation. (2008). *Medicaid: overview and impact of new regulation.* Washington. DC: Rudowitz R.

Kroll. T. (2008). "Rehabilitative needs of individuals with spinal cord injury resulting from gun violence: The perspective of nursing and rehabilitation professionals." *Applied Nursing Research* 21, pp. 45-49.

Krouse. W. (2011). *Gun Control Legislation* (Washington DC: Congressional Research Service).

Levitz, J. and Radnofsky. L. (January 15. 2013). "Delays in Medicaid pay vex hospitals." *The Wall Street Journal*. Retrieved from: http://online.wsj.com/news/articles/SB10001424127887324442304578234020690323296

Moore, N. (October 11. 2011). "Trauma patients on Southeast Side take more time to reach trauma centers." *National Public Radio*. Retrieved from: http://www.wbez.org/story/trauma-patients-southeast-side-take-more-time-reach-trauma-centers-93012

United States Census Bureau. (2012). *Statistical Abstract of the United States: 2012.* Available at: www.census.gov/compendia/statab/2012/tables/12s0002.pdf Accessed 20 November 2012.

United States Department of Justice Bureau of Alcohol. Tobacco. Firearms and Explosives, *Firearms commerce in the United States 2011* (Washington DC: BATF, 2011).

Yuen-Jan Hsia R. and Yu-Chu Shen. (2011). "Rising closures of hospital trauma centers disproportionately burden vulnerable populations." *Health Affairs* 30/10, pp. 1912-1920. http://www.kaiserhealthnews.org/stories/2012/september/25/trauma-centers.aspx

Chapter Nine

Gun Violence in the U.S.: A Muted Type of Terrorism?

Introduction

This is the true tragedy of culture
(as opposed to merely sad or calamitous plights):
that the forces threatening a culture arise from deep within that culture itself:
that with its destruction an inner destiny is fulfilled,
which represents the logical culmination and completion of that very structure
on which the culture's most brilliant achievements are built.

Georg Simmel

Since the September 11th attacks, the U.S. has shifted most of its attention in countering violence by investing in the *war on terrorism*. While terrorism is not a new phenomenon, it has become a main topic of public discourse, focusing mainly on international threats as well as homegrown terrorist groups. Research has categorized different types of terrorism, including political, dissident, state and religious terrorism to explain motivations behind terrorist organizations. In general, the U.S. seems to be more outraged over so-called terrorist attacks than it is with the severe intensity of gun violence and the deaths associated with it. Most of the debates over gun violence have primarily focused on gun control policies and a citizen's rights to bear arms. This chapter, however, focuses on how gun violence can also be categorized as a type of terrorism, due to the characteristics it shares with terrorism: fear, threat, violence, and most significantly, the number of innocent civilians killed in the commission of the act. The chapter will further show number of deaths associated with gun violence as well as its frequency, compared with terrorist attacks.

Historical Background

Everyone's worried about stopping terrorism.
Well, there's really an easy way: stop participating in it

Noam Chomsky

Embedded in world history and human civilizations, terrorism has symbolized different forms of state repression and tyranny, violent demonstrations of power, assassinations, and executions (Martin 2006). From antiquity, through different revolutions (e.g. The French Revolution), and into the midst of our modern day era, the social and political dynamics within which society experiences terrorist related events encompass a myriad of conflict issues that have continued to give rise to new dimensions of terrorism. As a result, terrorism has become a challenge to societal norms, particularly with the new magnitudes of terrorism which include bioterrorism, eco-terrorism, and even nuclear terrorism.

The September 11, 2001 attacks then become one of many violent crimes and terrorist attacks that have taken place, in the U.S. and around the world. The attacks were particularly sensationalized through the media, and had an impact on domestic and foreign policy. While it is true that the attacks on the World Trade Center and Pentagon on September 11, 2001, were heinous and senseless, it is a *cliché* that these events were a *turning* point in U.S. history (Forst 2009). The U.S. has experienced many different acts of terrorism throughout its history: e.g. lynching of African Americans, extreme violence from Ku Klux Klan (KKK) during the 1950s and 1960s, radicalism from the American leftists (e.g. The Black Panthers), and other rebellious groups such as the Weatherman/Weather Underground organization, to name a few. Furthermore, attacks on the World Trade Center, in fact, began as early as 1993, when a group of terrorists detonated a truck bomb below the North tower. Perhaps what was different about the September 11th, 2001 attacks is that they were more global, terrorizing, and resulted in a massive number of deaths: 2,996 people (including the 19 hijackers).

Also, the September 11th, 2001 attacks gave rise to a more globalized perspective on "terrorism," with policies created to combat it. For instance, different law enforcement agencies, such as the FBI, Bureau of Alcohol, Tobacco, and Firearms, and the Drug Enforcement Administration began working more in collaboration with each other to investigate possible terrorist threats against U.S. soil, both at the national and international levels. Other examples include, tightened airport security, implementation of the Patriot Act, the creation of the Department of Homeland Security (DHS), and increased efforts in emphasizing counterintelligence functional areas. Approaches to combating terrorism have thus become more proactive than reactive in nature, but also expensive in terms of funding, training, and hiring personnel. What the U.S. government has *failed* to do, however, is invest its efforts to combating other overlooked violent crimes in America that may occur in more frequency and be more lethal than Terrorism, one of which being gun violence.

Gun Violence in American Society: Realities and Dangers

Force and mind are opposites:
morality ends where a gun begins

Ayn Rand

Historically, guns have been a part of U.S. culture since before the 1700s (Lindgren 2002). Today, however, the argument is that guns are more sophisticated and accurate than they were in colonial times: "simpler guns manufactured one at a time to more sophisticated mass-produced guns" (Lindgren, 2002, p. 4). As a result of that, more guns in American society have led to more violent acts and deaths associated with the use and misuse of guns. Guns have also proved to be more lethal than knives, sticks, or any substitutes. With this breakdown in societal norms and threat to morals and ideals, gun violence have become a threatening issue at the local, state and federal levels of government. Gun violence in American society has further fueled many controversial political debates in an attempt to counter the problems associated with it. What has been even more challenging is trying to come up with gun policies that are likely to reduce gun violence and gun-related deaths. While stricter gun control policies *may be* significant in reducing gun violence and deaths associated with it, they are also controversial as to whether or not they are an infringement on a citizen's second Amendment which *protects the right of the people to keep and bear arms from infringement.* However, some opponents to gun control policies may argue that the question of whether or not stricter gun control policies will reduce gun violence and deaths associated with it is debatable. This is due to the fact that criminals will continue to obtain their firearms illegally. For example, at the State and Federal levels, 33 percent and 39.2 percent (respectively) of inmates reported obtaining their last gun through illegal sources, while 39.6 percent and 35.4 percent (respectively) "borrowed" it from a friend or family member (Scalia, 2000; Wolf Harlon, 2001).

Discussion on perhaps how and when the Supreme Court began closely examining the second Amendment dates back to the 1876 case of United States v. Cruikshank. The Court, in this case, concluded that while the right to keep and bear arms shall not be infringed by Congress, States should be given freedom to protect or restrict this right under their police power (United States v. Cruikshank, 92 U.S. 542). The ruling of the Supreme Court in Cruikshank was later affirmed in Presser v. Illinois (1886) that while Congress and the national government may have limited powers upon the freedom to bear arms, the states shall maintain their power to protect or restrict that right, so long as the State is also not in violation of a citizen's Fourteenth Amendment (United States v. Cruikshank, 92 U.S. 548-549).

This is significant because it shows how a citizen's right under the second Amendment can be interpreted differently depending on the circumstances of the case in point. As a result, today, conflict over the *right* to bear arms is challenged by advocates of gun control policies. To what extent does a U.S. citizen have the right to keep and bear arms? The answer to this question may not be as clear as we think. However, conflict situations that have involved a firearm in the commission of a crime have put more emphasis on the importance of giving gun control policies and *enforcement* of these policies a closer look. Regardless of how the second Amendment is interpreted, society has had its long battle with guns, making the U.S. one of the most industrialized countries with the highest number of gun-violence incidents and gun related deaths.

The early 1990s, for instance, showed an increase in the number of people killed or wounded by firearms. Statistics show that more than 17,000 Americans were killed in 1993 alone during the commission of some violent crime (Blumstein 1995; Cook and Laub 1998, 2002). On September 13, 1994 Title XI, Subtitle A of the violent Crime Control and Law Enforcement Act of 1994, banned the "manufacture, transfer, and possession" of certain semiautomatic firearms. Since then, the U.S. has experienced a drop in deaths related to firearms, particularly in 1999, which was 15533, the lowest in 33 years. While there are no clear or direct reasons for the drop, some argue that perhaps the economic boom contributed to more employment opportunities and therefore giving people little motivation to commit crime. Another reason may be attributed to mandatory sentences, for drug possession and crimes involving guns, contributing to specific deterrence among those who are likely to offend or reoffend.

Prior to this period, the War on Drugs during the late 1980s also saw an increase in the use of handguns among juveniles and young adults (between the ages of 18-27) and their death rates. Responses and efforts directed toward reducing the availability of handguns are therefore necessary in reducing gun-related deaths. One such effort that has been implemented focuses on police methods targeted at getting guns off the street. Another is tougher regulations on the sale of handguns (Blumstein and Wallman 2000). While banning assault weapons is always in question on whether or not it will likely reduce crimes associated with it, it is believed to reduce the *lethality* of semiautomatic weapons (Koper and Roth 2001). The challenge is that there will always be controversies on strict regulations or even bans on firearms (Koper and Roth 2001).

The increase and decrease of gun violence has kept Americans puzzled about what could be the best strategy, or rather policy to control this phenomenon. In 2000, gun homicide decreased by 40 percent (10,203 incidents) and remained at a relatively low rate until 2004. Then, according to the Bureau of Justice Statistics, gun homicides increased again by 6 percent to (11,346) and then decreased to 10,086 in 2007. One of the attempts, by gun control advocates, in trying to control gun violence and deaths associated with it, is to implement a stricter gun control policy. Stell (2004) defines strict gun control policy as "an array of legally sanctioned restrictions designed to impose firearm scarcity on the general population" (p.38). The main problem then behind gun control measures may not necessarily be the strict policies trying to control it, but rather the loose policies that make guns easily accessible to criminals as well as law abiding citizens.

As a result, the controversial second Amendment which focuses on the right to keep and bear arms, should be addressed more closely, not only by looking at the percentage of felons who have used a weapon during their commission of a crime, but rather upon the entire gun ownership population in the U.S. (Zimring, 2004). Zimring (2004) also argues that gun control laws can contribute to a marginal decrease in homicide rates by making guns scarcer in the social environment. While the scarcity of guns in society may not dramatically decrease gun related crimes, the policies behind controlling the gun epidemic should still be pursued and re-examined in an attempt to reduce deaths associated with it. Although the debates surrounding the issue of gun ownership and its legality primarily focuses on the adult population, it is very significant to take a closer look at gun shooting incidents on school campuses among the youth population in the U.S.

School Shootings: The Realities Behind the "Unsafe School Zones"

> The students of Columbine High School and
> children everywhere have a basic right to learn in an
> environment free of fear and violence.
> We must redouble our efforts to see that this is a reality
>
>   John McCain

The past two decades in American society have seen a negative impact of gun violence, particularly among the juvenile and young adult population (Sheppard et al 2000). A teenager in America is more likely to die of a gunshot than of all other natural causes or disease (Fingerhut 1993). According to a 1997 national youth risk behavior survey, among students in the ninth to twelfth grades: almost 6 percent reported carrying a gun outside the home in the past 30 days (Kahn et al 1998). Of those same students, 8.5 percent reported carrying a weapon to school within the past 30 days (Brener el al 1999). While these numbers may seem alarming, this issue is even more problematic among youth living in the inner city. A study with 800 inner-city high school students, 22 percent said they carried weapons to school (Sheley and Wright 1993). The problem of guns and youth associated with them has become very severe in American society, leading to deaths, injuries, and disturbances to the social norms in society. Furthermore, the increase in school shootings in the U.S. has contributed to feelings of unsafety among students (Kaufman et al 1998). As a result, the problem associated with guns is not only an epidemic among the adult population, but also among juveniles. Gun shootings contribute to the majority of deaths at schools, particularly with the increased accessibility and use of firearms among juveniles (Snyder and Sickmund 1999).

Whether it's for self-protection or with the intention of attacking someone at school, an estimated 135.000 students carry guns to schools (Maginnis 1995). The problem, however, is that approximately 6.000 of those students are expelled per school year for bringing a firearms to school (U.S. Department of Education 1998), which means that punishment is not severe enough to deter juveniles from continuing to carry firearms to schools. Otherwise, perhaps the argument is that those firearms being brought to school are not being detected, making security and safety issues very problematic (Redding and Shalf 2001). The U.S., with its more accessible guns and permissive gun laws, faces a very serious problem associated with gun violence and deaths, particularly among its youth population, which are more likely to die by firearms at a much higher rate than in the rest of the developed world.

Carrying guns to schools has been attributed to various reasons. For instance, some youth, particularly those living in the inner city, carry guns to schools because they are scared (Hausman, Spivak and Prothrow-Smith 1994: Everett and Price 1995). Part of that stems largely from the reason that inner city youth perceive their environment within which they live, as dangerous. It is also noteworthy that according to the Children's Defense Fund (CDF), children in the U.S. are at a much higher risk of death or injury from a firearm than their counterparts in other industrialized countries.

To further emphasize this reality, in 2005, there were 3006 firearms-related deaths among U.S. children aged 15 years and under. In this particular statistic 822 committed suicide. 1972 suffered a gun-related homicide, and 212 died in an accidental death that was related to firearms (Obeng 2010). Taking into consideration the prevalence of guns and gun-related incidents, the issue should be more of concern to policy makers due to its frequency and lethality. It is therefore only appropriate to classify gun violence as a type of terrorism. Following is a chart from 2010, showing the number of murders in the U.S. as a result of handguns, compared with other substitutes.

Table 9.1. Murders in the U.S. 2010

Weapon	Number of Murders
Rifles	358
Handguns	6.009
Shotguns	373
Unknown Guns	2.035
Knives/Blades	1.704
Other Weapon	1.772
Hands/fists/feet	745

Source: FBI.

Gun Violence Vs. Terrorism:
Different or Similar

I don't care if I fall
as long as someone else picks up my
gun and keeps on shooting

Che Guevara

One of the most significant time periods when terrorism was largely seen and experienced, was during the French Revolution of 1789, followed by the "Reign of Terror" (1793–1794). The conflict, which was primarily an opposition to the Jacobin dictatorship, resulted in mass executions to those who were perceived as enemies of the new revolutionary republic, with a death toll that ranged in the tens of thousands. British statesman and philosopher Edmund Burke (1993) is known as one of the first to use the word terrorism to describe the Reign of Terror (la Terreur). However, specific definitions to terrorism are difficult to find. According to Cooper (2001) "there has never been, since the topic began to command serious attention, some golden age in which terrorism was easy to define" (Cooper, 881). Attempts in trying to define terrorism have resulted in more than 100 definitions (Laqueur, 1999).

Bruce Hoffman defines terrorism as "the deliberate creation and exploitation of fear through violence or the threat of violence in the pursuit of political change" (Hoffman, 2006, 41; Howard & Sawyer, 2004, 23). According to the Federal Bureau of Investigation (FBI) terrorism refers to "the unlawful use of force or violence against persons of property to intimidate or coerce a Government, the civilian population, or any segment thereof, in furtherance of political or social objectives" (U.S. Department of Justice, 1996, ii.). The Department of Defense's definition of terrorism is described as "the unlawful use of, or threatened use, of force or violence against individuals or property to coerce and intimidate governments or societies, often to achieve political, religious, or ideological objectives" (U.S. Departments of the Army and the Air Force 1990, 3–1). Finally, in Cooper's words, terrorism is "the international generation of massive fear by human beings for the purpose of securing or maintaining control over other human beings" (Cooper, 2001, 883). Some of the interesting findings though that researchers have come up with in finding the most common elements in the proposed definitions were as follows: violence or force (84 percent of the definitions), political motivation (65 percent), engendering fear or terror (51 percent), using a threat (47 percent), psychological effects (42 percent), and victim-target differentiations (38 percent; Schmid& Jongman, 1988). However, for the purpose of this chapter, Kofi Annan's (Former Secretary General of the United Nations) redefinition of terrorism seems to be the most fitting. In Annan's words, terrorism is any act that is intended "to cause death or serious bodily harm to civilians." While this redefinition may have been directly interpreted to refer to terrorism, it certainly encompasses a much wider range of other criminal and violent acts; one of which includes gun violence.

In general, society has put so much emphasis on terrorism that it tends to treat it far more seriously than gun shootings in terms of countering terrorism rather than countering gun violence. While the U.S. has clearly pursued the War on Terrorism, it had yet to wage war against gun violence. The question remains: why can't gun shootings be referred to as terrorist acts or attacks? Though terrorists' motivations may somewhat differ than those of gun shooters, both have some common characteristics. For instance, they instill fear, change societal norms, challenge the status quo, intimidate civilians, and are damaging to society as a whole. It is therefore very significant as to how and what society *chooses* to label as terrorism. This is important because it would largely impact policies that are made in an attempt to prevent different forms of terrorism (Greene, 2009), such as gun violence, as this chapter argues. Framing attacks is largely impacted by how policy makers interpret them: "if policy making is a struggle over alternative realities, then language is the medium that reflects, advances, and interprets these alternatives" (Rochefort and Cobb, 1994: 9).

With respect to gun violence, the issue surrounding its control has been interpreted by different entities: politicians, interest groups, as well as the media, in a way that is likely to benefit them. Regardless of how seriously the issue is perceived and interpreted, it is clear to the average citizen that there is a social epidemic engraved in every life. From a political perspective, however, the issue is surrounded by competing views that revolve around an individual's civil liberties and the limitation of government in not violating these liberties (Edel 1995). For example, while the National Rifle Association (NRA) believes that gun control is a threat to a person's liberty by opening doors to government intervention, the Brady Center to Prevent Gun Violence frames the issue as reasonable, with the intention that it will save lives by reducing crime and violence (Kleck 1991).

Research has shown that terrorists are engaged in crimes such as assassinations, kidnappings, racketeering (Hamm, 2007) rather than simply being involved in "other" criminal acts that are somewhat committed haphazardly (Gottfredson and Hirschi, 1990). While this shows that terrorists may differ in their motivations and criminal behavior (Legault and Hendrickson, 2000), guns *remain popular* among them. For instance, Clarke and Newman (2006) identified that terrorists prefer weapons that are: "multipurpose, undetectable, removable, destructive, enjoyable, reliable, obtainable, uncomplicated, and safe" (2006:108) which guns do possess. What makes guns even more attractive among terrorists is their legal accessibility (Lichtblau, 2005). For instance, if and when a terrorist has lacked an evident criminal history (Sageman, 2006), they would experience little scrutiny when entering the U.S. (Meissner, 2004), which may increase their access to firearms in the U.S. The relationship then between guns and terrorism is very intimate. Terrorists will use guns to commit their acts of violence whenever and wherever possible, and similarly, gun shooters will use terrorist like behavior to commit their acts of violence. A common theory surrounding this issue is that loose gun laws help terrorists commit their acts: "As demonstrated by recent attacks, terrorists will use any weapons—explosives, firearms, and even knives—to carry out their deadly schemes. Congress must close gaps in our laws—such as the gun show loophole—that criminals, potentially, terrorists, exploit to obtain such weapons" (Brady Center Press Release 9/20/2001).

The National Rifle Association, however, may have an opposing idea about linking acts of terrorism to guns: "The national public policy debate had plunged to a new low . . . [making] an outrageous attempt to link terrorist strikes against this country to a national tradition as old as America itself—gun shows . . . It's time for full disclosure" (NRA Press Release 10/26/01). The NRA also made the point that an American citizen's liberties are being compromised by becoming a casualty in the war against terrorism, and emphasized that the increase in gun sales following the September 11, 2001 attacks were needed for self-protection: "True American public opinion is telling its own story. Since the attacks of September 11, media outlets have been filled with reports of Americans purchasing their first firearms and learning to use them safely and responsibly for self-protection" (NRA Press Release 10/26/01).

There is no question that gun-related shootings and deaths are tragic, but it is the percent of gun ownership in the U.S. that is more tragic and alarming. The United States has more private guns per capita and higher levels of household gun ownership than other developed countries (Killias 1993, SAS 2007). Even though the *intent* to kill may not necessarily preside as the overarching argument among gun owners, the consequences of owning them are somewhat predictable.

While owning or having access to a gun is just as serious and lethal as an act of terrorism, the latter has made its way through to the public, impacting them in a more dramatic way, particularly with the support of the media. Once an act is labeled as an act of terrorism, it becomes a national and international issue. To further illustrate this contention, this chapter presents the Boston Marathon bombing as a case in point to show how impacting a so-called terrorist attack may be: by simply labeling it as an act of terrorism. .

The Boston Marathon Bombing: A Case in Point

On April 15, 2013, two bombs exploded during the Boston Marathon. According to reports, 3 people were killed and more than 200 were injured. Once the FBI identified and released photographs of the suspects, Tamerlan and Dzhokhar Tsarnaev, the suspects continued with their acts of violence, killing an MIT police officer and getting involved in a gunfire exchange with police in Watertown, Massachusetts. The manhunt for Dzhokhar, who survived his injuries but escaped from police, began on April 19, with thousands of police officers searching for him. Residents of Watertown were asked to stay in their homes, and most businesses and schools were closed, while other city functions were cancelled. The suspect was later found hiding in a Watertown resident's boat in his backyard, where he was arrested and transported to a nearby hospital. While the two brothers were not connected to any terrorist organization, Dzhokhar admitted later that they both learned how to make explosives through an online magazine linked to Al-Qaeda. In response to the Boston Marathon bombings, the Federal Aviation Administration issued an airspace restriction over Boston, in addition to a temporary ground stop for Boston's Logan International Airport. Police throughout Massachusetts and other states put their police force on high alert and the U.S. Attorney General, Eric Holder, issued that "full resources" of the U.S. Department of Justice should be directed at investigating the attacks. The Boston Police Department encouraged people to call and provide information if they had any, while a helpline was provided for people who were concerned about family and friends that may have been at the marathon area or close to it. Government agencies, including the Federal Bureau of investigations (FBI), acting as the lead investigating agency, along with the Bureau of Alcohol, Tobacco, Firearms and Explosives (BATFE), the Central Intelligence Agency (CIA), the National Counterterrorism Center (NCC), and the Drug Enforcement Agency (DEA), all worked in order to gather information and help resolve the conflict.

There is no question that the Boston Marathon bombing was a heinous crime. However, the fact that it was labeled a *terrorist* attack, as opposed to a violent crime or a bombing, made it more sensational and prompted a more active response. For instance, in addition to closing various businesses and schools, and cancelling events in the city, there was a massive investment in countering the problem by having different government agencies work in collaboration to fix the problem. What was noteworthy about Boston is that even though it may not have necessarily experienced a *noted* terrorist attack until the marathon bombing in 2013, it has certainly experienced the gun violence epidemic. For instance, during the late 1980s (with the rise of the crack cocaine epidemic) and early 1990s Boston experienced a series of gun violence incidents (Kennedy et al. 1996; Braga 2003). Between 1980-198, Boston averaged 40 gun homicide per year, 57 in 1989 and 86 in 1990 (Braga et al 2010). In the early 1990, Boston averaged 62 gun homicides per year. In 1996, the number dropped to 38, and decreased all the way to 19 by 1999. However, the decrease was not long lived, as the number rose again in the early 2001, reaching 55 victims in 2006, 52 in 2007 and 49 in 2008 (Braga et al. 2010).

Overall, shootings and deaths associated with them have been very dramatic and traumatic in the U.S., perhaps even more than terrorism as a whole. The likelihood that America would experience a gun shooting with a large number of fatalities is higher than its experience with terrorism. Also for terrorists to act upon their beliefs and ideologies, they would require to have some criminal intent and behavior. The challenge is in trying to define and classify the type of criminal activity that they commit. The use of firearms in the commission of a violent crime is one way that we can classify these violent acts as acts of terrorism, due to the fear, intimidation, and death and/or injury inflicted upon the victims. Furthermore, while profiling terrorists in an attempt to prevent any future attacks by them may be beneficial, it can also be misleading. For instance, the infamous face of Osama bin

Laden. for years, was over-emphasized by the media, and made such an impact on people's perception of what the "typical" terrorist looks like. While this image may hold true in some instances. it clearly overlooks the reality behind what a terrorist *really* looks like.

Six Decades of Mass Gun Shootings in the U.S.

To further illustrate the epidemic of gun violence and gun related deaths in the U.S., following is a selected list of mass gun shootings that have taken place in the U.S. since 1966 committed by senseless. unpredictable. violent, and more importantly, armed citizens.

August 1, 1966—After killing his mother and wife, Charles Joseph Whitman. a former U.S. Marine. killed 16 people and wounded more than 30 from a tower at the University of Texas. He was later shot and killed by two police officers.

May 4, 1970—The Ohio National Guard fired 67 rounds in 13 seconds against students protesting against the U.S. incursion into Cambodia. killing four students and injuring nine.

May 15, 1970—At Jackson State University (South Carolina), police fired against protestors (primarily African Americans). killing one student and wounding one passerby.

January 7, 1973—In New Orleans. Louisiana. 23-year-old Mark Robert James Essex. shot and killed nine people in a rampage at a Howard Johnson motel. He was later shot and killed by police.

August 20, 1982—A 51 year old History teacher. Carl Robert Brown. who was armed with a shotgun. killed eight people at a machine shop in Miami. Florida. He was later shot by a witness who pursued him. Reports show that he was on leave from school for psychological treatment.

September 25, 1982—A prison guard in In Wilkes-Barre. Pennsylvania. George Banks. killed 13 people including five of his own children. In September 2011. the Pennsylvania Supreme Court overturns his death sentence stating that Banks is mentally incompetent.

May 17, 1984—A 25-year-old drifter Army veteran. Michael Silka. killed eight people in a three-hour rampage in Manley Hot Springs. Alaska. Two days later, he was shot and killed by police during a shootout.

July 18, 1984—41-year-old James Huberty, armed with a long-barreled Uzi, a pump-action shotgun and a handgun shot and killed 21 peoples (including children) at a local McDonalds in San Ysidro, California. He was later shot and killed by police.

September 14, 1989—In Louisville, Kentucky, 47-year-old Joseph Wesbecker armed with a AK-47 semiautomatic assault rifle, two MAC-11 semiautomatic pistols, a .38 caliber handgun, a 9-millimeter semiautomatic pistol and a bayonet killed eight co-workers at Standard Gravure Corporation before killing himself. Resports show that he was placed on disability leave from his job due to mental problems.

October 16, 1991—35-year-old, George Hennard, shot and killed 23 people before committing suicide in Killeen, Texas.

July 1, 1993—In San Francisco, California, 55-year-old Gian Luigi Ferri, shot and killed eight people in a law office before killing himself.

April 20, 1999—At Columbine High School in Littleton, Colorado, 18-year-old Eric Harris and 17-year-old Dylan Klebold killed 12 fellow students and one teacher before committing suicide in the school library.

July 29, 1999—In Atlanta, Georgia, 44-year-old Mark Barton killed his wife and two children at his home. He then opens fire in two different brokerage houses killing nine people and wounding 12. He later kills himself.

September, 1999—A gunman opened fire at a prayer service in Fort Worth, Texas, killing six people before committing suicide.

October, 2002—A series of sniper-style shootings occurred in Washington DC, leaving 10 dead.

August, 2003—In Chicago, a laid-off worker shot and killed six of his former workmates.

November, 2004- In Birchwood, Wisconsin, a hunter killed six other hunters and wounded two others after an argument with them

March 21, 2005—In Red Lake High School, Minnesota, 16-year-old Jeff Weise killed his grandfather and another adult, four fellow students, a teacher and a security officer, before killing himself.

March, 2005—A man opened fire at a church service in Brookfield, Wisconsin, killing seven people.

October, 2006—A truck driver killed five schoolgirls and seriously wounded six others in a school in Nickel Mines, Pennsylvania before killing himself.

April 16, 2007—A gunman, 23-year-old student Seung-Hui Cho, goes on a shooting spree at Virginia Tech killing 32 people and wounding an undetermined number of others on campus, before committing suicide.

August, 2007- Three Delaware State University students were shot and killed in "execution style" by a 28-year-old and two 15-year-old boys.

September, 2007—A freshman student at Delaware State University shot and wounded two other students at a campus dining hall.

December 5, 2007—At an area mall in Omaha, Nebraska, 19-year-old Robert Hawkins killed eight people before killing himself.

December, 2007—A woman and her boyfriend shot dead six members of her family on Christmas Eve in Carnation, Washington.

February, 2008—A shooter tied up and shot six women at a suburban clothing store in Chicago, leaving five of them dead and the remaining one wounded.

February, 2008—A man opened fire in a lecture hall at Northern Illinois University in DeKalb, Illinois, killing five students and wounding 16 others.

July, 2008—A student shot three people in a computer lab at South Mountain Community College, Phoenix, Arizona.

September, 2008—A mentally ill man who was released from jail one month earlier shot eight people in Alger, Washington, killing six and wounding two others.

October, 2008—A group of men drove up to a dormitory at the University of Central Arkansas and opened fire, killing two students and injuring one other.

December, 2008—A man dressed in Santa Claus suit opened fire at a family Christmas party in Covina, California, then set fire on the house and killed himself. Police later found nine people dead in the debris of the house.

March 10, 2009—In Alabama, Michael McLendon of Kinston, killed 10 people before killing himself.

March 29, 2009—In Carthage, North Carolina, 45-year-old Robert Stewart killed a nurse and seven elderly patients at a nursing home.

March, 2009—Six people were shot dead in a high-grade apartment building in Santa Clara, California.

April 3, 2009—In Binghamton, New York, Jiverly Wong killed 13 people and injured four othersduring a shooting at an immigrant community center, before killing himself.

April, 2009—An 18-year-old student followed a pizza deliveryman into his old dormitory, shot the deliveryman, a dorm monitor, and himself at Hampton University, Virginia.

July, 2009—Six people, including one student, were shot in a drive-by shooting at a community rally on the campus of Texas Southern University, Houston.

November 5, 2009—Major Nidal Malik Hasan killed 13 people and injured 32 others at Fort Hood, Texas, during a shooting rampage.

January 19, 2010—Christopher Speight, 39, killed eight people at a house in Appomattox, Virginia.

February, 2010—A Professor at the University of Alabama killed three colleagues and wounded three others, at a faculty department meeting.

August 3, 2010—In Manchester, Connecticut, Omar Thornton killed eight co-workers at Hartford Distributors before killing himself.

January, 2011—A Gunman opened fire at a public gathering outside a grocery in Tuscon, Arizona, killing six people including a nine-year-old girl and wounding at least 12 others. Congresswoman Gabrielle Giffords was severely injured with a gunshot in the head.

October 12, 2011—Eight people were killed during a shooting at the Salon Meritage in Seal Beach, California. The suspect was 41 year old, Scott Evans Dekraai, who was armed with three guns—a 9 mm Springfield, a Smith & Wesson .44 Magnum, and a Heckler & Koch .45.

July 20, 2012—James E. Holmes, 24, shot and killed 12 people and wounding 58 at an Aurora, Colorado movie theater screening of the new Batman film.

August, 2012—A white supremacist, Wade Michael Page, killed six people at a Sikh temple in Wisconsin before being shot dead by police.

December 14, 2012—At Sandy Hook Elementary School in Newtown, Connecticut, Adam Lanza, 20, gunned down 20 children, six adults, and himself. Reports show that his mom was later found dead from a gun wound as well.

September 16, 2013—Aaron Alexis, 34, fired shots inside the U.S. Navy Yard killing 12 people. He was later shot and killed by police. (Canning, 2012)

Conclusion

> Gun violence has terrible
> consequence for our society
> and if we can only do one thing to stop it,
> we should all try and do that
>
> President Barack Obama

While the correlation between stricter gun control measures and death rates may open doors for controversial debates, the issue remains significant and calls for further examination. Perhaps even more significant is whether or not more strict *enforcement* of gun control policies for gun-related offenses may act as a deterrent for future predators. In this regard the cost-benefit analysis of choosing to commit a gun-related offense may be altered.

What is also key in countering the gun violence epidemic is that American society *classifies* gun related offenses as a type of terrorism. Until then, the gun violence epidemic will continue to coexist in American society with policies only circling around a citizen's right to bear arms and its infringement. For example, the most recent incident of the Navy reservist, Aaron Alexis, who killed at least 12 people on September 16, 2013, in a mass shooting at a military facility, led to a partial lockdown at the nation's capital. Reports showed that even after he was captured and killed, authorities believed that there were two other men who fled the scene but were *armed*. Shortly after, the act was classified as a "lone gunman" shooting. In response to this shooting, Dr. Janis Orlowski, the Chief Medical Officer for MedStar Washington Hospital Center said:

> There's something wrong in our society that we as Americans have to work on to try and eradicate . . . I may see this every day, but there is something wrong when we have these multiple shootings, these multiple injuries, there's something wrong.

Despite the seriousness of the act and the reactions it spurred in Washington, as well as the U.S. as a whole, it was never once classified as a terrorist attack. So the question is: are terrorist acts and attacks only classified as such when they are committed by a foreign person or country? The answer to this question should simply be no. Violent acts, that involve a firearm in their commission, and meet the characteristics of a terrorist-related act, should be classified as one type of terrorism regardless of the racial, ethnic, or religious background of the armed individual. In Alexis's case, three weapons were found on him: an AR-15 assault rifle, a shotgun and a semiautomatic pistol. At what point will America classify him as a terrorist and his act as a terrorist attack?

Just as the media have globalized terrorism at both the national and international levels, it is necessary that it does so with gun violence and the deaths associated with it. The emphasis that the media has put on terrorism vs. gun related offenses, has instilled much fear in the minds and hearts of Americans about the beast they call terrorism (Martin 2006). The relationship between terrorism and the media in all its different forms (e.g. internet, radio, television, print) has therefore become very unique. In the words of Carlos Marighella, who wrote the manual for urban guerillas, "The media are important instruments of propaganda for the simple reason that they find terrorist actions newsworthy" (Weimann & Winn, 1994, p. 112). However, while the public is open to receiving information about violence in their society, the media may be guilty of disseminating terrorist propaganda. As a result, the media may be seen as an entity that may be promoting more violence committed by terrorists rather than discouraging it.

With respect to gun violence and gun control policies, the media played a role in publicizing these issues particularly during urban riots in the 1960s and the assassinations of Robert Kennedy and Martin Luther King. While advocates of gun control emphasized that strict gun laws may cure the crime and violence associated with firearms, opponents believed that this would be an infringement on freedom and a citizen's right to bear arms (Cobb & Elder 1972). Another incident that also sparked a new wave in the media and among the American public as a whole, including government, is when Jim Brady, former White House Press Secretary to Ronald Reagan, was critically injured in an assassination attempt in 1988. One year later, there was also a proposed ban on assault weapons introduced at the federal level. On March 2, 2000, President Bill Clinton stated that "the Brady Bill is saving people's lives and keeping guns out of the wrong hands." This was particularly true due to the number of people who were denied to purchase a handgun as a result of the law. For example, during the first five years of the Brady Act, 312,000 applications to purchase handguns from dealers (2.4 percent of the total) were denied due to a felony record or other disqualifying characteristic (Bowling et al. 2010). This does not include the people who were deterred from purchasing a firearm. Since guns are more lethal than any other substitute, a reduction in their accessibility and use would likely contribute to a reduction in the number of homicides (Zimring 1968, 1972).

Despite efforts made to combat the gun violence epidemics, terrorism has taken over the media and public's attention, particularly since the September 11th 2001 attacks. The reality, though, is that the likelihood of dying from a gunshot is much higher than that of a terrorist-related act, though reactions to counterterrorism have been more evident compared to those countering gun violence (e.g. funding, collaboration between government agencies, intelligence, investigations, tighter security, etc . . .). In fact, America has launched its War on Terrorism following the September 11th attacks in 2001, and it has yet to officially launch its *War on Guns*. Notwithstanding efforts made to enact stricter gun control policies, gun violence incidents, particularly those that result in deaths and injuries, should be classified as an act of terrorism. Perhaps then, enforcement of gun laws will become stricter and serve as an effective deterrent. Statistics show that the number of Americans killed in gun deaths is much larger than the number of those killed in terrorist attacks around the *world* every year. In 2010, 13,186 people died in terrorist attacks worldwide. In that same year, in America, 31,672 people died in gun related deaths. Furthermore, since 2005, international terrorism has taken an average of 23 American lives annually, while 30,000 people are killed by firearms in the U.S. each year, including suicides, murders and accidents (CDC). In the words of Charles Collier, a Professor of Law and Philosophy at the University of Florida Gainesville, "will we recognize this form of terrorism for what it is, even as it arises-so chillingly familiar-in our very midst?"

References

Blumstein, A. (1995). Youth Violence, Guns, and the Illicit Gun Industry. *Journal of Criminal Law and Criminology*. 86: 10-36.

Blumstein, A., & Wallman J (eds). (2000). *The Crime Drop in America*. Cambridge University Press, New York.

Bowling, M., Frandsen, R., Lauver, G., Boutilier, A., and Adams, D. (2010). Background Checks for Firearms: Statistical Tables. *Bureau of Justice Statistics Bulletin* NCJ 231679.

Braga, AA. (2003). Serious Youth Gun Offenders and the Epidemic of Youth Violence in Boston. *Journal of Quantitative Criminology*, 19:33-54.

Braga, A., Papachristos, A., & David M. Hureau. (2010). The Concentration and Stability of Gun Violence at Micro Places in Boston, 1980–2008. *Journal of Quantitative Criminology*, 26:33-53.

Brener, N.D., Simon, T.R., Krug, E.G., and Lowry, R. (1999). *Recent Trends in Violence-Related Behaviors Among High School Students in the United States*. Hyattsville, MD:U.S. Department of Health and Human Services, Centers for Disease Control and Prevention, National Center for Health Statistics.

Burke, Edmund. (1993). *Reflections on the Revolution in France*. New York: Oxford University Press.

Canning, E. A. (2012). Guns and mass murder in U.S. since 1966. The Brad Blog. December 16. http://www.bradblog.com/?p=9781

Cobb, R.W., and Elder, C. D. (1972). *Participation in American Politics: The Dynamics of Agenda Building*. Allyn and Bacon. Boston.

Collier, Charles W. (2013). *Gun Control in America: An Autopsy Report*. Dissent.

Cook, P., & Laub J. (1998). The Unprecedented epidemic in Youth Violence. In: Tonry M, Moor, M. (eds). *Youth Violence*. Vol. 24. "Crime and Justice" a review of research. University of Chicago Press, Chicago. 27–64.

Cooper, H. H. A. (2001). Terrorism: The Problem of Definition Revisited. *American Behavioral Scientist,* 44(6), 881–893.

Dwivedi, O.P. (2000). Reducing Gun Deaths in the USA. *The Lancet,* Vol. 356, No. 9239.

Edel, W. (1995). *Gun Control: Threat to Liberty or Defense Against Anarchy?* Westport, CT: Praeger.

Everett, Sherry A., & James H. Price. (1995). Students' Perceptions of Violence in the Public Schools: The Metlife Survey. *Journal of Adolescent Health,* 17:345–53.

Fingerhut, L.A. (1993). Firearm mortality among children, youth, and young adults 1–34 years of age, trends and current status: United States, 1985–1990. *Advance Data From Vital and Health Statistics.* Number 231. Hyattsville, MD: U.S. Department of Health and Human Services, Centers for Disease Control and Prevention, National Center for Health Statistics.

Fischman, Harris. (2012). *Gun Control and the Second Amendment: Developments and Controversies in the Wake of District of Columbia v. Heller and McDonald v. Chicago.* Introductory Remarks to the Fordham Urban Law Journal's Volume XXXIX Symposium.

Forst, Brian. (2009). *Terrorism, Crime, and Public Policy.* Cambridge University Press.

Gottfredson, Michael R., & Travis Hirschi. 1990. *A General Theory of Crime.* Stanford, CA: Stanford University Press

Hausman, Alice J., Howard Spivak, and Deborah Prothrow-Stith. (1994). *Adolescents' Knowledge and Attitudes about and Experience with Violence.* Journal of Adolescent Health, 15:400–406.

Hoffman, B. (2006). *Inside Terrorism.* (Rev. ed.). New York: Columbia University Press.

Howard, R.D., & Sawyer, R.L. (2004). *Terrorism and Counterterrorism: Understanding the New Security Environment, Readings and Interpretations.* New York: McGraw-Hill.

Kaufman, Philip, Xianglei Chen, Susan P. Choy, Sally A. Ruddy, Kathryn A. Chandler, Christopher D. Chapman, & Kleck, G. (1991). *Point Blank: Guns and Violence in America.* New York: Aldine de Gruyter.

Lindgren, J. (2002). Fall from grace: Arming America and the Bellesiles scandal. *Yale Law Journal* (2195), 1–34.

Michael E. Rand, & Cheryl Ringe. (1998). *Indicators of School Crime and Safety.* Washington, D.C.: U.S. Dept. of Education, Office of Educational Research and Improvement, National Center for Education Statistics; U.S. Dept. of Justice Office of Justice Programs, Bureau of Justice Statistics.

Kennedy, D.M., Piehl A.M., & Anthony Braga. (1996). Youth Violence in Boston: Gun Markets, Serious Youth Offenders, and a Use-Reduction Strategy. *Law and Contemporary Problems* 59:147–196.

Killias, M. (1993). International correlations between gun ownership and rates of homicide and suicide. *Canadian Medical Association Journal* 148 (10):1721–1725.

Koper, Christopher S., and Jeffrey A. Roth. (2001). The Impact of the 1994 Federal Assault Weapon Ban on Gun Violence Outcomes: An Assessment of Multiple Outcome Measures and Some Lessons for Policy Evaluation. *Journal of Quantitative Criminology,* Vol. 17.

Laqueur, W. (1999). *The New Terrorism: Fanaticism and the Arms of Mass Destruction.* New York: Oxford University Press.

Maginnis, Robert. (1995). *Violence in the Schoolhouse: A Ten-Year Update.* Washington, D.C.: Family Research Council.

Mahan, Sue, & Pamala Griset. (2008). *Terrorism in Perspective.* Second Edition. Sage Publications, Inc.

Martin, Gus. (2006). *Understanding Terrorism: Challenges, Perspectives and Issues.* Second Edition. Sage Publications, Inc.

Obeng, Cecilia. (2010). Should Gun Safety be Taught in Schools? Perspectives of Teachers. *Journal of School Health.* Vol. 80, No. 8.

Redding, Richard., & Sarah M. Shalf. (2001). The Legal Context of School Violence: The Effectiveness of Federal State, and Local Law Enforcement Efforts to Reduce Gun Violence in Schools. *Law & Policy.* Vol. 23, No. 3. Blackwell Publishers Ltd.

Rochefort, D.A. and Cobb, R.W. (1994). "Problem Definition : An Emerging Perspective." In D.A. Rochefort and R.W. Cobb (Eds.). *The Politics of Problem Definition: Shaping the Political Agenda* (1–31). Kansas: University Press of Kansas.

SAS. 2007. "Completing the count: Civilian firearms: Annexe 1: Seventy-nine countries with comprehensive civilian ownership data." In *The small arms survey: Guns in the city,* ed. Small Arms Survey Geneva. Cambridge, UK: Cambridge University Press.

Schmid, A., & Jongman, A. (Eds.). (1988). *Political Terrorism: A New Guide to Actors, Authors, Concepts, Data Bases, Theories, and Literature.* New Brunswick, NJ: Transaction.

Sheley, J.F., and Wright, J.D. (1993). *Gun Acquisition and Possession in Selected Juvenile Samples.* Research in Brief. Washington, DC: U.S. Department of Justice, Office of Justice Programs, National Institute of Justice.

Sheppard, D., Grant, H., Rowe, W., and Jacobs, N. (2000). *Fighting Juvenile Gun Violence.* U.S. Department of Justice Office of Justice Programs *Office of Juvenile Justice and Delinquency Prevention.* Juvenile Justice Bulletin.

Simonich, Milan. (2000). *Victims Left in Wake of Rampage.* Pittsburgh Post-Gazette.

Snyder, Howard N., and Melissa Sickmund. (1999). *Juvenile Offenders and Victims: 1999 National Report.* Pittsburgh: National Center for Juvenile Justice.

Stell, Lance K. (2004). *The Production of Criminal Violence in America: Is Strict Gun Control the Solution?* Journal of Law, Medicine and Ethics. Terrorist Research and Analytical Center, National Security Division, Federal Bureau of Investigation. *Terrorism in the United State 1995.* Washington, DC: U.S. Department of Justice, 1996, p. ii.

U.S. Departments of the Army and the Air Force. *Military Operations in Low Intensity Conflict.* Field Manual 100- 20/Air Force Pamphlet 3–20. Washington, DC: Headquarters, Departments of the Army and the Air Force, 1990.

United States v. Cruikshank, 92 U.S. 542, 548-49 (1876).

Vernick, Jon S., & Julie Samia Mair. (2002). How the Law Affects Gun Policy in the United States: Law as Intervention or obstacle to Prevention. *Journal of Law, Medicine & Ethics,* 30:692–704.

Weimann, G., & Winn, C. (1994). *The Theater of Terror: Mass Media and International Terrorism.* New York: Longman.

Zimring, Franklin E. 1968. "Is Gun Control Likely to Reduce Violent Killings?" *The University of Chicago Law Review* 35: 721–737.

———. 1972. "The Medium is the Message: Firearm Calibre as a Determinant of Death from Assault." *Journal of Legal Studies.* 1: 97–124.

———. (2004). Firearms, Violence, and the Potential Impact of Firearms Control. *Journal of Law, Medicine and Ethics.*

Selected Bibliography

Blendon R.J., Young J.T., and Hemenway D, "The American Public and the Gun Control Debate," *Journal of the American Medical Association* 275, no. 22 (1996):1719–1722. 9. Teret SP.

Brady Center to Prevent Gun Violence. On Target: The Impact of the 1994 Federal Assault Weapon Act. 2004. www.bradycenter.org/xshare/pdf/reports/on_target.pdf

Rand, M. R. (1990). *Handgun Crime Victim* (Special Report). Bureau of Justice Statistics, United States Department of Justice. Washington, DC.

———. (1994). *Guns and Crime* (Crime Data Brief). Bureau of Justice Statistics, United States Department of Justice. Washington, DC.

Randall, T. (1993). Clinicians' forensic interpretations of fatal gunshot wounds often miss the mark. *JAMA* 269: 2058-2061.

Roth, J. A., & Koper, C. S. (1997). *Impact Evaluation of the Public Safety and Recreational Firearms Use Protection Act of 1994*. Urban Institute. Washington, DC.

Schmidt, M.S., Gaps in FBI Data Undercut Background Checks for Guns. *New York Times*, December 20, 2012. http://www.nytimes.com/2012/12/21/us/gapsinfbidataundercut background checks for guns .html ?pagewanted=all & r=0

Teret S.P., Webster D.W., Vernick J.S., et al., "Support for New Policies to Regulate Firearms," *New England Journal of Medicine* 339, no.12 (1998): 813–818.

Chapter Ten

Applying a Disaster Process Framework to Studying Gun Violence: The Gun Assisted Violence as Disaster (Gavad) Model

Lisa A. Eargle

Introduction

This chapter examines the issue of Gun Violence from the theoretical framework of disaster research. A disaster is a process that poses a threat to human life or property (Keller and Blodgett, 2007), that is usually marked by some destructive event produced by nature or humankind (World Health Organization. n.d.). All disasters have some components in common and progress through a series of phases. However, the precursor conditions. catalysts or triggering events, impacts, and duration of effects do differ among disasters (Picou and Marshall, 2007). One common way of thinking about disaster phenomena is to classify them into different types according to their catalysts or origins.

Natural disasters involve acts of nature or God, such as hurricanes, earthquakes, and extreme temperatures (Picou and Marshall, 2007). Technological disasters are created by human error leading to the failure of equipment, buildings. or infrastructure, such as oil spills, levee breaks, and bridge collapses (Aini and Fakhrul-Razi, 2010). Biological or epidemiological disasters are threats to human health created by the spread of disease and pestilence, to create epidemics (World Health Organization, n.d.). Terrorism disasters are created by lapses in security and crime prevention efforts, which allow individuals and organizations to attack others in order to achieve a socio-political objective (Morley and Leslie, 2006).

Of these disaster types, gun violence has been discussed in the context of terrorism and epidemiological disasters. Mass shootings, such as the attack on

Russian school children by separatists from Chechnya in 2004 (CNN Library, 2013), have political objectives and are clearly acts of terrorism. To date these types of terror events (involving gunfire) have been limited in number and scale in the United States (Plumer, 2013).[1] From an epidemiological perspective, which examines health patterns of populations (World Health Organization, n.d.), repeated gun violence from other types of shooting incidents—whether mass shootings like the 2009 Virginia Tech incident, serial shootings like the 2002 DC Snipers incidents, the 243 single-shooting incident homicides in Chicago in 2012, or firearm suicides—can be viewed as a "disease", creating injury, death, and other disastrous effects on a society over time (Slutkin, 2015). Like a disease, there is also the concern that "contagion" will occur—that individuals with grievances will copy these behaviors to get publicity and notoriety if action is not taken to stop them (Mesoudi, 2013).

However, there are also similarities between what takes place in gun violence incidents and other types of disasters as well. For example, before the BP Deepwater Horizon oil spill, there were warning signs that an explosion was possible. Workers on the oil rig reported sparks occurring from the ignition of methane gas being released (Kirkham, 2010). After the Santa Barbara shooting incident in 2014, there were discussions in the media about warning signs (i.e. postings in social media with a violent content) that were issued by the gunman, long before he shot anyone (ABC News, 2014).

Like other disasters, the impacts of gun violence are wide ranging. Mass shootings can occur anywhere, victimizing anyone. People can be affected directly if they were shot, witnessed a shooting, or have an interpersonal connection to someone shot. Moreover, family members of the shooter, if not the victims of the shooting, are also affected by the event. Members of society at large can be affected by the indiscriminate acts of violence and the fear that it induces (Garbarino, Bradshaw and Vorrasi, 2002).

Moreover, as with other types of disasters, there are certain groups in society that face higher risks of experiencing gun violence. Firearm homicide and assault victimization occurs more often among people in their teens and twenties, African Americans, and males than among other groups; it is also one of the leading causes of death for these groups (Allen, 2013). Suicide by firearm occurs more often among young people, whites, and males than among other groups; it is also one of the leading causes of death for these groups (Drexler, 2013). The risks or vulnerabilities to gun violence are discussed further in this chapter.

Using a disaster research framework to study these phenomena allows us to see how the conditions present in a society can lead to a destructive event, produce undesirable outcomes, and how our responses can either exacerbate or ameliorate the situation. It also allows us to take action to reduce the chances of a similar event occurring again in the future (Congressional Record, 2002). Viewing the phenomena as being a process that unfolds over time, with Pre (Before), During, and Post

(After) phases, allows us to develop strategies to better respond at any given time to the phenomena (Bjelopera, Bagalman, Caldwell, Finklea, and McCallion, 2013).

In the next sections of this chapter, several different disaster models are examined in detail and how they can be applied to understand gun violence. In these discussions, key aspects and stages in the unfolding of a disaster will be highlighted. They are then used to develop a theoretical model that explains gun violence from a disaster process perspective.

Disaster Process Models

In this section, four different disaster models are discussed: Pressure And Release (PAR), Socio-Technological, Corrosive Community and Disaster Resilience of Place (DROP) model. The important stages and aspects of these models are presented, first in the context of the type of disaster they were originally created to explain. Then the relevance or the applicability of these models towards understanding gun violence is discussed.

Pressure and Release (Par) Model

This model was originally proposed by Blaikie et al (1994) to examine the conditions in society that contribute to creation of natural disasters. According to this model, there are Root Causes, Dynamic Pressures, and Unsafe Conditions that all lead to disaster. *Root Causes* are political and economic inequities that have long existed in society.

Root Causes lead to *Dynamic Pressures* that appear as forms of over- and under- development or utilization of resources and institutions in society. Dynamic Pressures produce *Unsafe Conditions*, which are exemplified by the vulnerability of social groups and institutions in society.

These Root Causes, Dynamic Pressures, and Unsafe Conditions can all be considered Precursors to a disaster. They are conditions that existed in society prior to a disaster that contribute to or facilitate the creation of the disaster. Additionally, they are embedded in a society's structure and are not easily removed or altered (Anderskov, 2004).

As with natural disasters, researchers have also documented that there are pre-existing factors in society that can give rise to or promote gun violence. If one examines the communities in which gun violence routinely occurs, these communities are characterized by economic disinvestment, household instability, gang activity and deteriorating infrastructure (Sherman, 1998). These communities lack influence in the political system as well, often seen as a drain on society at best and totally invisible at worst. If we examine cases of mass murder involving middle class perpetrators, we see the mental health care system and others failed to identify and serve offenders before the incidents (i.e. Aurora, Newtown, and Tucson). There's the ready accessibility of firearms and ammunition as well as the routine exposure to violence through media outlets that they are desensitize individuals (Scarf et al., 2013).

Socio-Technological Disaster

The Socio-Technological model was developed by Aini and Fakhrul-Razi (2010) to explain technological disasters, such as chemical leaks, industrial fires, and building collapses. According to this model, there are numerous stages involved in the unfolding of a disaster. These stages are Operation, Incubation, Forewarning, Activation, Response, Inquiry, Reporting, Feedback, Social Justice and Reform.

Operation refers to the decision to construct a facility. Operation and Incubation can be considered as the Precursors to a disaster. *Forewarning* refers to the warning signs that a disaster event is likely to occur in the near future. Clues that a disaster is in the making are ignored, misinterpreted, or not reported to the right people.

Activation refers to a triggering event occurring, which sets the disaster into creation. Short-term impacts would the immediate disaster results, while long-term impacts are those that would be felt long after the danger has receded. While Aini and Fakhrul-Razi (2010) combined the disaster event itself and the disaster impacts together, it might be useful to consider these as separate stages in the disaster process. In order for impacts to occur, there must be an event that creates them first.

Response refers to the actions taken immediately to address the disaster and limit its potential impact on society. *Inquiry* refers to determining the cause or who is to blame for the disaster. *Reporting* is providing the information that was learned to the public for consumption. *Feedback* is the actions taken by government agencies and others to hold those responsible for the disaster accountable. Inquiry, Reporting and Feedback are different aspects of assigning blame in a disaster.

Social Justice refers to the punishments meted out to those responsible for the disaster, to compensate victims and communities. *Reform* refers to new regulations and possibly new agencies created to address to prevent future disasters. These actions can also be considered as being part of the prevention and mitigation efforts against disasters reoccurring in the future (Aini & Fakhrul-Razi, 2010).

While this model has been used to explain technological disasters, many of its stages can also be applied to gun violence as well. In gun violence, the Operation stage would be the decision to build a large public place (such as a mall or theater). The Incubation stage would be not providing enough security to detect the presence of a shooter and his multi-shot weapons, and allowing his entry into the facility (National Counter Terrorism Committee, 2010). These serve as precursors to the disaster.

Forewarning or warning signs are indications that gun violence is about to occur. Examples of warning signs include someone making remarks about shooting another person or buying large amounts of ammunition (Huffington Post, 2012). Activation or the presence of catalysts includes someone being fired, the termination of a tumultuous relationship, or being arrested (Borum, et al., 1999). Onset or the disaster event itself would be the actual shooting incident itself and its features (number of shots fired, location(s) of the shooting, and victim(s)—offender(s) relationship). Impacts of the event would be the number of victims, property damage incurred, and disruption of normal routines in the shooting location (Blair and Schweit, 2014).

In a gun violence incident, Response would include the arrest of the shooting suspect, sending the injured to the hospital, and sealing off the shooting site from public entry (Police Executive Research Forum, 2014). In the Inquiry, Reporting and Feedback stages or Blame Assignment stage, there are efforts to determine the guilt of the perpetrator, if he/she had any accomplices to the crime (Sennewald and Tsukayama, 2015), and what may have motivated the offender to engage in gun violence (Petherick, 2015).

Social Justice contributing to the recovery of victims would be providing compensation to them for the crime (Malsch and Carriere, 1999). Reform efforts leading to the prevention of or mitigation against gun violence would include tougher restrictions on gun access (Hahn et al., 2005), training of personnel in workplaces to notice warning signs (White, 2014), and providing access to mental health care for those needing it (Montgomerie et al., 2015).

Corrosive Community Model

The processes involved in the Corrosive Community model was identified by Erikson (1976), Couch and Kroll-Smith (1985), and Levine (1982) and has been subsequently elaborated upon by others (Freudenberg, 1993; Picou and Gill, 2000; Picou, Marshall and Gill, 2004; Picou and Marshall, 2007) to better understand the processes taking place in a community before, during and after man-made or hybrid natural/man- made disasters. One distinguishing feature of these disasters (and of this model) is the recognition that some communities never fully recover from disaster, but remain trapped in a cycle of trauma over time that eventually leads to the disintegration of the community. The cycle of trauma lies in part with the origins of man-made disasters: they are created by human activity, whose negative consequences could have been averted by not engaging in the hazardous activity at all or by taking extra precautions.

As with natural disasters, Picou et. al (2004) argue there are *Warning Signs*, that some hazard in the community poses a possible risk to the community. This can escalate into a *Threat*, whereby it is obvious that a disaster will occur. This is followed by *Impact*, where the disaster event occurs and leaves its marks on a community and its population. This is followed by *Rescue*, where endangered individuals and property are removed from the disaster location. From there, movement toward community *Restoration*, *Reconstruction* and *Recovery* occurs. Restoration involves repairing damaged facilities and healing injured people. Reconstruction refers to replacing lost or severely damaged facilities. Recovery refers to returning to the normal functioning of a community, as it was prior to the disaster.

However, after man-made disasters, there are often secondary disasters that occur. These subsequent disasters can prevent the community from engaging in full recovery because there are additional new threats and impacts to address before resolving the initial disaster event.

In such disasters, the process of determining the causes and who are to blame (*Blame Assignment* phase) commences, which can prove to be a complex undertaking. The Blame Assignment phase can often last for decades as litigation surrounding responsibility, injury, punishment, and reparations unfolds in the court system (Picou and Marshall, 2007). The community is required to keep "re-living" the disaster repeatedly, as documentation and testimony are presented in court cases, and the media continues to report on these cases (Sheoin and Zavestoki, 2012). The disintegration of the community occurs as members of the community are often divided against one another in the assignment of responsibility and payment of reparations (Haney, 2012). Also, trauma can be maintained (possibly even magnified) when one disaster follows immediately after another disaster, before the community can adequately address the previous disaster (Picou and Marshall, 2007).

As criminological researchers have documented, some communities disproportionately experience high levels of gun violence repeatedly over time. A constant state of heightened awareness and trauma settles into the communities as more members witness gun violence, and/or experience injury, or death from the use of firearms (Bieler, 2014). Like other man-made disasters, gun violence originates with the choice of humans to engage in activities that produce negative outcomes. Gun violence is an activity that is optional[2], with the intent of inflicting harm upon another (Wilkinson and Fagan, 1996).

Blame Assignment also occurs as families and communities try to comprehend what may have enticed or driven someone to shoot another person (Haider-Markel and Joslyn, 2001).[3] The "re-living" of the violent incidents by victims (Singer et al, 1995) and witnesses (Shakoor and Chalmers, 1991) can occur repeatedly over a long period of time, as the apprehension, prosecution, and punishment of crime perpetrators by the criminal justice system unfolds (Orth, 2002) and the media covers the stories (Coté and Bucqueroux, 1996). The disintegration of the community, even particular families, can occur as members have victimized one another, and as others leave these communities to find safer environments (Barbee, 2010).

Disaster Resilience of Place (Drop) Model

The Disaster Resilience of Place (DROP) model was originally developed by Cutter and associates (2008) for natural disasters such as hurricanes, earthquakes and floods, but as the model's creators acknowledge, it can potentially be applied to other types of disasters as well. The model argues there are numerous stages involved in the unfolding of a disaster, including the Disaster Event, Impacts, Mitigation and Preparedness. Although many of these disaster stages delineated within the DROP model are also applicable to gun violence events, I will discuss only a few of these below (as previous discussions of other models have already highlighted many of the stages).

Disaster Event refers to the characteristics of the disaster itself, such as its location of occurrence, length of duration, size of area or populations affected, and frequency of similar events in the past. *Impacts* refer to the different ways the disaster event affected the natural, built, and social environments and those that inhabit them.

Social Learning involves developing new strategies to address the event. Some of these strategies may be actions developed and taken during the event, or in the middle of the event to address emerging situations. Those actions could be considered as part of the Immediate Response stage. Other new strategies may be developed later after the event is over, after evaluating the response to the event. These later developed strategies can be considered as part of Preparedness and Mitigation.

Degree of Recovery is the extent that a community can return to normal, pre-disaster functioning after a disaster event. It also encompasses the actions taken to return a community back to normal functioning. *Mitigation* refers to the actions taken by a community to prevent a future disaster event from occurring. *Preparedness* refers to a community's ability to respond to similar events in the future (Cutter et al., 2008). Since some of the same actions can be taken as part of both Mitigation and Preparedness efforts, for the purposes of this chapter, I combine Mitigation and Preparedness into one stage that occurs at the end of the disaster process.

Looking at gun violence incidents as disaster events, they can vary in terms of their duration (single shooting incident versus serial shootings), locations (private residence, along a sidewalk, or in a movie theater), victim-offender relationship (strangers, acquaintances, co-workers, or intimate partners), and number of offenders (single or multiple perpetrators) (Gun Violence Archive, 2015). The impacts can vary as well, in terms of the number of victims, extent and type of injuries, property damage, and magnitude of public fear (Bjelopera, Bagalman, Caldwell, Finklea, and McCallion, 2013).

Response includes the arrival of police and medical personnel on the shooting scene, public statements by politicians condemning the violence, and using social media to alert the public about a shooting incident (U.S. Department of Homeland Security, 2008). Recovery includes providing medical treatment to help the injured get well, providing financial and social support to victims and their families, and repairing or replacing any damaged property (Buchanan, 2014). Prevention and mitigation would involve passing new laws to restrict access to weapons, restricting the types of firearms sold, installing additional security personnel and cameras in public areas, and increasing public awareness about gun violence (Bilchik, 1999).

Gun-Assisted Violence as Disaster (GAVAD) Model

Now that I have discussed the applicability of these different models to understanding gun violence. I use the important components of these models to construct a theoretical model of how gun violence as a disaster phenomenon unfolds. I refer to this model as the Gun-Assisted Violence As Disaster (GAVAD) model. Table 10.1 below displays the stages of a gun violence disaster. as revealed by the GAVAD model. and its overlap with the other disaster models previously discussed.

Table 10.1. Disaster Models and Their Stages

(GAVAD)	Pressure And Release (PAR)	Socio-Technological	Corrosive Community	(DROP)
Precursors	Root Causes, Dynamic Pressures & Unsafe Conditions	Operation & Incubation	—	Antecedent Conditions
Warning Signs	—	Forewarning	Warning	—
Catalysts	Hazard	Activation	—	—
Disaster Event	Disaster	Onset	Threat	Disaster Event
Impacts	—	Onset	Impact	Impact
Immediate Responses	—	Response	Rescue	Absorptive Capacity, Coping Response. Improvise & Social Learning
Blame Assignment	—	Inquiry. Reporting & Feedback	Blame	—
Recovery	—		Restoration. Reconstruction & Recovery	Degree of Recovery
Prevention and Mitigation	—		—	Social Learning. Mitigation & Prepared-ness

[4]See notes at the end of the chapter for references. GAVAD (Gun Assisted Violence As Disaster): DROP (Disaster Resilience of Place)

In the GAVAD model. there are nine stages of a gun violence disaster. Those stages are Precursors. Warning Signs. Catalysts. Disaster Event, Disaster Impacts. Disaster Response. Blame Assignment. Recovery. and Prevention and Mitigation.

Table 10.2 presents a list of these stages and their definitions. as well as where in the Pre-. During, and Post-Disaster phases each stage occurs. Some of the component stages within phases may overlap in terms of their temporal occurrence and duration (i.e. Blame Assignment and Disaster Recovery stages); however. for the sake of clarity, they listed here as occurring in chronological order.

Table 10.2. Disaster Phases. Component Stages and Definitions

Phase	Component Stage	Definition of Stage
Pre-Disaster	Precursors	Conditions that make possible or facilitate a disaster
	Warning Signs	Indicators that a disaster event is developing
	Catalysts	Triggering events or conditions that cause a disaster
During Disaster	Disaster Event	Event that inflicts damage on people. property and environment
	Disaster Impacts	Types and extent of damage inflicted
	Immediate Disaster Responses	Actions taken to limit further damage from occurring or worsening
Post-Disaster	Blame Assignment	Who is responsible for the disaster event. directly and indirectly
	Disaster Recovery	Actions taken to restore society back to normal functioning
	Disaster Prevention	Efforts to reduce the likelihood of a similar disaster in the future
	Disaster Mitigation	Efforts to limit the impacts of a similar disaster in the future

[5]See notes at the end of the chapter for references.

Tables 10.3 through 10.11 provide extensive examples of the components that comprise each stage of a gun disaster. These tables are accompanied by a brief discussion of each stage.

Disaster Precursors

Long before a disaster event occurs, there are conditions present in a society that make it possible for a disaster to happen. These conditions can be found in the characteristics of the social, economic, legal, security, technological, built and .natural environments of a society (Cutter et al., 2008). The social environment refers to the nature of interactions between different groups in society. These interactions are influenced by and reflect the inequalities in status and power between groups in society. Closely associated with the conditions of the social environment are conditions present in the economic environment (Barnett and Casper, 2001). Issues of unequal wealth and income distribution, employment instability, and employment discrimination can give rise to a sense of injustice among groups of individuals (Leon- Guerrero, 2009).

The legal environment dictates what behaviors are condoned in society and which behaviors are considered deviant and threatening to the well-being of society. Those behaviors considered the most threatening to society are harshly punished via fines and imprisonment. Law enforcement and security are charged with preventing these damaging behaviors from occurring, and when they do occur, to detect and terminate them (Schmalleger, 2008). The legal environment also serves as a guide to how society will respond to and recover from a disaster (Birkland and Schneider, 2007).

The technological environment influences how members of societies communicate with one another, the content of information that is shared in those communications, and how quickly/easily the information is transmitted (Carl, 2013). Technology is also a factor in the disaster event itself (Scigliano, 2002) and is used in responding to (Meredith, 2012) and recovering from disasters (Kiniry, n.d.).

The built environment refers to the physical structures (buildings, highways, and railways) present in a society and how they are distributed over a physical space. It also refers to how those built structures are constructed and arranged internally (Bartuska, 2007). Finally, the natural environment consists of the vegetation, waterways, and terrain of an area (Harper, 2012). Table 10.3 provides examples of precursor conditions found in society.

These examples of Precursor Conditions by no means are exhaustive for gun violence and do not necessarily apply to every single shooting incident. Precursor conditions may not be mutually exclusive, but can be interrelated and influence one another. For example, internet technology makes the recruitment of alienated youth into violent organizations possible (Kaplan, 2009). However, the presence of no single precursor alone creates conditions that produce gun violence, but rather it is the combination of precursors makes gun violence possible (PoliceOne. Com, 2013; Felson and Pare, 2010). The presence of these precursors in society, a community, or an individual's life does not mean that a particular person will *definitely* engage in acts of firearm violence. The presence of these precursors increases the *probability* of that person engaging in firearm violence (Papachristos, Wildeman, and Roberto, 2015).

Table 10.3. Precursor Conditions and Their Examples, for Gun Violence

Precursor Conditions	Examples
Social	Grievances against others based on some interaction at home, workplace, or school; Recruitment of alienated youth by gangs, hate groups, and terror organizations
Demographic	Large numbers of teenaged and young adult males; Densely populated areas
Health	Untreated and under-treated mental health issues; Substance abuse issues
Cultural	Glorification and prevalence of violence in entertainment; Racial and religious animosity; Disdain for authority figures; Stigma associated with mental health diagnosis/treatment; Emphasis on individualism and hyper-success; Desire to preserve one's "honor" when disrespect is perceived
Familial	Poor socialization into normative roles; Instability in familial membership and roles; Lack of law abiding authority figures and role models; Lack of parental support for children and youths
Economic	Employment instability and income inequality; Intense competition for employment with others of different backgrounds/characteristics; Anger towards big business and Wall Street
Political	Disenfranchisement, unrest, and rapid change; Open disrespect and hostility towards those with different views; Leaders out of touch with public's concerns; Anger towards big government involvement in people's lives

Table 10.3 (Continued)

Precursor Conditions	Examples
Educational	High school dropout and under-performance rates; Problems with student discipline; High turnover in teachers and other key personnel
Religious	Over/under influence of institutions in community; Cults and extremist views regularly propagated
Legal	Weak restrictions on firearm possession and use; Ineffective punishment for violations; Easy access to weapons on the black market
Security	Lapses in patrol coverage of an area; Lack of surveillance and rapid crime detection; Easy entry into unlocked facilities and premises
Technological	Multi-shot capacity firearms; Accessibility of information and communication via internet and cell phones; Quick, repeated and pervasive coverage of shootings by media
Built Environment	Easily accessible, open public spaces where crowds congregate make people easy targets; Interstate highways for easy shooter escape; Abandoned buildings for killing/dumping victims; Porous national borders for easy entry/exit by drug cartel members, terrorists, etc.
Natural Environment	Forests, swamps, and rugged terrain where shooters can hide after a rampage; Location where victims can be killed/dumped without being seen; Good weather and pleasant temperatures encourage more people to engage in leisure activities outside of the home, making more people potential crime targets

[6]See notes at the end of the chapter for references.

Disaster Warning Signs

There are many different warning signs presented (by a potential shooter) that a gun violence incident is emerging. Unfortunately, these signs are often recognized after the disaster has taken place, as associates of the shooter and law enforcement begin to examine the disaster's evidence and events prior to the shooting incident(s) (Malsch and Carriere, 1999).

These warning signs can be emotional, mental and/or behavioral in nature (College of Southern Nevada, n.d.). While no one example of a warning sign alone is an indication of a potential firearm disaster, a multitude of these examples combined together for an individual does increase the likelihood of a gun violence disaster in the making. Table 10.4 presents examples of different warning signs that may be present in a gun violence disaster.

Table 10.4. Warning Signs for Gun Violence

Warning Sign Category	Examples
Emotional	Out of control emotions like extreme rage; Lack of emotional expression
Mental	Acute episodes of mental illness; Obsessions with violent incidents or violent offenders
Behavioral: Social Interaction	Social isolation from others; New group of associates replacing former associates; Appears to be under someone else's "spell" or command; Increased communications and visits with known gang, hate or terrorist group's members
Preparation for /Engaging in Violent or Destructive Behavior	Acts of cruelty towards others; Acts of vandalism; Making threats of violence; Substance abuse; Carrying firearms regularly; Regular visits to violent or extremist group websites; Expressed interest in joining a gang, hate or terror group; Enjoying violent entertainment to the exclusion of other activities; Repeated surveillance of a location; Stalking an individual or group; Stockpiling firearms and bullets; Frequent participation in paintball and other pseudo military exercises
Neglectful Behavior	Declining performance at school or work; Chronic absenteeism at school or work; Radical change/decline in physical appearance

[7]See notes at the end of the chapter for references.

Disaster Catalysts

Catalysts are the events that trigger or spark an act of gun violence. These catalysts can come from a variety of sources, such as loss of status, negative interactions with others, mental health issues, or criminal activity (Wilkinson & Hamerschlag, 2003). However, the mere presence of one of the catalyst examples (see Table 10.5) in a person's life does not mean that he/she will engage in gun violence. There are other factors that come into play such as a person's history of interactions, how they have learned to resolve conflict, and society's response to violence. These factors influence whether or not if a situation turns into a catalyst for violent actions (Kennedy and Forde, 1998). Moreover, the presence of multiple catalysts in a person's life can increasingly stress that individual to point of seeking release. This release can be in the form of the individual harming his self or others (ABC News, 2004).

Table 10.5. Catalysts for Gun Violence

Catalyst type	Examples
Dramatic Event: Loss of Status	Fired from a job; Failing grade on assignment or class; Failure to receive a promotion at work; Eviction from home by landlord or mortgage company; Divorce or separation
Negative Interactions	Physical attack at home; Intense argument over money, drugs, and/or lovers; Arrest, court subpoena, lawsuit, or other negative experiences with the law; Bullied at school or work; Romantic advances spurned
Mental Health Issues	Worsening PTSD symptoms; Deepening psychosis; Increasing paranoia
Criminal Activity	Robbery victim fights back; Gang warfare over turf; Inflict death and fear against others who are different or government officials to advance a socio-political agenda

[8]See notes at the end of the chapter for references.

Disaster Events

This is the event or action that damages or destroys populations, their possessions, and/or the built and natural environments. Gun Violence Disaster Events contain many aspects, such as the type of shooting incident, number of shooters, victims, accessories, and witnesses, the relationships between those involved, environment of event, and motives for the shooting(s). Examples of different Gun Violence Event Aspects are presented in Table 10.6.

Table 10.6. Gun Violence Event Aspects

Event Aspects	Example
Type of Incident	Single shooting, mass shooting, spree shooting, or serial shooting; Were other types of weapons also involved?
Shooter(s)	One or more shooters
Victim(s):	
Number	One or more
Relationship	Known or unknown to offender
Witness(es)	None, one or more
Accessories to event:	
Number	None, one or more contributors
Type	Supply weapons
	Provide surveillance information
	Involved in planning
Environment	Location
	Time of day or night
	Day of week
	Time of year
	Weather
Shooter(s) Motive(s)	Suicide; Revenge; Retaliation; Terror; Theft; Notoriety; Protection; Carelessness; Mercy Killing; Fear; War
Type of firearm used	Handgun, shotgun, rifle, assault rifle; small capacity vs. large capacity clip

[9]See notes at the end of the chapter for references.

Disaster Impacts

Disaster Impacts are the types and extent of damage that the gun disaster event had on population, property and the environment. Some impacts are immediate and short-term, while other impacts take more time to unfold and/or are enduring. Also, impacts can be localized or broad in scope. Examples of Disaster Impacts are presented in Table 10.7.

Table 10.7. Gun Violence Impacts. Immediate and Long-term

Type of Impacts	Examples
Social	Distrust of strangers; Traffic delays due to blocked streets and facilities
Demographic	Declining population for certain groups. such as young black males. where firearm homicide is a leading cause of death
Health	People killed and injured: Survivors and witnesses traumatized; Long-term disability of victims; General public fearful
Cultural	Increase in "live by the gun. die by the gun" mentality for certain groups
Familial	Loss of family members; Trauma of loss for family members of victims and offenders; Shame and regret experienced by offender's family
Economic	Loss of workers and wages: Repair costs for damaged facilities; Loss of business due to public's fear of location as a "shooting" location
Political	Public pressure on politicians to create restrictive legislation
Educational	Learning impeded by school violence
Security	Copycat offenders emerge: Repeat offenders returning to scene
Built Environ-ment	Damage to facilities
Natural Environ-ment	Tainted soil and water from decaying bodies dumped in woods

[10]See notes at the end of the chapter for references.

Immediate Disaster Responses

Disaster Responses are the actions that society takes to limit the extent of damage that can continue to occur after a disaster event. These responses can take many forms and often multiple responses are used to address a gun violence disaster. Examples of different Disaster Responses are presented in Table 10.8.

Table 10.8. Immediate Gun Violence Disaster Responses

Immediate Responses	Examples
Security	Lockdown of school or facility where incident is occurring; Keeping the public away from the scene; Apprehending or killing the shooter Seize all weapons brought on scene by shooter; Search and seize all other potential stockpile locations; Seize important evidence
Health	Removing the wounded and transfer them to hospital ER unit; Remove deceased to city morgue; Counseling services for those traumatized
Familial	Contact next of kin for victims and shooter
Technological	Use public address system, text alerts, Twitter, robo calls, etc. to alert people of a shooter on a premises and in the community; Use of robot equipped with camera to enter scene to locate a hiding shooter or shooter's body
Political	High status and local representatives denounce act to discourage copycat offenders
Educational	If event occurs at a school, top administrator makes public statement once event is over
Social	Public wary of those around them
Economic	If event occurs in a business facility, work stops temporarily; Top manager makes statement to reassure workers and customers once the event is over and to re-establish a sense of normalcy; Increase in gun purchases, for protective purposes, by consumers

[11]See notes at the end of the chapter for references.

Blame Assignment

Immediately after every gun violence incident, questions emerge about the assailant and what may have influenced him/her to engage in such destructive behavior. Obviously, the person who shoots the firearm is directly responsible for the violent action. Yet, many discussions in the media and elsewhere focus on the lack of prohibitive measures in place and other potential social-cultural factors as being indirect influencers of gun violence. Since these indirect influencers often lack conclusive scientific evidence supporting their role in creating gun violence, prolonged intense debates swirl around any legislative attempts to restrict their presence in society (PBS, 2000).

Table 10.9 provides examples of some of the factors often mentioned as being responsible for gun violence. For the purposes of the GAVAD model, it does not matter if these factors have not been proven to cause gun violence. What is important is how gun violence is often attributed to these factors in societal discussions and actions.

Table 10.9. Blame Assignment for Disaster Event, Directly and Indirectly

Who is Responsible (Blamed)	Examples
Direct	The shooter
Indirect	Weak security measures in place at facilities; Producers and vendors of violent entertainment
	Lawmakers instituting weak firearm purchase/ possession regulations and penalties for firearm violations; Law enforcement for not responding to warning calls from family/ friends about impending incident; Family, friends and others not recognizing warning signs in time to stop incident
	Inadequate mental health care system; Incompetent and lenient parents; Weapons manufacturers and sellers; National Rifle Association and pro-gun enthusiasts
	Extremist groups for propagating hate and violent solutions; Media for providing publicity for the offender and event with non-stop coverage

[12]See notes at the end of the chapter for references.

Disaster Recovery

Disaster Recovery refers to the efforts made to restore society, as much as possible, back to its pre-disaster state of routine functioning. These recovery efforts can take place in many different ways. To what extent this can occur depends upon many factors, including the extent of devastation that occurred and how easily the damage can be reversed. For someone who lost a loved one to gun violence, returning back to the pre-disaster state is not easily accomplished. For society, the more gun violence incidents occur, the harder it is to erase their impacts on the collective memory and behavior (Buchanan, 2014). Table 10.10 presents examples of recovery efforts taken after a shooting.

Table 10.10. Recovery Efforts

Recovery Efforts	Examples
Built Environment	Clean and repair damaged facilities
Economic	Provide financial support to those with long-term disability from incident; Victim compensation
Health	Heal the injured; Counsel traumatized victims and witnesses
Social	Reassure public steps are being taken to prevent future tragedies; Hold public memorial services for victims

[13]See notes at the end of the chapter for references.

Disaster Prevention and Mitigation

After a disaster event, an assessment of the disaster situation takes place. This assessment is used to determine what actions can be taken to reduce the likelihood of a similar disaster event occurring in the future (prevention) and to lessen the impact if one does occur (mitigation) (Moran, 2012). Since many actions that can be taken are both preventive and mitigative in nature, they are combined into one stage in the GAVAD model.

Prevention and mitigation efforts must focus on those precursor conditions that gave rise to the gun violence disaster. These efforts, once implemented, create social change and become part of the characteristics of society. Their goal is to become the components of society that attempt to eliminate the precursor conditions which led to the disaster event. Their success depends upon many things, including the number of gun violence supporting and negating features in society, as well as veracity of their application. Table 10.11 presents examples of different prevention and mitigation efforts that a society can take in response to gun violence.

Table 10.11. Firearm Violence Prevention and Mitigation Efforts

Prevention Efforts	Examples
Cultural	Reduce violence in entertainment; Efforts to counteract and denounce extremist views; Non-violent solutions to problems emphasized and violent solutions de-emphasized/denounced
Educational	Faculty, staff, students, and co-workers taught to recognize warning signs and how to prevent a shooting; Training drills on what to do if a shooter appears at work, school or elsewhere; Educate facility personnel not to let other personnel use their passes/keys to enter facilities
Legal	Restrict firearm access, especially for mentally ill; Increase registration requirements for firearms purchased at any venue; Toughen sanctions for firearm violations; Lobby for new gun violence prevention programs
Security	Increase number of law enforcement personnel; Increase surveillance; Install metal detectors and scanning devices; Alarm systems to alert public of threat; Combat firearm black markets; increase public awareness of potential threats
Technological	Develop "smart guns" that won't function for non-owners
Social	Affected communities come together as a social movement
Religious	Organizations (i.e., Methodists) calling for gun violence prevention and lobbying state legislatures on the issue; Faith leaders emphasizing nonviolent aspects of religious texts

[14]See notes at the end of the chapter for references.

In summary, the GAVAD model identifies nine different stages that occur in the unfolding of a gun violence disaster. These stages are Precursors, Warning Signs, Catalysts, Disaster Event, Impacts, Immediate Responses, Blame Assignment, Recovery, and Prevention and Mitigation. Within each of the stages, there are many different aspects at work influencing the gun violence disaster process. Examples of these aspects were shown in the preceding tables (Tables 10.3 through 10.11).

Conclusion

This chapter has examined the issue of gun violence from the theoretical framework provided by disaster research. Many similarities exist between gun violence and disaster phenomena, in terms of the ways that they unfold and can affect society. Four different models of disasters—Pressure And Release, Socio-Technological, Corrosive Community, and Disaster Resilience of Place—are applied to the issue of gun violence and used to inform the creation of the Gun Assisted Violence As Disaster (GAVAD) model.

The next step in this research agenda will be to apply the GAVAD model to many different gun violence cases, to fully determine the scope and limitations of the model. To do this, the GAVAD model will need to be tested using cases from different time periods and societies, with different perpetrator motives and impacts. Factors that influence the features of each of the disaster stages will be examined as well (Neuman, 2011).

While the development and refinement of the GAVAD model makes contributions to the scholarly literature, it also has the added benefit of assisting those in law enforcement, healthcare, community activism, and other professions in the field develop practices to address gun violence issues. GAVAD examines gun violence as a *process* embedded in society, with distinct stages of unfolding, not as a societal aberration or as an event that occurs out of nowhere that is short in duration.

Notes

The author would like to thank Dr. Jessica Doucet, Dr. Jessica Burke, and Dr. Nwamaka Anaza for their comments on previous drafts of this paper.

1.   The surviving victims and families of deceased victims in the Fort Hood 2009 shooting are requesting that the incident be classified as a terrorist attack by the US Government, because the shooter shouted Islamist remarks before opening fire on fellow soldiers. However, the shooter was not prosecuted as a terrorist because there are no provisions in military law that address fellow soldier-on-soldier attacks as a terrorist event. Hence, it has been classified as an act of workplace violence (Kreider, 2012). Major Nidal Hasan, an Army psychiatrist, fatally shot 13 and wounded 30 fellow soldiers and reservists. He was sentenced to death by a military court for his actions (Graczyk and Merchant, 2013).
2.   Like homicide, suicide by firearm also negatively impacts family members, friends and communities, including an increased risk of suicide attempts by survivors (Zhang, Tong, and Zhou, 2005; Lippman, 2010; Ali, 2015)
3.   A similar process of seeking explanations for and someone or something to blame for a suicide or an accident also occurs (Marcus, 2012; Peters, 2015).
4.   References used for Table 10.1 are: Anderskov (2004) for the Pressure And Release model; Aini and Fakhrul-Razi (2010) for the Socio-Technological model; Picou,

Brunsma, and Overfelt (2010) for the Corrosive community model; and Cutter et al. (2008) for the Disaster Resilience of Place model.

5. References used for Table 10.2 are: Bjelopera et al. (2013) for the three disaster phases and placement of stages; Blaikie et al. (1994), Aini and Fahkrul-Razi (2010), Cutter et al. (2008), and Picou and Marshall (2007) for the definitions of stages.

6. References used for Table 10.3 are: For social, Neuman and Baron, 1998; Felson, Berg, and Rogers, 2014; White and Cunnen, 2006; For health, Arseneault et al. 2000); For cultural, Cantor, 2000; Levin and McDevitt, 2008; Cukier and Sheptycki, 2012; Qian and Zhang, 2014; Felson and Pare, 2010; Patton, Eschmann, and Butler, 2013; For familial, Loeber and Hay, 1997; For economic, White and Cunnen, 2006; For political, Southern Poverty Law Center, 2014; For educational, Ramirez et al., 2011; For legal, Taylor and Li, 2015; Braga, 2008; Lee, 2015. For technological, Helfgott, 2015. For built environment, Wilcox 2015 and Marzbali et al., 2011; Spelman, 2002; Ting, 2006; For natural environment, Marzbali et al. 2011; Cohn, 1990; For security, Wayland, 2014. For religious, Southers, 2013.

7. References used for Table 10.4 are: For emotional American Psychological Association (n.d.) and Kerr, 2010; For mental Hall and Friedman, 2013; For behavioral Muscari, 2004; Freedman and Hemenway, 2000; Gold, Gold and Herkov, 2008; Stroebe, 2013; Gunter and Daly, 2012; Skoler, 1998; White, 2012.

8. References used for Table 10.5 are: for loss of status Neuman and Baron, 1998; Ellis, Stuckless and Smith, 2015; for negative interactions Glicken, 2009; Freedman and Hemenway, 2000; for mental health Montgomerie et al., 2015; Wachtel and Shorter, 2013; for criminal activity Peron, 2013; Warner, 2007.

9. References used for Table 10.6 are Altheimer et al., 2013; Greenberg, 2013.

10. References used for Table 10.7 are: for social Kaminiski et al., 2010; Forest and Brown, 2015; Kwong, 2014; for demographic Bell, 2013; for health Kerr, 2010; Helfgott, 2015; Steffen and Harlow, 2014,, for cultural PBS, n.d.; for familial Jany, 2015; Buchanan, 2014; for economic Corso et al., 2007; for political Singh, 2003, for educational Juvonen, 2001; for security Everson and Pease, 2003; for built environment Law Center to Prevent Gun Violence, 2015; for natural environment Harris, 2013.

11. References used for Table 10.8 are: for security, Australia-New Zealand Counter-Terrorism Committee, 2013; Indiana University, n.d.; Lohr, 2012; for health, Linkous and Caret, 2009; Jaycox et al., 2014; for technological, College of Southern Nevada, n.d.; Knight (2014); for familial Sapakie, 2015, for political, Kindy, 2014; for Educational, Hedgpeth and Bui, 2015; for Social, Martinez, 1993; for economic, Caronated.tv, n.d.; Thompson, 2012.

12. References used for Table 10.9 are: for direct Hickman, 2014; for indirect Ross and Bryant, 2010; Karlinsky and Przygoda, 2012; Pearson, 2014; Ellis and Sidner, 2014; Puffer, 2014; Blake, 2013; Belkin, 2013; Schecter, 2014; Dorelien et al., 2009; and Grenny, 2012.

13. References used for Table 10.10 are: for built environment Clean Scene Services, LLC, n.d.; McLemore, 2014; for economic National Association of Crime Victimization Compensation Boards, n.d.; Robert Wood Johnson Foundation, 2012; for social Williams, 2014; Dial, 2014.

14. References used for Table 10.11 are: for cultural, Busch, 2014, and Center for Nonviolent solutions, n.d.; for educational, Hanson, 2014; for legal, Kellerman, 2004; for security, Hefling et. al, 2014; Johnson, 2013; for social, Hawdon et al., 2012; Dial, 2014; for religious, United Methodist Church, 2012, and Jenkins and Towns, 2013.

References

ABC News (2004). Direct link between stress and aggression. *ABC News*, October 13. http://abcnews.go.com/Technology/DyeHard/story?id=158266

ABC News (2014). Inside the Santa Barbara killer's manifesto. *Good Morning America*, May 25. http://abcnews.go.com/US/inside-santa-barbara-killers-manifesto/story?id=23860511

Aini, M. S., & Fakhrul-Razi, A. (2010). Development of a Socio-Technological Disaster Model. *Safety Science*, 48: 1286–1295.

Ali, F. (2015). Exploring the complexities of suicide bereavement research. *Procedia- Social and Behavioral Sciences*, 165 (6): 30–39.

Allen, F. (2013). Gun violence leading cause of death of black children. *The Black Voice News*, August 5. http://www.blackvoicenews.com/news/news-wire/48950-gun-violence -leading-cause-of-death-of-black-children.html

Altheimer, I., Duda, J., DiPoalar, A., & Bower, K. (2013). Toward a research agenda for the Rochester Shooting Database. Working paper #2013-04. *Center for Public Safety Initiatives*, February 6. https://www.rit.edu/cla/criminaljustice/sites/rit.edu.cla. criminal justice/files/ docs/WorkingPapers/2013/2013-04.pdf

American Psychological Association. (n.d.) Warning signs of youth violence. http://www.apa.org/helpcenter/warning-signs.aspx

Anderskov, Christina. 2004. Anthropology and disaster. Thesis for Aarhus University. http://www.anthrobase.com/Txt/A/Anderskov_C_03.htm.

Arseneault, L., Moffitt, T. E., Caspi, A., Taylor, P. J., & Silvia, P. A.(2000). Mental disorders and violence in a total birth cohort: Results from the Dunedin study. JAMA Psychiatry, 57 (10): 979–986.

Australia-New Zealand Counter-Terrorism Committee. (2013). Active shooter guidelines for places of mass gathering. Commonwealth of Australia.http://www.nationalsecurity. gov.au/Media-and-publications/Publications/documents/active-shooter-guidelines-places-mass-gathering.doc

Barbee, E. (2010). *The solution for black America: Reclaiming, rebuilding* and restoring the urban ghettos in America. Xlibris Corporation.

Barnett, E., & Casper, M. (2001). A definition of 'social environment.' *American Journal of Public Health*, 91 (3): 465.

Bartuska, T. (2007). The built environment: Definitions and scope. In W. R. McClure & T. J. Bartuska. *The built environment: A collaborative inquiry into design and planning, Second edition.* Wiley and Sons.

Belkin, L. (2013). Should we blame the parents of the Nevada school shooter? *Huffington Post*, October 23. http://www.huffingtonpost.com/2013/10/23/should-we-blame-the-parents-of-the-nevada-school-shooter_n_4151476.html

Bell, L. (2013). Disarming realities: As gun sales soar. Gun crimes plummet. *Forbes*, May 14. http://www.forbes.com/sites/larrybell/2013/05/14/disarming-realities-as-gun-sales-soar-gun-crimes-plummet/

Bieler, S. (2014). Raising the voices of gun violence. *Urban Institute*. http://www. datatools.urban.org/Features/raising-the-voices-of-gun-violence/

Bilchik, S. (1999). *Strategies to reduce gun violence*. Washington: Office of Juvenile Justice and Delinquency Prevention.

Birkland, T. A., & Schneider, C. A. (2007). Emergency management in the courts: Trends after September 11 and Hurricane Katrina. *The Justice System Journal*, 28 (1): 20–35.

Bjelopera, J.P., Bagalman, E., Caldwell, S. W., Finklea. K. M., & McCallion, G. 2013. *Public mass shootings in the United States: Selected implications for federal public health and safety policy.* Congressional Research Service. March 18. http://www.fas.org/sgp/crs/misc/R43004.pdf

Blaikie, P., Cannon, T., Davis. I. & Wisner. B. (1994). *At risk: Natural hazards, people's vulnerability, and disasters.* London: Routledge.

Blair, J. P., & Schweit, K. W. (2014). *A study of active shooter incidents, 2000–2013.* Texas State University and Federal Bureau of Investigation, U.S. Department of Justice, Washington D.C.

Blake, A. (2013). On gun violence, Americans blame mental health system over gun laws. *Washington Post.* September 20. http://www.washingtonpost.com/blogs/post-politics/wp/2013/09/20/on-gun-violence-americans-blame-mental-health-system-over-gun-laws/

Borum, R., Fein. R., Vossekuil, B., & Berglund. J. (1999). Threat assessment: Defining an approach to assessing risk for targeted violence. Mental Health Law & Policy Faculty Publications. Paper 146. http://scholarcommons.usf.edu/mhlp_facpub/146

Braga, A. A. (2008). Pulling levers focused deterrence strategies and the prevention of gun homicide. *Journal of Criminal Justice.* 36 (4): 332- 343.

Buchanan, C. (2014). *Gun violence, disability and recovery.* Xlibris Corporation.

Busch, A. (2014). Reducing violence in movies is a start. *The Denver Post.* March 1. http://www.denverpost.com/ci_25250722/reducing-violence-movies-is-start

Byron, J. & Braden, J. (2013). Toward an informed rebuilding: documenting Sandy's impacts. *Pratt Center for Community Development,* June 4.

Cantor, J. (2000). Media violence. *Journal of Adolescent Health.* 27 (2) supplement 1: 30–34.

Carbonated.tv. (n.d.) Deadly shooting means business interruption for Hartford distributors. http://www.carbonated.tv/news/deadly shooting means

Carl, J. D. (2013). *Think social problems 2013.* Boston: Pearson

Center for Nonviolent Solutions. (n.d.). Education for youth. http://www.nonviolentsolutions.org/youth

Clean Scene Services, LLC. (n.d.) Trauma and death scene cleaning and restoration. http://www.cleanscenellc.com/media.html

CNN Library. 2013. Belsan School siege fast facts. www.cnn.com/2013/09/09/world/europe

Cohn, E. G. (1990). Weather and crime. *British Journal of Sociology,* 30 (1): 51–64

College of Southern Nevada. (n.d.). Active shooter community response plan. http://www.csn.edu/pages/1687.asp

Congressional Record. 2002. Proceedings and debates of the 107th Congress, second volume. Washington, DC: United States Government Printing Office. https://books.google.com/books?id=et1MeIF41-QC&printsec=frontcover#v=onepage&q&f=false

Coté, W., & Bucqueroux, B. (1996). Covering crime without re-victimizing victims. *Victims and the Media Program. Michigan State University School of Journalism.* http://www.victims.jrn.msu.edu/public/articles/nashvill.html

Corso, P. S., Mercy, J. A., Simon, T. A., Finkelstein, E. A., & Miller, T. R. (2007). Medical costs and productivity losses due to interpersonal and self-directed violence in the United States. *American Journal of Preventive Medicine,* 32 (6): 474–482.

Couch, S. R., & Kroll-Smith, J. S. (1985). The chronic technical disaster: Toward a social scientific perspective. *Social Science Quarterly* 66:564–75.

Cukier, W., & Sheptycki, J. (2012). Globalization of gun culture transnational reflections on pistolization and masculinity. flows and resistance. *International Journal of Law, Crime and Justice*, 40 (1): 3–19.

Cutter, S. L., Barnes, L., Berry, M., Burton, C., Evans, E., Tate, E., & Webb, J. (2008). A place-based model for understanding community resilience to natural disasters. *Global Environmental Change*, 18: 598–606.

Dial, S. (2014). Unusual memorial for victims of gun violence. *WLTX*, Channel 19. http://www.wltx.com/story/news/local/2014/06/25/gun-violence-columbia/11385791/

Dorelien, A., Miller, M., & Brody, P. (2009). *Guns and hate*. Brady Center to Prevent Gun Violence: Washington, D.C. http://www.bradycampaign.org/sites/default/files/guns-hate.pdf

Drexler, M. (2013). Guns and suicide: the hidden toll. *Harvard School of Public Health Magazine*, Spring. http://www.hsph.harvard.edu/magazine-features/guns-and-suicide-the-hidden-toll/

Ellis, D., Stuckless, N., & Smith, C. (2015). Separation and lethal intimate partner violence. *Marital separation and lethal domestic violence*, 29–43.

Ellis, R. & Sidner, S. (2014). Deadly California rampage: Chilling video, but no match for reality. *CNN*, May 27. http://www.cnn.com/2014/05/24/justice/california-shooting-deaths/

Erikson, K. (1976). *Everything in Its Path: Destruction of Community in the Buffalo Creek Flood*. Simon & Schuster.

Everson, S., & Pease, K. (2003). Crime against the same person and place: Detection opportunity and offender targeting. *Crime Prevention Studies*, 12: 199–220.

Felson, R. B., Berg, M. T., & Rogers, M. L. (2014). Bring a gun to a gunfight: Armed adversaries and violence across nations. *Social Science Research*, 47: 79–90.

Felson, R. B., & Pare, P-P. (2010). Firearms and fisticuffs: Region, race, and adversary effects on homicide and assault. *Social Science Research*, 39 (2): 272–284.

Forest, A., & Brown, G. (2015). Update: Lots of questions about person found shot on I-240. *WREG, News Channel 3*. Memphis, TN, March 29. http://wreg.com/2015/03/29/traffic-alert-accident-on-i-240-causes-delays/

Freedman, D., & Hemenway, D. (2000). Precursors of lethal violence: A death row sample. *Social Science and Medicine*, 50 (12): 1757–1770.

Freudenburg, W. R., & Jones, T. R. (1991). Attitudes and stress in the presence of technological risk: A test of the Supreme Court Hypothesis. *Social Forces* 69:1143–68.

Garbarino, J., Bradshaw, C. P., & Vorrasi, J.A. (2002). Mitigating the effects of gun violence on children and youth. *Future of the Children*, 12 (2). http://futureofchildren.org/publications/journals/article/index.xml?journalid=42&articleid=166&sectionid=1068

Glicken, M. D. (2009). Evidence-based practice and school violence.*Evidence-Based Practice with Emotionally Troubled Children and Adolescents*, 2009: 335–355

Gold, M. S., Gold, S. T., & Herkov, M. (2008). Drugs and violence in the USA. In L. Kurtz. *Encyclopedia of violence, peace and conflict. Second edition*. Pp.590–606.

Graczyk, M., & Merchant, N. 2013. Nidal Hasan death sentence: Fort Hood shooter will be executed for 2009 rampage. *Huffington Post*, August 28. http://www.huffingtonpost.com/2013/08/28/nidal-hasan-death-sentence_n_3831672.html

Greenberg, S. (2013). Characteristics of gun violence: Information from three roundtable discussions with senior law and front line enforcement personnel. *Committee on Priorities for a Public Health Research Agenda to Reduce the Threat of Firearm-*

related Violence, April 23. http://www.iom.edu/~/media/0A49FA78043C40A8A9AF 1A3FB0946FF2.ashx

Grenny, J. (2012). The media is an accomplice in public shootings: A call for a "Stephen King" law. *Forbes*, December 13. http://www.forbes.com/sites/josephgrenny/2012/ 12/13/the-media-is-an-accomplice-in-public-shootings-a-call-for-a-stephen-king-law/

Gun Violence Archive. (2015).General methodology. http://www.gunviolencearchive. org/methodology

Gunter, W. D., & Daly, K. (2012). Causal or spurious: Using propensity score matching to detangle the relationship between violent video games and violent behavior. *Computers in human behavior*, 28:1348–1355.

Hahn, R. A., Bilukha, O., Crosby, A., Fullilove, M. T., Liberman, A., Moscicki, E., Snyder. S. Tuma, F., & Briss, P. A. (2005). firearm laws and the reduction of violence: A systematic review. *American Journal of Preventive Medicine*, 28: 40–71.

Haider-Markel, D. P., & Joslyn, M. R. (2001). Gun policy, opinion, tragedy, and blame attribution: The conditional influence of issue frames. *The Journal of Politics*, 63 (2): 520–543.

Hall, R. C. W., & Friedman, S. H. (2013). Guns, schools and mental illness: Potential concerns for physicians and mental health professionals. *Mayo Clinic Proceedings*, 88 (11): 1272–1283.

Haney, T. J. (2012). The gulf oil spill, ecological debt, and environmental justice in Louisiana: Lessons from sociology. In L. A. Eargle & A. Esmail, *Black beaches and bayous: The BP Deepwater Horizon oil spill disaster*, pp. 105–118. Lanham: University Press of America.

Hanson, H. (2014). Ultra-realistic school shooting 'drill' terrifies students, teachers, parents. *Huffington Post*, November 17. http://www.huffingtonpost.com/2014/11/17/jewett-middle-academy-shooter-drill-_n_6174096.html

Harper, C. L. (2012). *Environment and society. Human perspectives on environmental issues, fifth edition*. Upper Saddle River: Prentice Hall.

Harris, M. (2013). Arsenic contamination in graveyards: How the dead are hurting the environment. *Utne Reader*. June. http://www.utne.com/environment/arsenic-contamination-ze0z1306zpit.aspx

Hawdon, J., Rasanen, P., Oksanen, A., & Ryan, J. (2012). Social solidarity and wellbeing after critical incidents: Three cases of mass shootings. *Journal of Critical Incident Analysis*. Fall: 1–25.

Hedgpeth, D., & Bui, L. (2015). Police continue search for clues in shooting outside Frederick High school. *Washington Times*, February 5. http://www. washingtonpost.com/local/crime/police-continue-to-search-for-clues-in-shooting-outside-frederick-high-school/2015/02/05/f92a0b66-ad2c-11e4-abe8-e1ef60ca26de_story.html

Hefling, K., Brumback, K., Burke, S., Scolforo, M., Anderson, J., & Elliott, D. (2014). Despite increased security, school shootings continue. *PBS Newshour Rundown*. February 2.

Helfgott, J. B. (2015). Criminal behavior and the copycat effect: Literature review and theoretical framework for empirical investigation. *Aggression and Violent Behavior*. 22:46–64.

Hickman, D. R. (2014). Soapbox: Don't blame the gun: Blame the shooter. *Coloradoan*. June 24. http://www.coloradoan.com/story/opinion/contributors/2014/06/24/blame-gun-blame-shooter/11310129

Huffington Post. (2012). James Holmes, Aurora shooting suspect, purchased 6,000 rounds of ammunition online. *Huffington Post*, July 21.

Indiana University. (n.d.). Responding to an active shooter. https://protect.iu.edu/police/active-shooter

Jany, L. (2015). Gun violence victims remembered by family and friends. *Star Tribune Minneapolis*, January 31. http://www.startribune.com/local/blogs/290433531.html

Jaycox. L. H., Stein, B. D., & Wong, M. (2014). School intervention related to school and community violence. *Child and Adolescent Psychiatric Clinics of North America*, 23 (2): 281–293.

Jenkins, J., & Towns, E. (2013). Thou shall not kill: Faith groups and gun-violence prevention. *Center for American Progress*, April 23. https://www.americanprogress.org/issues/religion/report/2013/04/23/61165/thou-shall-not-kill-faith-groups-and-gun-violence-prevention

Johnson, F. (2013). Why gun control can't eliminate gun violence: Advocates push measures that might reduce everyday crime, but absent a ban on ownership, no recent tragedy would have been averted by regulation. *National Journal*, September 18. http://www.nationaljournal.com/domesticpolicy/why-gun-control-can-t-eliminate-gun-violence-20130918

Juvonen, J. (2001). School violence: prevalence, fears and prevention. *Issue Papers*, IP-219: Rand Corporation. http://www.rand.org/pubs/issue_papers/IP219/index2.html

Kaminiski, R. J., Koons-Witt, B. A., Thompson, N. S., & Weiss, D. (2010). The impacts of Virginia Tech and Northern Illinois University shootings on fear of crime on campus. *Journal of Criminal Justice*, 38 (1): 88–98.

Kaplan, E. (2009). Terrorists and the internet. *Council on Foreign Relations*. http://www.cfr.org/terrorism-and-technology/terrorists-internet/p10005

Karlinsky, N., & Przygoda, D. (2012). Video games and violence: Every generation blames newest media. Expert says. *ABC Nightline*. December 18. http://abcnews.go.com/Technology/video-games-violence-generation-blames-latest-media-expert/story?id=18009898

Keller, E. A., & Blodgett, R. H. (2007). *Natural hazards: Earth's processes as hazards, disasters and catastrophes*. Upper Saddle River, NJ: Prentice Hall.

Kellerman, A. L. (2004). Treating gun violence before the 911 call. *Annals of Emergency Medicine*, 43: 743–745.

Kerr, K. M. (2010). *Workplace violence: Planning for prevention and response*. Burlington, MA: Butterworth-Heinemann

Kindy, K. (2014). Father of victim in Santa Barbara shootings to politicians: 'I don't care about your sympathy.' *Washington Post*. May 27. http://www.washingtonpost.com/politics/father-of-victim-in-santa-barbara-shootings-to-politicians-i-dont-care-about-your-sympathy/2014/05/27/8a030d10-e5ad-11e3-a86b-362fd5443d19_story.html

Kiniry, L. (n.d.). 9 disaster-relief inventions. *Popular Mechanics*. http://www.popularmechanics.com/science/environment/g1025/9-disaster-relief-inventions/?

Kirkham, C. (2010). Deepwater Horizon oil well was increasingly out of control before fatal explosion, widows testify. *The Times-Picayune*, August 12.

Knight, Claire. 2014. Oregon shooting leaves 2 dead, 1 injured: Tech tools that helped restore order. *Education Technology News Weekly Newsletter*, June 11. http://educationtechnews.com/2-dead-1-injured-technologys-role-in-oregon-shooting/?pulb=1

Kreider, R. 2012. Fort Hood victims demand attack be deemed 'terrorism'. *ABC News*, October 20. http://abcnews.go.com/Blotter/fort-hood-victims-demand-attack-deemed-terrorism/story?id=17525656

Kwong, J. (2014). Fatal police shooting causes traffic delays in SF. *San Francisco Examiner*, September 25. http://www.sfexaminer.com/sanfrancisco/shooting-involving-multiple-officers-causes-delays-in-financial-district/Content?oid=2907325

Law Center to Prevent Gun Violence. (2015). Fifty caliber rifles in California. January 12. http://smartgunlaws.org/fifty-caliber-rifles-in-california/

Lee, K. (2015). Federalism, guns and jurisdictional gun policies. *Regional Science and Urban Economics*, doi: 10.1016/j.regsciurbeco.2015.03.005

Leon-Guerrero, A. (2009). *Social problems: Community, Policy and Social Action*. Los Angeles: Pine Forge.

Levin, J., & McDevitt, J. (2008). Hate crimes. In L. Kurtz, *Encyclopedia of violence, peace, and conflict, second edition*, pp. 915–922.

Levine, A. G. 1982. *Love Canal: Science, Politics, and People*. Lexington Books.

Linkous, D., & Carter, K. F. (2009). Responding to the shootings at Virginia Tech: Planning and preparedness. *Journal of Emergency Nursing*, 35: 321–325.

Lippman, G. (2010). Guns: Dangerous, especially for suicide, and costly for America. *Psychiatry*, 7(2): 14–15.

Loeber, R., & Hay, D. (1997). Key issues in the development of aggression and violence from childhood to early adulthood. *Annual Review of Psychology*, 48: 371–410.

Lohr, D. (2012). Sandy Hook crime scenes: Police 'indefinitely' seize all sites connected to shooting. *Huffington Post*, December 17. http://www.huffingtonpost.com/2012/12/17/sandy-hook-crime-scenes-seized_n_2315843.html?

Malsch, M., & Carriere, R. (1999). Victims' wishes for compensation: The immaterial aspect. *Journal of Criminal Justice*, 27 (3): 239–247

Marcus, E. (2012). The blame game: Dharun Ravi and Tyler Clementi. *Why Suicide? Blog*, February 4. http://whysuicideblog.com/?p=154

Martinez, M. (1993). Pool-goers wary after shooting. *Chicago Tribune*, July 24. http://articles.chicagotribune.com/1993-07-24/news/9307240163_1_drive-by-shooting-emil-schullo-pool-deck

Marzbali, M. H., Abdullah, A., Razak, N. A., & Tilaki, M. J. M. (2011). Validating crime prevention through environmental design construct through checklist using structural equation modelling. *International Journal of Law, Crime and Justice*, 40: 82–99.

McLemore, A. (2014). After Friday shooting, repairs begin for bullet-riddled buildings. *Austin-American Statesman*, November 30. http://www.mystatesman.com/news/news/local/after-friday-shooting-repairs-begin-for-bullet-rid/njJLK/

Meredith, L. (2012). Cellphones are changing school emergency plans. *Discovery News*, December 16. http://news.discovery.com/tech/cellphones-changing-school-emergency-plans-121216.htm

Mesoudi, A. (2013). Mass shooting and mass media: Does media coverage of mass shootings inspire copycat crimes? *ITHP*, February 11. http://ithp.org/articles/media copycatshootings.html

Montgomerie, J. Z., Lawrence, A. E., LaMotte, A. D., & Taft, C. T. (2015). The link between posttraumatic stress disorder and firearm violence: A review. *Aggression and Violent Behavior*, 21: 39–44.

Moran, B. R. (2012). Shooting incident reconstruction: Part 1. In W. J. Chisom & B. Turvey, *Crime Reconstruction, Second Edition*. Pp. 365–421. Waltham, MA: Elsevier.

Morley, B. & Leslie, G.D. 2007. Terrorist bombings: motives, methods and patterns of injuries. *Australasian Emergency Nursing Journal*, 10: 5–12.

Muscari, M. (2004). Juvenile animal abuse: practice and policy implications for PNPs. *Journal of Pediatric Healthcare.* 18 (1): 15–21

National Association of Crime Victimization Compensation Boards. (n.d.). Crime victim compensation: an overview. http://www.nacvcb.org/index.asp?bid=14

National Counter-Terrorism Committee. (2010). *National guidelines for the protection of places of mass gathering from terrorism.* http://www.nationalsecurity.gov.au/... publications/...

Neuman, J. H., & Baron, R. A. (1998). Workplace violence and workplace aggression: Evidence concerning specific forms. Potential causes, and preferred targets. *Journal of Management.* 24 (3): 391–419.

Neuman, W. L. (2011). *Social research methods: Qualitative and quantitative approaches, Seventh edition.* Boston: Allyn and Bacon.

Orth. U. (2002). Secondary victimization of crime victims by criminal proceedings. *Social Justice Research.* 15 (4): 313–325.

Papchristos, A. V., Wildeman, C., & Roberto, E. (2015). Tragic, not random: The social contagion of nonfatal gunshot injuries. *Social Science and Medicine.* 125: 139–150.

Patton, D. U., Eschmann, R. D., & Butler, D. A. (2013). Internet banging: New trends in social media, gang violence, masculinity and hip hop. Computers in Human Behavior. 29 (5): A54–A59.

PBS. (n.d.). Gun violence. *In The Mix Show.* http://www.pbs.org/inthemix/shows/show_gun_violence.html

PBS. (2000). The lawsuits. *Frontline.* January. http://www.pbs.org/wgbh/pages/frontline/shows/kinkel/blame/summary.html

Pearson, M. (2014). Blame weak gun laws for holiday violence. Chicago's top cop says. *CNN*, July 7. http://www.cnn.com/2014/07/07/justice/chicago-shootings/

Peron, J. (2013). Drug warriors and gun violence: The war on drugs fuels violence. *Huffington Post.* May 19. http://www.huffingtonpost.com/james-peron/violence-war-on-drugs_b_3300781.html

Peters, J. (2015). Stop calling children's gun deaths 'accidental': They're the fault of criminally negligent parents and guardians—who must be prosecuted. *Slate.com.* March 4. http://www.slate.com/articles/news_and_politics/crime/2015/03/three_children_shot_in_houston_these_weren_t_accidents_they_were_the_result.html

Petherick, W. (2015). Motivations. *Applied Crime Analysis.* 148–171.

Picou, J. S., & Gill, D. A. (2000). The *Exxon Valdez* Disaster as localized environmental catastrophe: Dissimilarities to Risk Society Theory. In M. J. Cohen, *Risk in the Modern Age: Social Theory,Science, and Environmental Decision-Making.* (pp. 143–170). Macmillan.

Picou, J. S., Marshall, B. K., & Gill, D. A. (2004). Disaster, litigation and the corrosive community. *Social Forces.* 82(4):1493–1522

Picou, J. S. & Marshall, B. K. (2007). Introduction: Katrina as a paradigm shift: Reflections on disaster research in the twenty-first century. In D. L. Brunsma, D. Overfelt, and J. S. Picou, *The sociology of Katrina: Perspectives on a modern catastrophe* (pp. 1–22). Lanham, MD: Rowman and Littlefield.

Picou, S. J., Brunsma, D. L., & Overfelt (2010). Introduction: Katrina as a paradigm shift: Reflections on disaster research in the twenty-first century. In D.L. Brunsma, D. Overfelt & J. S. Picou, *The sociology of Katrina: perspectives on a modern catastrophe. Second edition* (pp. 1–21). Lanham: Rowman and Littlefield

Police Executive Research Forum. (2014). *The police response to active shooter incidents*. Washington, D.C. http://www.policeforum.org/assets/docs/Critical_Issues_Series /the%20police%20response%20to%20active% 20shooter%20incidents%202014.pdf

PoliceOne.com (2013). P1 gun control survey: Top 10 reasons for gun violence. *Police One*. May 30. http://www.policeone.com/Gun-Legislation-Law-Enforcement/ articles/6253478-P1-Gun-Control-Survey-Top-10-reasons-for-gun-violence/

Plumer, B. (2013). Nine facts about terrorism in the United States since 9/11. *Washington Post*. September 11. http://www.washingtonpost.com/blogs/wonkblog/wp/2013/09/11/ nine-facts-about-terrorism-in-the-united-states-since-911/

Puffer, M. (2014). Warning signs ignored: Report: System missed opportunities to help troubled Lanza. *Republican-American*. November 22. http://www.rep-am.com/articles/ 2014/12/21/news/local/844742.txt

Qian, Z. & Zhang, D-J. (2014). The effects of viewing violent movie via computer on aggressiveness among college students. *Computers in Human Behavior*, 35: 320–325.

Ramirez, M., Ferrer, R.R., Cheng, G., Cavanaugh, J. E., & Peek-Asa, C. (2011). Violation of school behavioral policies and its relationship with crime. *Annals of epidemiology*, 21 (3): 214–220.

Robert Wood Johnson Foundation. (2012). For gunshot survivors, wounds that don't heal. RWJF scholar examines how victims' lives are disfigured, physically and 'existentially,' by the lingering effects of gunshot injuries. http:// www.rwjf.org/ en/library/articles-and-news/2012/07/for-gunshot-survivors--wounds-that-don-t-heal.html

Ross, C. & Bryant, J. 2010. After shooting, Wilson High students wary about security. *PilotOnline.com*, April 30. http://hamptonroads.com/2010/04/after-shooting-wilson-high-students-wary-about-security

Sapakie, R. (2015). Nine dead after Missouri mass murder. News10.com. February 27. http://news10.com/2015/02/27/nine-dead-after-missouri-mass-murder/

Scarf, P., Calderon-Abbo, J., Gordon, J., Chodroff, C., Scott, R. C., Vassar, B., & McDonald, A. (2013). *Averting the prevalence and consequences of mass shooting and urban gun violence*. Report to the United States House Judiciary Subcommittee on Crime, Terrorism, and Homeland Security. http://bobbyscott.house.gov/ sites/bobby scott.house.gov/files/migrated/uploads/YPAWhitepaperfinal011913_Scharf_FINAL .pdf

Schecter, C. (2014). How the NRA enables massacres. *The Daily Beast*. May 24. http://www.thedailybeast.com/articles/2014/05/24/the-nra-s-all-out-assault-on-accurate-information-about-gun-deaths.html

Schmalleger, F. J. (2008). *Criminology today: An integrative introduction, fifth edition*. Upper Saddle River: Prentice Hall.

Scigliano, E. (2002). 10 technology disasters. *MIT Technology Review*. http://www. technologyreview.com/featuredstory/401465/10-technology-disasters

Sennewald, C. A., & Tsukayama, J. K. (2015). Identifying suspects: The who of investigation. *The Process of Investigation. Fourth Edition*. 213–224.

Shakoor, B. H., & Chalmers, D. (1991). Co-victimization of African-American children who witness violence: Effects on cognitive, emotional, and behavioral development. *Journal of the National Medical Association*. 83(3): 233–238.

Sheoin, T. M., & S. Zavestoki. (2012). Corporate catastrophes from UC Bhopal to BP Deepwater Horizon: Continuities in causation, corporate negligence, and crisis management. In L. A. Eargle & A. Esmail. *Black beaches and bayous: The BP Deepwater Horizon oil spill disaster*, pp. 53–93. Lanham: University Press of America.

Sherman, L. W. (1998). Communities and crime prevention. In L. W. Sherman, D. Gottfredson, D. MacKenzie, J. Eck, P. Reuter, & S. Bushway (Eds.), *Preventing crime: What works, what doesn't, what's promising* (pp. 3-1–3-52). College Park: University of Maryland.

Singer, M. I., Anglin, T. M., Song, L. Y., & Lunghofer, L. (1995). Adolescents' exposure to violence and associated symptoms of psychological trauma. *The Journal of the American Medical Association*, 273 (6): 477–482.

Singh, R. (2003). *Contemporary American politics and society: Issues and controversies*. Thousand Oaks, CA: Sage

Skoler, G. (1998). The archetypes and psychodynamics of stalking. *The psychology of stalking*, 85–112.

Slutkin, G. (2015). Why we should treat violence as a contagious disease. *National Public Radio*, February 6. http://www.npr.org/2015/02/06/379185265/why-should-we-treat-violence-like-a-contagious-disease

Southern Poverty Law Center. (2014). Guns of April: the Bundy standoff. July. http://www.splcenter.org/get-informed/publications/War-in-the-West-Guns-of-April-The-Bundy-Standoff

Southers, E. (2013). Ideological motivation. *Homegrown Violent Extremism*, 2013: 21–52

Spelman, W. (2002). Abandoned buildings: Magnets for crime? *Journal of Criminal Justice*, 21 (5): 481–495.

Steffen, S. & Harlow, P. (2014). Gang violence: What happens when you don't die? *CNN*, July 9. http://www.cnn.com/2014/07/08/us/paralyzed-by-gun-violence

Stroebe, W. (2013). Firearm possession and violent death: A critical review. *Aggression and violent behavior*, 18 (6): 709–721.

Taylor, B. & Li, J. (2015). Do fewer guns lead to less crime? Evidence from Australia. *International Review of Law and Economics*, 42: 72–78.

Teret, S. P., & Lewin, N. L. (2003) Policy and technology for safer guns: An update. *Annals of Emergency Medicine*, 41 (1): 32–34.

The Lancet. (2013) Editorial. Reducing gun violence: Facts are stubborn things. *The Lancelet*, 381 (9883): 2055.

Thompson, M. (2012). Why gun sales often rise after mass shootings. *CNBC*, December 17. http://www.cnbc.com/id/100321785

Ting, J. C. (2006). Immigration and national security. *Orbis*, 50 (1): 41–52.

United Methodist Church. 2012. Gun violence. The book of resolutions of the United Methodist Church. United Methodist Publishing House. http://www.umc.org/what-we-believe/gun-violence

U.S. Department of Homeland Security. (2008). *Active shooter: How to respond*. Washington, DC.

Wachtel, L. E., & Shorter, E. (2013). Autism plus psychosis: A one-two punch risk for tragic violence? *Medical Hypotheses*, 81 (3): 404–409.

Warner, B. D. (2007). Robberies with guns: Neighborhood factors and the nature of crime. *Journal of Criminal Justice*, 35: 39–50.

Wayland, B. A. (2014). Facility security design. Security for business *professionals*. Pp. 101–106. Butterworth Heiman publishing.

White, J. (2012). Lee Boyd Malvo. 10 years after D.C. area sniper shootings: 'I was a monster.' *Washington Post*. September 29.

White, J. M. (2014). Workplace violence risks and vulnerabilities. *Security Risk Assessment*, 113–123.

White. R.. & Cunnen. C. 2006. Social class. youth crime and justice. In B. Goldson & J. Muncie. *Youth crime and justice: Critical issues* (pp. 18–29). London: Sage Publications.

Wilcox. P. (2015). Routine activities. criminal opportunities. crime and crime prevention. *International Encyclopedia of the Social and Behavioral Sciences*. 772–779.

Wilkinson. D. L.. & Fagan. J. (1996). The role of firearms in violence scripts: The dynamics of gun events among adolescent males. *Law and Contemporary Problems*. 59 (1): 55–89

Wilkinson. D. L.. & Hamerschlag. S. J. (2003). Situational determinants in intimate partner violence. *Aggression and Violent Behavior*. 10: 333–361.

Williams. B. (2014). Harteau again seeks to reassure Minneapolis residents after more gun violence. *MPR News*. July 10. http://www.mprnews.org/story/2014/07/10/harteau-tours-north-minneapolis

World Health Organization. (n.d.). Epidemiology. http://www.who.int/topics/epidemiology/en/

Zhang. J.. Tong. H. Q.. & Zhou. L. (2005). The effect of bereavement due to suicide on survivors' depression: A study on Chinese samples. *Omega*. 51(3): 217–227

Chapter Eleven

Framing Mass Gun Violence:
A Content Analysis of Print Media Coverage
of the Virginia Tech and Sandy Hook
Elementary School Tragedies

James Hawdon, Laura Agnich, Robert Wood and John Ryan

Introduction

The deadliest school shooting in American history occurred on April 16, 2007 when a student killed 32 people and wounded 17 others at Virginia Tech. The heinous event attracted the media as domestic and foreign journalists from every major media outlet descended on the campus. Five years later, on December 14, 2012, a 20-year-old Newtown, Connecticut community member entered Sandy Hook Elementary School. The gunman committed the second deadliest school shooting in U.S. history by fatally shooting 20 students and six staff members. Once again, gun violence had shocked the nation; once again, gun violence had destroyed the lives of children and rattled the social fabric of a community. And, of course, once again, the media flocked to the scene of the tragedy, and, once again, the world saw images of fragile individuals and a community united in grief.

While it is understandable that the media covered these horrific events, we must realize that the media did more than simply tell the stories of these tragedies. Journalists, editors, and other media members expressed their opinions about the causes and consequences of these tragedies, as well as possible means of averting such tragedies in the future. The media undoubtedly frames our understanding of tragedies, and these frames can influence us negatively (e.g. Ahern et al., 2002; 2004; Pfefferbaum et al., 2001; Pfefferbaum et al., 2002) or positively (e.g. Boomgaarden & de Vreese, 2007; Letukas, Olofsson, & Barnshaw, 2009; Hawdon,

Oksanen, and Räsänen 2012; Hawdon, Agnich, and Ryan forthcoming). Realizing the power of frames for the wellbeing of individuals and communities, we must ask if media outlets tell the story of a tragedy the same way across various outlets. Or, is it the case that the story that is told depends on spatial and temporal factors? Understanding the possible influences of spatial and temporal factors on the framing of tragic events is important because these frames have implications for victims and victimized communities.

Therefore, we examine how the framing of the VT and Sandy Hook tragedies vary by the distance between the reporting media and the community in which the tragedy occurred. Thus, the fundamental goal of our research is to investigate how the distance between a print media outlet and a community victimized by a tragedy influences the coverage of the tragedy. To achieve our goal, we conduct content analyses of all stories related to the shootings published in the *New York Times*, *Washington Post*, *Chicago Tribune*, *Los Angeles Times*, *Wall Street Journal*, and the *Roanoke Times* between 4–16–2007 and 6–17–2007 for the Virginia Tech tragedy, and in the *Hartford Courant* between 12–14–2012 and 2–15–2013 for the Sandy Hook incident.

Theoretical Background

Visual and print media coverage of tragedies is common, publicly desired, and profitable (Croteau & Hoynes, 2000), but such extensive coverage may influence public perceptions and interpretations of the tragedy (Lawrence & Birkland, 2004; Scharrer et al., 2003; Nurmi, 2012). Long term coverage may not only influence public opinion on related issues (Boomgaarden & de Vreese, 2007; Hawdon, 2001; Terkildsen & Schnell, 1997), but it may in fact expand the effects of a tragedy beyond those originally affected (see Boomgaarden & de Vreese, 2007; Brezina & Kaufman, 2008; Catalano & Hartig, 2001; Schlenger et al., 2002). Indeed, coverage may even increase the likelihood of similar events occurring in the future (Kupchik & Bracy, 2009; Lawrence & Birkland, 2004; Lawrence & Mueller, 2003). Because of these potential effects, it is important to understand the factors influencing media coverage.

After a disaster or mass tragedy, the media tends to operate in "media hype mode," providing extensive and amplified coverage of the event (e.g. Vasterman, Yzermans, & Dirkzwager, 2005). Under these conditions, reporters often base their coverage on rumors, and their reports are often oversimplified and rely on emotional responses from victims rather than more objective sources (Thevenot, 2006; Muschert, 2007; Kupchik & Bracy, 2009). Thus, media operating in "hype mode" often disseminate a biased view of the events. The nature and direction of the media bias following a tragedy can be consequential, and research suggests that the media can hinder or hasten the recovery process, depending on the nature of the coverage (see Hawdon, Oksanen, & Räsänen, 2012).

For example, coverage following school shootings often provokes fear by framing school violence as a common occurrence (Lawrence & Mueller, 2003; Kupchik & Bracy, 2009). In addition, sensationalized coverage of violent events can lead to exaggerated concerns and fears amongst the public (see Boomgaarden & de Vreese, 2007; Brezina & Kaufman, 2008), and this fear can have detrimental effects on the levels of solidarity in a community (see Hawdon et al. 2013). This heightened fear can also manifest in communal bereavement (see Catalano & Hartig, 2001) or posttraumatic stress (Pfefferbaum et al. 2003; Schlenger et al., 2002; also see Ahern et al., 2004).

Conversely, the media can be a valuable asset during and after tragic events, mediating the effects of a disaster or providing vital information, even saving thousands of lives in cases of hurricanes and earthquakes (see, for example, Cruz, 1993). Media coverage can also express shared beliefs, collective emotions, and the community's assessment of the consequences of a disaster, helping individuals make sense of and provide meaning for an event, and helping victims to cope with their grief and sense of loss (Gortner & Pennebaker, 2003; Hawdon et al., forthcoming; Boomgaarden & de Vreese, 2007; Gauthier, 2003) and promoting social cohesion (Boomgaarden & de Vreese, 2007; see also: Argothy, 2005; Letukas, Olofsson, & Barnshaw, 2009).

Given that the media can produce either positive or negative outcomes depending on how they frame a story, we must ask what determines how the media frames events. One possible factor is the media's distance from the event. Generally, the closer the media's targeted audience is to the community affected by a tragedy both geographically and culturally, the greater probability the media will cover the event (McQuail, 2005; Hawdon et al. forthcoming). While catastrophic events are typically covered by all major media, the nature and duration of the coverage varies according to, among other things, such factors as the newsroom resources available for deployment, accessibility to the site, the intended audience, the salience of the story for that audience, and competing events (Albarran, 2002; Van Belle, 2000). There is also a growing body of literature that suggests that coverage also varies with the geographic and cultural distance between the tragic event and the reporting media (e.g. Wenger & Friedman, 1986; Garner, 1996; Hawdon et al., forthcoming).

Garner (1996), for example, found that national and international coverage of floods provided depersonalized accounts that emphasized the massive damage associated with the flooding, the disaster's economic cost, and the potential national consequences of the disaster. Conversely, the local media focused primarily on the victimized individuals and community (Garner, 1996). Similarly, after the Texas A&M bonfire tragedy, the Texas A&M student newspaper's orientation was significantly more community focused than was the coverage provided by the University of Texas's student paper. In addition, the Texas A&M paper was more likely to include articles that searched for causes and meaning than did the University of Texas newspaper (Gortner & Pennebaker, 2003). Finally, Hawdon, Agnich and Ryan (forthcoming) found that geographically close newspapers focused on the victims and reported evidence of community solidarity more than national papers after the mass murder of 32 people on Virginia Tech's campus in 2007. Conversely, more distant papers tended to publish stories about the tragedy's perceived underlying causes (e.g. issues related to mental health, issues related to gun control, and issues related to campus security). Thus, compared to more national media outlets, local media tends to provide personalized and collectively oriented coverage of tragedies. But why would this be the case?

.Variations across Newspaper Markets: Local versus National Papers

How might the needs, desires, and tastes of the audiences, and therefore the journalistic styles, differ? First, we must realize that the U.S. newspaper industry is heavily concentrated as the top 50 papers account for approximately one-third of the nation's total newspaper circulation (Kirchhoff, 2010). Most newspapers are "local" in that they are based in a metropolitan area; for example, among the top 20 U.S. daily newspapers by circulation, only the *Wall Street Journal* and *USA Today* are not directly associated with a metropolitan area (see Kirchhoff (2010, p. 11) for a list of the top 20 daily newspapers). However, a handful of these papers, including the *New York Times, Washington Post,* and *Chicago Tribune*, have a national readerships in excess of a half million (Kirchhoff, 2010). Moreover, these widely circulated papers are known for their international reporting, general news coverage, or intensive coverage of national issues (Letukas et al., 2009). These "national" papers devote significantly more space to national and international affairs than do "local" papers. In comparison, local papers typically focus on events that "national" papers would likely consider "un-newsworthy." Simply put, these papers serve different markets, and this distinction has implications for how the papers report a tragedy.

Hawdon, Agnich, and Ryan (forthcoming) argued that Pennebaker and Harber's (1993) social stage model of coping can help explain the differences in how local and national papers cover tragedies. According to the social stage model of coping, during the first two to three weeks after a disaster (the emergency phase), individuals openly sharing their thoughts and feelings about the tragedy. During this stage, people are processing the events and trying to make sense of the tragedy (Pennebaker & Harber, 1993; also see Stone & Pennebaker, 2002). During the next stage (the inhibition phase), there is a sudden decrease in people discussing the event despite their continuing to think about it. In the final stage of the model (the adaptation phase), both thoughts and talking about the disaster substantially decrease (Pennebaker & Harber, 1993). Hawdon and his colleagues (forthcoming) argue that since the media both creates and reflects a community's framing of an event, it is likely that coverage of a tragedy will follow the social stage model of coping. In essence, the media can help individuals understand, work through, and cope with the traumatic event (see, for example, Muschert & Carr, 2006;

Pennebaker & Harber. 1993: Gortner & Pennebaker. 2003: Stone & Pennebaker, 2002; Scharrer et al.. 2003).

In general. during the emergency phase. which lasts approximately two weeks after the tragedy, we would not only expect a substantial number of articles to be written about the tragedy (see McQuail. 2005). we would also predict that the articles would reflect attempts to "work through" the tragedy collectively. However, since attempts to understand the tragedy by members of the victimized community would likely differ from those in less affected communities. national and local media sources would likely report the tragedy in a manner that best serves their own parochial markets.

People in markets most directly affected would likely need to "work through" the tragedy more so than those in distant markets: thus. stories in papers most proximate to the tragedy would likely use a "frame of solidarity" when reporting a tragedy. Reporters generate a "frame of solidarity" when their stories focus on the tragedy's victims and the afflicted community (see Hawdon. Oksanen. & Räsänen, 2012: Hawdon et al.. forthcoming). By doing so. local papers serve similar functions as public memorials that are often held after tragedies: they simul-taneously allow readers to experience the emotions of grief and the collective's strength. Such stories both acknowledge the community's loss while also reaffirming its resolve to confront and overcome the loss. In addition. shortly after the tragedy. local papers will likely avoid controversial issues concerning the underlying cause or causes of the tragedy such as the treatment of the mentally ill or handgun legislation. Instead. stories in local papers will disproportionately focus on the victims to make the tragedy more personalized and the local community to evoke the sense of collective loss. Thus. local papers. in their attempt to assist in "meaning making" for their customers. will likely publish articles that depict the community as collectively suffering grief.

By contrast. those in more distant markets would be less focused on the victims and traumatized community. Although both national and local papers will use personalization to produce solidarity with the afflicted community (see Letukas et al.. 2009). the national papers' targeted audiences' attempts to understand the tragedy would require less solidarity-producing efforts than would the local papers' audiences. For national papers. parochialism would be less about how the local community is confronting the tragedy and more about what *their community* should do to avoid such tragedies in the future. Thus. we anticipate that national papers would meet their market's needs by discussing issues of causation that could be applied to any community. Therefore. relative to local papers. national papers would contain fewer stories about the victims and local community and more stories about the mentally ill. handgun legislation. the shooter or shooters. campus safety, and other broad issues.

Next. following the social stage model of coping. we predict that during the "inhibition phase" local coverage would likely begin to focus more on issues of causation in a manner similar to the how national papers did in the initial phase. Muschert and Carr (2006). for example. found that when the media report on rampage school shootings. they initially emphasize individual and community aspects of the story; however. after some time. media stories tend to focus more on societal aspects of the shooting. Consequently. we expect to find support for the following hypotheses:

* In the emergency phase. compared to national papers, a greater percentage of stories in proximate papers will focus on the victims of a tragedy.
* In the emergency phase. compared to national papers, a greater percentage of stories in proximate papers will focus on community solidarity.
* In the emergency phase. compared to local papers, a greater percentage of stories in national papers will focus on underlying causes of the tragedy (issues of mental health. access to handguns. etc.).
* In the inhibition phase." an increasing number of stories in local papers will focus on the underlying causes of the tragedy.

Variations Across Tragedies:
Virginia Tech compared to Sandy Hook

While there is likely variation in the reporting of tragedies across newspapers that reflect the different needs of the papers' markets. there may also be cross-tragedy differences. Not all tragedies will have identical impacts. and the specific details of the Virginia Tech and Sandy Hook tragedies can provide examples. As noted earlier, frames of solidarity focus on victims (as opposed to perpetrators or broader issues) and the afflicted community. While we would predict that both tragedies were framed in this way. it is possible that this frame was adopted more when journalists reported the Sandy Hook shooting than when they reported the Virginia Tech shooting. Two possible factors could have led to the increased use of a frame of solidarity during the Sandy Hook coverage: (1) the age of the victims. and (2) the characteristics of the attacker. Research suggests that crimes (see Yanich. 2005) and specifically homicides (Sorenson. Manz. & Berk. 1998). with juvenile victims receive heightened media coverage. In addition. a generally elevated cultural importance of youth may influence approaches to media coverage. In short. the younger victims. many as young as six years old. at Sandy Hook compared to the adult victims of the Virginia Tech shooting may result in a greater focus on the victims in coverage of Sandy Hook.

Similarly. the shooters' characteristics may influence the media coverage of the tragedy. The Virginia Tech shooter. Seung-Hui Cho. was a student. a part of the community. Since he was a community member. it is possible that a frame that blames the community in some way for the incident will emerge. For example. after a school shooting in Jokela. Finland. residents expressed a sense of collective guilt and stigmatization (see Nurmi. Räsänen & Oksanen. 2012: Hawdon et al.. 2012). When this occurs. it can threaten the use of a frame of solidarity because the community is deemed culpable instead of victimized (see Ryan & Hawdon. 2008). In contrast. when the shooter is clearly an outsider. as was the case in the Sandy

Hook tragedy, the community's blamelessness is unquestioned. As a result, the community is clearly a "moral victim" and, therefore, a frame of solidarity is likely to emerge (see Ryan & Hawdon. 2008). Since an "insider" committed the Virginia Tech tragedy and an "outsider" committed the Sandy Hook tragedy, we expect an increased focus on the community in the Sandy Hook coverage. Thus, we anticipate finding support for two additional hypotheses:

- Stories about the Sandy Hook tragedy will focus on the victims more so than the stories reporting the Virginia Tech tragedy.
- Stories about the Sandy Hook tragedy will focus on the community more so than the stories reporting the Virginia Tech tragedy.

Methods

The content of all news articles written about the two shootings published in five major U.S. newspapers and in two newspapers considered local to the two communities (Blacksburg. Virginia and Newtown. Connecticut) were analyzed. The "national" papers were the *New York Times. Washington Post, Chicago Tribune, Los Angeles Times,* and *Wall Street Journal.* These were selected based on their geographic coverage in each U.S. Census designated region, and because these five papers constitute half of the top ten U.S. daily newspapers based on circulation and market shares at the time of each incident (BurrellesLuce. 2012; 2007). The two local papers, the *Roanoke Times* and *Hartford Courant,* were selected because they are the most widely read publications in close proximity to the sites of the tragedies.

All published news articles on the Virginia Tech shooting published in the national newspapers and local paper between April 16, 2007 and June 20, 2007, were coded and analyzed. In addition, all news articles on the Sandy Hook incident published in the five national and one local newspaper between December 14, 2012 and February 15, 2013 were coded for analysis. Only those with a clearly evident focus were included in the analysis. In all, 1,484 news articles published in five national papers and two local papers were coded and analyzed: 725 articles on the Virginia Tech incident, and 759 articles on the Sandy Hook incident. The content of each story was coded for its focus (e.g. stories about victims, the perpetrator(s), underlying causes such as mental health care or access to firearms, or "news," that simply relays facts and information about the event), and indicators of community solidarity. We analyze these aspects of coverage along three dimensions: the *media's locale, the phase of social coping,* and *the incident.*

Measures

Our central dependent variable is the article's focus. The focus of each article was coded into one of the following categories based on the main overarching theme about which the article was written: *victims, the perpetrator, underlying causes,* or *news.* Articles that focused primarily on victims and their personal lives were coded as *victim-focused*. An article published in the *Wall Street Journal* (Hollander & Strickler, 2012) exemplifies a victim-focused story on the Sandy Hook incident. An excerpt reads,

Gilles Rousseau and his wife rushed to Newtown Town Hall after learning of the shooting at the workplace of their 30-year-old daughter, Lauren Rousseau, a substitute teacher. They consoled themselves with the thought that their daughter never brought her cellphone into the school and couldn't have called them.

Articles were coded as *perpetrator-focused* if they provided details about either Seung-Hui Cho in the Virginia Tech case, or Adam Lanza in the Sandy Hook case. Articles that discussed their backgrounds or families were coded as *perpetrator-focused*. A *Los Angeles Times* article (Serrano, Drogin & Zucchino, 2007) provides an example of a perpetrator-focused article.

Seung-hui Cho, a child immigrant from South Korea who grew up in the Washington suburbs, was portrayed by fellow students and teachers as an insecure loner who ate by himself night after night, watched TV wrestling shows alone and, when spoken to, had little to say.

A story was coded as focusing on *underlying causes* if it centered on any number of issues relating to potential causes of the tragedy. These issues included access to mental health care, gun control, campus security and the response by officials, violent media, and societal morals as a whole. A *Washington Post* article (Dennis & Kane, 2013) illustrates a focus on underlying causes.

A bipartisan group of senators, citing renewed urgency after the shooting massacre at Sandy Hook Elementary School, introduced legislation Thursday aimed at strengthening the nation's fragmented mental health-care system and improving access at the community level.

Finally, an article was coded as focusing on *"news"* if it solely reported facts about the case and did not discuss details of the victims, their lives, the perpetrators or their backgrounds, or issues related to potential underlying causes of the crimes.

Our next variable of central interest is *indicators of community solidarity*. These were stories that depicted the community as displaying signs of unity, solidarity, togetherness, or collective resolve. This variable was not treated as a mutually exclusive category with respect to the articles' focus. That is, articles with any of the aforementioned foci may have depicted indicators of community solidarity. The following excerpt from a *Roanoke Times* article (Johnson, 2007) illustrates such a depiction of the Blacksburg, Virginia community in an article focusing on a wounded victim of the Virginia Tech tragedy, Heidi Miller:

Heidi Miller and her family appreciate all the love and support they have received following this week's tragic event at Virginia Tech. Heidi recognizes the beauty of growing up in a strong community and realizes what a great resource that is, now more than ever.

Our central independent or predictor variables include *media locale, phase of social coping,* and *incident. Media locale* was coded as either national or local.

Articles published in the *New York Times, Washington Post, Chicago Tribune, Los Angeles Times*, and *Wall Street Journal* were coded as national. For the Virginia Tech incident, the *Roanoke Times* was coded as a local newspaper given its proximity to Blacksburg, Virginia, and for the Sandy Hook incident the *Hartford Courant* was considered local to Newtown, Connecticut.

Next, the *social coping phase* during which each article was published was coded (see Pennebaker & Harber, 1993). According to Pennebaker & Harber, 1993, Phase 1, the emergency phase, is the three weeks that follow a tragic event. Phase 2, the inhibition phase, is the following three weeks, and Phase 3, the adaptation phase, is the next three weeks after that. For the Virginia Tech incident, the emergency phase was April 16 to May 7, 2007. Phase 2, the inhibition phase was between May 8 and May 29, 2007, and Phase 3, the adaptation phase, is from May 30 through June 20, 2007. For the Sandy Hook incident, the emergency phase was December 14, 2012 to January 4, 2013. The inhibition phase was January 5 through January 26, 2013, and the adaptation phase was January 27 to February 17, 2013. Finally, the *incident* was indicator coded as either Virginia Tech or Sandy Hook. Sandy Hook was coded as 0 and used as the reference category.

Two researchers coded the articles on both the Virginia Tech and Sandy Hook incidents, and cross-coded approximately 20 percent of the total articles to establish inter-rater reliability. The inter-rater reliability was calculated as the percent agreement between the two researchers on each variable for which articles' content were analyzed: the focus of the article, and indicators of community solidarity. In addition, a more conservative estimate used to evaluate the pairwise agreement of the coders, Cohen's kappa statistic, was calculated. For the articles about the Virginia Tech shooting, the researchers had 92.9 percent agreement on the articles' focus (Cohen's kappa=.90) and 93.5 percent agreement on indicators of community solidarity (Cohen's kappa=.86). For the Sandy Hook articles, the two researchers had 86.4 percent agreement on the articles' focus (Cohen's kappa=.83), and 88.1 percent agreement on community solidarity indicators (Cohen's kappa=.83). Kappa coefficients greater than .80 are typically considered reliable in the field of content analysis (see Carletta, 1996; Krippendorff, 1980), therefore, the measures in the present analyzed in the present study should be considered reliable.

Results

Tables 11.1 through 11.3 present the results for the relationship between media location and stories about victims or that adopt the victim frame for each phase of the social coping model. In the following analyses we combine stories about Sandy Hook and stories about Virginia Tech. We also analyzed the data with Sandy Hook and Virginia Tech separated; however, the results were nearly identical to those for the combined data. We report the combined analysis to conserve space, but the separated analyses are available upon request.

Table 11.1 presents data for the Emergency Phase. As seen in the table, there is a significant (p < .01) relationship between media locale and stories focusing on victims. Over a third (39.5 percent) of the local media stories focused on the victims or the victim frame, compared to only 22.0 percent of the stories in national media stories. Also, as predicted by the third hypothesis, a greater percentage of stories in national papers focused on underlying causes of the tragedy. While 44.6 percent of stories in the national paper were about "issues," only 21.9 percent of those in the local papers were issue-focused.

Table 11.1. Article Focus by Newspaper Location: Emergency Phase

Article Focus	Newspaper		Total
	National	Local	
Victims	137	90	227
	22.0%	39.5%	26.6%
Shooter	70	14	84
	11.2%	6.1%	9.9%
Issues	278	50	328
	44.6%	21.9%	38.5%
News	139	74	213
	22.3%	32.5%	25.0%
Total	624	228	852
	100.0%	100.0%	100.0%

$X^2 = 52.72$; p < .001

Table 11.2. Article Focus by Newspaper Location: Inhibition Phase

Article Focus	Newspaper		Total
	National	Local	
Victims	18	22	40
	5.5%	16.9%	8.8%
Shooter	10	7	17
	3.1%	5.4%	3.7%
Issues	234	58	292
	71.6%	44.6%	63.9%
News	65	43	108
	19.9%	33.1%	23.6%
Total	327	130	457
	100.0%	100.0%	100.0%

$X^2 = 32.64$ p < .001

Table 11.2 presents the same relationship for the Inhibition Phase. The table shows a statistically significant (p < .001) relationship between location and the use of a victim frame with local media devoting 16.9 percent of their incident-related stories on the victims while national media focused only 5.5 percent of their incident coverage on victims. Again, the national media is dominated by issue-related stories (71.6 percent); however, it should be noted that the percentage of local stories devoted to "issues" increases dramatically from the Emergency Phase (21.9 percent) to the Inhibition Phase (44.6 percent). This increase supports the fourth hypothesis that in the Inhibition Phase, an increasing number of stories in local papers will focus on the underlying causes of the tragedy.

Table 11.3. Article Focus by Newspaper Location: Adaptation Phase

Article Focus	Newspaper		Total
	National	Local	
Victims	9	11	20
	7.3%	21.6%	11.4%
Shooter	1	0	1
	0.8%	0.0%	0.6%
Issues	101	35	136
	81.5%	68.6%	77.7%
News	13	5	18
	10.5%	9.8%	10.3%
Total	124	51	175
	100.0%	100.0%	100.0%

$X^2 = 7.67$ $p = .05$

Table 11.3 reports the relationship between media locale and victim-focused stories for the Adaptation Phase. As can be seen in the table, here too there is a significant ($p < .05$) relationship between the variables, with local media devoting 21.6 percent of its stories to the victims compared to only 7.3 percent of the stories in the national media. Taken together, these findings strongly support our contention that local media focuses more on victims than will national media. In addition, it should be noted that by the Adaptation Phase, both the national and local media are primarily publishing articles about the underlying issues related to the tragedy (81.5 percent and 68.6 percent, respectively).

Next, we analyze the relationship between the location of the media and the likelihood the media focused on aspects of the community, specifically on signs that the community was solidified. Tables 11.4–11.6 report the results of these bivariate analyses. As reported in Table 11.4, during the Emergency Stage, 49.6 percent of local stories compared to only 35.6 percent of stories in national papers reported signs of community solidarity. This relationship is statistically significant ($p < .001$).

Table 11.4: Signs of Solidarity by Newspaper Location: Emergency Phase

		Newspaper		
		National	Local	Total
Signs of solidarity	None mentioned	402	115	517
		64.4%	50.4%	60.7%
	Sign mentioned	222	113	335
		35.6%	49.6%	39.3%
Total		624	228	852
		100.0%	100.0%	100.0%

$X^2 = 13.69$ $p < .001$

In the Inhibition Phase, once again we find that local papers are significantly more likely to report signs of solidarity than are national papers (45.4 percent vs. 29.7 percent, respectively). This pattern remains in the Adaptation Stage too: 52.9 percent of stories in the local papers compared to only 24.2 percent in the national papers report signs of community solidarity. Both of these relationships are statistically significant ($p < .001$), and these are reported in tables 11.5 and 11.6, respectively. Once again, these findings strongly support our contention that local media is more likely to report signs that the traumatized community is solidified than will national media outlets.

Table 11.5: Signs of Solidarity by Newspaper Location: Inhibition Phase

		Newspaper		
		National	Local	Total
Signs of solidarity	None mentioned	230	71	301
		70.3%	54.6%	65.9%
	Sign mentioned	97	59	156
		29.7%	45.4%	34.1%
Total		327	130	457
		100.0%	100.0%	100.0%

$X^2 = 10.22$ $p < .01$

Table 11.6: Signs of Solidarity by Newspaper Location: Adaptation Phase

		Newspaper		
		National	Local	Total
Signs of solidarity	None mentioned	94	24	118
		75.8%	47.1%	67.4%
	Sign mentioned	30	27	57
		24.2%	52.9%	32.6%
Total		124	51	175
		100.0%	100.0%	100.0%

$X^2 = 13.59$ $p < .001$

Logistic Regression Results

In the second stage of the analysis we conducted a logistic regression to assess whether the predictor variables, media locale, and incident (Sandy Hook or Virginia Tech), affected the number of stories that focused on victims or adopted a victim frame. Taken together our predictor variables significantly predict the number of victim stories (x^2 =53.63, df=2, N=1512, p<.001). Table 11.7 presents the odds ratios from the analysis, which suggest that, as predicted, the chances of a story being about victims or adopting the victim frame increase if the story is in the local media and decrease if the story is about Virginia Tech rather than Sandy Hook. Indeed, local papers were over twice as likely to report about the tragedies' victims than were national papers (odds ratio = 2.55; p < .001), and stories about the Virginia Tech tragedy were approximately half as likely to report about the victims than were stories about the Sandy Hook tragedy (odds ratio = 0.598; p < .001).

Table 11.7. Logistic Regression Predicting the Prevalence of Stories about Victims or Taking the Victim Frame

Variable	B	SE	Wald	Odds ratio	p-value
Local	.935*	.139	44.97	2.546	< .001
VT	−.515*	.136	14.31	.598	< .001
Constant	−1.489*	.101	218.83	.226	< .001

* p < .001

Finally, we conducted a logistic regression to determine whether our variables of interest (media locale and incident) could predict the number of stories adopting a solidarity frame by focusing on the community as a solidified entity. Taken together, our variables significantly predict the number of solidarity stories (x^2 = 34.52, df=2, N=1512, p<.001). Table 11.8 presents the odds ratios from this analysis. As predicted, the chances of a story adopting the solidarity frame increase if the story is in local media. Local papers were twice as likely to report about signs of solidarity as were national papers (odds ratio = 2.00; p < .001). If the story is about Sandy Hook as compared to Virginia Tech, it was also more likely to be reported; however, this relationship was not statistically significant.

Table 11.8. Logistic Regression Predicting the Prevalence of Stories Adopting the Solidarity Frame

Variable	B	SE	Wald	Odds ratio	p-value
Local	.695*	.119	33.98	2.00	< .001
VT	−.147	.110	1.79	.863	.180
Constant	−.663*	.083	63.66	.516	< .001

Discussion

Overall. the evidence strongly supports our predictions that a media outlet's location shapes how it frames a tragedy's story. Newspapers geographically close to the tragedy not only publish more tragedy-related articles than do papers that are distant from the tragedy. they are also likely to frame the tragedy differently. We argue that the differences between local and more distant papers in the framing of a tragedy are the result of the media's attempt to meet market needs or desires.

The market for local or proximate media sources are likely traumatized: thus. the members of that market would benefit from a "frame of solidarity." This frame emerges when published articles focus on the victims and report evidence of community solidarity (Hawdon et al.. forthcoming). Focusing on the victims and depicting the community as unified in their grief reaffirms the group's resolve and helps promote the social solidarity on which community members often rely. Evidence suggests that social solidarity promotes community resiliency and individual wellbeing after a tragedy (Hawdon et al.. 2012; Hawdon. Räsänen. Oksanen. & Ryan. 2012; Hawdon & Ryan. 2012); therefore. the local media can help their readers recover from the tragic incident by using a frame of solidarity. Moreover. by focusing on the individuals affected by the tragedy instead of the institutional problems that led to the event. the media promotes a frame that offers support and ultimately alleviates the social guilt associated with a tragedy (see Ott & Aiki. 2002).

National papers. by comparison. are more likely to publish stories that focus on the potential causes of the tragedy. In the case of school shootings. these issues typically include gun control and the provision of mental health services. Their readers do not need the emotionally supportive. highly personalized frames that help generate solidarity: instead. their readers' meaning-making needs are likely centered on the event's underlying causes. As a result. national papers distant from the tragedy publish significantly more "issue focused" stories than proximate papers do. These broader-issue stories help readers understand the alleged causes of the event in hopes of averting a similar one from occurring in their communities.

We also found support for our assertion that the characteristics of the Virginia Tech and Sandy Hook tragedies would influence the framing of the events. While the reporting of both tragedies adopted a "frame of solidarity." the Sandy Hook tragedy's framing followed this script even more so than did the Virginia Tech tragedy. The coverage of the Sandy Hook tragedy was twice as likely to focus on the victims and twice as likely to mention signs of community solidarity as were the stories about Virginia Tech's tragedy. We speculate that this is because the victims in the Sandy Hook shooting were younger than the Virginia Tech victims. Moreover. the perpetrator of the Sandy Hook murders was clearly a community outsider; this was not the case at Virginia Tech. These two factors made it far more difficult for a frame that blamed the community to emerge in Sandy Hook than it was after the Virginia Tech murders. In fact. alternative frames that blamed the community, and the university in particular, did emerge, they just did not become the dominant frame (see Ryan & Hawdon, 2008).

Our research provides additional evidence that the social stage model of coping (Pennebaker & Harber, 1993) can account for observed variations in the framing of tragedies overtime. While there is a stark contrast in how local and national papers frame tragedies initially, as time passes and we move from the emergency to the inhibition stage, the issues covered become increasingly similar. Although local papers are still more likely to adopt a "frame of solidarity," both local and national papers tend to focus on the underlying causes of the tragedy.

Our research also improves our understanding of the role media plays in framing tragedies. As previously mentioned, how the media frames a tragedy can influence how the tragedy unfolds, the likelihood of a similar tragedy occurring again, who is blamed for the tragedy, perceptions of what caused the tragedy, public opinion about issues related to the tragedy, policy decisions, and the resiliency and recovery of both individuals and their communities. It is therefore important to understand how different media sources frame tragedies since different frames will lead to different understandings and conclusions. This research should alert media scholars as well as journalists and editors to exercise care when framing tragic events.

While we researched only two tragedies, we believe our results are generalizable. First, similar results were found when the media coverage of other tragedies were studied (e.g. Pennebaker & Harber, 1993; Gortner & Pennebaker, 2003; Stone & Pennebaker, 2002; Scharrer et al., 2003; Hawdon et al forthcoming). Second, there is little reason to think that the media coverage of these tragedies was unique. Both cases dominated the news for a short while and both cases were used to stimulate discussion of larger issues such as gun control laws. At least superficially, this level of media attention and the subsequent generation of widespread public debate that is covered by the media occurred after other tragedies such as the mass shootings in a Pennsylvanian Amish elementary school in 2006, an Illinois university in 2008, a Tucson shopping mall in 2011, and a Colorado movie theater in 2012. Unfortunately, there are numerous other examples of how the media reports tragedies, and most of these examples appear to follow a familiar pattern. Thus, we believe similar results would be found if the media coverage of other tragedies were analyzed.

However, we should note that digital media is changing journalism (for example, see Horrigan, 2005). Nearly half of Americans get local news on a mobile device and mobile news applications (Purcell et al., 2011) or Social Networking Sites such as Facebook (see Mitchell, Ronsenstiel, & Christian, 2012). With the increasing use of social media, distances are becoming less important in all aspects of life, including the more tragic events we experience. Moreover, in response to budget cuts and declining profits for print media, media sources have been recently outsourcing local news reporting. This outsourcing may result in not only less accurate reporting of local perspectives, but also inferior coverage of local events (see Tady, 2008). Given these trends, it is likely that distance is becoming less important for determining how the story of a tragic event is told. Nevertheless, journalists will still need to consider the needs of different markets while they cover tragic events.

Conclusion

Tragedies, heinous crimes, disasters, and critical incidents attract media attention. As journalists flock to cover these events, they begin to tell the story. Depending on what they write and editors decide to print the media constructs our understanding of the event. Several media critics have warned about the hyper-sensationalistic and often overly simplistic nature of the coverage of tragedies. Our research adds to these criticisms and should be considered as a cautionary warning. Our research clearly shows that not all media sources tell a story in the same way. The location of a media outlet relative to a tragedy influences how the story is framed. It not only influences what aspects of the story are emphasized, it ultimately can influence the communities it serves. Therefore, our study has important implications for journalists who cover tragic events and any communities affected by one.

The fact that the location of media sources influences how a tragedy is reported raises an issue about the "truth" of reporting. Can the "truth" about a tragedy ever be discerned from media accounts if different sources do not tell the same story or focus on the same facts? Probably not; however, how the media frames an event is probably less important for discovering "the truth" than it is for meeting the needs of its readers. Although mass tragedies may affect "all of us" in some way, those closest to the tragedy in both geographic and social space disproportionately bear the brunt of the tragedy's physical, economic, and emotional harm. Our research demonstrates that the media can play a crucial role for those trying to make sense of and recover from a tragedy. The media assists in meaning making, and they appear to do it in a manner that is most appropriate for the audiences they serve.

References

Ahern, J., Galea, S., Resnick, H., Kilpatrick, D., Bucuvalas, M., Gold, J., & Vlahov, D. (2002). Television images and psychological symptoms after the September 11 terrorist attacks. *Psychiatry: Interpersonal and Biological Processes*, 65, 289–300.

Ahern, J., Galea, S., Resnick, H.S. & Vlahov, D. (2004). Television images and probable posttraumatic stress disorder after September 11: The role of and background characteristics, event exposures, and perievent panic. *Journal of Nervous and Metnal Disease*, 192, 217–226.

Albarran, A. B. (2002). *Media Economics: Understanding Markets, Industries, and Concepts (Second Edition)*. Ames, IA: Iowa State Press.

Argothy, V. (2005). *Framing Volunteerism in a Consensus Crisis: Mass Media Coverage of Volunteers in The 9/11 Response*. Disaster Research Center, Preliminary Paper 335.

Boomgaarden, H. G., & de Vreese. C.H. (2007). Dramatic real-world events and public opinion dynamics: Media coverage and its impact on public reactions to an assassination. *International Journal of Public Opinion Research,* 19, 354–366.

Brezina, T., & Kaufman, J.M. (2008). What really happened in New Orleans? Estimating the threat of violence during the Hurricane Katrina disaster. *Justice Quarterly,* 25, 701–722.

BurrellesLuce. (2007). Top media outlets: Newspapers. blogs, & consumer magazines. Retrieved from http://www.burrellesluce.com

BurrellesLuce (2012). Top media outlets: Newspapers, blogs, consumer magazines, websites, & social networks. Retrieved from http://www.burrellesluce.com

Catalano, R., & Hartig. T. (2001). Communal bereavement and the incidence of very low birthweight in Sweden. *The Journal of Health and Social Behavior,* 42, 333–342.

Carletta, J. (1996). Assessing agreement on classification tasks: the kappa statistic. *Computational Linguistics,* 22(2), 249–254.

Croteau, D., & Hoynes, W. (2000). *Media/Society: Industries, images, and audiences.* Thousand Oaks, CA: Pine Forge Press.

Cruz. J. d. (1993). *Disaster and society: The 1985 Mexican earthquakes.* Lund, Sweden: Lund University Press.

Dennis, B., & Kane. P. (2013, February 7). Measure would strengthen mental health care system. *The Washington Post.* Retrieved from http://articles.washingtonpost.com/2013-02-07/national/36970733_1_mental-health-mental-disorders-health-centers

Garner, A.C. (1996). The cost of fighting Mother Nature: News coverage of the 1993 Midwest Floods. *Journal of Communication Inquiry,* 20, 83–98.

Gauthier, C. C. (2003). News media coverage of national tragedies: Public discourse as public grieving. *International Journal of Applied Philosophy,* 17, 33–45.

Gortner, E.M., & Pennebaker. J.W. (2003). The archival anatomy of a disaster: Media coverage and community-wide health effects of the Texas A&M bonfire tragedy. *Journal of Social and Clinical Psychology,* 22, 580–603.

Hawdon, J. (2001). The role of presidential rhetoric in the creation of a moral panic: Reagan, Bush, and the War on Drugs. *Deviant Behavior,* 22, 419–445.

Hawdon, J., & Ryan, J. (2012). Wellbeing after the Virginia Tech mass murder: The relative effectiveness of face-to-face and virtual interactions in providing support for survivors. *Traumatology,* 18(4), 3–11. doi:10.1177/1534765612441096

Hawdon, J., Agnich. L., & Ryan, J. (in press). Media framing of a tragedy: A content analysis of print media coverage of the Virginia Tech tragedy. *Traumatology.*

Hawdon, J., Oksanen A., & Räsänen. P. (2012). Media coverage and solidarity after tragedies: Reporting school shootings in two nations. *Comparative Sociology,* 11, 1–30.

Hawdon, J., Oksanen, A., Räsänen. P., & Ryan. J. (2012). *School shootings and local communities: An international comparison between The United States and Finland.* Turku, Finland: University of Turku Press.

Hawdon, J., Räsänen P., Oksanen A., & Ryan J. (2012). Social solidarity and wellbeing after critical incidents: Three cases of mass shootings. *Journal of Critical Incident Analysis,* 3, 2–25.

Hawdon, J., Vuori, M., Räsänen. P., & Oksanen. A. (2013). Social responses to collective crime: Assessing the relationship between crime-related fears and collective sentiments. *European Journal of Criminology.* Advance online publication. doi:10.1177/1477370813485516

Hollander, S., & Strickler. A. (2012, December 14). Hope turns to sorrow as families wait for word. *Wall Street Journal*. Retrieved from http://online.wsj.com/news/articles/SB10001424127887324296604578180073713040306

Horrigan, J.B. (2005). Americans' consumption of news and information. Presentation to the Associated Press Broadcast Meeting. *Pew Internet and American Life Project, Pew Research Center*. Retrieved from http://www.pewinternet.org/Presentations/2005/Americans-Consumption-of-News--Information.aspx

Johnson, R. (2007, April 20). Heidi Miller: Road to recovery is getting shorter. *The Roanoke Times*. Retrieved from http://ww2.roanoke.com/vtvictims/wb/113863

Kirchhoff. S. M. (2010). The U.S. newspaper industry in transition. Congressional Research Service Report for Congress. Retrieved from http://www.fas.org

Krippendorff. K. (1980). *Content analysis: An introduction to its methodology*. Thousand Oaks. CA: Sage Publications.

Kupchik. A., & Bracy, N.L. (2009). The news media on school crime and violence: Constructing dangerousness and fueling fear. *Youth Violence and Juvenile Justice*. 7, 136–155.

Lawrence. R. G., & Birkland, T.A. (2004). Guns. Hollywood, and school safety: Defining the school-shooting problem across public arenas. *Social Science Quarterly*. 85, 1193–1207.

Lawrence. R., & Mueller, D. (2003). "School shootings and the man-bites-dog criterion of newsworthiness. *Youth Violence and Juvenile Justice*, 1, 330–345.

Letukas. L.. Olofsson. A., & Barnshaw. J. (2009). Solidarity trumps catastrophe? An empirical and theoretical analysis of post-tsunami media in two Western nations. Preliminary Paper #363.

University of Delaware Disaster Research Center. Retrieved from http://dspace.udel.edu

McQuail. D. (2005). *Mass Communication Theory (Fifth Edition)*. London: Sage Publications.

Mitchell. A., Rosenstiel, T., & Christian. L. (2012). What Facebook and Twitter mean for news. *Pew Internet and American Life Project. Pew Research Center*. Retrieved from http://stateofthemedia.org/2012/mobile-devices-and-news-consumption-some-good-signs-for-journalism/what-facebook-and-twitter-mean-for-news/

Muschert. G. W. (2007). The Columbine victims and the myth of the juvenile superpredator. *Youth Violence and Juvenile Justice*. 5, 4, 351–366.

Muschert. G. W., & Carr, D. (2006). Media salience and frame changing across events: Coverage of nine school shootings. 1997–2001. *Journalism and Mass Communication Quarterly. 83*, 2, 747–766.

Nurmi. J. (2012). Making Sense of School Shootings: Comparing Local Narratives of Social Solidarity and Conflict in Finland. *Traumatology*. 18(3), 16–28.

Nurmi. J., Räsänen, P., & Oksanen. A. (2012). The norm of solidarity: Experiencing negative aspects of community life after a school shooting tragedy. *Journal of Social Work*. 12(3), 300–319.

Ott. B. L., & Aoki. E. (2002). The politics of negotiating public tragedy: Media framing of the Matthew Shepard murder. *Rhetoric and Public Affairs*. 5, 483–505.

Pennebaker. J. W., & Harber, K.D. (1993). A social stage model of collective coping: The Loma Prieta Earthquake and the Persian Gulf War. *Journal of Social Issues*, 49, 125–145.

Pfefferbaum. B., Nixon. S., Tivis. R., Doughty. D., Pynoos. R. Gurwitch. R., & Foy. D. (2001). Television exposure in children after a terrorist incident. *Psychiatry*, 64, 202–211.

Pfefferbaum, B., Doughty, D.E., Reddy, C., Patel, N., Gurwitch, R.H., Nixon, S.J., & Tivis, R.D. (2002). *Journal of Urban Health.* 79, 3, 354–363.

Pfefferbaum, B., Sconzo, G., Flynn, B., Kearns, L., Doughty, D., Gurwitch, R., Nixon, S. & Nawaz, S. (2003). Case finding and mental health services for children in the aftermath of the Oklahoma City Bombing. *Journal of Behavioral Health Services and Research.* 30, 215–228.

Purcell, K. Rainie, L., Rosenstiel, T., & Mitchell, A. (2011). How mobile devices are changing community information environments. *Pew Internet and American Life Project. Pew Research Center.* Retrieved from http://www.pewinternet.org/Reports/2011/Local-mobile-news.aspx

Ryan, J., & Hawdon, J. (2008). From individual to community: The 'framing' of 4–16 and the display of social solidarity. *Traumatology.* 14, 43–52.

Scharrer, E., Wiedman, L.M. & Bissel, K.L. (2003). Pointing the finger of blame: News media coverage of popular-culture culpability. *Journalism and Communication Monographs.* 5, 49–98.

Schlenger, W. E., Caddell, J. M., Ebert L., Jordan, B. K., Rourke, K., Wilson, D., Thalji, L., Dennis, J. M., Fairbank, J. & Kulka, R. K. (2002). Psychological reactions to terrorist attacks: Findings from the National Study of Americans' reactions to September 11." *Journal of the American Medical Association.* 288, 581–588.

Serrano, R. A., Drogin, B., & Zucchino, D. (2007, April 18). Shooter plotted in silent rage. *Los Angeles Times.* Retrieved from http://www.latimes.com/la-na-shooter18apr18.0.1843841.story

Sorenson, S. B., Peterson Manz, J. G., & Berk, R. A. (1998). News media coverage and the epidemiology f homicide. *American Journal of Public Health.* 88, 1510–1514.

Stone, L.D., & Pennebaker, J.W. (2002). "Trauma in real time: Talking and avoiding online conversations about the death of Princess Diana. *Basic and Applied Social Psychology.* 24, 3, 173–183.

Tady, M. (2008). Outsourcing journalism: Localism threatened by offshore reporters and editors. *FAIR: Fairness and Accuracy in Reporting.* Retrieved from http://fair.org/extra-online-articles/Outsourcing-Journalism

Terkildsen, N., & Schnell, F. (1997). How media frames move public opinion: An analysis of the women's movement. *Political Research Quarterly.* 50, 879–900.

Thevenot, B. (2006). Myth-making in New Orleans. *American Journalism Review.* 27, 30–37.

Van Belle, D. A. (2000). New York Times and network TV news coverage of foreign disasters: The significance of insignificant variables." *Journalism and Mass Communication Quarterly.* 77, 50–70.

Vasterman, P., Yzermans, C.J., & Dirkzwager, A.J.E. (2005). The role of media and media hypes in the aftermath of disasters. *Epidemiologic Reviews,* 27, 107–114.

Wenger, D., & Friedman, B. (1986). Local and national media coverage of disaster: A content analysis of the print media's treatment of disaster myths. *International Journal of Mass Emergencies and Disasters.* 4, 3, 27–50.

Yanich, D. (2005). Kids, crime and local television news. *Crime & Delinquency,* 51, 103–132.

Chapter Twelve

Satirizing Mass Murder:
What Many Think, Yet Few Will Say

Jaclyn Schildkraut, H. Jaymi Elsass and Glenn W. Muschert

Introduction

Littleton, Colorado. Blacksburg, Virginia. Fort Hood, Texas. Tucson, Arizona. Aurora, Colorado. Newtown, Connecticut. And, most recently, Navy Yard in Washington, D.C. Each of these towns and cities has unexpectedly become part of a infamous group of places that have become the home to mass shootings. Still, despite the infrequency of such events, the level of media attention they command make them seem far more commonplace than their actual occurrence (Elsass, Schildkraut, & Stafford, 2013; Schildkraut, 2012a; Schildkraut & Muschert, 2014; Schildkraut, Elsass, & Stafford, 2013). Lynch (2012), for example, notes that between January 2003 and August 2012, 195 people were killed and an additional 207 people injured in mass shooting events. By comparison, an estimated 14,827 people were killed in the U.S. in 2012 alone (FBI, 2013). Still, it is the sensational characteristics of mass shootings that keep these events in the public focus and dominate media coverage with each occurrence.

In many instances, both the public and the media discourses toe the line between right to know and avoidance of the larger issues. These "disaster narratives" provide comfort and commentary, but little resolution, as the real heart of the issues rarely is addressed (Schildkraut & Muschert, 2014). Several satirical news outlets, including *The Onion, The Daily Show,* and *The Colbert Report,* however, have taken a "no sugar-coating," tell-it-how-it-really-is approach to chronicling the narratives of these events. Using truth wrapped in humor and satire, these sources often make the statements other sources shy away from. This chapter examines the news reports offered by these sources following recent mass shooting events.

Media Coverage and Disaster Narratives

It's been 2 months since the tragedy at Sandy Hook, but the media just won't let this story go. Meanwhile, other news just gets completely ignored. Where's the in-depth report on the salsa dog? Salsa dog—could it happen in your town?
—Stephen Colbert (2013a)

Gotta say, the coverage is really improving. Quick conveyance of details, good b-roll of the shooters' houses, and they've stopped getting so weepy with the vigils.
—Janelle Hamer[1] ("Rash of School Shootings, 2006, para. 2)

When mass shootings occur, regardless of location, the media, politicians, and at times, the public, often treat these events as a new and unexpected phenomenon. Millions of viewers tune in to around-the-clock coverage waiting for some novel idea or approach to explain these events. Whether it is how the events are covered, who is interviewed, what statements are made, or even how long the coverage lasts, there also is the anticipation that it will be new and different. Yet, in reality, these shootings all are part of a larger "disaster narrative," whereby audiences are faced with the same, redundant marathon of news coverage (Schildkraut & Muschert, 2014), the format of which rarely differs from event to event.

Why, then, are audiences surprised when they get the same neatly packaged content they always have gotten? In July 2012, following the Aurora movie theater shootings, writers at *The Onion* tackled precisely this issue in an article entitled "Sadly, Nation Knows Exactly How Colorado Shooting's Aftermath Will Play Out":

The nation's 300 million citizens told reporters they can pinpoint down to the hour when the first candlelight vigil will be held, roughly how many people will attend, how many times the county sheriff will address the media in the coming weeks, and when the town-wide memorial services will be held . . . Some sort of video recording, written material, or disturbing photographs made by the shooter will be surfacing in about an hour or two . . . Calls for a mature, thoughtful debate about the role of guns in American society started right on time, and should persist throughout the next week or so . . . The debate will soon spiral out of control and ultimately lead to nothing of substance . . . Questions will be raised as to whether or not violence in the movies and video games has something to do with the act . . . [Further, as resident Amy Brennan notes,] "In exactly two weeks this will all be over and it will be like it never happened."

Mass shootings have become what Douglas Kellner (2003, 2008a, 2008b) calls a "media spectacle," whereby the news media inundate audiences with repetitive coverage of the aftermath of these tragedies. These may include "rushed and often inaccurate reports of the number of dead and injured, interviews with badly shaken witnesses, candlelight vigils, and often pointless debates over gun control" ("Desperate Nation Tries Getting On Board," 2013, para. 6). More recently, the media also have begun to incorporate eyewitness accounts, including footage captured on cell phone cameras into the loop (Elsass et al., 2013; Kellner, 2008b; Schildkraut, 2012b; Sutter, 2012; Wigley & Fontenot, 2009).

Despite the visceral reaction that often accompanies these events, thousands upon thousands of people flock to televisions, newspapers, and the Internet to get more news. Following the 2007 Virginia Tech shootings, 1.4 million people tuned in to CNN to watch coverage of the event (Garofoli, 2007), when viewership averages 450,000 people per day (Pew Research Center's Project for Excellence in Journalism, 2006). Similarly, while Fox News has an average of 900,000 viewers per day (Pew Research Center's Project for Excellence in Journalism, 2006), viewership on the day of the shooting doubled to 1.8 million people (Garofoli, 2007). When CNN first broke into coverage of Columbine in 1999, six hours of uninterrupted live coverage were aired (Muschert, 2002), and similar practices have been witnessed following other mass shooting events (Tucker, 2012). Nightly news broadcasts devote inordinate amounts of coverage to follow up stories from the scene for days and, depending on the audiences' response to the shooting, sometimes even weeks (Maguire, Weatherby, & Mathers, 2002; Muschert, 2002; Robinson, 2011; Tucker, 2012). Newspapers crank out article after article (Chyi & McCombs, 2004; Muschert & Carr, 2006; Newman, 2006; Schildkraut, 2012a; Schildkraut & Muschert, 2014), each with attention-grabbing, sensationalized headlines. More recently, people have begun to gravitate to the Internet and social media sites for quicker updates (Elsass et al., 2013; see also Schildkraut, 2012a; Schildkraut & Muschert, forthcoming).

Though previous research in agenda setting (see, for example, McCombs & Zhu, 1995) have found the average life-span of many hot-button issues in the public and political discourses to be around 18.5 months, interest in mass shootings tends to be considerably shorter. While it may not be the two weeks as noted in the earlier quote, rarely does coverage of a high profile mass shooting last for more than 30 days (Chyi & McCombs, 2004; Muschert & Carr, 2006; Schildkraut, 2012a; Schildkraut & Muschert, 2014). For events that are perceived as less salient (e.g., the 2012 Sikh Temple shooting in Oak Creek, Wisconsin) or are replaced with news of a different, putatively more important shooting (e.g., the 2012 Clackamas, Oregon mall shooting that occurred two days prior to the shooting at Sandy Hook), coverage may last an even shorter time.

In an article following the Sikh Temple shooting, an event which took place about two weeks after the Aurora shooting, *The Week* magazine, which features political news and cartoons, examined why two mass shootings occurring so close in temporal proximity were treated completely different in the media. Writers proposed four theories as to why Aurora received more coverage: (1) victims of the Sikh shooting were being treated as second-class victims because their religion is not mainstream; (2) people can relate more with being in a movie theater than in a

Sikh temple; (3) the Sikh temple had less drama – meaning that there were less victims, the shooter was killed rather than being taken alive, and the event wasn't dubbed "The Batman murders" complete with a killer who allegedly claimed to be The Joker; and (4) media fatigue ("Why the Sikh Temple Shooting Got Less Coverage," 2012, para. 2). Inevitably, what these writers are getting at is that Aurora was just more newsworthy than Oak Creek, particularly in a year when there were multiple mass shooting events to cover (Lynch, 2012).

The media, as well as society in general, assign different values to victims of these mass shootings. For the media, this figure of newsworthiness typically falls to those victims that are viewed as the most vulnerable – females, children, the elderly, and whites (Sorenson, Manz, and Berk, 1998). Still, in coverage of mass murder, not all victims, despite the heinous nature of their deaths, are considered newsworthy. Following the Columbine shooting, the media focused on four main victims – students Cassie Bernall, Rachel Scott, and Isaiah Shoels, and teacher Dave Sanders – despite that 13 people (excluding the shooters themselves) were killed that day (Muschert, 2007b; see also Schildkraut & Muschert, 2014). Other victims, such as student Kyle Velasquez, receive little to no coverage in the mainstream media. Though more recent events, such as the 2012 shootings in Aurora, Colorado and Newtown, Connecticut have given way to a more victim-centered focus, rather than reporting focused primarily on the offenders (Schildkraut & Muschert, 2014), varied amounts of attention are allocated to each victim based on their personal histories or circumstances surrounding their deaths. Further, beyond assigning different levels of newsworthiness to the victims, the events as a whole also are ranked based on perceived importance. Those that receive more attention typically have higher death tolls and either sensational (e.g., Aurora) or symbolic (e.g., Newtown) characteristics. Other events, such as the 2007 shootings at malls in Salt Lake City, Utah and Omaha, Nebraska, the 2008 Northern Illinois University (NIU) shooting, and the 2009 shooting at a Binghamton, New York immigration education center, have failed to garner equitable coverage, especially in the national media (Elsass et al., 2013; Schildkraut et al., 2013).

Another problem plaguing the exorbitant amounts of media coverage of mass shootings is inaccuracies in the reporting. Following the 2007 shooting at the Westroads Mall in Omaha, Nebraska, reporters incorrectly reported the racial identification of the shooter, suggesting that a black male was still on the loose when the shooter, Robert Hawkins, a white male, was lying dead in one of the mall's department stores (Lipschultz & Hilt, 2011). In the first few hours after news of the shooting at Sandy Hook Elementary School in 2012 broke, reporters splashed Facebook photos of Ryan Lanza, brother of the actual shooter, across screens and identified him as the suspect (Hack, 2012; Soliwon & Nelson, 2012). These photos were reposted on the social media platform nearly 10,000 times before reporters correctly identified Adam Lanza as the shooter (Soliwon & Nelson, 2012). Even the identification of Aurora shooter James Holmes as "The Joker" is suspect, as this rumor circulated once it was revealed that Holmes had dyed his hair a curious shade of orange before the massacre, and despite the fact that the Joker's hair in all

Batman movies is green. Such problems stem not only from rushed, unchecked stories and public accounts (Lipschultz & Hilt, 2011), but also from the increasing use of media, such as photographs and videos, from third party information subsidiaries (Wigley & Fontenot, 2009). In sum, the media's coverage of mass shootings have led to reports that are "not necessarily complete, balanced, or accurate" (O'Toole, 2000, p. 3).

There Has To Be A Reason

> There's no clear motivation for my horrendous act.
>> —Roland Walling ("Victims Sought," 2005, para. 2)

> Let me just say there's no use looking for answers at a time like this. An event as tragic as what I will be carrying out . . . never has any easy explanation.
>> —Edwin Gregory Teach ("If It's Any Consolation," 2008, para. 3)

> Who gives a [expletive] what they were watching? What ever happened to crazy?
>> —Chris Rock (Vasilev, 2011)

Once the initial shock of the shooting wears off, one of the first questions to enter the public discourse is, "Why?" Why here? Why now? Why did this happen? Why were there no warning signs? Following the December 12, 2012 shooting at a Portland area mall, *The Onion* suggested that shooter Jacob Tyler Roberts simply "shot random, innocent strangers for no reason at all, because he was terrible" ("Authorities Not Even Going To Bother," 2012). This simplistic response rarely, if ever, is accepted as an answer to the larger question of "why?"

More commonly, the discourse following mass shooting events typically focuses on "usual suspects,"—guns, mental health, and violent video games (Schildkraut & Muschert, forthcoming). Typically, this discussion involves banter back and forth about whether more or less guns are needed or how they should be kept out of the hands of the mentally ill. Other times, it is suggested that the desensitization offered by violent media has turned "normal" people into killing machines with the underlying suggestion that such content should be outlawed. As Jon Stewart (2013) pointed out, "the Dutch spend more than twice as much on video games as we do and have less than a tenth of the gun violence. Maybe we need to talk about whether our culture is adding to the soup." Still, despite the attention these dialogues receive, they rarely bring us closer to a solution, perhaps because the true intention of the message is lost in translation.

Gun Violence

> You would not be stunned or perplexed to discover that the gunmen used automatic or semi-automatic rifles with high-capacity magazines to carry out the shootings, and the fact that the weapons and ammunition were all acquired legally would likely otherwise not leave you the least bit astonished.

("It Wouldn't Surprise You," 2013, para. 6)

As noted in the article, "Desperate Nation Tries Getting On Board With Mass Shootings," these events often lead to "fiery, often pointless debates over gun control" (2013, para. 6). Those in favor of gun control often call for stricter regulations, such as the banning of assault weapons and large capacity magazines, as was present from Columbine to Aurora to Sandy Hook. As one article points out, written from the perspective of Senator Harry Reid.

> Under our current laws, there exist virtually no rules preventing assault rifles or other deadly weapons that serve no legitimate purpose except to kill human beings from falling into the hands of anyone who wants them. ("The Time Is Now," 2013, para. 3)

Alternately, those in favor of gun rights suggest that lesser restrictions should be imposed so that people are able to protect themselves and others. As noted in *The Onion* following the 2011 shooting of Congresswoman Gabrielle Giffords and others outside of a Tucson, Arizona political rally, "we can only hope that if he [Jared Loughner] acts out again, another Arizona citizen will be legally carrying a concealed firearm and be able to stop him" ("Shooting Suspect Released," 2011).

Despite research (e.g. Cohen, 1963; Entman, 2007; McCombs, 1997; Reese, 2007) that has shown that the public's opinion about a particular issue often is shaped by the agenda set forth by claims makers via the media, studies have shown that mass shootings typically do not have an effect on views about gun control. Following the mass shooting in Aurora, the Pew Research Center for the People & the Press (2012) found that public opinion over both gun rights and gun control remained virtually unchanged. Specifically, support for gun control increased two percentage points (from 45 percent to 47 percent), while preference for gun rights decreased three percentage points (from 49 percent to 46 percent) from when the same questions were asked three months earlier (Pew Research Center for the People & the Press, 2012). The lack of visible change was also evident following the 2011 Tucson, Arizona shooting (gun control −4 percent, gun rights +3 percent) and the 2007 Virginia Tech shootings (gun control +2 percent, gun rights −5 percent) (Pew Research Center for the People & the Press, 2012).

The lack of a definitive public opinion still does not prohibit politicians from rushing hundreds of pieces of legislation to the floor in an effort to "fix the problem." Following Columbine, over 800 pieces of legislation were introduced, with around 10 percent being enacted into law (Schildkraut & Hernandez, 2013; Soraghan, 2000). All of the measures aimed at closing the gun show loophole, which was identified as a leading reason that the shooters were able to acquire their firearms with such ease, failed to pass, despite being reintroduced over and over again on the taxpayers' dime (Schildkraut & Hernandez, 2013). Early after the Newtown shooting, New York state passed a strict gun control package, which included a ban on assault weapons and large capacity magazines (Kaplan, 2013;

Schildkraut & Muschert, 2014; Schildkraut & Muschert, forthcoming). A number of other measures introduced in the weeks and months following the shooting, however, either have failed to pass or have little chance of being enacted into law.²

The underlying issue with such responses to mass shootings is that the corresponding response is one of "feel good" legislation rather than that which is effective (Schildkraut & Hernandez, 2013). Speaking as Senator Harry Reid, *The Onion* noted that:

> While it may not be politically convenient for them to do so, lawmakers must be willing to step up, band together, and go to work on a diluted, insubstantial bill that will essentially do nothing to address this problem. Moreover, once they've drafted such a bill, they must ensure it is torturously wrung through the Congressional legislative process until it bears virtually no resemblance to the law that was initially envisioned. ("The Time Is Now," 2013, para. 3)

In many events, bills that have little chance of passing, such as legislation aimed at closing the gun show loopholes following Columbine, are continually reintroduced in both the House and the Senate, each attempt as unsuccessful as the next. In fact, several pieces of legislation following Columbine were reintroduced in five different legislative sessions, and did not ever pass (Schildkraut & Hernandez, 2013). One potential consideration, then, becomes whether the continual introduction of new legislation does more than provide temporary comfort, and as such, if the resources spent drafting such bills would be better allocated to enforcing those laws currently in place and providing the much needed help for groups such as the mentally ill and at-risk youth.

One problem in the discursive battle between gun control and gun rights is that, at least in the media, there never seems to be an appropriate time to talk about it. As Jon Stewart (2012) pointed out in a monologue on *The Daily Show* following the Aurora shootings:

> Are we ever going to get a handle on how to prevent these types of tragedies? It's a very complex issue, obviously, the intersection of the mental health system and cultural influences, a balance between individual freedoms and public safety, availability of guns. If we draw lines on weaponry, obviously the question is have we drawn them right? So while we also talk about societal factors and moral factors, you know, we should also talk about [sic] more and more powerful destructive weaponry. You're telling me, that to discuss the epidemic of gun violence in this country, for that there is a waiting period?

In addition to when the discussion about gun violence is appropriate, the question also is raised as to how such a discourse should be carried out. In an episode of *The Colbert Report* two months after the Sandy Hook shootings, host Stephen Colbert (2013a) tackles the issues of individual gun rights: "Sure, with a gun in the house, my family is less safe. But isn't that a small price to pay for my family's safety?" Yet such a simplistic question rarely is the focus of the gun violence discourse. Instead, the media parade politicians, pundits, and so-called "experts" across television screens, one after the next, to either support or refute the issue at hand. Perhaps it is, as Colbert (2013a) noted in the same monologue, "This morbid obsession with the tens of thousands of people who are killed every year with guns is just all part of the media's anti-gun agenda . . . To the media, a smoking gun is always a smoking gun."

Mental Health

> You certainly wouldn't be alarmed to read that each of the 12 shooters had a well-documented history of mental instability and had exhibited worrying signs in the prior days, weeks, and even years.
>
> ("It Wouldn't Surprise You," 2013, para. 6)

The media's fascination with mental health as a causal factor for gun massacres is undeniable. Following mass shooting events, this is one of the earliest topics to enter the discourse, besides the obvious discussion on guns. Whether the shooters were on antidepressant medications, as was Eric Harris, one of the Columbine shooters, or had previous indicators of mental illness, as did Jared Loughner, perpetrator of the 2011 shooting of Congresswoman Gabrielle Giffords in Tucson, Arizona, mental illness typically is a common buzzword that encapsulates these events. Yet such a discourse may be misplaced. Following the shooting at Sandy Hook, for example, the media latched onto the fact that shooter Adam Lanza had Asperger's syndrome (Schildkraut & Muschert, forthcoming). Despite that this condition is a highly functioning form of autism, and people diagnosed with the disorder rarely are violent, particularly to those outside of their family (Harmon, 2012), the media pointed to the disease as a causal factor for the shooting, thus criminalizing people with Asperger's. As one Asperger's advocate noted:

> The media's continued mention of a possible diagnosis of Asperger syndrome implies a connection between that and the heinous crime committed by the shooter. They may have just as well said, 'Adam Lanza, age 20, was reported to have had brown hair.' (Lori Shery, in Harmon, 2012)

One of the earliest shootings where mental health was front and center was the 2007 Virginia Tech massacre. The shooter, Seung-Hui Cho, had a long documented history of mental illness. Two years prior to the shootings, he had even been involuntarily hospitalized and declared an imminent danger to himself and others (Schildkraut & Muschert, forthcoming; Virginia Tech Review Panel [VTRP], 2007). Due to overcrowding in Virginia's mental health facilities, however, Cho was ordered to outpatient treatment (Bonnie, Reinhard, Hamilton, & McGarvey, 2009; VTRP, 2007) and the entire exchange was never reported to the Central Criminal Records Exchange (Schildkraut & Hernandez, 2013). Subsequently, when Cho went to purchase his firearms, he was able to do so legally (Bonnie et al., 2009;

Roberts, 2009; Schildkraut & Hernandez, 2009). Similar warning signs were noted in shooters Jared Loughner, who was initially found incompetent to stand trial (though later was determined to be sane and pled guilty) and James Holmes, who months after his arrest, decided to forward an insanity defense (Schildkraut & Muschert, forthcoming).

In 2008, as a response to Virginia Tech, then-President George W. Bush signed into law the NCIS Improvement Amendments Act (Schildkraut & Hernandez, 2013). In order to improve, update, or establish reporting systems for mentally ill individuals who should be disqualified from gun purchases, this act allocated over $1.3 billion dollars in federal grants made available to states (Schildkraut & Hernandez, 2013). As of 2012, however, most of these funds went unclaimed and millions of records were never added to the background check systems (Brady Campaign Press Release, 2011; Witkin, 2012). Further, these measures, even when implemented, failed to account for those people who are never diagnosed as mentally ill or never receive any form of mental health counseling (Schildkraut & Hernandez, 2013). Why, then, are we surprised when later shooters were legally able to purchase their firearms because of similar failures?

Mental illness has become one of the easiest scapegoats in the ongoing narrative of mass shootings. Yet, most of this discourse focuses on criminalizing mental illness, particularly as it intersects with gun violence, rather than offering a solution. As Stephen Colbert (2013b) pointed out following the Navy Yard shooting.

> While we may never know what motivated the shooter, we do know that he had a troubled and violent past and evidence of mental illness. So it's time to admit, all of us, that some dangerous items shouldn't fall into the hands of the disturbed. No not guns, I mean, we didn't even do anything about guns after Sandy Hook . . . but for the last time, guns have nothing to do with gun violence. We all know what the real problem is.

Further, as Jon Stewart (2013) noted following Sandy Hook:

> We closed the mental institutions in many respects and now our mentally ill live on the streets or are in prison and it is untenable. It is up to us to help them find compassionate, proactive care. This is what we have to address in our mental health system. . . . Yes, mental healthcare absolutely has to be on the table, has to be improved, but someone is always going to slip through the cracks, and our mental health problem leads to other problems—crime, guns, violence. It is a complex problem and all solutions have to be on the table.

The real problem, as identified in Colbert and Stewart's monologues, ties back to this failure of the system. Such a failure includes an inability to adequately detect warning signs, to do something once such signs are evident, and to provide adequate help to those people struggling with mental illness. Access to mental health services also is problematic. The rising costs of health care and lack of affordable treatment options, coupled with overcrowded facilities and inundated caseworkers, block opportunities for those with serious mental conditions to access the help they need.

Duh! There Were Warning Signs

Once in a while, though, a student hands in something that is an absolute delight to read. A student like Brian Petersen, who wrote an incredible short story about a deadly school shooting and how nobody picked up on all the warning signs until it was too late.

("This Short Story," 2009, para. 2)

In the days directly following a mass shooting, the inevitable search begins for indications that the perpetrators were capable of and considering carrying out such an event. Acquaintances of the shooter—including family, friends, teachers, and coworkers—flock to the media with illustrations of warning signs, including the perpetrator's antisocial behavior, propensity for violence, examples of emotional disturbance, tales of bullying and victimization, and/or serious mental health concerns. The media discourse typically includes some discussion as to warning signs present in the shooter and the need to recognize similar red flags in others before another mass shooting takes place. The consistently repeated decree is that by identifying warning signs, potential shooters may be stopped before ever firing a weapon. Such an assertion, while noble in cause, however, fails to be realistic. Predicting mass shooting events is virtually impossible as there exist a large portion of individuals who exhibit warning signs, but never act out, thereby inflating the rate of false positives (Fox & Savage, 2009, p. 1471). Most juveniles and young adults go through periods of time in which they are withdrawn (especially from adults), are quick to anger, or are rebellious, often as a result of fluctuating hormones, rapid brain development, and social and emotional maturation that naturally occur during adolescence (Arredondo, 2003; Lamb & Sims, 2013). Even when warning signs are clearly present and should serve as red flags that the individual in question is in need of some professional psychological and/or emotional intervention, it is not uncommon for those behaviors to be explained away and the person in need not receive any real assistance. Once warning signs are ignored, the individuals violent planning is unconstrained, a point touched on by *The Onion* in the following:

A few days into his summer vacation, local 16-year-old John Vucinich told reporters Tuesday that he is excited to have the next three months to do nothing but sit back, relax, and *meticulously* plot out the details of the mass shooting he is planning for the upcoming school year. ("16-Year-Old Excited", 2013)

Why then, when extreme warning signs are present, does there exist a near refusal by law enforcement, school officials, and the public to acknowledge them? It is not uncommon for people to go to great lengths to explain away red flags, when faced with evidence of completed mass shooting events with similar characteristics. In a recently reported case from New Jersey, an 11-year-old, fifth grade student was found to have drafted detailed plans for a mass-casualty event, including a hit list containing the names of more than 40 people (Dodero, 2013). Interestingly, though the police lieutenant compared the plot as "similar to Columbine or Newtown," in one breath, he dismissed the scheme as one the child was unlikely to be able to execute in the next, saying that the plan was "not something he was capable of actually carrying out" (Dodero, 2013, para. 2). This characterization of the scheme as unrealistic was arrived at based on the youthful age of the child, the inclusion of a few celebrity names in the hit list, and the statement by a family member of the child that though they possess firearms, the youth never has access to them. The dismissal of the legitimacy of the plot as nothing more than violent fantasy unable to be translated into action effectively ignores the same warning signs that we search for in the days following a completed mass casualty event and claim to be so vital in preventing similar attacks. This response has become characteristic, and as such, has not gone unnoticed by satirical writers:

Investigators agreed Beyer's plan was ill-conceived, saying they had confiscated a journal from the boy's home filled with amateur depictions of violence, several poorly drawn band logos, a "completely juvenile" manifesto detailing his personal grievances, and a diagram of the intended massacre suggesting the student lacked strong grasp of the layout of the school he has attended for two and a half years. ("Student Had Embarrassingly Bad Plans," 2011)

Why do we classify one child's plot as unrealistic when completed attacks have occurred which possess similar, if not identical, characteristics? In 1998, 13-year-old Mitchell Johnson and 11-year-old Andrew Golden opened fire at their middle school in Jonesboro, Arkansas killing five and injuring 10 others (Schildkraut & Hernandez, 2013). Johnson and Golden's youthful ages did not make their plot mere violent fantasy. Columbine shooters Eric Harris and Dylan Klebold also included a few famous targets within the lists of their classmates and teachers in their mass casualty plan, which they executed in 1999 killing 13 (excluding themselves) and wounding 21 (Schildkraut & Hernandez, 2013). Harris and Klebold's plan was not unrealistic. Lastly, a number of mass shooters have acquired firearms from family members who believed that their weapons were unattainable. Mass shooting perpetrators often have used restricted access firearms from family members to carry out their attacks, including (1) the aforementioned Johnson and Golden who shot up their middle school in Jonesboro, Arkansas (Schildkraut & Hernandez, 2013); (2) Kipland Kinkel, who after murdering his parents, opened fire on his high school in Springfield, Oregon killing two and wounding 25 (Swanson, 2000); (3) Luke Woodham, who after murdering his mother, opened fire on his high school in Pearl, Mississippi killing two and injuring seven (Pompilo, 1998); (4) Charles "Andy" Williams, who killed two and injured 13 others at his high school in Santee, California (Leary, Kowalski, Smith, & Phillips, 2003); and most recently, (5) Adam Lanza, who killed his mother before murdering 26 and injuring two in an elementary school in Newtown, Connecticut (Schildkraut & Hernandez, 2013). The fact that their families believed that these perpetrators did not have access to their firearms did not stop these shooters from killing.

How important to the thwarting of future mass shooting events can warning signs be if they are written off as inconsequential by those who recognize them, especially when those are the individuals tasked with protecting society? Even when detailed plans are discovered, we are quick to devalue the legitimacy of the plot because "it could never happen here." Yet, after an event does take place somewhere no one thought it could happen, we all scream about the warning signs that were missed or ignored. Still, the question remains as to whether anything can realistically be done when red flags are present, assuming that they are noticed and not explained away.

A Failure of the System

After a school shooting at their high school, the school board in Granton, Kansas has enacted a new proactive plan for removing emotionally disturbed students from the school before they can strike. . . . Displaying at least two of the five defined characteristics will result in immediate expulsion. ("School Board Acts To Remove," 2011, para. 1)

It is comforting in the days after a mass shooting to cling to the idea that warning signs exist and if we just identify them and address them, then future attacks will be greatly diminished, if not eliminated. This point has not been overlooked by satirical publications, as is exemplified in an article published by *The Onion* in which it was reported that "federally funded 'depressed-teen mobile response units' [will] swiftly move in on youths displaying anger, low self-esteem" ("The Columbine Legacy," 2000). Though the article is draped in sarcasm, it is actually a reflection of reality, as similar plans of action are introduced without fail after nearly every mass casualty event perpetrated by a youth (see, for example, Douglas & Lurigio, 2010). What little consolation lies in such strategies, however, is virtually destroyed when the realistic outlets for providing psychological and emotional intervention and care in the United States are examined. Nowhere does this ring truer than in this country's juvenile justice system.

Beginning in the 1960s, there occurred a massive shift from methods of long-term institutionalized treatment to a now heavily relied upon short-term, community-based treatment system and psychotropic medication regime for those suffering from mental illness and/or emotional disturbance (Shields, 2011, p. 4). This change, together with soaring healthcare costs, the reluctance to view mental illness and emotional disturbance on the same plane with other medical illnesses, and a middle class that increasingly does not qualify for government assistance for such services, has resulted in the criminal and juvenile justice systems becoming warehouses for those in need of mental health services (Shields, 2011). This stark reality is even more pronounced when the individual in need of mental illness and/or emotional disturbance treatment is a minor. As expressed by the Coalition for Juvenile Justice (2000): "It's tragic. If you are a young person and mentally ill, you have to get arrested to receive treatment" (p. 11).

Mentally ill youth today often are whisked away by the juvenile justice system under the guise that they will receive the mental health services that they require. Take for example, the recent case of an 11-year-old, fifth grader in New Jersey who was found to be in possession of plans for a mass shooting at his school. He was placed in an "alternate program" while awaiting "impending juvenile charges" (Dodero, 2013, para. 4). In a letter distributed to parents of children attending the school, however the interim superintendent asserted that they would be addressing "the needs of the juvenile suspect" (para. 5). It is clear that in this case, addressing a child's needs – which are likely to be emotional or psychological in nature – is equated with the filing of juvenile charges. As Shields (2011) points out, "mentally ill juveniles today are now left with two less than desirable supervisory treatment options: their families or their local correctional system, which now serves as the de facto mental health system in the United States" (p. 14).

Such a supposition would be less of an issue if mentally ill youths actually were receiving thorough mental health care while in juvenile justice facilities. Yet, when it comes to mentally ill youths in this system, punishment seems to reign supreme. The juvenile justice system is punitive in nature and largely ignores mentally ill children's diseases (Garascia, 2005; Shields, 2011). The original purpose of the juvenile justice system, as entailed in the doctrine of *parens patriae*, was to be rehabilitative in nature, taking into account the inherent differences between children and adults, which results in different levels of culpability (see generally Arredondo, 2003; Garascia, 2005; Lamb & Sim, 2013, Sims, 2009). Today's juvenile justice system, however, closely resembles the adult criminal system thanks to "get tough" legislation focused on punitive responses to juvenile crime (Garascia, 2005).

Though there have been steps in the right direction – such as the introduction of mental health courts into the juvenile justice system – there remains much work to be done before any pronouncement of adequate, much less high-quality, mental health services for youths in the system can be made. We must strive for interagency collaboration between the child welfare and juvenile justice systems (Chuang & Wells, 2010). More comprehensive wraparound services would not only facilitate information sharing between systems charged with addressing juvenile health needs, but also may facilitate earlier intervention, thereby creating a real system for addressing red flags and warning signs, hopefully both inside and outside of the juvenile justice system.

The More Things Change, The More They Stay The Same

I'm getting in the elevator, and these two high school white boys tried to get on with me and I just dove off. I'm saying, y'all ain't killing me. I am scared of

young white boys. If you are white and under 21, I am running for the hills. What
the hell is wrong with these white kids shooting up the school? They don't even
wait until 3 o'clock either.

—Chris Rock (Vasilev, 2011)

Mass shootings have evoked a changing discourse in American society, particularly
as violent crime appeared, through the disproportionate media coverage, to shift
from a problem plaguing inner-city and urban communities to suburban and even
rural areas (Schildkraut et al., 2013). Further, the portrayal of these events in the
media also give the perception that crime rates are rising when, in fact, they are on
the decline (Best, 2006; Burns & Crawford, 1999; Wike & Frasier, 2009). In the
days and weeks after these shootings, an endless rhetoric about gun violence, mental
health, violent media, and what needs to change fills the air. Yet for the few changes
that are imparted after these tragic events, there remains a more consistent absence
of any substantial differences in how members of society change their daily lives as
a result of the impact of the shootings.

Several months following the Columbine shootings, *The Onion* published an
article entitled "Columbine Jocks Safely Resume Bullying" (1999). The article
discusses how, despite such a tragedy, high schools returned to their normal culture
of the in-groups and out-groups with little noticeable change from before the
shooting:

> Thanks to stern new security measures, a militarized school environment and a
> massive public-relations effort designed to obscure all memory of the murderous
> event, members of Columbine's popular crowd are once again safe to reassert their
> social dominance and resume their proud, longstanding tradition of excluding
> those who do not fit in . . . As the school year begins under the watchful eye of
> 24-hour electronic monitoring and police protection, a sense of normalcy has
> returned to Columbine. Just like at any other school, the computer geeks are
> mocked, the economically disadvantaged kids are barely acknowledged, and the
> chess-club, yearbook and debate team members are universally reviled.
> ("Columbine Jocks," 1999, para. 2, 8).

Satire aside, this passage underscores just how little has changed in U.S. high
schools over the last 15 years. Bullying, the favored buzzword for the motive for
school shootings, has remained as prevalent in the discourse (see, for example,
Leary et al., 2003; Weisbrot, 2008). Since Columbine, there have been several high
profile cases of bullying in U.S. schools, particularly cases such as Phoebe Prince
and Megan Meier, where the harassment led to these students' suicides. Still, no
amount of legislation aimed at preventing bullying or cyber-bullying has changed
the social structure of schools around the nation.

Similarly, changes enacted at college and university campuses across the
country have done little to change the environment that hundreds of thousands of
students face each year. In another article, *The Onion* suggested that, following the
shootings at Virginia Tech and NIU, changes implemented on such campuses

should include: "Security cameras shut off to prevent any potential heart-wrenching footage in the event of a shooting . . . Dormitory RAs have been formally deputized and are now armed . . . Campus bookstores to carry Kevlar hoodies . . . Depressed loners to be banned from college" ("Campus Security Measures Increased," 2008).

There is a clear absence of a productive and meaningful discourse about mass shootings. We act in horror when these events occur, yet just as quickly, "with the attention spans of newborns," we move on to the next hot story ("Let's Just Go Ahead," 2011, para. 4). Perhaps then the answer to what is needed to address the problem of mass shootings is what is right in front of us:

> [After the Giffords shooting] There seemed to be a clarion call to have an open dialogue about gun control, a thoughtful conversation about the way this country treats its mentally ill, and a long overdue discussion about the consequences of overly inflammatory political rhetoric . . . The violence was far too brutal and the loss of life far too tragic for the American people to treat the Arizona shooting like any other news event that consumes the country for a brief moment and is then virtually forgotten . . . Because after all, if we had just brushed aside the life-altering assassination attempt of a congresswoman, as well as the death of a federal judge and a 9-year-old girl *without* seizing the opportunity to address our nation's glaring problems, then all the shooting victims would have died in vain. ("Let's Just Go Ahead," 2011, para. 1, 3, 4).

Despite the number of changes that occur following mass shootings, the overarching problem is largely ignored. Countless pieces of ill-conceived and ineffective legislation are introduced, little of which passes. That which passes, or has passed prior to the shooting, rarely is enforced. Clearly identified gaping holes in our mental health and juvenile justice systems are left wide open, despite promises and calls for reform. More importantly, however, the greater discourse after mass shootings fails to account for the cultural meanings and causes of mass shootings (Schildkraut & Muschert, 2013). An examination is needed into how this country has come to accept violence as part of its fabric, and how we have become socialized to act so complacent in addressing violence. What is needed then, as these articles are really saying, is change.

A Time For Change

> I can already see the expressions of shock on everyone's faces . . .
> No one's going to expect this.
>   —*Adriana Simons* ("Everyone At Office," 2013, para. 6)

Mass shootings have left an indelible mark on our culture. These events elicit emotions of shock and horror, both for those who directly are a part of the event and those who witness from afar. As we noted at the outset of this chapter, when these events occur, the reaction often is one of surprise, like something we never saw coming. Yet. in other ways. we have come to expect acts of violence to occur. and. much like an automobile accident. we cannot look away. It may be then. as written in an article following the shooting at the Washington. D.C. Navy Yard. that the American public is:

> Totally into and [has] indeed fully embraced deadly public shootings as part of the rich tapestry of American life. akin to baseball or apple pie . . . They are undeniably an American tradition at this point. ("Desperate Nation Tries Getting On Board." 2013. para. 2. 5)

It is not so much that people are not shocked by these events as it is that. due to the amount of coverage these acts of episodic violent crime receive. they have come to expect these events to occur. As another article from *The Onion* points out:

> Should you. during the course of your day. see pictures of thousands upon thousands of shaken and weeping bystanders standing outside . . . with countless ambulances and police cars behind them. it would elicit in you emotions of sadness and disgust. but no feeling remotely close to disbelief. ("It Wouldn't Surprise You." 2013. para. 7)

So what will it take for real change to occur? The following quotes in various editions of *The Onion* perhaps shed some light on the true nature of just how far the discourse after mass shootings truly has strayed: "If only the gunmen of 2012 had killed more people." ("Democrats Give Up," 2013, para. 4)

It would take much more than brutally gunning down a congresswoman. a federal judge. a nine-year-old girl. and 17 others for the nation to rise above its current corrosive state of politics. ("Report: It's Going To Take Way More." 2011)

> Somewhere around 1.000 kids would have to die in a school shooting in order for the [N.R.A.] organization to reconsider their longstanding opposition to gun control . . . Anything less than 1.000 dead kids would not be enough for the NRA to stop urging Congress to pass pro-gun legislation . . . The shooter would also have to use 30 different types of guns in the shooting in order for us to rethink what the Founding Fathers intended when they wrote the Second Amendment. (NRA Sets 1.000 Killed. 2012).

While we do not suggest by citing these passages that the answer is a greater loss of life. we do argue there is a need for a more meaningful discourse about these events (see also Henry. 2000. 2009; Muschert 2007a. 2010; Muschert et al.. 2014; Schildkraut & Muschert. forthcoming). By and large. the discourse following mass shootings, both in the media and in other areas of society, typically focus on the immediate – bringing some sort of resolution to a grieving public. This response often involves added criminalization of the shooters for some flaw beyond their control (e.g.. mental health). impromptu public memorials and tributes to the victims. and an introduction of "feel good" legislation that fails everywhere except perhaps giving people a much needed peace of mind that something, even if ineffective at best, is being done to acknowledge the problem. Such responses, however, are akin to a wheel stuck in the mud – we keep spinning in the same circle, but never get free. We never get the real answers and solutions being demanded.

Such a discussion also must be protracted (Schildkraut & Muschert, forthcoming). It simply is not enough to look for a "quick fix" to the problem of mass shootings or even homicide in a broader sense, nor is it enough to address one event at a time. Though we treat all of these shootings as somewhat fundamentally different, typically because of location (e.g., school shooting, workplace shooting, domestic terrorism), the reality is that there is a certain commonality among these events (see Harris & Harris, 2012 for a call for such research). In order to implement effective preventative measures, we must look beyond a single place and time to all like events, connect the dots, and see where improvement really is needed. Society cannot simply react in a knee-jerk fashion with a quick fix to a single event. Rather, what is needed is cognizant and intelligent analysis of events among a variety of disciplines, collaborative efforts between academics, the media, and politicians, and the creation of responsible, well-informed legislation, in addition to the enforcement of existing laws and policies.

We must learn from these events, and not simply allow them to fade into the background without resolution. If we as a society allow this to happen, then the shooters win and, more importantly, people have lost their lives in vain. There are lessons within the lines of these disaster narratives, but we must be willing to read between them, be willing to see the signs that are present, and be willing to act in a well-thought out, fully researched, and responsible manner to implement change that has some chance of actually working. We must share information and educate the public on what these events truly mean, and how we can overcome the disproportionate fear that these tragedies bring to offer a proper contextualization and, ultimately, an effective solution. We owe it to the victims of these tragic events to do better.

> We are facing the threat. The threat of information. The fact is that the only thing out there that can stop a bad guy with good information is a good guy with bad information . . . they can take our ignorance when they pry it from our cold, dead minds. (Stephen Colbert, 2013a)

Notes

1. Janelle Hamer is a fictional person, as are all persons included in this chapter as portrayed by *The Onion*, even those whose names are identical to living persons, as in the case of Senator Harry Reid.
2. For passage projections on all related legislative bills, see www.GovTrack.us.

References

16-year-old excited to have whole summer to plan shooting for next school year. (2013. July 2). *The Onion*. Retrieved from http://www.theonion.com/articles/16yearold-excited-to-have-whole-summer-to-plan-sho.33019/.

Arredondo. D.E. (2003). Child development, children's health and the juvenile justice system: Principles for effective decision making. *Stanford Law & Policy Reviews, 14*(1), 13-28.

Authorities not even going to bother looking for motive behind Oregon shooting. (2012. December 12). *The Onion*. Retrieved from http://www.theonion.com/articles/authorities-not-even-going-to-bother-looking-for-m.30708/.

Best. J. (2006). The media exaggerate the school-shooting problem. In S. Hunnicutt (Ed.) *School Shootings* (pp. 18-27). Farmington Hills, MI: Greenhaven Press.

Bonnie. R.J., Reinhard. J.S., Hamilton. P., and McGarvey. E.L. (2009). Mental health system transformation after the Virginia Tech tragedy. *Health Affairs, 28*(3), 793-804.

Brady Campaign Press Release. (2011, January 7). One million mental health records now in Brady background check system. *BradyCampaign.org*. Retrieved from http://brady campaign.org/media/press/view/1336/.

Burns. R., & Crawford. C. (1999). School shootings, the media, and public fear: Ingredients for a moral panic. *Crime, Law & Social Change. 32*(2), 147-168.

Campus security measures increased. (2008. April 23). *The Onion*. Retrieved from http://www.theonion.com/articles/campus-security-measures-increased.8405/.

Cartwright, B. (2009, January 14). This short story about a school shootings is actually pretty good. *The Onion*. Retrieved from http://www.theonion.com/articles/this-short-story-about-a-school-shooting-is-actual.11441/.

Chuang. E., & Wells. R. (2010). The role of interagency collaboration in facilitating receipt of behavioral health services for youth involved with child welfare and juvenile justice. *Children & Youth Services Review. 32*(12), 1814-1822.

Chyi. H., & McCombs. M. (2004). Media salience and the process of framing: Coverage of the Columbine school shootings. *Journalism and Mass Communication Quarterly. 81*(1), 22-35.

Coalition for Juvenile Justice. (2000). Hand with care: Serving the mental health needs of young offenders. *Coalition for Juvenile Justice Annual Report*. Washington. D.C. Retrieved from http://www.ncmhji.com/resource_kit/pdfs/Overview/Readings/Handle WCare.pdf.

Cohen. B.C. (1963). *The press and foreign policy*. Princeton. NJ: Princeton University Press.

Colbert. S. (2013a, February 25). The word— silent but deadly [Episode # 09066]. *The Colbert Report*. Retrieved from http://www.colbertnation.com/the-colbert-report-videos/424142/february-25-2013/the-word---silent-but-deadly.

Colbert. S. (2013b. September 18). Navy Yard shooting & gun violence causes [Episode # 09151]. *The Colbert Report*. Retrieved from http://www.colbertnation.com/the-colbert-report-videos/429165/september-18-2013/navy-yard-shooting---gun-violence-causes.

Columbine jocks safely resume bullying. (1999. September 8). *The Onion*. Retrieved from http://www.theonion.com/articles/columbine-jocks-safely-resume-bullying.661/.

Democrats give up on assault weapons ban. (2013. March 20). *The Onion*. Retrieved from http://www.theonion.com/articles/democrats-give-up-on-assault-weapons-ban.31746/.

Desperate nation tries getting on board with mass shootings. (2013, September 17). *The Onion*. Retrieved from http://www.theonion.com/articles/desperate-nation-tries-getting-on-board-with-mass.33894/.

Dodero, C. (2013, September 9). Fifth grader found with mass casualty hit list of 40 classmates' names. *Gawker*. Retrieved from http://gawker.com/fifth-grader-found-with-mass-casualty-hit-list-of-40-cl-1277875759.

Douglas, A.V., & Lurigio, A.J. (2010). Youth Crisis Intervention Teams (CITs): A response to fragmentation of the educational, mental health, and juvenile justice systems. *Journal of Police Crisis Negotiations, 10*(1/2), 241-263.

Elsass, H.J., Schildkraut, J., & Stafford, M.C. (2013). *Breaking news of social problems: Examining media effects and panic over school shootings*. Manuscript submitted for publication (copy on file with author).

Entman, R.M. (2007). Framing bias: Media in the distribution of power. *Journal of Communication, 57*(1), 163-173.

Everyone at office planning shooting spree for same day. (2013, January 3). *The Onion*. Retrieved from http://www.theonion.com/articles/everyone-at-office-planning-shooting-spree-for-sam,30793./.

Fox, J. A., & Savage, J. (2009). Mass murder goes to college: An examination of changes on college campuses following Virginia Tech. *American Behavioral Scientist, 52*(10), 1465-1485.

Garofoli, J. (2007, April 20). New-media culture challenges limits of journalism ethics. Retrieved from http://articles.sfgate.com/2007-04-20/news/17242016_1_new-media-traditional-media-traditional-news-sources/3. Garascia, J.A. (2005). The price we are willing to pay for punitive justice in the juvenile detention system: Mentally ill delinquents and their disproportionate share of the burden. *Indiana Law Journal, 80*(2), 489-515.

Hack, C. (2012, December 17). Former Jersey Journal reporter helped clear up misidentification of Connecticut school gunman. *The Jersey Journal*. Retrieved from http://www.nj.com/jjournal-news/index.ssf/2012/12/confusion_about_killers_name_i.html.

Harmon, A. (2012, December 18). Fearing a stigma for people with autism. *The New York Times*. Retrieved from http://www.nytimes.com/2012/12/18/health/fearing-a-stigma-for-people-with-autism.html.

Harris, J.M., & Harris, R.B. (2012). Rampage violence requires a new type of research. *American Journal of Public Health, 102*(6), 1054-1057.

Henry, S. (2000). What is school violence? An integrated definition. *Annals of the American Academy of Political and Social Science, 567,* 16-29.

Henry, S. (2009). School violence beyond Columbine: A complex problem in need of an interdisciplinary analysis. *American Behavioral Scientist, 52*(9), 1246-1265.

If it's any consolation, I am going to shoot myself after I kill all of you. (2008, April 9). *The Onion*. Retrieved from http://www.theonion.com/articles/if-its-any-consolation-i-am-going-to-shoot-myself,11378/.

It wouldn't surprise you if this headline was about 318 people being shot in 12 different public places. (2013, February 7). *The Onion*. Retrieved from http://www.theonion.com/articles/breaking-it-wouldnt-surprise-you-if-this-headline,31210/.

Kaplan, T. (2013, January 15). Sweeping limits on guns become law in New York. *The New York Times*. Retrieved from http://www.nytimes.com/2013/01/16/nyregion/tougher-gunlaw-in-new-york.html.

Kellner, D. (2003). *Media spectacle*. London: Routledge.

———. (2008a). *Guys and guns amok: Domestic terrorism and school shootings from the Oklahoma City bombing to the Virginia Tech massacre.* Boulder, CO: Paradigm Publishers.

———. (2008b). Media spectacle and the "Massacre at Virginia Tech". In B. Agger & T.W. Luke (Eds.), *There is a gunman on campus* (pp. 29-54). Lanham, MD: Rowan & Littlefield Publishers, Inc.

Lamb, M. E., & Sim, M. (2013). Developmental factors affecting children in legal contexts. *Youth Justice, 13*(2), 131-144.

Leary, M.R., Kowalski, R.M., Smith, L., & Phillips, S. (2003). Teasing, rejection, and violence: Case studies of the school shootings. *Aggressive Behavior, 29*(3), 202-214.

Let's just go ahead and assume we've learned the lessons of the Gabrielle Giffords shooting. (2011, May 24). *The Onion.* Retrieved from http://www.theonion.com/articles/lets-just-go-ahead-and-assume-weve-learned-the-les,20525/.

Lipschultz, J.H., & Hilt, M.L. (2011). Local television coverage of a mall shooting: Separating facts from fiction in breaking news. *Electronic News, 5*(4), 197-214.

Lynch, R. (2012, August 6). Sikh temple rampage: List of mass shootings grows – and grows. *The Los Angeles Times.* Retrieved from http://articles.latimes.com/2012/aug/06/nation/la-na-nn-sikh-temple-rampage-20120806.

Maguire, B., Weatherby, G.A., & Mathers, R.A. (2002). Network news coverage of school shootings. *The Social Science Journal, 39*(3), 465-470.

McCombs, M.E. (1997). Building consensus: The news media's agenda-setting roles. *Political Communication, 14*(4), 433-443.

McCombs, M.E. & Zhu, J.H. (1995). Capacity, diversity, and volatility of the public agenda: Trends from 1954 to 1994. *Public Opinion Quarterly, 59*(4), 495-525.

Muschert, G.W. (2002). *Media and massacre: The social construction of the Columbine story.* (Unpublished doctoral dissertation). University of Colorado at Boulder, Boulder, CO.

———. (2007a). Research in school shootings. *Sociology Compass, 1*(1), 60-80.

———. (2007b). The Columbine victims and the myth of the juvenile superpredator. *Youth Violence and Juvenile Justice, 5*(4), 351-366.

———. (2010). School shootings. Pp. 73-89 in Martine Herzog-Evans (ed.) *Transnational Criminology Manual.* Volume 2. Nijmegen, Netherlands: Wolf Legal Publishing.

Muschert, G.W., & Carr, D. (2006). Media salience and frame changing across events: Coverage of nine school shootings, 1997-2001. *Journalism and Mass Communication Quarterly, 83*(4), 747-766.

Muschert, G.W., Henry, S., Bracy, N.L., & Peguero, A.A. (eds.). (2014). *Responding to school violence: Confronting the Columbine effect.* Boulder, CO: Lynne Rienner.

Newman, K.S. (2006). School shootings are a serious problem. In S. Hunnicutt (Ed.), *School Shootings* (pp. 10-17). Farmington Hills, MI: Greenhaven Press.

NRA sets 1,000 killed in school shooting as amount it would take for them to reconsider much of anything. (2012, May 25). *The Onion.* Retrieved from http://www.theonion.com/articles/nra-sets-1000-killed-in-school-shooting-as-amount,28352/.

O'Toole, M.E. (2000). *The school shooter: A threat assessment perspective.* Washington, DC: Federal Bureau of Investigation. Retrieved from http://www.fbi.gov/publications/school/school2.pdf.

Pew Research Center for the People & the Press. (2012). Views on gun laws unchanged after Aurora shooting. Retrieved from http://www.people-press.org/2012/07/30/views-on-gun-laws-unchanged-after-aurora-shooting/.

Pew Research Center's Project for Excellence in Journalism. (2006, March 13). Cable TV audience: 2006 annual report. Fox News vs. CNN. Retrieved from http://www.journalism.org/node/507.

Police: Student had embarrassingly bad plans for school shooting. 2011, November 10). *The Onion.* Retrieved from http://www.theonion.com/articles/police-student-had-embarrassingly-bad-plans-for-sc.26593/.

Pompilio, N. (1998). Finding grace in the face of tragedy. *American Journalism Review, 20*(1), 14-15.

Rash of school shootings. (2006, October 4). *The Onion.* Retrieved from http://www.theonion.com/articles/rash-of-school-shootings.15082/.

Reese, S.D. (2007). The framing project: A bridging model for media research revisited. *Journal of Communication, 57*(1), 148-154.

Report: It going to take way more than an inconceivable act of violence for country to rise above politics. (2011, January 13). *The Onion.* Retrieved from http://www.theonion.com/articles/report-it-going-to-take-way-more-than-an-inconceiv.18816/.

Roberts, J. (2009, February 11). Gun used in rampage traced to Va. shops. *CBS News.* Retrieved from http://www.cbsnews.com/2100-500690_162-2695059.html.

Robinson, M.B. (2011). *Media coverage of crime and criminal justice.* Durham, NC: Carolina Academic Press.

Sadly, nation knows exactly how Colorado shooting's aftermath will play out. (2012, July 20). *The Onion.* Retrieved from http://www.theonion.com/articles/sadly-nation-knows-exactly-how-colorado-shootings.28857/.

Schildkraut, J. (2012a). Media and massacre: A comparative analysis of the reporting of the 2007 Virginia Tech shootings. *Fast Capitalism, 9*(1). Retrieved from http://www.uta.edu/huma/agger/fastcapitalism/9_1/schildkraut9_1.htm.

————. (2012b). The remote is controlled by the monster: Issues of mediatized violence and school shootings. In G.W. Muschert & J. Sumiala (Eds.), *School Shootings: Mediatized Violence in a Global Age* (pp. 235-258). Bingley, United Kingdom: Emerald Publishing Group Limited.

Schildkraut, J., & Hernandez, T.C. (2013). *Laws that bit the bullet: A review of legislative responses to school shootings.* Manuscript submitted for publication (copy on file with author).

Schildkraut, J., & Muschert, G.W. (2014). Media salience and the framing of mass murders in schools: A comparison of the Columbine and Sandy Hook massacres. *Homicide Studies, 18*(1).

————. (Forthcoming). Violent media, guns, and mental illness. In B. Agger and T. Luke (eds.) *Gun Violence and Public Life.* Boulder, CO: Paradigm Publishers.

Schildkraut, J., Elsass, H.J., & Stafford, M.C. (2013). *Could it happen here? Moral panics, school shootings, and fear of crime among college students.* Manuscript submitted for publication (copy on file with author).

School board acts to remove emotionally disturbed students. (2011, February 11). *The Onion.* Retrieved from http://www.theonion.com/articles/school-board-acts-to-remove-emotionally-disturbed.19135/.

Shields, D.M. (2011). Warehoused: The plight of 'mad' youths in the juvenile justice system. *Justice Policy Journal, 8*(1), 48-84.

Shooting suspect released after not breaking any Arizona laws. (2011, January 12). *The Onion.* Retrieved from http://www.theonion.com/articles/shooting-suspect-released-after-not-breaking-any-a.18809/.

Sims, G.L. (2009). The criminalization of mental illness: How theoretical failures create real problems in the criminal justice system. *Vanderbilt Law Review, 62*(3), 1053-1083.

Soliwon, D., & Nelson, S. (2012, December 14). Was an innocent person wrongly identified as the Ryan Lanza responsible for the Connecticut elementary school shooting? *US News & World Report.* Retrieved from http://www.usnews.com/news/articles /2012/12/14/was-an-innocent-person-wrongly-identified-as-ryan-lanza-responsible-for-connecticut-elementary-school-shooting.

Soraghan, M. (2000). Colorado after Columbine: The gun debate. *State Legislatures. 26*(6). 14-21.

Sorenson, S.B., Manz, J.G., & Berk. R.A. (1998). News media coverage and the epidemiology of homicide. *American Journal of Public Health, 88*(10), 1510-1514.

Stewart, J. (2012, July 23). Aurora shootings—gun control [Episode # 17127]. The Daily Show with Jon Stewart. Retrieved http://www.thedailyshow.com/watch/mon-july-23-2012/aurora—gun-control.

———. (2013, January 8). Scapegoat hunter [Episode # 18040]. The Daily Show with Jon Stewart. Retrieved from http://www.thedailyshow.com/watch/tue-january-8-2013/scapegoat-hunter.

Sutter, J.D. (2012, July 20). Theater shooting unfolds in real time on social media. *CNN News.* Retrieved from http://www.cnn.com/2012/07/20/tech/social-media/colorado-shooting-social-media.

Swanson, E. (2000). "Killers start sad and crazy": Mental illness and the betrayal of Kipland Kinkel. *Oregon Law Review. 79*(1), 1081-1119.

The Columbine legacy. (2000, April 19). *The Onion.* Retrieved from http://www. theonion.com/articles/the-columbine-legacy,7760/.

The time for watered-down and effectively meaningless gun laws is now. (2013, March 20). *The Onion.* Retrieved from http://www.theonion.com/articles/the-time-for-watered down-and-effectively-meaningle,31751/.

Tucker, K. (2012, December 14). How TV is covering the Newtown, CT, school massacre: For the most part, badly, inevitably. *Entertainment Weekly.* Retrieved from http://watching-tv.ew.com/2012/12/14/adam-lanza-newtown-ct-massacre-sandy-hook/.

U.S. Department of Justice. Federal Bureau of Investigation. (2013). *Crime in the United States, 2012: Annual Uniform Crime Report.* Washington, DC. Retrieved from http://www.fbi.gov/about-us/cjis/ucr/crime-in-the-u.s/2012/crime-in-the-u.s.-2012.

Vasilev, B. (2011, February 28). *Chris Rock – Crazy kids* [Video file]. Retrieved from http://www.youtube.com/watch?v=mq32_26Vpno.

Victims sought in next week's shooting. (2005, March 9). *The Onion.* Retrieved from http://www.theonion.com/articles/victims-sought-in-next-weeks-shooting,1756/.

Virginia Tech Review Panel. (2007). *Mass Shootings at Virginia Tech April 16, 2007: Report of the Review Panel.* Arlington: Governor's Office of the Commonwealth of Virginia. Retrieved from http://www.governor.virginia.gov/TempContent/techpanel report.cfm.

Weisbrot, D. M. (2008). Prelude to a school shooting? Assessing threatening behaviors in childhood and adolescence. *Journal of the American Academy of Child & Adolescent Psychiatry, 47*(8), 847-852.

Why the Sikh temple shooting got less coverage than the Aurora massacre. (2012, August 8). *The Week.* Retrieved from http://theweek.com/article/index/231650/why-the-sikh-temple-shooting-got-less-coverage-than-the-aurora-massacre.

Wigley, S., & Fontenot, M. (2009). Where media turn during crises: A look at information subsidies and the Virginia Tech shootings. *Electronic News, 3*(2), 94-108.

Wike, T.L., & Fraser, M.W. (2009). School shootings: Making sense of the senseless. *Aggression and Violent Behavior, 14*(3), 162-169.

Witkin, G. (2012, April 16). On anniversary of Virginia Tech shooting, law to close loophole hasn't accomplished much. *iWatchNews.org.* Retrieved from http://www.iwatchnews.org/2012/04/16/8660/anniversary-virginia-tech-shooting-law-close-loophole-hasnt-accomplished-much.

Chapter Thirteen

Voices from Gun Violence Prevention Interest Groups: Prescriptive Solutions to Reducing the Problem

Selina Doran

Introduction

The first section of this chapter provides a historical context to the issue of "gun control" and its key developments throughout the years. Following that, the next section gives more information on the methodological process of retrieving the empirical data for this chapter. Interest groups occupy an important position in U.S. policy-making (see Kingdon 1994; Nownes 2013; or Spitzer 2004, for more specific information on gun-related interest groups). For that reason, qualitative interviews were conducted with interest groups' current campaigns and challenges they have faced to gain a better insight into the policy-making processes around gun violence prevention. These interviews were semi-structured in nature, consisting of predefined topics for all, as well as questions specific to each organization's campaigns. The interviewing took place in two stages: autumn 2012, prior to the election results; summer 2013 to monitor changes in the second term of the Obama administration. Six interviewees formed the sample: five were from interest groups specializing in gun violence prevention and one was from a centrist think tank which has a partial focus on gun violence. For reasons that will be explored further in section two, the sample was limited to interest groups specializing in gun violence prevention rather than also including all organizations that have a vested interest in all gun policies.

The purpose of this chapter is to explore the ongoing work of interest groups working to combat gun violence and their recommendations for ways to solve the problems. For these interest groups, their goal is, as one interviewee stated, to "go out of business" by improving the gun violence situation so much that they become unnecessary. The key prescriptive policy areas of interviewees may be grouped into three main categories: improving background checks by extending them to all private sales and clarifying the criteria of restricted persons to ensure that dangerous categories of people are unable to procure firearms: given that large capacity magazines have been used in a number of other mass shootings, interviewees were keen to reinstate the "Assault Weapons Ban" which was in place from 1994 to 2004, as this limited magazines to ten rounds: enforcing accountabilities and responsibilities of gun owners and the gun industry are prescribed as ways to deal with the volume of accidental shootings that occur. Each of these categories will be discussed and deliberated within three separate sections of this chapter.

In the next two sections of this chapter, the findings from interviews were put into the contextual framework within which the interest groups are intending to enact policies. The first of these is the case *Heller et al V. District of Columbia (United States Supreme Court* 2008), which overturned the Washington DC handgun ban on the basis that the second amendment protected an individual right to self-defence, has put some legal parameters on this debate. The consequences of this ruling are that the government has jurisdiction to restrict firearms to some extent but an outright blanket ban—like the one in the U.K.—is constitutionally forbidden. This ruling is thus significant to shaping future solutions to address gun violence. The second factor is the fact that public support regarding an issue must be located within current social values (Spitzer, 2004, 15). Public sentiment on the issue of gun violence is of key importance in gauging the viability of policy proposals. When it comes to the issue of gun violence, it tends to be 'focusing events' which give it prominence, triggering media attention and expanding the issues to be discussed (Kingdon, 1994/2003; Birkland 1997). An event like a mass shooting like the one at Sandy Hook elementary school certainly fits that criteria and this was one which was a catalyst in reigniting the debate—probably due to the horrific nature of twenty very young children being killed at school alongside six members of staff. The penultimate section also discusses the consequences—and lack thereof—of the work of the Obama administration in this area and state-level actions.

The final section of this chapter is a discussion of the most achievable and beneficial solutions for the future. The political terrain surrounding policy—especially something as contested as gun policy—is fundamental to the values of interest groups being translated into concrete policy objectives. For that reason, the prescriptive proposals of interviewees and researchers in this area are deliberated, in relation with the current political climate post-Sandy Hook and taking the 2008 Supreme Court ruling into consideration. The conclusion is reached that background checks, licensing and some modest changes to gun dealers are the most viable at the federal and state levels, but that it will probably fall to individual states to decide about matters such as whether to limit large capacity magazines. Depoliticizing the debate and framing it as a matter of public safety will be useful in guiding future research into ways to reduce the level of gun violence in the U.S.

Historical Context of Gun Control
and Gun Violence Debate

It is important to note that, within public discourse, discussions of reducing gun violence bring about the highly politicized and divisive debates about "gun control" and "gun rights": this is something which has developed throughout history. Up until the early twentieth century, any type of regulation of guns revolved around restricting *where* guns could be carried—such as the banning of guns in public spaces like Saloons—rather than *who* could own various types of firearms (Dizard et al., 1999, 5–6; emphasis added). In 1813, Kentucky passed a law prohibiting concealed carry, attaching with it a large fine of one hundred dollars; following suit were Alabama, Georgia, Louisiana, Ohio and Virginia (Cornell, 2006, 141–142). "Sullivan's Law" (1909), implemented in New York, was the major one and this commanded permits for handgun possession (Vizzard, 1999, 131).

The next noticeable change in gun control came about following the implementation of the eighteenth amendment, in place from 1920–1933, which banned the sale and production of alcohol. During the Prohibition era, organized crime became prolific with heavily-armed criminals controlling underground drinking. In 1929, the horrendous St. Valentine's Day Massacre occurred: Al Capone's hit men murdered seven rival mobsters with Thompson submachine guns. Following the killings, images of the deceased men shown in the media culminated in the start of a movement towards gun control spearheaded by President Franklin Roosevelt, with a particular emphasis on regulating Thompson submachine guns and sawed-off shotguns. Consequently, the "National Firearms Act" (1938) was implemented to make the sale and possession of such firearms illegal, as these were the preferred weapons of choice for gangsters (Dizard et al., 1999, 10–11; Winkler 2012). Thereafter, the "Federal Firearms Act" (1938) was passed, mandating gun dealers to be licensed and for gun purchases to be tracked; however, this law was difficult to enforce (Vizzard, 1999, 132).

Following the implementation of these two federal-level laws, declining crime rates meant that no further action was taken until the "Gun Control Act" of 1968: this was enacted in response to public outrage about the assassinations of President John F. Kennedy and Mather Luther King. This law circumscribed banning guns for certain categories of people and tightened seller regulations, such as restricting mail-order sales (Cornell, 2006, 205; Vizzard, 1999, 131-132; Winkler, 2012, 2). The translation of this law into regulatory action was not as successful as it could have been, with it being described as a "statement of intended policy than a framework for policy implementation" (Vizzard, 1999, 133). Consequently, those in favor of gun control perceived this act as just a "smokescreen" with limited usefulness; however, for activists campaigning for gun rights this law was seen as the first major challenge to constitutional rights. As a result, the "Gun Control Act"

(1968) paved the way for the formation of advocacy groups affected and motivated by gun policies (Vizzard, 1999, 133)—more will be said on the role of interest groups in the next section of this chapter.

In 1988, the attempted assassination attempt on President Ronald Reagan and the serious wounding of his press secretary, James Brady, led to the passage of the "Brady Handgun Violence Prevention Act" (1994)—more commonly referred to in public discourse as the "Brady Bill." This prescribed a five day waiting period for federal firearm licenses before conducting purchases and the provision of federal funding for states to improve the background check system to check whether the person is prohibited by state or federal law (Cuthbertson, 2011, 11; Spitzer, 2004, 130). Criticisms of the law are mainly directed at its "loophole," meaning background checks are not required for private transactions: the means by which the majority of banned persons obtain their guns (Vizzard, 1999, 135). Cook and Ludwig (2013) tested the usefulness of the law: the thirty-two "change" states where the "Brady Act" was implemented were compared and contrasted with the "control" group of the eighteen other states and District of Columbia not affected by the law, as they already met the minimum requirements of the law. The findings revealed that there was "no statistically discernible difference in homicide trends between the Brady (treatment) and non-Brady (control) states among people aged 21 or older" (Cook and Ludwig, 2013, 26). Problems highlighted were the disqualification criteria being too narrow and the incompleteness of the background check system (Cook and Ludwig, 2013, 30-31)—these are issues that also came up for my interviewees.

Of particular interest from this historical overview is the fact that two major federal gun control laws—the "Gun Control Act" (1968) and the "Brady Handgun Violence Prevention Act"—were proposed in the aftermath of highly-publicized assassinations and attempted assassinations: this raises the issue of whether action was taken because the attacks were directed at Presidents and political leaders rather than ordinary citizens. Possibly, if no action had been taken on either of these occasions, public outrage might have ensued.

At the present time, the debate on "gun control" and "gun rights" is still ongoing. Dizard et al. (1999, 13) accused the opposing positions of "feeding each other's fears" via hyperbolic portrayals of the issue: "The pro-gun folks portray a nation of the verge of anarchy that requires law-abiding people to arm themselves in self-defence. The anti-gun folks portray a nation awash in guns, held hostage to the impulsive acts of unstable people." This statement perhaps exaggerates, given it would only likely apply to certain extreme segments of either side. A further criticism would also be that it uses the term "anti-gun" to describe gun control advocates, which has negative—and often false in a number of instances—connotations. The significance of language to politics has been documented by Edelman (1964), who notes that the allocation of values—in this case, the perception that certain groups have disdain/hatred for guns—has the ability to secure political success: in this case, it is positioning that group as being in conflict with U.S. cultural traditions and values and thus rendering their arguments invalid. Such a simplistic binary can only serve to further polarize the issue.

To contextualize this debate of "pro-gun" and "anti-gun"—two categories which are too restrictive and reductive to actually be reflective of how people view this issue—it is of key importance to look at the two different ideological bodies of thought surrounding the second amendment (for further information see Cornell 2006; Malcolm 1994; Williams 2003): "individual rights" and "states rights." van Dijk (1998, 98) questioned whether those who hold ideologies are "aware" of them; the true power of ideology lies in the "naturalization" of these into viewpoints that become part of everyday "common sense" thinking. The prevalence of ideologies in group discourse become explicated when each side defend their points of view and criticises any opposing stances. The influencing nature of group interests in the way they portray social problems to legitimate or oppose power relations (van Dijk, 1998, 5, 98)—this is something which is of key important to the gun violence debate. Lane (1996, 660) posited that ideological thinking is driven by dogmatism, where information is selected and interpreted in a particular way *as to fit* with current-held beliefs (emphasis added). To take this idea further, Stone (1989, 283) pointed to the use of ideas from each opposing side being utilised to frame policy options. With that in mind, the term "gun control" is now a highly charged and politicized term, lacking any nuanced understandings given it is embedded within a cultural framework (Kohn, 2004, 148)—one which is against the traditional values of the "individual rights" paradigm.

To explore the "individual rights" paradigm now, it has been purported by those supporting it that the "militia" part of the Second Amendment, at the time of writing, was intended for all White adult males and this has now been upgraded to all adult citizens (Davidson, 1998, 135). The "individual rights" interpretation denotes that the right to bear arms is for individual as well as state protection (Malcolm, 1994, 136). The first real example of this link between an armed citizenry and self-defense was Mississippi's contention in the early nineteenth century that every citizen had the right "to bear arms in defense of himself and the state" (Cornell, 2006, 142). More recently, NRA vice-president Wayne La Pierre (1994/1999, 173, 175) proposed counterattack self-defense by armed citizens as a deterrent to crime; to illustrate this, he used the example of two murders of European tourists in Florida targeted specifically because the attackers knew they would not be carrying guns. The entrenchment of self-defence within the individual rights paradigm is probably attributable to the historical roots of the Second Amendment:

> it emerged from a tradition which viewed general possession of arms as a positive social good, as well as an indispensable adjunct to the individual right of self-defense. In the absence of a police, the American legal tradition was for responsible, law abiding citizens to be armed and to see to their own defence. (Kates, 1992, 99)

Kates has questioned, however, whether the founders would still have had the same thoughts today, given the militia has since been replaced by modern law enforcement agencies. (1992, 99)

The second component of the individual: rights paradigm is "insurrectionism": the right to revolution against a tyrannical government (Spitzer, 2012, 42). In a similar vein, debunking the 'myths of gun rights.' Spitzer (2012, 43) pointed out that the Constitution, in articles I and III respectively, clearly states that militias are intended to "suppress insurrections" and that the crime of treason is "levying war" against one's government. Furthermore, it is claimed that the Constitution Framers distinguished between "revolutions," by the people for the good of the collective and "insurrection," resistance by a faction (Williams, 2003, 57). The notion of "individual armed people" in an insurrectionist movement raises a number of issues: who leads the movement; how will these individuals decide where, when and how to act. Individual right theorists are said to fail to address these issues, instead presuming that "revolting, spontaneously and independently, individual Americans will mould into a body." Williams, 2003, 155). In a similar vein, Cornell (2006, 214) was critical of the two dimensions of "individual rights" thinking, claiming they promote an "anti-civic" notion of guns as a way to repel other citizens and the government.

The other side of the debate, gun control advocates promote the "states right"—sometimes known as "collective rights"—interpretation of the Second Amendment: it is there to protect the power of states—as opposed to individual citizens—to maintain militias (see Williams 2003). The argument was made that the phrase 'Body of the People' cannot apply to all individuals because they have the collective powers only to initiate rebellions and civil war. (Williams, 2003, 70). This militia is therefore believed to take the form of state military forces offering protection from a corrupt federal government, with the point being made that gun owners have not had militia training (Davidson, 1998, 135; Williams, 2003, 71). To "states rights" believers, therefore, individual states are well within their scope to mandate gun regulations in an effort to reduce gun-related crimes (Squires, 2000, 75). One thing to note is that the terminology of "control" as opposed to "rights" contradicts the fundamental values of U.S. culture—the symbolic value of gun rights will be discussed in more detail in section eight of this chapter. Cornell (2006, 214-215) was critical of "states right" supporters for this reason, accusing them of failing to position gun control within a constitutional framework that would appeal to American values of liberty.

In an attempt to depoliticize the issue, gun control has been promoted via various frames. One of these is "crime control"—predicated on assumptions that criminals and crime are controllable via gun regulatory laws—drawing upon the conflation of low crime rates with gun restrictions (Vizzard, 1999, 138). Such an approach has been effective in justifying strict gun restrictions in countries like the U.K., which happens to have very low levels of gun crime; in the U.S., however, "crime control" argument have been less convincing (Squires, 2000, 7). Another more neutral way to address gun violence has been via "public health" framing, started in 1983 by the Centers for Disease Control and Prevention (Spitzer, 2012, 49). What this does is treat gun violence like any other harmful substance or activity, such as alcohol usage and smoking, producing safety responses like child-safety locks on guns (Davidson, 1998, 281; Vizzard, 1999, 139). Kohn (2004, 134) is critical of gun violence being framed this way, maintaining that it is predicated on a notion of "risky behaviour" rather than acknowledging the roots of the problem. Moreover, it is said to be an insidious way of legitimizing certain ideologies: "Public health rhetoric provides the aura of scientific fact to the political agenda of gun control" (Kohn, 2004, 134). Having said that, Davidson (1998, 281) makes the point that although safety restrictions would only have a limited impact on gun-related injuries and fatalities, it is still worthwhile as a first step towards addressing the problem of gun violence. The viability of these approaches will discussed later on in this chapter when deliberating over concrete action that could be taken to reduce gun violence. For the moment, this paper will now turn to look at the role of interest groups in U.S. policy-making and thereafter outlining the sample and methodology used in this chapter.

Interview Results

Brief Overview of Interest Groups and Interviewees

When the focus of interest groups is narrow and singular—like gun rights or gun violence prevention—they tend to adopt and stick firmly to polarized positions (Spitzer, 2004, 15). Their power is said to lie in their ability to "mobilise and sway popular sentiment in the aftermath of a pivotal event" (Spitzer, 2004, 74)—an event like a highly publicized shooting would fit that description. In a sense, it could be said they act as a conduit between the public and legislators: "They perform a useful, even indispensable, function of supplying legislators with information about policies and legislation under consideration" (Egger and Harris, 1963, 89). Kingdon's (1994) three-fold model outlined the processes involved in policy-making: the political stream, referring to the wider political climate at that point in time; the policy stream, consisting of prescriptive recommendations to solve the issue; the problem stream, based upon the dimensions of the issue and how it is being perceived in public consciousness. The conflation of all three streams increases the chances of an issue gaining "agenda" status: the list of subjects or problems to which officials are paying attention to (Kingdon, 1994/2003, 3). Interest groups have the potential to shape the "policy" and "problem" streams, by framing issues in certain ways that are translatable into policy outcomes and how it is portrayed to the public (Callaghan and Schnell, 2005, 7; Gabrielson, 2005, 84). With expertise in their area of interest and resources behind them, interest groups have the potential to encourage or stall proposals and to provide the "decision agenda" of alternative options to those currently being considered by the government (Kingdon, 1994/2003, 4, 49).

The role of interest groups should not be overestimated. however, for whilst they can try to give momentum to an issue, their ability to actually "control" the debate surrounding it is limited (Kingdon, 1994/2003, 50, 52). When it comes to the issue of gun violence, it tends to be 'focusing events' which give it prominence, triggering media attention and expanding the issues to be discussed (Kingdon. 1994/2003; Birkland 1997). Birkland (1997, 22, 25) advanced the concept of "focusing events" by setting out four criteria, occurring suddenly with little or no warning; being rare and unpredictable; impacting upon a group or community of persons; the public and policy members learn about the event simultaneously. Although mass shootings are relatively rare in the overall spectrum of gun violence, they tend to act as a prism through which to discuss ways to solve this issue. In particular, an event like Sandy Hook has been instrumental in guiding some recent debates around gun violence prevention efforts.

To turn to the methodology of this chapter now, a sample of six interviewees were used, five representatives from interest groups specializing in reducing gun violence; one representative from a centrist think tank, which focuses partially on gun violence and a range of other issues from the economy to climate change. For organizations focusing on preventing gun violence, their goal is, as one interviewee. Cathie Whittenburg (SUPGV) stated, to "go out of business" by improving the gun violence situation so much that they become unnecessary. I was interested in speaking to the "ideologues"—those in leadership positions expected to be able propagate ideologies due to their "privileged access" to public discourse (van Dijk, 1998, 172, 186)—and so my selection of interviewees involved those in presidential or public relations positions. The research participants[1] are:

- Eileen McCarron, president of Colorado Ceasefire Capitol Fund, which lobbies the state legislature: Tom Mauser, president of Colorado Ceasefire Political Action Committee, which endorses political candidates, and the spokesman for and board member of Colorado Ceasefire Capitol Fund— both organizations are part of a non-partisan political action committee Colorado Ceasefire (CC)[2] formed in 2000;
- Andrew Goddard, president of Virginia Center for Public Safety (VCPS), formed in 1992 in response to a crime wave in Norfolk, Virginia;
- Cathie Whittenburg, communications director, of States United to Prevent Gun Violence (SUPGV), an organization formed in 1999 to bring together state gun violence prevention groups and to give them a voice at the national level;
- Ladd Everitt, communications director of Coalition to Stop Gun Violence (CSGV), formed back in the middle of the civil rights movement;
- Jim Kessler, formerly Director of Policy and Research at Americans for Gun Safety (AGS); this has now merged into the centrist think tank Third Way (TW), of which Jim Kessler is both co-founder and Senior Vice President.

Three of the groups operate at the national level: CSGV and TW are based in Washington D.C. and focus on federal efforts; SUPGV is interested in action in all member state groups (a list of these is available on the website). The other two groups CC and VCPS are state-specific groups based in Colorado and Virginia respectively. It was believed these states are particularly appropriate to the issue of gun violence prevention, given they have suffered some of the worst massacres in U.S history: the Columbine High School shooting (1999) and the Aurora Theater attack (2012) both took place in Colorado, as did the tragic hostage situation at Platte Canyon High School (2006); whilst Virginia was home to the Virginia Tech massacre (2007), which has the highest death toll of any mass shooting incident at thirty-two deaths. What makes these two states particularly interesting to study is that Colorado is a Western state with traditionally conservative values and Virginia is a pro-gun state commonly cited as a source of illegal firearms in the state of New York. With this in mind, it would seem reasonable that efforts to reduce gun violence would centre on extending gun rights; however, as this chapter will demonstrate, this has not exactly been the case.

Of particular interest is the fact that some of the gun violence prevention groups have links to gun victims. CSGV's Ladd Everitt summarized this link in the following way: "We are victims of gun violence." On the CSGV staffs are gun violence survivors like Lori Haas, whose daughter was seriously wounded during the Virginia Tech (2007) shooting. Similarly, VACPS's president, Andrew Goddard, first got involved in the issue of gun violence because his son, Colin, was shot in the Virginia Tech (2007) massacre. Probably the most prominent example out of my interviewees is CC's Tom Mauser, whose son, Daniel, was one of the victims of the Columbine High school shooting; in the past, he was heavily involved in the campaign to close the "gun show loophole" in Colorado—this will be discussed in more detail later on.

To keep this article at a reasonable scope, the focus was exclusively on organizations dedicated to reducing gun violence (or those which had been in the past, like Americans for Gun Safety) to get behind their thinking and what they prescribe as solutions to address this problem. For that reason, other interest groups interested in gun policy but not *exclusively* focusing on gun violence, such as the National Rifle Association (NRA), have not been included in the sample. Groups representing gun owners and the industry are pertinent to strengthening the U.S.'s "gun culture," alongside influencing the political agenda (Squires, 2000, 204). Future research could involve speaking such groups to find out more about alternative solutions suggested to negate gun violence. As it stands, it was felt that the most prudent article for this volume would be one which looked at interest groups specializing in gun violence prevention. A very small sample of interest groups is used here, so findings cannot be seen to be reflective of nation-wide efforts.

Material from qualitative interviews and additional information shared via email correspondences provided the empirical data for this chapter about interest groups' current campaigns and challenges they have faced. Interviews can be seen as "a construction site for the generation of knowledge" (Kvale, 1996, 14); those which are qualitative in nature allow for the examination of the opinions, ideas and experiences of interviewees (Arksey and Knight, 1999, 96). These interviews were semi-structured in nature, consisting of predefined topics, wherein there was a topic guide of word or phrases to facilitate discussion, as well as questions specific to each organization's campaigns; there was enough flexibility to allow interviewees to "stray" from it on occasions where they were providing useful information relevant to the research questions (Arksey and Knight, 1999, 96-97). The interviewing took place in two stages: the first of which was in the autumn of 2012, prior to the election results; the second stage, more crucially, took place in the summer 2013 to monitor changes in the second term of the Obama administration that were taking place in the aftermath of the Sandy Hook shooting (December 2012). This chapter will now move on to discuss the findings from interviews as they pertain to recommendations for ways to reduce gun violence.

Background Checks and Why These Are Needed

Probably the most pressing concern of all interviewees was the need to ensure that the wrong people are not able to gain access to firearms—these are all vital concerns, especially since "we're seeing so many horrific acts of violence by people who are legally armed." (Everitt, CSGV). Discussion in this section will revolve around the three major problems in gun laws as they relate to background checks:

> For starters, background checks are not required on all gun sales, and in forty or more states you can buy a gun in a private sale without even undergoing a background check. That's a major problem. And then even when you do undergo a background check, the database they check through is missing out millions of disqualifying records because the states, in many cases, they do not submit those to the FBI. Then the third problem—and this has come up because of some of the mass shootings recently—is that the disqualifications for gun purchasers, that would prohibit people from buying guns, are very narrow." (Everitt, CSGV)

In terms of the first issue, "Brady Bill" loophole allowing private sales to forego background checks, with it only being illegal if the seller has "reasonable cause" to suspect the buyer is a prohibited person (Wintemute, 2013a, 96–97). Jim Kessler pointed out how simple private transactions can be: "If you lived in, let's say, Virginia, and I lived in Virginia, and I wanted to sell you my gun . . . that's like selling lemonade: there's no ID; there's no check." (Kessler, TW) The most prolific site of private sales is at gun shows:

> The classic example, of course, is the gun show where you can have two tables side by side: one of them with a nice professional sign on it and a table full of handguns; one of them next to it with a handwritten piece of cardboard which says guns and [has] a table full of handguns. Now, if you go to the table with the pretty sign and the guy with the clipboard, you're going to have to do a background check before you go buy that gun. Go to the guy with that cardboard sign who has nothing written on the guns at all—no boxes, no manuals, no nothing—you can

buy exactly the same gun: you might spend twenty dollars more but he won't ask
you who you are. (Andrew Goddard. VACPS)

Most notably, the "gun show loophole" is commonly linked to a source of
weapons for criminals and terrorists. The Bureau of Alcohol. Tobacco and Firearms
estimated about 30 percent of guns in illegal trafficking investigations were sold this
way (Samaha 2010). The point remains that the loophole does allow prohibited
persons to circumvent the law: ". . . yeah. they're [criminals] not stupid—so if you
give them an opportunity to buy a gun with no background check. they're gonna use
it." (Tom Mauser. CC). A particularly prominent and tragic example of this is the
Columbine High shooting (1999) where two friends of the perpetrators procured
weapons for them at gun shows. Robyn Anderson. who was a "straw buyer" for the
shooters since they were not old enough. admitted that she would not have done so
had there been paperwork to fill out (Spitzer. 2012. 77).

Following Columbine. when action on gun shows failed to transpire in
Congress and the Colorado House rejected a package of gun control measures. the
Colorado-based organization Sane Alternatives to the Firearm Epidemic—CC's
Tom Mauser was a lobbyist for them at that time—gathered signatures to put
"closing the gun show loophole." on the public ballot. Kleck (2009. 1451)
counteracted the need for background checks at gun shows. claiming that
Columbine has been the only mass shooting where weapons were procured at a gun
show. with perpetrators commonly stealing guns to carry out their attacks. However.
the fact that it even happened once and caused such devastating loss for the
community of Littleton is enough for it to at the very least be considered as an
option for policy action. As it transpired. this measure was passed in Colorado and
thus required background checks on all gun buyers at gun shows: however it still
exists in a number of states. Surprisingly. Virginia currently has it. despite recommendations made by the 2007 report of the Virginia Tech Review Panel—formed
in the aftermath of the tragic 2007 shooting to assess the incident and make policy
recommendations—that there should be universal background checks in Virginia
and increased penalties for selling guns without background checks which are later
used in a crime.

Taking this argument further. Eileen McCarron believes that background
checks in Colorado need to go beyond gun shows: "we've closed the gun show
loophole in Colorado. but they [prohibited persons] could go online. they could go
to newspaper ads. they could go to friends: there's nothing stopping them. until we
close that background check loophole." (McCarron. CC) Wintemute (2013a, 104)
made a similar recommendation saying that "closing the gun show loophole" only
goes a limited way to solving the problem. as it is only addressing a small portion
of private sales. Backing up this point was Webster. et al.'s (2013) analysis from a
survey of fourteen hundred and two inmates at a state correctional facility. which
found that the largest source of handguns for criminals was actually from friends
and family members (37.5 percent). whilst the smallest portion (1.7 percent) was
from gun shows and flea markets. With those results in mind. the *accountability* of

the seller is something which really needs to be addressed and redefined. At the moment, this is something which is really lacking: "Right now the seller's not in any trouble if you sell a gun and someone else uses it." (Jim Kessler, TW). It was recommended that this be changed so the seller has to have some degree of responsibility. In our interview, Andrew Goddard of VACPS said:

Goddard:	"If you give a gun to your grandchild because it's a family heirloom shotgun, you don't need to do a background check on your grandchild, because that is your own responsibility; that's an internal thing."
Interviewer:	"It's somebody you know."
Goddard:	"Yeah, if it's somebody you know, you are taking on the responsibility. [For instance] if it's your brother-in-law who you know has just got out of jail last week and you give him a gun, that's a different story—then you should be in big trouble."

The second problem with the background checks system is, currently, a number of states still submit partial or little data to the background checks system, rendering it ineffective to a certain extent: "Now, if you check somebody against a database that's incomplete, then there's a chance for that person to slip through, because they've not been recorded on that database."(Goddard, VACPS). The three- day limit on conducting the background checks further exacerbates matters because the federal firearms licensee is legally allowed to sell the firearm after this time period, even if they have been unable to retrieve the records (Cuthbertson, 2011, 12). Consequently, VACPS have been working on encouraging states to submit complete reports to the system and so far has convinced Virginia's governor to send round a letter requesting that governors from other states submit full records to the background check systems. Ladd Everitt of CSGV recommended a thorough examination of potential buyers to ensure that the wrong people do not "slip through" any loopholes:

We have to make sure that when people buy guns in this country that they're having a background check . . . that we're really looking into their history and seeing if they're a threat to public safety.

The main way to solve this issue is ensure the system is thorough and complete, with all mental illness, criminal, and drug abuse records. One of the key findings of the report to the president conducted after Virginia Tech (Leavitt et al. 2007) was that an "accurate" and "complete" national instant criminal background check system (NICS) was pertinent to ensuring current federal guns laws prohibiting persons are effective. It was discovered that only 23 states provided information to NICS. The issue of information-sharing is a barrier here: some states cannot share information about such persons with the *NICS* because of state privacy laws preventing them from doing so. The state-level recommendations thus were to make the issue of addressing any legal and financial barriers to submitting records a priority. Prescribed federal-level action was for the US Department of Justice. in conjunction with the ATF Bureau and the FBI. to provide information to NICS about banned persons and to offer states guidance and encouragement to submit records (Leavitt et al.. 2007. 10–11). In January 2008. the president signed into law the "NICS Improvement Amendments Act" (2008). strengthening the ability of the Attorney General to procure information from federal agencies and departments regarding prohibited persons. requiring annual reports are provided to Congress. and authorizing incentives for states. tribes and court systems to provide records for the NICS. Financial grants totaling almost forty million dollars were divided up and awarded to twenty-five states from 2009–2011. Consequently. in 2011. the amount of records n the NICS index increased by forty-one percent to seven point two million (Cuthbertson. 2011. 12–13).

Even though this appears to be a positive change. this figure is still only half of what it should be, with some states still being lackadaisical about this issue: Arizona submitted three percent of its cases of disqualifying mental illness: Nebraska and Pennsylvania failed to submit any: only thirty-two states in total have ever submitted anything to it (Thornburgh. 2011). Moreover. despite federal money being donated to states as incentives to donate records (as per the recommendations of the VT Review Panel) only five percent of that funding was available (Romano and Wingert, 2011). Another major problem is that states lack the resources to manage and maintain records (Cuthbertson. 2011, 15).

Finally. the criteria for putting people into the prohibited category are problematic and very narrow in their parameters. CC's Eileen McCarron recommended exploring the role of misdemeanors in gun prohibition:

> To be able to buy a gun means you can't have a felony on your record: misdemeanors are allowed unless they were domestic violence And there are a lot of not nice people out there—not people you'd call 'law abiding'—who don't have felony records for whatever reason: they haven't been caught . . . or they got plea-bargained down to a misdemeanor.

In terms of misdemeanors. the "Gun Control Act" (1968) was amended in 1996 to include any misdemeanor that was committed by an intimate partner of the victim and "has. as an element. the use of attempted use of physical force or the threatened use of a deadly weapon." The main problem lies in the distinctions between state and federal laws. where some states do not have any criteria and thus have to rely solely on federal law (Zeoli & Frattaroli. 2013. 55–56). Concurrently. something that CC has considered pursuing is trying to add persons who have been convicted of violent offences onto the list of prohibited persons. In her interview. Eileen McCarron said:

> McCarron: "Another thing I would like to do is expand the background checks to ban sales of weapons to people who have been committed of violent misdemeanors. people who have been committed of violent

	misdemeanors—assaults and other things that are acts of violence that currently do not prohibit people from buying guns."
Interviewer:	"But if it involves violence you think it should be an automatic ban."
McCarron:	"Yes, California already has that. There's a professor named Garin Wintemute, who is a leading research on gun violence ... He's in one of the universities in California and years ago I asked him where we should be heading: if we want to advance progressive legislation. He indicated the number one thing we should attempt is the banning of firearms to those with violent misdemeanors.

California's law is thus being adopted as a model framework for developing proposals around domestic violence: this legislation enforces a ten year ban for crimes such as assault, battery and brandishing of a firearm (Wintemute, 2013b, 79). Further recommendations were made by Zeoli and Frattaroli (2013, 60-61) about ways to ensure those who commit violent or threatening acts against their intimidate partners are unable to purchase guns: providing incentives for states to report domestic violence misdemeanants: expanding the criteria to include past partners, especially those who have been convicted of stalking misdemeanors: those who violate domestic violence court orders should be banned for life.

Another major issue to consider is that of mental health criteria. The fact that the Virginia Tech perpetrator, Seung-Hui Cho, legally procured the semiautomatic weapons he used during the attack—ordering one weapon from the internet and collecting at a local pawnshop and buying another at a store—highlighted flaws in the system (Spitzer, 2012, xi). The worrying part here was that Cho had been issued with a temporary detention order a year and a half prior to the shooting, where a Virginia magistrate found him to present "an imminent danger to self or others as a result of mental illness" (Isikoff 2007). In Virginia, gun purchases must comply with both federal and state law. The federal-level "Gun Control Act" (1968) prohibited Cho from purchasing firearms, as he met the definition of someone who was "mentally defective":

[a] determination by a court, board, commission, or other lawful authority that a person, as a result of ... mental illness ... [i]s a danger to himself or to others.

Under Virginia law, however, because Cho was only "temporarily detained" rather than "committed," he was able to circumvent the federal restrictions and be eligible to buy firearms (VTRP, 2007, 71–72). What is notable here is that such a purchase perhaps could not have occurred in a state with different criteria for prohibition (Spitzer, 2012, xii). There was some state-level action in this area after the Virginia Tech shooting. After the VTRP (2007, 75) recommended that "anyone found to be a danger to themselves or others by a court-ordered review should be entered ... regardless of whether they voluntarily agreed to treatment," the Governor of Virginia acted upon this recommendation using executive order. Swanson et al. (2013, 35) pointed out that the requirements of the "Gun Control Act" need to be thoroughly scrutinized. CSGV's Ladd Everitt made a similar point, recommending this be updated to reflect changes in the mental health system:

> The only people disqualified because of mental health reasons are those who have been forced into a psychiatric institution, or people who have been formally adjudicated by a court as a danger to themselves and/or others. Unfortunately, because of how really archaic the mental health treatment in this country is, very few people who are dangerously mentally ill fall into one of those two categories.

Swanson *et al.* (2013, 48) also made the recommendation that prohibition criteria should focus on individual *dangerousness* rather than whether someone fits into a certain category (emphasis added).

This discussion on background checks has highlighted the flaws in the current system and ways to possibly improve it, as suggested by interviewees and backed up by other experts. Clearly, to make such changes will be a lengthy and costly process, and there will need to be assurances that these do not infringe the rights of responsible gun owners. Survey analysis conducted by McGinty et al. (2013) found that public support was strong in this particular area: 85 percent of the sample supported state requirements to report individuals who have been involuntarily committed or declared mentally incompetent; 75 percent of the sample were in favor of healthcare providers reporting people making threats against themselves or others to the background check system; sixty percent wanted government to fund more mental health screenings and treatments (McGinty et al., 2013, 247). This issue was not particularly partisan in nature with eighty-six percent of Republican and ninety-two percent of Democrat supporters respectively in favor of universal background checks (McGinty et al., 2013, 253).

Assault Weapons Ban Related to Mass Shootings

Also highlighted as a contributing factor to gun violence were high capacity magazines that allow multiple rounds to be fired. Interviewee Andrew Goddard, VACPS, pointed to the deadly potential of such magazines: "the more rounds you can fire without reloading, the more victims you can create." Unsurprisingly, perhaps, these are commonly used in mass shooting incidents—defined by the FBI as attacks involving four or more victims—and this is something my interviewees were very concerned about: "If you look at these mass shootings, one thing they all have in common is large ammunition magazines . . . the Aurora [cinema shooter] guy had a magazine that held a hundred bullets." (Cathie Whittenburg, SUPGV). Eileen McCarron, CC, used the 2011 attack on Gabrielle Giffords in Tuscon, Arizona, which resulted in the deaths of six people, to demonstrate why there should be limits on magazine sizes:

> Luckily, he [the perpetrator] was tackled when he was changing his magazines. If he had had a higher capacity magazine like James Holmes [the Aurora theatre

shooter] had, far more people would have been killed. But some very brave individuals—who were unarmed—took him down when he went to reload.

When one considers that the Virginia Tech shooter—the shooting with the highest death toll—used a magazine holding thirty bullets meaning he had to reload less often (Spizter, 2012, xi, xiii), there certainly seems to be a correlation between the devastating toll in mass shootings and large capacity magazines.

It was recommended by a couple of interviewees that laws should also begin to consider the type of weapons used in mass shootings. Cathie Whittenburg, SUPGV, supports a ban on military assault rifles, describing them as "a certain category of guns that belongs on the battlefield not in the homes." Tom Mauser, CC, made a similar argument:

> Assault weapons that are really designed to mow people down . . . we have to identify the ones that are most dangerous and used by people for mass shootings and we have to say "You know what? Those are military weapons and don't belong in the hands of civilians."

One of the ways to do this is renewing the ten year-old ban in Title XI of the "Violent Crime Control and Law Enforcement Act" (1994)—most commonly known as the federal assault weapons ban—that expired under George W Bush's administration back in 2004. The ban was very specific in the types of semi-automatics that were prohibited: threaded barrels, pistol grips, and ammunition magazines. However, it was also possible for the "banned weapons" to be trans-formed into a "legal" copy by removing certain cosmetic features; also, weapons manufactured before the law was implemented were "grandfathered" making them legal to own and transfer. For that reason, it has been said that the ban was more about *firearm accessories* than weapons themselves (Koper, 2013, 159–160). Doherty (2008, 50) was critical of the ban's "demonization" of the "scary cosmetic elements" and theorized that the next law could target all semiautomatic weapons. The law's most useful feature was the large capacity magazine ban, limiting them to ten rounds. Given the number of loopholes the ban had, Koper (2013, 159) came to the conclusion that it only had "mixed effects" on reducing crime levels. My interviewees told a similar story: "It probably didn't have that much of an impact on crime." (Kessler, TW).

Action on this issue came at the start of Obama's second term as a result of the tragic Sandy Hook shooting: the legislative package put together involved renewing the assault weapons ban, limiting magazines to ten rounds, and banning the possession of armor-piercing bullets. My interviewees, however, were a bit dubious about what was actually achievable in terms of the assault weapons ban. Jim Kessler, of TW, made the points that ". . . with the current configuration of Con-gress, I don't think it looks like a great environment for this issue" and "I think, as president, it's not just what you want to do but it's what you can do." When it comes to an issue like gun regulation, the president possesses only a "relatively marginal role" (Spizter. 2004. 15). Correspondingly, on March 19, 2013. the "assault weapons" portion of the package was removed—with the Senate citing a lack of votes as the main reason (*BBC News*, 2013).

In terms of the future of this issue, its failure in the Senate showed there will be difficulty in getting it passed at the federal-level, despite modest public support for the issue. A study by McGinty, et al. (2013) found that 69 and 68 percent of those surveyed supported a ban on assault weapons and large capacity magazines of more than ten bullets respectively. This result was highly polarized though—77 and 76-six percent of the sample in support were non-gun owners; forty-six and forty-eight percent were gun owners; fifteen and nineteen percent were members of the National Rifle Association (McGinty *et al.*, 2013. 214–215). Moreover, the assault-weapon ban is a partisan issue, with a Pew Research Center poll of one and a half thousand participants finding that support was split 84 and 44 percent for Democrats and Republicans respectively. It is also gendered: two-thirds of females polled in favor of a ban compared to fewer than half of the men sampled (cited in Page, January 2013. News 6A). It has been advised that any policy proposals centering solely on large capacity magazines rather than assault weapons have a better chance gaining support (Koper, 2013, 168).

On the state-level there has been more action in this area. In Colorado, a bill signed into law in 2013 by Governor Hickenlooper limited gun ammunition magazines to fifteen rounds. The combination of three factors in Colorado, argued CC's Eileen McCarron, led to the optimum climate for legislative change: the November election that changed the configuration of the Colorado Legislature; the Aurora Theater Shooting in Aurora. Colorado (July 2012); and, lastly, the Sandy Hook shooting in Newtown. Connecticut (December 2012). The perception was that Colorado citizens had had enough of gun violence:

> [Colorado is] a state that had already suffered quite a bit of gun violence: Columbine in 1999, and there was the Platte Canyon [2006 hostage] shooting later, and then the [2012] Aurora theatre [shooting]. It's just like—something's gotta change (McCarron. CC).

The importance of gun violence as an issue was evident in the 2012 Colorado election: "candidates reported that they were being asked about 'what are you going to do about assault weapons?'" (McCarron. *CC*.)

In response to the Colorado laws enacted in 2013. counter challenging forces have begun to take action. Senator Greg Brophy (Republican-Wray) showed condemnation for Governor Hickenlooper: "I am so committed to making sure he isn't re-elected in 2014. Colorado deserves a Governor that has Colorado values not East Coast values" (quoted in *Fox 31. Denver* 2013)—such a comment is framing the law as an infraction upon Colorado's traditional. Western state values. Further. a faction of sheriffs in Colorado have called the magazine ban "unconstitutional" because it deprives citizens of their rights—this is drawing upon the individual rights paradigm advocating an unbridled right to firearms, particularly to ensure the ability to defend themselves. Concurrently, one of the counter-arguments made to the law is that it violates the "Americans with Disabilities Act" (1990), as certain disabilities may limit people from changing magazines quickly if needed in a situation of self-defense. Further challenges come in the form of Concerned Citizens for a Safer Colorado, a group which has formed. The main strategy of this group is to collect signatures in an attempt to overturn the magazine ban, framing it via the prism of "self-defense."

It will be interesting to see what transpires with this counter-movement to the laws enacted will have: will the sheriffs, political actors and citizen group continue to push to repeal laws currently in place, or is it more likely that these laws will remain and further restrictions—for instance, the idea that Tom Mauser (CC) mentioned, of identifying dangerous assault weapons—discussed? If it comes to an appeal at the Colorado Supreme Court, will there be a similar conclusion to the *Heller et al. v. District of Columbia* (2011) ruling that restrictions on magazines do not violate the second amendment.

Accountability, Regulation and Redefining Safety

The final prescriptive proposal interviewees made was that stronger accountability and responsibility from gun owners and the gun industry itself was urgently needed. TW is particularly focused on tightening penalties for gun traffickers who buy guns and sell them illegally. Andrew Goddard, *VACPS*, believes that forcing gun owners to report stolen guns is the best way to regulate gun trafficking practices:

> We want them to have to report that [stolen guns] to the police, so if you're a gun trafficker and you buy ten guns and sell nine of them, you're not going to go down to the police station and say "You're not gonna believe this: I bought ten guns this weekend and nine of them got stolen from me."

Of particular concern is the inter-state trafficking of firearms as a means to circumvent strict state-level laws. Cathie Whittenburg, SUPGV, drew upon the example of Maine, where she lives:

> Maine has very, very weak gun laws and we are close to Massachusetts which has some of the strongest gun laws in the nation; as a consequence, Maine is a source for crime guns into Massachusetts because it's so easy to get guns here, and people will come up from Massachusetts and buy guns and bring them back down there and sell them on the street. It's a bad situation.

There is also a similar problem with guns from Virginia, which has more lenient gun laws, up to New York, which has some of the strictest gun laws in the nation. Looking at some of the newspapers based in New York shows a definite feeling of contempt and anger towards Virginia because of this. Just after the Virginia Tech shooting (2007), a *Daily News* article had the provocative title "Yes, Virginia, Guns

Kills Innocents," implying that the state of Virginia is in denial over this. The tone of the article seemed to be one of anger with the writer accusing Virginia of being "nonchalant" about their gun laws "plaguing our city [New York]" through the infiltration of illegal guns (Daly, 2007). Braga and Gagliardi (2013, 147–149) also made the recommendations that all private sales should involve paperwork to trace any trafficking practices and also to increase the penalties for trafficking due to its potential for causing serious harm.

One way to deal with the aftermath of criminal usage of guns and to ascertain whether this was attributable to gun trafficking would be to track crime guns using modern technology: a current *CSGV* campaign revolves around this. At the moment, CSGV's Ladd Everitt argued, the "microstamping" technology used in tracing crime guns is very outdated and thus highly ineffective. Microstamping, by contrast, means "every time you fire a round from a handgun, you are stamping a code that identifies the serial number of that gun on to the extended cartridge case." (Everitt, CSGV). The 2007 microstamping law in California is still to be implemented; even if this was finally employed, any progress is predicted to be slow:

> With the law now having been implemented in California, every new handgun model sold in the state moving forward will have to incorporate microstamping technology; but, as we all know, in the US there are many handguns already in circulation. (Everitt, CSGV).

Other ways of effectively tracing gun crimes would be to: develop protocols at local, state and federal levels; give more power to the Bureau of Alcohol, Tobacco and Firearms to regulate gun dealers; the annual publication of a report tracking all gun crime trends (Braga and Gagliardi, 2013, 150–151). Combining these practices with "micro-stamping" technology and a tougher stance on interstate gun trafficking should go some way to dealing with the issue of the illegal distribution of guns.

A way to address responsibility and accountability of gun owners has been to highlight the importance of gun storage. A lackadaisical attitude to storing guns, firstly, can be dangerous because of its link to criminal activity:

> Bottom line is a large number of guns in the illegal market come from thefts from homes or people who just leave them in their car or they leave them hanging around the house not put away safely. (Andrew Goddard, VACPS).

Moreover, Jim Kessler, TW, recommends gun storage measures predicated on a redefinition of "safety":

> The way you store it in your home, you make it so that it can't be stolen, so you might start seeing guns which takes a fingerprint or a combination that you need to do on the gun itself to make it work . . . So, there might be a whole series of other things that define safety in a way that helps keep them out of the hands of criminals.

CC's Tom Mauser advocated that safe storage laws are implemented "to make it clear that adults have a responsibility to keep guns away from kids—it's a matter of public policy." CC's Eileen McCarron. however. noted the difficulties in the practicalities of safe storage laws:

> And there are penalties invoked if a child uses a gun in a shooting of some sort . . . not only to the child but also for the gun owner: usually the parent. A lot of police and people don't like safe storage. because they hate going and charging parents with crimes . . . when they've just lost their child. (McCarron. CC)

Aside from my interviewees' advice. there has also been the suggestion of modifying guns themselves in order to reduce the risk of gun theft—one of the ways to do this would be to personalize guns so they can only be fired by authorized users. For instance. the New Jersey Institute of Technology has been working on a "grip recognition" device corresponding to the palm of the owner. In New Jersey. legislation has been passed requiring the personalization of manufactured guns (Teret & Mernit. 2013. 173. 179).

The second concern is that careless and irresponsible handling of guns can often cause accidental deaths and injuries: "We have a thousand people die accidently every year: if we could stop that. [then] that would be massive for a thousand families." (Goddard. VACPS). The individual blog "Ooh shoot!" researched and written by SUPGV's Cathie Whittenburg looks at the problem of accidental shootings. A daily Google alert with the terms "accident" and "shot" provides her with a whole array of news stories to choose from—something she said is "really quite pitiful." She claimed this problem is caused in part by a lack of knowledge about how to handle a gun properly and carry it safely: "You don't have to know anything about a gun before you can buy one: you could never have touched a gun." (Whittenburg. SUPGV). It is. therefore. recommended that training become mandatory for all gun owners:

> Before you buy a gun. you should have to get a gun license. which means that you have to take a gun safety course: you need to learn how to shoot a gun. how to unload a gun: what the gun laws are."(Whittenburg. SUPGV).

Similarly. a gun insurance program similar to that of driving automobiles is prescribed to make owners accountable for any accidents which could potentially occur: "After you buy the gun. you should need to register it which means you're responsible for that gun." (Whittenburg). The issue of accountability and transparency is of key importance here:

> You wanna carry a concealed weapon. you have to have insurance against you dropping it in the bathroom and it firing and shooting somebody in the leg. (Goddard. VACPS).

and

> Everybody should be accountable for their guns . . . [For] an automatic weapon, the one category of guns that are heavily regulated, you need a federal license and you need to register at a federal level; and, consequently, those guns are not used in crimes because people who own those guns have to be responsible for them—and if they show up at a crime scene, those people who register those guns are in a lot of trouble. So, we need that for all guns." (Whittenburg, SUPGV).

Cornell (2006, 217) also noted the potential of gun insurance or firearms tax as a way of returning costs back to irresponsible gun owners; to negate the issue of government intrusion, insurance information could be held by private companies only. As this method would be an easily maintained and straightforward—as it has been with automobile insurance—it is probably one of the most realistic options of gun regulation.

Accountability does not just apply to gun owners but also to those that manufacture firearms. The gun industry has blanket immunity from faulty product litigation, legalized by the "Protection of Lawful Commerce in Arms Act" (2005). At the moment, it has been said that "You could make a gun that blows off people's hands and a gun which just explodes in your face. And nobody can say a word to that gun manufacturer." (Goddard, VACPS). On a similar note, CSGV are currently running a "counter-marketing" campaign to "encourage or require the gun industry to implement certain safeguards in the way they market and distribute their products." (Everitt, CSGV). This campaign has forged links between CGSV and with one of the gun industry's biggest customers: law enforcement officials. The involvement of law enforcement officials has been crucial to the success of this campaign: ". . . it's something that requires no legislation; you're not relying on the voters; you're no relying on the legislators; you're not even relying on grassroots organizations." (Everitt, CSGV). With that in mind, it seems that gun violence prevention groups will have to form relationships with law enforcement to get most of these measures—curbing gun trafficking, gun registration and taxation, lifting the blanket immunity of the gun industry, micro-stamping, personalizing guns—passed, making the argument that increasing the accountability and responsibility of gun owners and the industry is likely to reduce homicides and make crime guns easier to trace, as well as minimize the amount of careless accidental shootings that occur causing injuries and deaths. There is some marginal degree of support for; providing funding for developing smart guns with 47 percent of non-gun owners and 35 percent of gun owners; having safe storage laws to prevent children accessing guns, in 75 and 45 percent respectively; gun licensing before the purchase takes place, totaling 84 and 59 percent respectively (McGinty et al., 2013, 246).

Current Political Terrain: Supreme Court Ruling

It could be said that the 2008 Supreme Court ruling, in the case *District of Columbia et al. v. Heller* which overturned the Washington, D.C. handgun ban, has put some legal parameters on this debate. This adheres to Spitzer's (2004, 15) point that: "the courts provide a key avenue for definition and change of the [gun control] issue." The definition of what is achievable and constitutional in terms of gun regulation now has some boundaries. To that end, the Supreme Court ruling represents a turning point in the gun debate: "It establishes a new shape for the arena in which legal and political struggle over guns and gun control will be fought" (Doherty, 2008, xviii).

First, the history of the ruling will be outlined to give the issue some context. Following a rise in crime in the 1970s (596.6 incidents per 100, 000 populations), the District of Columbia enacted the very strict "Firearm Control Regulations Act" (1976): handguns purchased after 1976 could not be registered and it was illegal to own a handgun without registering it (the only exceptions were those in law enforcement and security): handgun carrying was banned: guns in the home had to be kept unloaded and secured with a trigger lock (Doherty, 2008, 26, 45; Spitzer, 2012, 36). The Supreme Court of the United States (2008, syllabus, 3) came to the conclusion that: "the handgun ban and trigger lock requirement violate the second amendment." Moreover, the ruling embodied elements of the "individual rights" paradigm by arguing that the second amendment *protects* "an individual right to possess a firearm . . . for traditionally lawful purposes, such as self-defense within the home" (Supreme Court of the United States, 2008, syllabus, 1; emphasis added) What is slightly problematic though is that the Court did not rigorously examine what could be considered "unconstitutional" in terms of gun regulations: the main point to take away from it is the correlation between the second amendment and self-defense (Rosenthal & Winkler, 2013, 228). Notably, Spitzer (2012, 42) is critical of the *Heller* ruling drawing parallels between modern day threats such as house invasions and the second amendment, maintaining that constitutional guidelines were originally designed around armies and militias

Further complicating matters is that fact that the ruling also made the point that the second amendment is not unlimited: "It is not a right to keep and carry any weapon whatsoever in any manner whatsoever and for whatever purpose" (Supreme Court of the United States, 2008: syllabus, 2). The ruling reinforced that there should be certain prohibitions on *where* firearms can be carried, making them off-limits in "sensitive places" like schools and government buildings and *who* is allowed to own them: dangerous groups like criminals and those suffering from mental illness should still be banned (Supreme Court of the United States, 2008, syllabus, 2: emphasis added). This argument is said to be consistent with the historical tradition of enforcing restrictions that are necessary to public safety (Rosenthal and Winkler, 2013, 228). Additionally, there is also the possibility for *certain* weapons to be regulated and for laws with storage requirements to be enacted (Spitzer, 2012, 36).

In terms of future implications after the decision, this requires careful consideration. Previous court rulings had all advocated in favor of the "states right" interpretation of the second amendment, which Spitzer (2012, 39) believes "lends credence to the criticism that the *Heller* ruling played fast and loose with history." This was something The ruling was not unanimous; rather the voting decision was five to four against the District of Columbia's "Firearm Control Regulations Act" (1976). The dissenting judges advocated the "states right" interpretation of the second amendment, with one even stating that even if there was an individualist right to bear arms D.C.'s strict law was legitimate as an effort to control crime (Spitzer, 2012, 36-37). The narrow victory of the *Heller* case means that Doherty's (2008, 115) argument that "most existing gun regulations and lots of future gun regulation may well survive *Heller*" seems rather convincing. Further adding to this are the fact that almost all of the challenges to gun laws brought forward in lower courts since the *Heller* ruling —such as the challenge to Chicago's gun law, which is extremely similar to the one the District of Columbia had—have been unsuccessful (Spitzer, 2012, 38). Probably the most important point to take from a post-*Heller* world is that the self-defense principle must always be taken into consideration when proposing future gun regulations, as must the benefit to public safety and whether it would be a compelling enough reason for enforcing a restriction, i.e., if it prohibited dangerous groups owning guns and firearms being in sites like government buildings. The consequences of this ruling are that the government has jurisdiction to restrict firearms to some extent but an outright blanket ban—like the one in the U.K.—is constitutionally forbidden. This renders "slippery slope" argument—deliberately amplifying the repercussions of an issue without any concrete evidence such as any restrictions would eventually result in gun confiscation and a blanket ban—counter-challenges to gun regulations obsolete. Such arguments can be convincing, however, leading onto the next topic of this chapter: the view of the public when it comes to guns and "gun control."

Current Political Terrain: Public and Guns

It has been said policy-making is dependent upon a triangular relationship between three pertinent groups: the media, the public and politicians (Burns & Crawford 1999). In terms of the importance of the public, citizens' concerns provide a base for issues to be covered and the other two groups address these (Burns & Crawford, 1999, 160). It is realistic to pursue an understanding of the media-public and public-politicians relationship as one which does have a power imbalance, given the media and politicians have the ability to control which information is released, but of acknowledging that the public do have the ability to engage with the process of governance as well as debate what is presented to them in the media. Gabrielson (2005, 83) offers a convincing interpretation of the influence of politicians over the public: those who are politically sophisticated and strongly ideological are more likely to have strong predispositions and be able to resist pre-packaged messages; conversely, the less ideological but attentive citizens are those who are more susceptible to such influences—in terms of the gun violence issue, those who are less ideological are more likely to be swayed by alternative interpretations of the problem.

When it comes to an issue like gun control, public support for change must be linked to social norms and values at that moment in time (Spitzer, 2004, 15). At the moment, gun control, more generally, has diminished in importance for the public. Even well-publicized mass shootings which are particularly horrific in nature only have a short-term impact on people's opinions. Eileen McCarron, CC, pointed to a general public complacency with mass shootings.

> I think that the mass shootings are becoming so common that people have become a little inured to it and people think "another mass shooting, there's nothing we can do except comfort the families, grieve the dead, heal the wounded and go on."

Without real support driving it, any temporary spikes in support for gun control after mass shootings just fade away:

> Even this recent shooting in Santa Monica, California, it's gonna be gone from people's memory within probably a week because it was only five deaths. Only five! The total amount Scotland has in a year. We won't be talking about it in another couple of weeks - that makes it very difficult to do anything about this.- (Mauser, CC).

Although mass shootings gain greater media attention and are more "spectacular" in nature, Andrew Goddard, VACPS, highlights that the "daily grind" of shootings, such as isolated incidents and single victim attacks, is the real issue that needs to be dealt with:

> There were thirty-two people who died at Virginia Tech; thirty-two people die every single day here." For that reason, any campaigns about gun violence really need to focus on the commonplace occurrence and what can be done about it: "We have now moved to a model of sustained activism that's not based on a given day's shooting." (Everitt, CSGV).

Looking at recent opinion polls reveals a paradigm shift towards public disinterest in the issue. A Gallup poll showed 55 percent of respondents were in support of lessening gun laws or keeping them as they were (cited in Shrum, 2012). This seems paradoxical when one considers the polling data showing support for *specific* gun control regulations—these are intermixed throughout the sections on background checks and the assault weapons ban. Discussions with my interviewees elucidated why this distinction exists:

Gallup asked people what do you support more gun rights or gun control? Well, that's silly. I mean, "control" or "rights?" I'd support rights! I mean, that's a word with a much more positive connotation for any American than I support "controlling you." (Everritt, CSGV).

It's the way it's presented. They support a basic right to bear arms but they most agree with the need to take reasonable steps to keep them from people who shouldn't have them—but they don't think of it as "gun control." (Mauser, CC).

It seems to be the particular phrase "gun control" that is the real problem: "when people hear the words "gun control" they think "gun ban." (Whittenburg, SUPGV).

Notably, it is the word "control" that is problematic:
I think if you put "control" in front of anything in America, it doesn't work. (Kessler, TW)

CSGV's Ladd Everitt explained why this term is now outdated for contemporary society:

It's a term that was created back in 1968 when Americans' view of government in general was much more positive . . . now people don't like terms like "control."

Tom Mauser, CC, made a similar point:

When they present gun control as "gun control," it's government controlling you; we are still a nation that likes its rights. People recognize the need to put limits on rights, but they don't like government telling them what those limits are. It's conflicted.

Lasswell *et al.* (1949, 8) theorised that the "political function of language" impacts upon decision making. In the case of the US, this is entrenched in ideals of "rights," "freedom," and "equality" (Lasswell, et al. 1949, 12)—it is clear that these underpin the thinking behind gun control. The conflation of rights with the American identity was a key feature for my interviewees. Ladd Everitt of CSGV commented: "Individual rights are central to the American identity: freedom is central to the American identity." While Jim Kessler of TV said, "we have a real history of freedom and liberty . . . it's more a part of America's history than just about any country.

At the crux of the gun debate in the United States is the notion of American identity and what that means to people. During the course of her investigation into shooters' relationship with guns, Kohn (2004, 61) found that guns tended to symbolize positive attributes such as "independence," "freedom" and "civic responsibility." These results indicate that there does exist some correlation between guns and one's national identity, where using them may be seen as a means of 'performing' it (see Billig, 1995).

Current political sentiment has also been shaped by the tragic Sandy Hook elementary school shooting. which has raised the issue of "guns in schools." The National Rifle Association questioned why other public locations such as banks and airports had armed guards and "children did not" (Mardell. 2012)—showing this issue is being framed around children's safety. Sixty-four percent of the one and a half thousand polled in a Pew Research Center survey favored more armed guards in schools: whilst. fifty-seven percent were opposed to the idea. This is a partisan issue: 56 percent of Republicans compared to 23 percent of Democrats supported armed teachers in schools. It is also gendered with almost half the men in the sample supporting it. compared to a third of female respondents (cited in Page, 2013, News 6A). This demonstrates that notions of protection and preempting attacks are driving current public sentiments.

Discussion on the Future of this Issue

In terms of projections for the future. Vizzard (1999. 140) said gun control is likely to become a more compelling issue when the paradigms shift enough to encompass widespread public compliance with news measures. With this in mind. Cathie Whittenburg of *SUPGV*. believed that attitudes about guns could someday mirror that of smoking:

> . . . if you had told me there would come a time where I couldn't smoke in a bar in Maine. I would've said 'you're crazy!' And now there are state beaches where you can't smoke and people accept it. So. there's been a huge change in the societal attitudes towards smoking and I think that there could be a huge change towards guns as well.

A similar point was made by CC's Tom Mauser using the example of social perceptions towards homosexuality in the US:

> It was because young people said. "No. this is changing" and we're seeing the change. Uh. the same could happen with the gun issue. It will take social change with younger people over a couple of generations that says "We want to make this someplace different."

Moving forward. interviewee. SUPGV's Cathie Whittenburg. also identified a lack of general knowledge about current gun laws and which areas need to be addressed. The most viable way to do this is to frame gun violence as a "public health problem" (see Kohn. 2004. 134: Spitzer. 2004. 43). with a reconceptualization of safety in mind as something which can be managed and researched. This would help depoliticize the issue from the contrasting paradigms guiding each side and may shift attention away to safety measures such as ensuring children are unable to obtain guns. This would only address a portion of gun-related deaths and injuries. however. so other options would have to explore exactly how criminals procured guns and expanding the criteria for prohibited persons. With President Obama making federal funding available for gun-related research. this seems an auspicious time for some further investigations into the most effective solutions to reduce gun violence in the United States.

The research conducted thus far indicates that the most viable options that will not infringe upon rights are: requiring universal background checks and states to update the NICS database more frequently and thoroughly. alongside redefining criteria of persons prohibited from purchasing firearms: having more accountability. education and transparency around ownership to attempt to improve gun safety. as well as gun licensing and registration similar to that of automobiles. Similarly. McGinty. et al.'s (2013, 255) study found that the majority of the public supported: gun licensing. universal background checks. regulating gun dealers' practices. and prohibiting certain groups (in particular. those with mental illness) from owning guns. More importantly. it is within the parameters of the Supreme Court ruling. which have indicated that certain dangerous groups—criminals. those with serious mental illness. and persons acting violently towards their intimate partner—should be prohibited (Rosenthal & Winkler. 2013, 231).

When it comes to the assault weapons ban. Rosenthal and Winkler (2013) came to the conclusion that such a ban would be "constitutional" under the parameters of the Supreme Court ruling. In fact. it was also maintained in the U.S. Court of Appeals in a challenge that an assault weapons ban "does not effectively disarm individuals" nor "prevent a person from keeping a suitable and commonly used weapon for protection in the home or for hunting" (*Heller et al. v. District of Columbia*, D.C. Cir. 2011: 4b 32. 4b 31). The onus is on the government to ascertain whether such a ban would be beneficial in protecting law enforcement and preventing mass shootings. since large capacity magazines are disproportionately used in those ways (*Heller et al. v. District of Columbia*, D.C. Cir. 2011: 4c 33. 4a 30). With the Senate rejecting the attempt to reinstate the assault weapons ban—which was already riddled with loopholes when it was in place from 1994–2004—it is unlikely. however. that this will ever be re-implemented at the federal level. In terms of the large capacity magazines. it will fall to individual states to decide what is an appropriate magazine size—for instance. Colorado compromised on fifteen rounds from initial proposals of limiting magazines to ten—and whether this is something worth pursing or not. This would certainly be something that could have a substantial impact on reducing the carnage of mass shootings and it is likely to gain more support than banning all assault weapons.

When policies are set they should be implemented in such a way that they are easily enforced and monitored (Vizzard. 1999, 141). Winkler (2012) says the only viable option is really to have federal laws that intertwine all state ones. However. CSGV's Ladd Everitt counteracted that sentiment with: "I think there's certainly room for individual states to regulate guns as they see fit. I don't think it's a one-size-fits-all thing." He advocated a strong federal laws overall. but maintained that state laws should vary based on a number of factors: "I think there's a case to be made for slightly weaker gun laws in a place like Montana or Vermont where you can drive a half hour without seeing another human being." (Everitt, CSGV). A stronger federal baseline would certainly create a foundation for gun regulation to prosper at the state level, with each individual one deciding what is appropriate for them based on factors such as geographical landscape, dangers from animals such as bears and wolves, crime levels, weaknesses in current laws, and levels of public support.

References

Arskey, Hilary & Knight, Peter T. (1999) *Interviewing for Social Scientists.* London. Thousand Oaks, CA: Sage.

BBC News. (2013) "Senate Democrats to drop assault weapon ban from gun bill." 19 March. News: US & Canada. Available at: http://www.bbc.co.uk/news/world-us-canada-21849814.

Billig, M. (1995) *Banal Nationalism.* London: Sage.

Birkland, Thomas A. (1997) *After Disaster: Agenda Setting, Public Policy and Focusing Events.* Washington DC: Georgetown University Press.

Braga, Anthony A. & Peter L. Gagliardi. "Enforcing Federal Laws Against Firearm Traffickers: Raising operational effectiveness by lowering enforcement obstacles." In Daniel W. Webster & Jon S. Vernick. *Reducing Gun Violence in America: Informing Policy with Evidence and Analysis.* Baltimore, Maryland: The John Hopkins University Press. 143–154.

Burns, Ronald & Charles Crawford. (1999) "School shootings, the media and public fear: ingredients for a moral panic." *Crime, Law and Social Change* 32, 147–168.

Cook, Philip J. & Jens Ludwig. (2013) "The Limited Impact of the Brady Act: Evaluation and Implications." In Daniel W. Webster & Jon S. Vernick. *Reducing Gun Violence in America: Informing Policy with Evidence and Analysis.* Baltimore, Maryland: The John Hopkins University Press. 21–32.

Cornell, Saul. (2006) *A Well-regulated Militia: The Founding Fathers and the Origins of Gun Control in America.* Oxford, UK; New York, N.Y.: Oxford University Press.

Cuthbertson, David. (2011) "FBI Testimony: The Fix Gun Checks Act: Better State and Federal Compliance, Smarter Enforcement." Statement before the Senate Judiciary, Subcommittee on Crime and Terrorism. Washington D.C.: 15 November. *http://www.fbi.gov/news/testimony/the-fix-gun-checks-act-better-state-and-federal-compliance-smarter-enforcement.*

Daly, Michael. (2007) "Yes, Virginia, Guns Kill Innocents." *Daily News (New York).* 17 April: News, 23.

Davidson, Osha Gray. (1998) *Under Fire: The NRA and the Battle for Gun Control.* Iowa City: University of Iowa.

Dizard, Jan E., Robert Merrill Muth & Stephen P. Andrews Jr.(1999) "The Rise of Gun Culture in America. Introduction: Guns Made US Free – Now What?" In Jan E. Dizard, Robert Merrill Muth & Stephen P. Andrews Jr. *Guns in America: A Reader.* London, New York: New York University Press. 1–8.

Doherty, Brian. (2008) *Gun Control in Trial: Inside the Supreme Court Battle over the Second Amendment.* Washington, D.C.: CATO Institute.

Edelman, Murray. (1964) *The Symbolic Uses of Politics.* Urbana, Ill.: University of Illinois Press.

FOX 31 Denver. (2013) "Gov. Hickenlooper signs landmark Colo. gun control bills into law." 20 March. *http://kdvr.com/2013/03/20/hickenlooper-sings-colo-gun-control-bills/*.

Gabrielson, Teena. "Obstacles and Opportunities: Factors that Constrain Elected Officials" Ability to Frame Political Issues." in Karen Callaghan & Frauke Schnell (ed.). *Framing American Politics*. Pittsburgh, PA.: University of Pittsburgh Press, 76–99.

Isikoff, Michael. (2007) "Did He Buy the Guns Legally?" *Newsweek*, 18 April.

Kates, Don B. Jr. (1992) "The Second Amendment and the Ideology of Self-Protection." *Constitutional commentary* 9, 87–104.

Kingdon, John W. (1994) *Agendas, Alternatives and Public Policies (second edition)*. New York: Longman.

Kleck, Gary. (2009) "Mass Shootings in Schools: The Worst Possible Case for Gun Control." *American Behavioral Scientist* 52 (10), June, 1447–1464.

Kohn, Abigail A. (2004) *Shooters: Myths and Realities of America"s Gun Cultures*. New York, Oxford: Oxford University Press.

Koper, Christopher S. (2013) "America"s Experience with the Federal Assault Weapons Ban, 1994–2004: Key Findings and Implications." In Daniel W. Webster & Jon S. Vernick. *Reducing Gun Violence in America: Informing Policy with Evidence and Analysis*. Baltimore, Maryland: The John Hopkins University Press, 159–171.

Kvale, Steinar. (1996) *InterViews: An Introduction to Qualitative Research*. Thousand Oaks, CA: Sage.

LaPierre, Wayne. (1994/1999) "Self-Defense: The Right and the Deterrent." In Jan E. Dizard, Robert Merrill Muth and& Stephen P. Andrews Jr. *Guns in America: A Reader*. London, New York: New York University Press, 173–177.

Lane, Robert E. (1966) "The Decline of Politics and Ideology in a Knowledgeable Society." *American Sociological Review* 31 (5), 649–662.

Lasswell, Harold D., Nathan Leites and Associates. (1949) *Language of Politics: Studies in Quantitative Semantics*. Cambridge, Massachusetts: The M.I.T. Press.

Leavitt, Michael O., Alberto R. Gonzales, & Margaret Spelling. (2007) "Report to the President on Issues Raised by the Virginia Tech Tragedy." 13 June, Washington, D.C.: U.S. Department of Justice.

Leinwald, Donna. (2008) "States bolster FBI gun database: Mental-health records swell since Va. Tragedy." *USA Today*, 19 February, News, 1A.

Lukes, Steven. (1974/2005) *Power: A Radical View (Second Edition)*. Basingstoke, UK; New York, N.Y.: Palgrave MacMillan.

Malcolm, Joyce Lee. (1994) *To keep and Bear Arms: The Origins of an Anglo-American Right*. Cambridge, Ma.; London, UK: Harvard University Press.

Mardell, Mark. (2012) "Can an emboldened President Obama address gun control?" *BBC News*. 15 December. *http://www.bbc.co.uk/news/world-us-canada-20738725*.

McGinty, Emma E., Daniel W. Webster, Jon S. Vernicle, & Colleen L. Barry. (2013) "Public Opinion on Proposals to Strengthen U.S. Gun Laws: Findings from a 2013 Survey." In Daniel W. Webster & Jon S. Vernick. *Reducing Gun Violence in America: Informing Policy with Evidence and Analysis*. Baltimore, Maryland: The John Hopkins University Press, 239–257.

Nownes, Anthony J. (2013) *Interest Groups in American Politics: Pressure and Power (second edition)*. New York, London: Routledge.

Page, Susan. (2013) "Poll spots activism in gun control debate." *USA Today*, 15th January, News 6A.

Rosenthal, Lawrence E. & Adam Winkler. (2013) "The Scope of Regulatory Authority under the Second Amendment." In Daniel W. Webster & Jon S. Vernick. *Reducing Gun Violence in America: Informing Policy with Evidence and Analysis.* Baltimore, Maryland: The John Hopkins University Press. 225–236.

Samaha, Omar. (2010) "Firearms Still Easily Available." *Richmond Times Dispatch.* 20 April. editorial. A09.

Shrum, Robert. (2012) "For Obama, Romney and America, Gun Control is Dead." *Newsweek.* 24 July. *http://www.thedailybeast.com/articles/2012/07/24/for-obama-romney-and-america-gun-control-is-dead.html.*

Spitzer, Robert J. (2004) *The Politics of Gun Control (3rd edition).* Boulder, Co., London: Paradigm Publishers.

Spitzer, Robert J. (2012) *The Politics of Gun Control (5th edition).* Boulder, Colorado; London: Paradigm Publishers.

Stone, Deborah A. (1989) "Causal Stories and the Formation of Policy Agendas." *Political Science Quarterly* 104(2), 281–300.

Squires, Peter. (2000) *Gun Culture or Gun Control? Firearms, Violence and Society.* London, New York: Routledge.

Supreme Court of the United States. (2008) *Supreme Court Ruling: District of Columbia et al. V. Heller.* Certiorari to the United States Court of Appeals for the District of Columbia Circuit. No. 07–290. Argued March 18, 2008; decided June 26, 2008.

Swanson, Jeffrey W., Allison Gilbert Robertson, Linda K. Frisman, Michael A. Norko, Nsiu-Jo Lin, Martin S. Swartz & Philip J. Cook. "Preventing Gun Violence involving People with Serious Mental Illnesses." In Daniel W. Webster & Jon S. Vernick. *Reducing Gun Violence in America: Informing Policy with Evidence and Analysis.* Baltimore, Maryland: The John Hopkins University Press. 33–51.

Teret, Stephen P. & Adam D. Mernit. (2013) "Personalized Guns: Using Technology to Save Lives." In Daniel W. Webster & Jon S. Vernick *Reducing Gun Violence in America: Informing Policy with Evidence and Analysis.* Baltimore, Maryland: The John Hopkins University Press. 173–182.

Thornburgh, Nathan. (2011) "After Tuscon: Why Are the Mentally Ill Still Bearing Arms?" *Time Magazine,* 10 January.

United States Court of Appeals for the District of Columbia. (2011) *Court of Appeal Ruling: Heller et al. v. District of Columbia.* Appeal from the United States District Court for the District of Columbia United States Court of Appeals. No. 10–7036. Argued 15 November, 2010; decided 4 October, 2011.

van Dijk. (1998) *Ideology: a multidisciplinary approach.* London: Thousand Oaks, CA.: Sage.

Virginia Tech Review Panel. (2009) "Mass shootings at Virginia Tech April 16, 2007: Report of the Virginia Tech Review Panel presented to Timothy M. Kaine, Governor, Commonwealth of Virginia (updated edition)." November. *http://www.vtreview panel.org/report/index.html.*

Vizzard, William J. (1999) "The Impact of Agenda Confliction Policy Formulation and Implementation: The Case of Gun Control." In Jan E. Dizard, Robert Merrill Muth & Stephen P. Andrews Jr. *Guns in America: A Reader.* London, New York: New York University Press. 131–144.

Webster, Daniel W., Jon S. Vernick, Emma W. McGinty & Ted Alcorn. (2013) "Preventing the Diversion of Guns to Criminals through effective Firearm Sales Laws." In Daniel W. Webster & Jon S. Vernick. *Reducing Gun Violence in America: Informing Policy with Evidence and Analysis.* Baltimore, Maryland: The John Hopkins University Press.

109–121.

Welch. William M. (2013) "Gun-law push faces slow start in most states." *USA Today*, 15th January. front page.

Williams. David C. (2003) *The Mythic Meanings of the Second Amendment. Taming Political Violence in a Constitutional Republic*. New Haven and London: Yale University Press.

Winkler. Adam. (2012) "Why Don"t Mass Shootings Lead to Gun Control?" *The Daily Beast*. 20 July. Shooting in Aurora. Available at: http://www.thedailybeast.com/ articles/2012/07/20/why-don-t-mass-shootings-lead-to-gun-control.html.

Wintemute. Garen J. (2013a) "Comprehensive Background Checks for Firearm Sales: Evidence from Gun Shows." In Daniel W. Webster & Jon S. Vernick. *Reducing Gun Violence in America: Informing Policy with Evidence and Analysis*. Baltimore. Maryland: The John Hopkins University Press. 95–107.

———. (2013b) "Broadening denial criteria for the purchase and possession of firearms: need. feasibility and effectiveness." In Daniel W. Webster & Jon S. Vernick. *Reducing Gun Violence in America: Informing Policy with Evidence and Analysis*. Baltimore. Maryland: The John Hopkins University Press. 77–93.

Zeoli. April M. & Frattaroli. Shannon. (2013) "Evidence for Optimism: Policies to Limit Batterers" Access to Guns." In Daniel W. Webster & Jon S. Vernick. *Reducing Gun Violence in America: Informing Policy with Evidence and Analysis*. Baltimore. Maryland: The John Hopkins University Press. 53–63.

Editors

Lisa A. Eargle

Lisa A. Eargle, Ph.D., is a Board of Trustees' Research Scholar, Professor and Chair of the Department of Sociology at Francis Marion University (FMU). Dr. Eargle is also the co-coordinator of the Criminal Justice Program at FMU. Her research focuses on a variety of issues, including development, environment, disasters, and social justice. She is the co-editor of the volumes. *Black Beaches and Bayous: The BP Deepwater Horizon Oil Spill Disaster* (University Press of America, 2012), *Savage Sand And Surf: The Hurricane Sandy Disaster* (University Press of America, 2015), and *Terrorism Inside America's Borders* (forthcoming, University Press of America).

Dr. Eargle has numerous book, chapter and journal article publications. These include Hurricane Katrina's impacts on education (in the first and second editions of *The Sociology of Katrina*). 'The Impact of Culture on Crime' (in the journal of *Race, Class and Gender*). 'Traditional Bullying to Cyber Bullying: A Criminal Pathology' (in *Alleviating Bullying: Conquering the Challenge of Violent Crimes*). 'Corporate Deviance' (in *The Encyclopedia of Social Deviance*). 'The Roles of Family Structure, Family Interactions and Gender on African American Delinquency' (in the *Journal of Education and Social Justice*). 'Economic Reforms, Values, and Politics as Determinants of Cross-National Sex Trafficking Network in Developing Countries: A Theoretical Overture Using Global Commodity Chain Approach' (in the journal of *Race, Class And Gender*), and 'Incorporating Peace Education Strategies in University Classroom: Approaches Used in Sociology Courses' (in *Youth Violence in American Schools: How It Can Be Alleviated*).

She has conducted workshops at professional conferences on integrating environmental issues into the Sociology curriculum (for the American Sociological Association and South Carolina Sociological Association), using Geographic Information Systems in teaching and research (South Carolina Sociological Association), and approaches to teaching theory to undergraduates (American Sociological Association and Southern Sociological Society). Papers presented at professional conferences include 'Disaster Preparedness Planning for Disabled Populations: The View through Marketing's Lens' (for Marketing and Public Policy), 'Applying the Disaster Resilience of Place Model to the BP Oil Spill' (for Mid-South Sociological Association), 'The Influence of Infrastructure Type and Prevalence on Crime Rates' (for Southern Criminal Justice Association), 'Abolishing or Limiting Parole: Potential Benefits and Costs' (for South Carolina Sociological Association) and 'Arizona SB 1070 'Paper Please' And Similar Laws' Impact on Whites in the U.S.' (American Society of Criminology). Dr. Eargle teaches a variety of sociology and criminal justice courses, including Population in Society, Environmental Sociology, Urban Sociology, Crime & Organizations, Alcohol, Drugs & Society, and Social Problems. Dr. Eargle has also created a course on Disasters and Extreme Events that she will teach in the Spring 2016 semester.

Ashraf M. Esmail

Ashraf M. Esmail, Ph.D., is the Program Coordinator of the Criminal Justice Program at Dillard University in New Orleans, LA. His research interests include criminology, social problems, deviance, urban, multicultural, and peace education, family, cultural diversity, and political sociology. He has co-edited numerous volumes, including the books *Youth Violence in American Schools: How Can it Be Alleviated* and *Black Beaches and Bayous: The BP Deepwater Horizon Oil Spill Disaster, Alleviating Bullying: Conquering the Challenge of Violent Crimes* and *Qualitative Study of Job Satisfaction Experiences of Forensic Scientists*. Dr. Esmail recently published articles entitled *A Brief History of Social Justice Among Juveniles and Teaching Social Justice to Urban Students, Cross-National Sex Trafficking Network in Developing Countries: A Theoretical Overture Using Global Commodity Chain Approach, Learning to Change: Does Life Skills Training Lead to Reduced Incident Reports Among Inmates in a Medium/Minimum Correctional Facility* and *The Roles of Family Structure, Family Interactions and Gender on African American Delinquency, and Impact of Culture on Crime*.

He currently serves as the senior editor of the *Journal of Education and Social Justice*. He also was elected as President of the National Association for Peace Education in 2010. He is the Proposal Review Lead for the National Association for Multicultural Education and serves on the Board of Directors for the National Association for Peace Education.

Contributors

Reem A. Abu-Lughod

Reem A. Abu-Lughod. Ph.D. is an Associate Professor of Criminal Justice at California State University, Bakersfield (CSUB). A graduate of the University of Texas at Arlington (M.A. 2001: Criminology & Criminal Justice and Ph.D. in Urban Policy & Public Administration-emphasis in criminology & Criminal Justice). Dr. Abu-Lughod joined the California State University, Bakersfield (CSUB) Criminal Justice Faculty in Fall 2006. Since then. Dr. Abu-Lughod has taught myriad classes, including: Terrorism. Criminal Justice Policymaking. Race. Ethnicity and Criminal Justice, and Theoretical Criminology. Over her academic career, Dr. Abu-Lughod was actively involved with the U.S. State Department, conducting cultural and religious sensitivity training to troops being deployed to Iraq. Afghanistan and the Palestinian/Israeli territories. She is also a certified instructor in teaching Arabic as a foreign language. Dr. Abu-Lughod is very passionate about teaching. and always makes certain that her students graduate with a well-rounded education. In her professional service. Dr. Abu-Lughod has served on various committees, including the Kegley Institute of Ethics, the Kern Threat Working Group. and the Intelligence Committee at CSUB. In her research experience. Dr. Abu-Lughod has published on issues involving the War on Iraq. Hezbollah and the Lebanese politics. the 1948 Arab-Israeli conflict. Arab-Americans in the U.S.. crime and the media. domestic violence among the Palestinian Refugee women population and crime in U.S. cities. Her most recent publications include a book titled 'In Spite of Being White: The Plight of Arab Americans'. and an article titled 'Altruistic and Anomic Suicide: A Durkheimian Analysis of Palestinian Suicide Bombers'. Currently. Dr. Abu-Lughod's research focus on counterterrorism strategies. Arab Americans pre/post 9/11, and the sociopolitical conflict in war zones. Away from her teaching and research. Dr. Abu-Lughod enjoys playing with her three little children. Ghazal. Rama and Ameer: exploring new learning activities and helping them discover their inner interests and hobbies.

Laura E. Agnich

Laura E. Agnich is an Assistant Professor of Criminal Justice and Criminology at Georgia Southern University. Her research focuses on school violence, specifically bullying and school mass violence incidents in cross-national contexts. In addition, she researches gender and sexual orientation-related victimization and drug use. Her research has been published in journals such as *Deviant Behavior*, the *Journal of Crime and Justice, American Journal of Criminal Justice, Journal of School Violence, and Addictive Behaviors.*

Dinur Blum

Dinur Blum is a graduate student at the University of California, Riverside. In addition to work on mass shootings, Dinur's areas of research interest include the sociology of sport, sociology of culture, media, and criminology. He has written about how better helmets in football and hockey contribute to more dangerous games and how fans evaluate referees in sports with respect to issues of fairness and justice. He is also currently working on projects focusing on student-athletes' experiences in academia. He has recently published two in-briefs for Contexts, entitled 'Rage Against the Refs' and 'Better Helmets, Worse Sports'.

Chantel D. Chauvin

Chantel Dufrene Chauvin is a doctoral graduate of Louisiana State University. She is currently an Adjunct Professor at River Parishes Community College. Her dissertation analyzed the spatial patterning of suicide rates in the US. Her other research interests include violent offending and victimization and the southern subculture of violence. She has published articles that test the influence of the southern subculture of violence on women in *Sociological Spectrum* and the *Journal of Interpersonal Violence.*

Julia D'Antonio-Del Rio

Julia D'Antonio-Del Rio graduated with her doctorate in sociology from Louisiana State University in 2010. Her research focuses on violent crimes, deviance, and gender, generally using macro-level quantitative methods to examine the relationship between female homicide offending and characteristics of counties and neighborhoods. She has published manuscripts on the influence of the southern subculture of violence on female homicide offending in *Sociological Spectrum* and the *Journal of Interpersonal Violence.*

Selina Doran

Selina Doran is a researcher in the School of Life and Health Sciences at Glasgow Caledonian University in Scotland. Her PhD dissertation used the social problem of school shootings in the United States as a prism through which to examine gun and emergency management policies. She has Bachelor's degree in journalism and sociology, a Master of Research degree in social research, and received a Doctorate in Sociology in May 2014. Her research specialties are: school/mass shootings, media and political framing, emergency management and fear of crime.

Jessica M. Doucet

Jessica M. Doucet is an Assistant Professor of Sociology at Francis Marion University. She joined FMU after receiving her PhD from Louisiana State University. Her research interests include violent offending (with an emphasis on homicide), the southern subculture of violence, gender and crime, as well as rural and urban crime. She has published manuscripts in *Sociological Spectrum* and the *Journal of Interpersonal Violence*. These articles examine the influence of the southern subculture of violence on female offending. Her most recent research analyzes the ability of the civic community perspective to explain homicides in urban areas.

H. Jaymi Elsass

H. Jaymi Elsass is a doctoral candidate in the School of Criminal Justice at Texas State University. Her primary research interests are juvenile justice, fear of crime, and moral panic. Her research has been published in Crime, Law and Social Change and Criminology, Criminal Justice, Law and Social Change.

James Hawdon

James Hawdon is a professor of sociology and director of the Center for Peace Studies and Violence Prevention at Virginia Tech. His research focuses on how community programs can reduce violence and how communities respond to tragedies. In addition, he and his colleagues have recently started the project, *Radicalization on the Internet: Virtual Extremism in the U.S. from 2012–2017,* which is funded the National Institute of Justice. He is also working on a similar project with colleagues from Finland and Germany investigating online hate groups. He has published dozens of articles in the areas of crime, the sociology of drugs, policing, media studies, and the sociology of disasters.

Christian Gonzalez Jaworski

Christian Gonzalez Jaworski is a PhD candidate in Sociology at the University of California Riverside. His research interests include criminology, conflict theory and inequality. Currently, he is performing his PhD research on socialist transition in Europe. He and his wife live in Warsaw, Poland.

Anna Johnson

Anna Johnson received her B.A. in Psychology from the University of Minnesota. She was able to further her education, and earned her MSW from DePaul University in 2014. In 2014 she completed grant funded individual research on homelessness and SSI, and gave a presentation at the National Social Work Conference in Washington, DC regarding her research results. She is currently gainfully employed by a social service organization working specifically with children that have been in literal homeless, or near homeless situations with their families. She has particular interest in mental health, homelessness, and trauma informed services.

Christopher A. Kierkus

Christopher A. Kierkus is an associate professor of criminal justice at Grand Valley State University in Grand Rapids, Michigan. He received his Ph.D. in criminal justice from the State University of New York at Albany. Professor Kierkus' research and writing is focused on the role of family, gender, and relationships in the causation of delinquency. He is also interested in evaluation research and applied criminal justice policy.

Alan Lizotte

Alan Lizotte is dean and a professor in the School of Criminal Justice. at The University at Albany and executive director of the Hindelang Criminal Justice Research Center. He is co-principal investigator on the Rochester Youth Development Study, a twenty year ongoing longitudinal study of juvenile delinquency and drug use covering three generations of subjects. His substantive interests include the ownership and use of illegal firearms and developmental criminology. In 2003, he and coauthors were awarded the American Society of Criminology's Hindelang Award for the book *Gangs and Delinquency in Developmental Perspective*.

Glenn W. Muschert

Glenn W. Muschert is Professor in the Sociology. Criminology, and Social Justice Studies Programs at Miami University in Oxford. Ohio. His scholarly interests lie in the sociological study of crime and social problems, including the mass media discourse of school shootings, moral panics, and surveillance technologies. His research has appeared in a variety of journals and volumes in the fields of sociology, criminology, and media studies.

Mary Ann O' Grady

Mary Ann O'Grady. PhD is an adjunct professor. dissertation chair. and course author at Nova Southeastern University. Grand Canyon University. Southern New Hampshire University. and the University of the Rockies. She has a doctorate in conflict and crisis management. and a master's and bachelor's degrees in psychology: the focus of her research includes homicide. school shootings. mass shootings, and intra-family murder.

Noam Ostrander

Noam Ostrander, PhD. LCSW. is the director for the Master of Social Work Program at DePaul University. Dr. Ostrander's research interests include the intersections of disability. masculinity, and gun violence. He has studied gun violence in Chicago for more than a decade and has published his work in numerous journals spanning the fields of social work and disability studies. Prior to entering academia, Dr. Ostrander worked in clinical and research positions within Chicago social service agencies.

John Ryan

John Ryan, is Professor and Chair of Sociology at Virginia Tech. He came to Virginia Tech as department chair in 2001, after serving six years as chair at Clemson University. A graduate of Vanderbilt University, his research interests include the study of culture production and consumption, as well as violence and crime control within communities. Recent research has focused on community recovery from mass violence in the United States and Finland. and the acquisition and use of cultural capital across the life course.

Jaclyn Schildkraut

Jaclyn Schildkraut is an Assistant Professor of Public Justice at the State University of New York (SUNY) at Oswego. Her research interests include school shootings, homicide trends, mediatization effects, and crime theories. Her work has been published in *Homicide Studies, American Journal of Criminal Justice, Fast Capitalism*, Criminal Justice Studies, and Crime, Law and Social Change, among other journals, as well as several edited volumes.

Nicole M. Schmidt

Nicole M. Schmidt is an analyst in the Institute on Urban Health Research and Practice at Northeastern University. Her research interests include youth risky behaviors and mental health, developmental theory, and longitudinal methodology. She received her Ph.D. in criminal justice from the State University of New York at Albany.

Martha Smithey

Martha Smithey is associate professor at Texas Tech University, Lubbock, Texas. She earned her PhD from Texas A&M University in 1994. She is the recipient of research grants from the National Institute of Justice, National Institute on Drug Abuse, and National Institutes of Health among others. She has published in various journals including Homicide Studies, Journal of Interpersonal Violence, Journal of Family Violence, and Deviant Behavior. Her research interests include violence toward children, and women & crime.

Sheryl L. Van Horne

Sheryl L. Van Horne is the Director and Associate Professor of Criminal Justice at Eastern University in Pennsylvania. She formerly served as the Director of Global Security and Emergency Management at Arcadia University. She has taught at Widener University, Penn State University, Radford University, and Rutgers University. She graduated from Rutgers University's School of Criminal Justice. Her recent research focuses on homicides from a macro-level perspective, though she has also published articles on pedagogy, drug policy, and media portrayals of crime.

Robert Wood

Robert Wood is a PhD student in Sociology at Virginia Tech, working with the Center for Peace Studies and Violence Prevention. His concentrations are in crime, deviance, and culture, and his research pursuits include fear of crime as well as explanations of digital piracy.